W9-CFX-728

# Diderot the satirist

*Le Neveu de Rameau* & RELATED WORKS / AN ANALYSIS

DONAL O'GORMAN

iderot the satirist

UNIVERSITY OF TORONTO PRESS

17, UNIVERSITY OF TORONTO ROMANCE SERIES

© University of Toronto Press 1971
Printed in Canada by
University of Toronto Press
Toronto and Buffalo
ISBN 0-8020-5245-2

# Foreword

"A mighty maze! but not without a plan"
Alexander Pope, *Essay on Man*

THE three studies that make up this volume need little by way of introduction. Each is a self-contained treatment of a Diderot text, and the results, I believe, speak for themselves. It is worth remarking, nonetheless, as more and more scholars concentrate their attention on the eighteenth century, that much groundwork of the kind offered herein remains to be done. As a well-known *dix-huitiémiste* has recently stated, perhaps a moratorium should be declared on purely theoretical interpretations of Diderot until more certain critical bases have been laid.

The studies here presented are striking justification of Jean Fabre's timely plea on behalf of solid erudition as a point of departure for critical evaluation of any kind (Preface to *Entretiens sur "Le Neveu de Rameau"*). The third study especially, which deals with *Le Neveu de Rameau*, is sure to excite widespread interest. For over a century and a half, this enigmatic dialogue has successfully withstood the assorted weaponry of criticism. The present state of the question is aptly summed up in the words of the most recent English translator of *Le Neveu*, L. W. Tancock, in his Introduction: "Behind this very readable conversation, with the frolics and outrageous opinions of an exuberant personality, who is a great comic creation of Rabelaisian proportions, there is an extremely complicated and difficult work which raises questions not yet all clearly answered by the researches and criticisms of generations of scholars. One man's guess is almost as good as another's" (*Penguin Classics*, 1966).

I am convinced that Professor O'Gorman has supplied a *fil conducteur* that will guide readers through this fascinating labyrinth in confidence that they are following the path traced by Diderot's mind when he constructed it. In clearing up some of the "mystification," moreover – and this is the touchstone of reliable criticism – he has succeeded in making the mystery more profound. The mystery of a masterpiece is properly the mystery of its author's genius: and Diderot emerges from this study a literary artist of the first magnitude – a rank which many heretofore have been unwilling to accord him.

Otis Fellows
New York
June 1970

# Preface

« La satire est d'un tartuffe, et la comédie est du Tartuffe.
La satire poursuit un vicieux, la comédie poursuit un vice. »
*Paradoxe sur le comédien*

THE purpose of this book is to explore the mind and art of Diderot the satirist as revealed by those works of his which belong in their entirety to the satirical genre: *Satire première, Lui et Moi,* and *Le Neveu de Rameau*. There is no question here of a general inquiry into the art of satire as understood and practised by Diderot, for this would demand a much broader approach than the one adopted and would encompass many more of his writings. It is nonetheless hoped that the material contained in these pages can serve as the foundation upon which such a study might be built.

In addition to the generic relationship of the three texts chosen for discussion in these essays, there are other grounds for treating them together under a single cover. The *Satire première* (1773) and *Le Neveu de Rameau* or *Satyre 2de* (undertaken in 1761–2) are linked by the numerical ordering of their titles.[1] *Lui et Moi* (1762) also shares certain characteristics with *Le Neveu de Rameau*, chief among them being the fact that these are the only dialogues of Diderot in which the interlocutors are named "Lui" and "Moi." These various points of resemblance cannot be lightly dismissed, for they suggest the possibility that other similarities may exist at a deeper level. It is reasonable, therefore, and perhaps even necessary, that *Le Neveu de Rameau* should be examined in conjunction with those works of Diderot to which it is most akin.

---

1 It would appear that Diderot, during the period after his return from Russia in 1774 when he began arranging and revising his manuscripts in view of a general edition, came to see the *Satire première* and the *Satyre 2de* as companion-pieces. The fact that he did not add *Lui et Moi* to this series, as he might justifiably have done, is perhaps explained by the absence of all reference to that satire in his family papers. This is an indication that he no longer had a copy of *Lui et Moi* in his possession in the late 1770s.

Generally speaking, the critical approach taken in this book tends to be historical in the sense given to that term by Douglas Bush in a recent paper entitled "Literary History and Literary Criticism": "Every work must be understood on its own terms as the product of a particular mind in a particular setting, and that mind and setting must be re-created through all the resources that learning and the historical imagination can muster – not excluding the author's intention, if that is known."[2] The three satires are here given individual treatment, the method employed in each case depending upon the particular difficulties presented by the text. The two minor works are considered first (Parts ı and ıı) with a view to determining what significance they may have for the analysis of *Le Neveu de Rameau* (Part ııı). An appendix has been added in which the reader will find for his convenience the annotated text of the *Satire première* and of *Lui et Moi*.

This book has been published with the help of grants from the Humanities Research Council of Canada, using funds provided by the Canada Council, and from the Publications Fund of the University of Toronto Press. In the course of its preparation, assistance has been cheerfully given by many friends. I wish to express my thanks to the University of Toronto Research Board for a grant in aid of research, and to my colleagues at the University of Toronto, Miss Elsie Gladwell, Professors R. Bolger, P. Collet, Ph. Lafaury, J. R. O'Donnell, J. Sablé, J. Sheridan, D. W. Smith, A. Waligore, and many others. Professors Dana Rouillard, Norman Torrey, and Arthur Wilson kindly read the manuscript; their suggestions for its improvement are gratefully acknowledged.

A special debt of gratitude is owed to Professor Otis Fellows of Columbia University, co-founder and editor of the *Diderot Studies* series, who has been in close touch with this work since its inception. His invaluable counsel and his unfailing generosity over the years are deeply and warmly appreciated.

Donal O'Gorman
St Michael's College
University of Toronto
June 1970

2 In *Acta of the Ninth Congress, International Federation for Modern Languages and Literatures,* ed. Leon Edel (New York, New York University Press 1965), 8. Professor Bush continues: "The doctrine that a work of art is self-sufficient and may not receive extraneous illustration is arbitrary and irrational. ... We can of course achieve only limited degrees of truth in trying to re-create the outward and inward conditions in which a work of art was engendered, but, unless we try, we cannot distinguish between its local and temporal and its universal and timeless elements; indeed we may not be able to understand some works at all."

# Contents

# Abbreviations

**A.T.**
Denis Diderot *Œuvres complètes* ed. Jean Assézat and
Maurice Tourneux 20 vols. Paris, Garnier 1875–7

Best.
Voltaire *Correspondence* ed. Theodore Besterman
107 vols. Geneva, Institut et Musée Voltaire 1953–65

*Corr.*, ed. Leigh
Jean-Jacques Rousseau *Correspondance complète* ed. R. A. Leigh
Geneva, Institut et Musée Voltaire 1965 ff. 10 vols. to date

*Corr.*, ed. Roth
Denis Diderot *Correspondance* ed. Georges Roth
Paris, Editions de Minuit 1955 ff. 14 vols. to date

*Corr. lit.*
Grimm, Friedrich Melchior, Diderot, Raynal, Meister, et al.
*Correspondance littéraire, philosophique et critique*
ed. Maurice Tourneux 16 vols. Paris, Garnier 1877–82

Fabre
Denis Diderot *Le Neveu de Rameau* Edition
critique par Jean Fabre, Geneva, Droz 1950

## PART I

# On learned digressions: *Satire première*

THROUGHOUT the works of Diderot we find dispersed a number of brief essays bearing so plainly the stamp of his personality that they deserve to be accorded the close attention usually reserved to an author's major writings. If his *Eloge de Richardson* and the essay *Sur les Femmes* are examples that spring immediately to mind, readers familiar with Diderot will give at least equal importance to the *Satire 1, sur les caractères et les mots de caractère, de profession, etc.*[1] This brilliant satirical epistle weaves together anecdotes, personal reminiscences, and moral observations with such originality of style that it stands as one of the most characteristic pieces to come from Diderot's pen.

In addition to its intrinsic literary worth, the *Satire première* poses certain technical problems of some interest: genesis and structure, date of composition, and the relationship, implied by the title, with Diderot's *Satyre 2*<sup>de</sup>, better known as *Le Neveu de Rameau*. In an article by Herbert Dieckmann devoted to these matters, the elements of the question have been ably exposed.[2] Professor Dieckmann sets out to examine the *Satire première* insofar as it is able to throw some light on Diderot's masterpiece; the present study, on the other hand, is primarily concerned with the *Satire première* for its own sake and only incidentally with its relationship to other works.

## TITLE AND STRUCTURE

When the *Satire première* appeared in Grimm's *Correspondance litté-*

---

1 *Œuvres complètes de Diderot*, ed. J. Assézat and M. Tourneux (Paris, Garnier, 1875-7, 20 vols.), VI, 303-16. This edition is henceforth cited as A.T. All further references to the *Satire première* will be to the critical text in Appendix I below (p. 226 ff.), which is based on the first edition of the work by Jacques-André Naigeon in *Œuvres de Denis Diderot* (Paris, Desray-Déterville, an VI-1798, 15 vols.), IX, 492-514.

2 "The Relationship Between Diderot's *Satire I* and *Satire II*," *Romanic Review*, XLIII (1952), 12-26.

*raire* (October 1778), it was introduced by these simple words: "Satire par M. Diderot."[3] The other manuscripts, however, bear a formal title – *Satire première* – followed by an epigraph taken from Horace: "Quot capitum vivunt, totidem studiorum/Millia."[4] A further variation is found in the first printed edition of 1798; Naigeon, Diderot's friend and editor, introduces between the title *Satire première* and the epigraph an explanatory subtitle: *Sur les caractères et les mots de caractère, de profession, etc.* There can be no doubt that it was Diderot who gave the title *Satire première* to his little work,[5] and we must presume that the epigraph from Horace is equally authentic; but the subtitle is of doubtful origin, having come down to us on the sole authority of the editor Naigeon.[6]

If the subtitle – *Sur les caractères et les mots de caractère, de profession, etc.* – was indeed added by Naigeon, it was because he realized that Diderot's text as it stood was most ambiguous. Such an editorial procedure, however reprehensible, is at least understandable in this particular case; for the title *Satire première* and its accompanying epigraph, which suggest that we are dealing with a satire on the diversity of human character, seem to be contradicted by the long dedicatory formula immediately following: "A Mon Ami M. Naigeon, sur un passage de la première satire du second livre d'Horace: Sunt quibus in satyrâ videar nimis acer, et ultra/Legem tendere opus."[7] Were the subtitle lacking (and it *is* lacking in the manuscripts), one would naturally expect that the central preoccupation of the author would prove to be the discussion of a passage from Horace's *Sat.* ii.i; but such is not the case. Only in the last two pages, in fact, does Diderot take up the question of Horace announced in the dedication; by far the larger part – fully nine-tenths – of his satire is devoted to a treatment of the variety of character among men. The subtitle, therefore, must have been in-

3 The manuscripts of Grimm's newsletter are described in Appendix 1 (below, p. 224). The *Satire première* does not figure in the printed edition of the *Correspondance littéraire* (Paris, Garnier, 1877–82, 16 vols.), from which the editor, Maurice Tourneux, excluded those writings of Diderot that had already appeared in A.T.

4 "For every thousand living souls, there are as many thousand tastes" (*Sat.* ii.i.27–8). Trans. Fairclough.

5 The title *Satyre 2<sup>de</sup>* appears in Diderot's own hand on the autograph manuscript of *Le Neveu de Rameau*. This fact suffices to establish the authenticity of the title *Satire première*.

6 The *Satire première*, in its final form, is a satirical epistle addressed to Jacques-André Naigeon. It is conceivable that the copy sent to Naigeon by the author (see below, p. 8) might have borne the subtitle; however, there is no evidence to show that this was the case.

7 "There are some critics who think that I am too savage in my satire and strain the work beyond lawful bounds" (*Sat.* ii.i. 1–2). Trans. Fairclough. These lines serve merely to identify the satire in question; the passage to be discussed by Diderot, as we shall see later, comprises vv. 34–9 of *Sat.* ii.i.

troduced in order to counterbalance the disproportionate weight given to the commentary on ancient literature by the words with which Diderot addressed his satire to Naigeon.

The subtitle, then, serves to put the emphasis more firmly where it belongs. Unfortunately, this is of small benefit to the reader, for the root of the ambiguity is the composite nature of the work itself. The author saw fit to combine therein a satire on characters with a letter à propos of ancient literature, and we can only agree with Professor Dieckmann that the *Satire première* consists of "two parts, which are not related by Diderot, but simply put together."[8] This does not mean, however, that artistic unity is lacking; the following pages will attempt to show that the second part – the discussion of the passage from Horace – is indeed intimately related to what precedes.

One interest that Diderot had in common with his friend and disciple Jacques-André Naigeon was the study of ancient literature; and perhaps the favourite pastime of amateur (and many professional) classicists in the eighteenth century was looking for possible ways to emend difficult texts. In the concluding pages of the *Satire première* it is a question of changing the accepted attribution of several lines in the first satire of Horace's second book.

The Roman poet had composed this satire in the form of a dialogue between himself and an old lawyer named Trebatius. Traditionally, critics had considered vv. 24–60 of the dialogue to have been spoken by Horace, not by Trebatius. In substance, these lines are a humorous defence of satire; since nature, Horace says, has made each man unique and has given to each animal species its peculiar weapons of self-defence, he (Horace) is merely following his natural bent and his instinct for self-preservation in writing satirical verses against those who antagonize him. Commentators had not failed to point out that, towards the mid-point of this passage, the speaker digresses abruptly from his topic to devote five lines to the history of his native region, Lucania (vv. 35–9).

In Diderot's view this digression, which he calls "un fastidieux détail d'antiquités," is most ill-fitting in the mouth of Horace. Consequently, he suggests to Naigeon a possible emendation: if these lines are given to Trebatius instead of to Horace, they are seen to constitute a striking *mot de caractère* ! The dialogue can be rearranged as follows: at the mention of Lucania by Horace (v. 34) the old savant with whom the poet is speaking, carried away by his enthusiasm for ancient history, interrupts

---

8 "The Relationship ...", p. 15. This opinion is accepted by Roland Desné in the Introduction to his edition of the *Satire première* (Denis Diderot, *Satires* [Paris, Club des Amis du Livre Progressiste, 1963], 157).

his interlocutor and delivers a little lecture on the region just named. In this interpretation, vv. 35–9 are no longer an awkward digression; on the contrary, they manifest a remarkable insight into character on the part of the poet! "Et [voilà] qu'un endroit d'Horace qui m'avoit paru maussade, devient pour moi d'un naturel charmant, et d'une finesse exquise" (below, p. 238).

The value of Diderot's interpretation need not detain us here.[9] The important point to note is that the preceding analysis shows the two parts of the *Satire première* to be related in several ways. First, according to Diderot's interpretation, vv. 35–9 of Horace's satire are to be given to Trebatius because they constitute a typical example of professional deformation in an old *érudit*. Seen in this light, the disputed lines can be classified with the other "mots de profession" announced in the subtitle and given abundant illustration in the body of the work. Secondly, Diderot had terminated the first part with a practical application of his ideas on character, showing how it is possible to ascertain certain facts about those whom we meet in society by studying their mannerisms of speech and gesture (below, p. 234). In the same way the Trebatius-Horace question is expressly introduced as another practical lesson: it shows us how to apply our knowledge of human individuality to the interpretation of literature. Thirdly, the whole of the Horatian passage (vv. 24–60) has to do with the variety of human character, as does the first part of the *Satire première*. The author links the two by choosing for his epigraph a verse from this section of Horace: "Quot capitum vivunt, totidem studiorum/Millia" (vv. 27–8). This classic statement of human individuality is paraphrased by Diderot in introducing his treatment of character: "Aussi, autant d'hommes, autant de cris divers" (below, p. 226).

In addition to these elements which preserve the work's internal unity, there is an aspect that might somewhat improperly be called "mystification": the subtle manner in which form and sense are intertwined.

---

9 Modern editors accept the traditional attribution of vv. 35–9, pointing out that, in the mouth of Horace, they are a humorous way of leading up to the next point that he wishes to make (Fairclough). There is, however, a break in the thought at this point, for Horace had been speaking of his predecessor Lucilius (vv. 29–34) when he abruptly opened the subject of the origins of his native region, Lucania (vv. 34–9). Diderot, as is explained below (p. 238, n. 69), tries to make the link by suggesting that Lucilius was Horace's countryman, which is false. (In fact, it was Trebatius who came from the same part of Italy as did Horace.) It is unfortunate that all the standard editions and commentaries have overlooked the explanation of the seeming digression given by Baron Walckenaer in his *Histoire de la vie et des œuvres d'Horace* (Paris, Michaud, 1840, 2 vols.): "Cette digression, ou traînante parenthèse, qui embarrasse tout le texte, a paru si peu conforme à la marche ordinairement si rapide d'Horace, que selon l'usage, on a proposé des changements. Les commentateurs n'ont pas vu qu'Horace dit ici qu'il imite Lucilius, et qu'il a voulu jeter un léger ridicule sur sa manière diffuse" (i, 504).

With the apparent intention of writing a letter aimed at absolving Horace of a five-line digression, Diderot indulges in a digression nine times the length of the part of his letter that treats of Horace! Just before closing, he has Naigeon remark jokingly on the length of the digression; and his reply is: "Il est vrai. Le tic d'Horace est de faire des vers, le tic de Trébatius ... de parler antiquités, le mien de moraliser, et le vôtre ..." (below, p. 239). This oft quoted statement is not merely an embarrassed excuse for a digression. Diderot's thesis, throughout both parts of the *Satire première*, is that individual character traits are unconsciously disclosed by language; and now he points out that he himself, in the very form that his presentation has taken, has betrayed his own ruling passion, the urge to moralize upon the slightest pretext! Only at the end does the playful irony become apparent, when the reader is made aware of the self-mockery in which the author has been indulging from the very beginning. What better way to demonstrate his thought, especially in a satirical work, than to allow his penchant for moralizing to stand as ironical proof of what he is attempting to say? And the words "et le vôtre ... " implicate Naigeon, and beyond him all mankind, in the irony of the human condition.

DATE AND PLACE OF COMPOSITION

Since the *Satire première* bears no formal indication of date or place of composition, we are forced to rely on evidence from internal and external sources. Herbert Dieckmann has marshalled the pertinent information. Two facts appear certain from internal indications: the letter did not originate from Paris, and it must have been written after June 1773, that is, after Diderot's departure for Holland en route to Russia.[10] Moreover, several external factors connect the satire with the year 1773, the most important of which is a statement of Diderot to the effect that he had composed "une petite satyre" during his stay at the Hague, June to August of that year.[11]

Are the *Satire première* and the "petite satyre" of 1773 one and the

10 "The Relationship ... ," 12–13. In the *Satire première* Diderot refers to an incident that occurred "la veille de mon départ pour le grand voyage," which Naigeon affirms in a note to be the journey to Holland and Russia (below, p. 234). In closing the letter, he asks Naigeon to remember him to his friends in Paris (below, p. 240).

11 In a letter to Madame d'Epinay, written probably on 18 August 1773, Diderot states: "Je me suis amusé à écrire une petite satyre dont j'avois le projet lorsque je quittai Paris" (*Correspondance*, ed. Georges Roth [Paris, Editions de Minuit, 1955–], XIII, 46). Professor Dieckmann indicates two further facts: (1) Naigeon, in his edition, places the *Satire première* immediately after the *Lettre à monsieur l'abbé Galiani sur la sixième ode du troisième livre d'Horace* (A.T., VI., 289), which Diderot himself dated 25 May 1773; (2) Diderot's review of *Le Jugement de Pâris* by B. Imbert (A.T., VI, 434), which work appeared in 1772, contains a paragraph that corresponds almost literally to the opening lines of the *Satire première*.

same? Professor Dieckmann concludes with the strong presumption that they are.[12] This presumption becomes certainty when we remark the many similarities of detail to be found between this work and the *Réfutation suivie de l'ouvrage d'Helvétius intitulé L'Homme*, which we know to have been begun during that same summer.[13] The *Réfutation* contains a half-dozen passages and allusions found equally in the first part of the *Satire première*.[14] Given Diderot's well-known propensity to repeat in one work thoughts that appear in others written about the same time, this can be taken, along with the facts adduced by Professor Dieckmann, as a conclusive indication of simultaneity.

There are two reasons, however, that forbid us to hold that the little work as we know it was completed in the summer of 1773. As its dedicatory words and its postscript indicate, the *Satire première* is in the form of a letter to Jacques-André Naigeon, and would seem to have been sent through the post.[15] If it was written and mailed on the eve of Diderot's departure for Russia, as the date of the letter referring to the "petite satyre" (18 August) would seem to indicate, it is difficult to imagine the writer making the casual request found in his postscript: "Je lirois volontiers le commentaire de l'abbé Galiani sur Horace, si vous l'aviez" (below, p. 240). Moreover, there is one definite, though minute, indication that at least part of the letter was composed in France. In the dialogued interchange concerning the historian Rulhière, Diderot has Naigeon ask: "N'y a-t-il pas sur son compte? ..." His answer is: "Oui, une certaine histoire de Bordeaux, mais je n'y crois pas. On

12 "The Relationship ... ," 13. The "petite satyre" begun at the Hague cannot be *Le Neveu de Rameau*, says Professor Dieckmann, which was composed over a long period beginning in 1761 or 1762; nor is there any evidence that it was the *Satire contre le luxe à la manière de Perse*, the date of composition of which is unknown but which Naigeon and all subsequent editors of the *Salons* insert in the *Salon de 1767* (A.T., XI, 89–94).

13 Although the *Réfutation* was taken up after Diderot's return to France in 1774, and completed in 1775, the work was considerably advanced before he left the Hague in August 1773. Galitzine, Diderot's host, had seen Helvétius' posthumous work through the press shortly before the arrival of the Encyclopedist in June. By 22 July Diderot could write to Madame d'Epinay: "J'ai lu trois fois le posthume d'Helvétius" (*Corr.*, ed. Roth, XIII, 37), and on 18 August he declared: "J'ai barbouillé toutes les marges du dernier ouvrage d'Helvétius" (*ibid.*, 46). These last words occur in the same paragraph as the reference to "une petite satyre" cited above.

14 The similarities between the two texts are pointed out below, p. 227, n. 7; p. 228, n. 17; p. 229, n. 24; p. 230, nn. 25, 29. There is also a remarkable parallel between the opening paragraph of the *Satire première* and a passage of the *Réfutation* (A.T., II, 312).

15 See Naigeon's note, reproduced below (p. 239), in which he states that Diderot was cautious in what he said for fear that the letter might be intercepted. In all probability, therefore, Naigeon had in his possession at one time the original letter, or at least a direct copy of the original. The list in the Fonds Vandeul which mentions "Original et deux copies de la Satyre I<sup>e</sup>" (H. Dieckmann, *Inventaire du fonds Vandeul et inédits de Diderot* [Genève, Droz, 1951], 174) is perhaps untrustworthy.

est si méchant dans ce pays-ci ..." (below, p. 237). It is the author himself who says these last words, and obviously "ce pays-ci" refers to
France, not to Holland. We may be certain, therefore, that this section
of the letter was written, or at least revised, after Diderot's return from
Russia.

From this conflicting evidence it is possible to make an hypothesis
that will explain some of the difficulties posed by the *Satire première*.
Herbert Dieckmann has suggested that Diderot, intending to write a
letter to Naigeon concerning the passage from Horace (*Sat.* II. i. 35–9),
became distracted by the words "Quot capitum vivunt" immediately
above (vv. 27–8), and permitted himself to digress at length on the
thought contained therein before returning to his original subject.[16] It
would perhaps be better to say that Diderot *pretended* to have been
distracted, for we have seen that he had an artistic reason for presenting
the satire on characters as a digression. In fact, the structure of the work
is so perfectly designed that it is difficult to conceive of any element of
chance entering into its composition. From what we have seen above,
it is reasonable to suppose that Diderot might have written the first part
independently in Holland ("une petite satyre"), and after his return to
France decided to incorporate it into a letter to Naigeon, changing what
had to be changed.[17] This, I believe, would explain satisfactorily all the
elements of the puzzle.

Reasons for such a procedure are not hard to find. Diderot's love of
mystification would perhaps be explanation enough, but it is more likely
that his motive was an artistic one. If he did indeed write the first part
of the satire in Holland, without the benefit of the familiar tone and
chatty remarks directed to Naigeon, the overall result would undoubtedly have resembled, as the author admits, "une satire à la manière de
Perse" (below, p. 238). This was probably the character of the "petite
satyre" in its original form, before it became part of a letter addressed
to Naigeon. Diderot, fortunately, with his keen sense for literature, found
a way to add a more personal note as well as an Horatian touch, turning
a somewhat sober essay into an imaginative satirical epistle marked by
self-mockery, elegant wit, and gentle irony.

THE AUTHOR'S INTENTION. GENESIS OF THE WORK

Diderot, as a philosopher and as a literary artist, was passionately interested in the science of language. His *Lettre sur les sourds et muets* and

16 "The Relationship ... ," 17.

17 As it appears in the *Correspondance littéraire* (October 1778), the *Satire première* does not have the postscript found in all the other manuscripts as well as in
Naigeon's edition. This could be an indication that Diderot had not yet sent his
epistle to Naigeon at that time.

the article "Encyclopédie" bear witness to this fact, as do the many careful definitions of near-synonyms that were his personal contribution to the *Encyclopédie*. His manuscripts seem to indicate that he intended some day to complete the *Synonymes français* of Abbé Girard, already amplified by Beauzée,[18] or even, as Naigeon avers, to crown his career with a "dictionnaire universel et philosophique de la langue."[19] It was not, however, this concern for the *mot juste* that led Diderot to compose his satire on "le cri de la nature" and "les mots de caractère." It is his aim in this work to isolate the unique expression that will perfectly translate impulses of nature, passion, and character; and nothing could be further removed from the classical ideal as stated by La Bruyère: "Entre toutes les différentes expressions qui peuvent rendre une seule de nos pensées, il n'y en a qu'une qui soit la bonne."[20] La Bruyère was concerned with the logical interpretation of a rational universe; Diderot is dealing with the irrational expression of a sensitive soul.

If Diderot's satire is not the work of a philologist, neither is it that of a rhetorician. Cicero had assembled a lengthy series of *bons mots* in the *De oratore*;[21] Macrobius had filled Book IV of his *Saturnalia* with examples of pathos found in poetry; but we may not consider the *Satire première* to be, in this tradition, a collection of sayings and anecdotes demonstrating to authors the art of dialogue. The spirit of the work is completely modern: we are dealing here with Diderot *moraliste*, and it is his intention to give an ordered exposition of the unconscious sources of language.

This aspect of human speech had always fascinated Diderot, and we have no grounds for doubting his word when he tells us that he had the idea for his "petite satyre" already in mind when he left Paris in June 1773. However, there is every reason to believe that his thought was crystallized after his arrival in Holland by his reading of Helvétius' posthumous book, *De l'homme*. We have seen that the first draft of the "petite satyre" and that of the *Réfutation d'Helvétius* were composed during the summer of 1773; and the substantial number of parallel passages that we have remarked between the two works is surely not due to mere coincidence. In fact, their relationship becomes apparent when we realize that the central theme of the *Satire première* – individuality – is the principal source of contention between the Encyclopedist and the late author of *De l'homme*.

Helvétius, both in *De l'esprit* (1758) and in *De l'homme* (1773), had

18 See Herbert Dieckmann, *Inventaire*, 43–5.
19 *Encyclopédie méthodique. Philosophie ancienne et moderne* (Paris, Panckoucke, 1791, 3 vols.), II, 219.
20 *Les Caractères*, I, 17.
21 *De orat.* II. liv. 217-lxxi. 291.

defended the paradoxical position that all men are equal in every way at birth, and that education and environment are the only factors responsible for the diversity of mind, character, and talent that we see around us. Diderot, on the other hand, while allowing that educational and environmental forces have much importance, insisted that each man has natural aptitudes and natural limitations imposed by his physical make-up that determine to a large extent his capabilities and his character. So fundamental is this debate concerning the natural individuality of man that it runs like a refrain from end to end of the *Réfutation*.

From this idea to the theory of "le cri de l'homme" is but a short, logical step. Such is the diversity from one individual to the next, says Diderot in the *Réfutation*, that no two men will have the same ideas or use the same words to express them:

est-il possible que l'organisation étant différente, la sensation soit la même ? Telle est sa diversité, que si chaque individu pouvait se créer une langue analogue à ce qu'il est, il y aurait autant de langues que d'individus; un homme ne dirait ni bonjour, ni adieu comme un autre (A.T., II, 279).

Reasoned language, Diderot is saying, necessary in that it serves the end of social communication, fails utterly to express the individuality of the speaker. This idea appears several times in the *Réfutation*: "Nous sentons tous diversement, et nous parlons tous de même. ... A proprement parler, les sensations d'un homme sont incommunicables à un autre, parce qu'elles sont diverses. Si les signes sont communs, c'est par disette" (A.T., II, 325). And, in the *Satire première*, he shows us how a student of human nature should strive to recognize behind the mask of conventional usage the affective colouring that each individual gives to his words.

We may be sure, therefore, that it was Diderot's dynamic version of empiricism and the linguistic doctrine implicit in it that gave rise to the "petite satyre" of 1773. These pages were written in the same spirit in which the *philosophe* composed his *Réfutation*, where he asserts, against the relentless mechanistic doctrine of Helvétius, the natural individuality of man. The *Satire première* is, in effect, an elaborate literary digression from the *Réfutation*. It is Diderot's affirmation of the unique character of each human being from a particular point of view, that of language.

LE CRI DE L'HOMME: THEORY AND PRACTICE

The central theme of the *Satire première* is the variety of human character as expressed in language. Each animal species, says Diderot in his opening paragraph, has its distinctive cry; and likewise every man expresses his individuality in a unique way: "Aussi, autant d'hommes, autant de cris divers." Thereupon he proceeds to run through a series of examples of human discourse which are characterized as "cris de la nature," "cris de la passion," "cris de la profession," etc., ending with several practical illustrations of the utility of such insights into human nature. By thus weaving his ideas on character into the framework of "le cri de l'homme," Diderot was able to present a psychological analysis of man in the context of one of his favourite aesthetic theories – namely, that literary artists must strive to exploit the affective qualities of language. It would be well to consider briefly this aspect of poetic creation, somewhat overshadowed by the spirit of French neo-classicism, which had come into its own only with the growing importance given to sentiment in the aesthetics of the eighteenth century.

According to etymologists, the use of the word "cri" to designate "un mouvement intérieur de l'être, de l'âme" (Robert) is attested first in 1691.[22] The idea, however, has a long history. A recent study by Clifton Cherpack traces its development in the motif of "le cri du sang," which he equates with "la voix de la nature," in French classical tragedy.[23] Alexis François, in several works,[24] treats the broader question of the theory and practice of affective language from its expression in the rhetorical doctrines of the seventeenth century, especially those of Bernard Lamy,[25] through Abbé Du Bos and his "langage du cœur"[26] to the full flowering of the "rhétorique naturiste" in Condillac's *Essai sur l'origine des connaissances humaines*. After 1746, the date of the *Essai*, it was popular to believe with Condillac that language had not been a gift of God, but had evolved naturally from the gestures and inarticulate cries of primitive man to a system of conventional signs and finally to reasoned

---

22 Walther von Wartburg, *Französisches etymologisches Wörterbuch*, II², 1485. The reference is to Racine, *Athalie*, v, 6: "De leur sang par sa mort faire cesser les cris."

23 Clifton Cherpack, *The Call of Blood in French Classical Tragedy* (Baltimore, The Johns Hopkins Press, 1958).

24 In F. Brunot, *Histoire de la langue française*, VI², 2055-60. See also Alexis François, *Histoire de la langue française cultivée des origines à nos jours* (Geneva, Jullien, 1959, 2 vols.), II, 79-87; and his "Précurseurs français de la grammaire 'affective'," in *Mélanges de linguistique offerts à Charles Bally* (Genève, Georg, 1939), 369-77.

25 Bernard Lamy, *La Rhétorique, ou L'Art de parler* (Paris, 1675). The fourth edition of this work (1701), reprinted in 1715 and 1741, is described by A. François as "l'un des bréviaires du XVIIIᵉ siècle" (*Histoire de la langue française cultivée*, II, 80).

26 Jean-Baptiste Du Bos, *Réflexions critiques sur la poésie et sur la peinture* (Paris, 1719): "Ces premieres idées qui naissent dans l'ame, lorsqu'elle reçoit une affection vive, & qu'on appelle communément *des sentimens*, touchent toujours, bien qu'ils soient exprimés dans les termes les plus simples. Ils parlent le langage du cœur" (1760 ed., I, 268).

grammatical expression.[27] Developing this idea, Condillac showed that not only language but also music, poetry, and dancing can be traced back to the same source.[28] Thus the currents of sentimentalism, primitivism, and naturalism that were sweeping Europe were channelled into a new aesthetics based on the philosophy of sensationalism.[29] "En effet, quel est le son le plus propre à rendre un sentiment de l'ame ?" asked Condillac. "C'est d'abord celui qui imite le cri qui en est le signe naturel, il est commun à la déclamation et à la musique."[30] It was not long before the word "cri" was on everyone's lips to characterize instinctive, spontaneous movements of the soul.[31]

Diderot, of course, had been closely associated with Condillac and Rousseau in the preparation and publication of the *Essai*. For him, as for all the Encyclopedists, the natural origin of language and of the arts was thenceforth accepted as a corollary of the sensationalist philosophy which they officially espoused. Rousseau, in his *Discours sur l'inégalité*, indicates the two essential characteristics that give the "cri" its aesthetic value – energy and universality: "Le premier langage de l'homme, le langage le plus universel, le plus énergique ... est le cri de la Nature."[32] Diderot, for his part, stresses the emotional power of primitive tongues, which, unlike modern languages, were marked by "ces expressions énergiques ... ces termes qui équivalent à un long discours."[33] This holophrastic quality, unknown to ordinary discourse, is essential to poetic diction. In addition, poets must imitate the vital rhythm of the "accent" that characterizes living speech: "Ecoutez le défi énergique et bref de cet enfant qui provoque son camarade. Ecoutez ce malade qui traîne ses accents douloureux et longs. Ils ont rencontré l'un et l'autre le vrai

---

27 *Essai*, 2ᵉ partie, Sect. ɪ, Ch. ɪ, in *Œuvres philosophiques de Condillac*, ed. Georges Le Roy (Paris, Presses Universitaires de France, 1947–51, 3 vols.), ɪ, 60–3.

28 Ibid., Ch. ɪɪ–vɪɪɪ (ed. Le Roy, ɪ, 63–82).

29 On Condillac, see Isabel F. Knight, *The Geometric Spirit. The Abbé de Condillac and the French Enlightenment* (New Haven, Yale University Press, 1968), 144–97. A similar analysis of Diderot's views on language is given by Herbert Josephs, *Diderot's Dialogue of Gesture and Language: Le Neveu de Rameau* (Columbus, Ohio State University Press, 1969), 3–83.

30 *Essai*, 2ᵉ partie, Sect. ɪ, Ch. vɪ (ed. Le Roy, ɪ, 77–8).

31 "Le cri de la nature" is found in Voltaire, *Mérope* (1741; ɪɪɪ, 6); Diderot, *Essai sur le mérite et la vertu* (1745; ᴀ.ᴛ., ɪ, 39); Gresset, *Le Méchant* (1747; ɪv, 4). Thereafter the expression is commonplace. *Le Cri de la nature* (1769) is a one-act comedy by François Huguet (*dit* Armand). Montesquieu speaks of "le cri de l'innocence" (*Esprit des lois*, xxɪx, Ch. v); the Archbishop of Auxerre appeals to "le cri de la foi" (ᴀ.ᴛ., ɪ, 442), Helvétius to "le cri de l'honneur" (*De l'esprit*, Disc. ɪɪɪ, Ch. xxvɪɪɪ); controversial pamphlets are entitled "Le Cri de l'honnête homme" and "Le Cri des Nations" (Bachaumont, *Mémoires secrets* [1780–9 ed.], ɪv, 212, 267).

32 *Œuvres complètes de Jean-Jacques Rousseau* (Paris, Gallimard, Bibliothèque de la Pléiade, 1959– ), ɪɪɪ, 148.

33 ᴀ.ᴛ., ɪ, 367 (*Lettre sur les sourds et muets*).

rythme, sans y penser."[34] Rationalized, analytic language leaves us un-
moved; but the language of sentiment penetrates to the heart. It is on
the sensitive level, therefore, where the true universality of human nature
resides, that all forms of communication will have their broadest and
deepest appeal. The poet must be able to reproduce this "cri de la nature" if he is to reach the pinnacle of the sublime.[35]

It must be admitted that, as an aesthetic theory, "le cri de l'homme"
leaves much to be desired. Its effect on Diderot's theatrical writings, in
which he sought to move his audience by "des cris, des mots inarticulés,
des voix rompues, quelques monosyllabes qui s'échappent par intervalles,
je ne sais quel murmure dans la gorge, entre les dents," was little short
of disastrous.[36] Applied to music, as in *Le Neveu de Rameau*, the "cri
animal de la passion" had perhaps slightly less serious consequences.
But these aberrations are more than compensated by the fact that the
primitive "language of the heart" is intimately linked to the language
of gesture, and that Diderot's interest in pantomime springs from this
same source. May we not bear with *Le Fils naturel* for the sake of the
priceless mime scenes of *Le Neveu de Rameau*? It is true, moreover, that
although Diderot often allowed his enthusiasm for the pathetic to falsify
his taste, he was capable of rising above his prejudices. We have proof
of this in his novel, *La Religieuse*: having searched for the perfect "cry
of passion" to put in the mouth of the repentant Mother Superior, he
finally accepted the classically simple words: "Mon père, je suis
damnée !"[37]

### Satire première AND Satyre 2^de

The question of the possible relationship between the *Satire première*
and *Le Neveu de Rameau* or *Satyre 2^de*, first posed by Maurice Tourneux, has received extensive consideration by Herbert Dieckmann in the
article already cited. The *Satyre 2^de*, as Professor Dieckmann points
out, having been begun some ten years before the *Satire première*, must
have been given its title in conjunction with that of the later work. This
does not necessarily mean, of course, that we should look for an internal

---

34 A.T., XI, 268 (*Salon de 1767*).
35 "Comment se fait-il que dans les arts d'imitation, ce cri de nature, qui nous
est propre, soit si difficile à trouver? Comment se fait-il que le poète qui l'a saisi,
nous étonne et nous transporte? Seroit-ce qu'alors il nous révèle le secret de notre
cœur?" (below, p. 227).
36 A.T., VII, 105–6 (*Entretiens sur le Fils naturel*). For Diderot's influence on the
"affective" style of his century, see F. Brunot, *Histoire de la langue française*, VI²,
2058–60; also the article by A. Brun, "Aux origines de la prose dramatique : le style
haletant," in *Mélanges de linguistique offerts à M. Charles Bruneau* (Genève, Droz,
1954), 41–7.
37 See A.T., V, 162, n. 1.

link between the two; any number of exterior circumstances might have arisen to bring this about. Nonetheless, the reader of Diderot's two satires is struck by an unmistakable "air de famille" which, Professor Dieckmann suggests, is due to the fact that "the prevalent interest in the moral trait as expressed in the *mot de caractère* or in gestures and its use for the purpose of satire are common to *Satire 1* and the *Neveu de Rameau*."[38]

There is no need here to go over the careful analysis by which Professor Dieckmann shows how the notion of natural individuality, common to the two satires, is fundamental to Diderot's theory of literary realism, and how the instinctive or unreflecting expression of individuality tends to be satirical by its very nature.[39] We can agree without hesitation that the same view of man is evident in the two works, at least insofar as the technique of artless self-revelation in words is prominent in both. Of equal importance, perhaps, is an observation that can be made as a result of the present investigation: if the treatment of individuality in the satire of 1773 was inspired by Diderot's reaction to the doctrine contained in *De l'homme*, is there not reason to believe that the same doctrine, already vigorously denounced when it appeared in Helvétius' first book, *De l'esprit* (1758), might have played a similar role in the creation of *Le Neveu de Rameau*, begun in 1761 or 1762? This matter will be considered at length in Part III, Ch. 2, below.

CONCLUSION

Despite the fact that it is written in prose and has the form of a familiar letter, the *Satire première* unquestionably belongs to the satirical genre as the author conceived it. That he gave the title "Satire" to a prose piece need hardly cause surprise; having explicitly abandoned verse in his theory of the drama for the sake of realism, he would have had equal justification for feeling that prose was more suitable than verse for capturing the unpretentious, even familiar, spirit of classical satire.[40] As for the particular form of satire adopted here, we have the author's own opinion: "je vous ai presque fait une satire à la manière de Perse," he tells Naigeon (below, p. 238). No doubt he had in mind the quality

---

38 "The Relationship ... ," 21.

39 Ibid., 18–23.

40 Horace invokes his prosaic muse (*Sat.* II. vi. 17) and claims to write "lines more akin to prose" (*Sat.* I. iv. 42). The suggestion that Diderot might have considered the French Alexandrine employed by Boileau to be far removed from the spirit of Roman satire is made by Karl Maurer, "Die Satire in der Weise des Horaz als Kunstform von Diderots *Neveu de Rameau*," *Romanische Forschungen*, LXIV (1952), 381–4. See Diderot's article "Alexandrin," A.T., XIII, 271.

commonly recognized as marking Persius off from his predecessor
Horace: unity of subject matter. Horace had called his satires "ser-
mones," that is, conversations, and indeed had avoided order and
method, imitating the easy tone of conversation that passes imperceptibly
from one matter to another. Persius, on the other hand, treats one determined subject from which he does not stray. We see this quality in
the *Satire première* and also in the *Satire contre le luxe à la manière
de Perse* (A.T., XI, 89–94). Persius' satires, moreover, have a more noble
and philosophical tone than do those of Horace. A list of the subjects
of his six satirical poems – "On Softness"; "On Opinion"; "On True
Freedom" – reads like the table of contents of a treatise on practical
ethics. Diderot, in treating the psychology of human language in the
*Satire première*, leans rather in the direction of the serious Stoic satirist
than in that of Horace, who preferred to speak, at least on the surface,
of trivialities.

As for the satirical outlook of the author in the *Satire première*, it
was dictated inescapably by the matter chosen for discussion. However
seriously Diderot may have taken his theory of "le cri de l'homme," he
was well aware that the narrow psychological determinism on which
it rested was an oversimplification that had greater possibilities for
humour than for scientific treatment. Other aspects of determinism
he had dealt with facetiously in two chapters of *Les Bijoux indiscrets*
(XIX and XXIX); later, in *Jacques le fataliste*, he would exploit all the
possibilities of the subject. In the *Satire première*, the "cri" is presented
as an instinctive reaction to stimuli that partakes necessarily of the
laughter-provoking qualities attributed by Bergson to automatism, with
the added benefit of the caricatural distortion that results from any
reductionist treatment of man. Given the additional fact that the foibles
of many contemporaries are here exposed, we need make no apology for
this work as satire.

The form chosen for the *Satire première* was the ideal vehicle for
Diderot's theory of "le cri de l'homme": a moralistic essay on the variety
of human character. Despite appearances, we have here a carefully
planned exposition of a single theme with nothing of the haphazard
composition that he was wont to associate with the epistolary style. His
treatment follows a strictly logical order: he considers first the sources
of language that pertain to the individual – nature, passion, and character – and then those that have to do with man in society – profession,
national character, and character of social groups. Except for the letter
form chosen by the author, the satire has all the elements of an essay
after the manner of Montaigne: moralizing tone, personal reminis-

cences, keen observations set down with an air of sage detachment from the human comedy.

His intention in the *Satire première* is to present a series of situations in which the individuality of man, often concealed beneath the veneer of manners or the cloak of hypocrisy, is manifested in all its primitive force and singleness of purpose by a brief but all-revealing sentence. The "cri de l'homme" will be heard only under conditions of stress, or in unguarded moments, when the inner man speaks out and exposes his true nature in all its stark nakedness. Lucretius, in a verse that Diderot was fond of quoting, had pointed out that one of the uses of adversity and danger is that they strip off the mask and allow us to see a man as he really is: "For then at last a real cry is wrung from the depths of his heart; the mask is torn away, and the truth [lit., "the thing"] remains behind."[41] The "verae voces" of Lucretius are for Diderot the various "cris de l'homme." The moralist alone can seize them; and only the literary artist who observes with the eye of a moralist can hope to paint human nature in its infinite variety.

41 *De rer. nat.* III. 57–58: "Nam verae voces tum demum pectore ab imo / Eliciuntur; et eripitur persona, manet res." Diderot quotes these lines in a note, A.T., I, 107 (*Essai sur le mérite et la vertu*), and refers to the "vraies voix" of the passions, A.T., VII, 106 (*Entretiens sur le Fils naturel*). Again in the *Entretiens* (ibid., 118) he uses the words "Tum verae voces."

## PART II
# Once bitten, twice shy: *Lui et Moi*

In the Assézat-Tourneux edition of Diderot's works there was published for the first time a brief dialogue entitled *Lui et Moi*.[1] These few pages are ostensibly the record of a conversation between the author (Moi) and a young man with literary ambitions, formerly a practising lawyer, who is designated as Lui. Tourneux pointed out in his "Notice prélimi-naire" (p. 477) that Lui is undoubtedly identical with an acquaintance of Diderot named Rivière who figures as the inglorious hero of an anecdote related in Madame de Vandeul's biography of her father.[2] And indeed the meeting of Lui and Moi in the dialogue, and the en-counter of Diderot and Rivière in the anecdote, have so many details in common that it is evidently one and the same incident described in both.

The existence of two versions of the same story makes it reasonable to suppose that *Lui et Moi*, like many of Diderot's dialogues, is based on an actual happening. Lui, therefore, was an historical personage and his name was Rivière. But who was Rivière? The dialogue itself gives scarcely a clue. Considerably more information about him is found both in the anecdote and elsewhere in Diderot's writings, enough to permit positive identification. It is my purpose here to add a few facts to what is already known concerning Rivière, and then to examine *Lui et Moi* in the light of those facts. For the sake of clarity it is first necessary to look more closely at the anecdote as told by Diderot's daughter.

1 A.T., XVII, 481–5. The reader should be advised at the outset that the ambiguities of this little work have raised doubts in some minds as to its authenticity. He ought also to be reminded that Maurice Tourneux based his edition of *Lui et Moi* on a manuscript which was undoubtedly the original. Tourneux implied that it was an autograph (p. 474), and it was later sold as such (see below, p. 242). The text given below in Appendix 2 (pp. 242–6) follows that of A.T.

2 First published in 1813, the *Mémoires pour servir à l'histoire de la vie et des ouvrages de Diderot* were reprinted in the first volume of A.T., xxix–lxii. The Rivière anecdote, which begins on p. xlviii of A.T., is reproduced below in Appendix 3, item 1 (pp. 247–8).

THE ANECDOTE[3]

It is well known that Diderot was exceedingly generous by nature, and his biographers are wont to enliven their books with anecdotes illustrating his great obligingness. Perhaps the most amusing of these stories, as it is recounted in Madame de Vandeul's *Mémoires*, describes an attempt made by the *philosophe* to reconcile an indigent author named Rivière with a brother, "ecclésiastique et fort riche," who had disowned him, it seemed, for conduct that had been more mischievous than malicious. Determined to help his protégé, Diderot pays a visit to the priest and presents his plea. It becomes clear that he has been victimized when his host interrupts, and proceeds to inform him of Rivière's real nature. "Alors il enfile un tissu de bassesses, de noirceurs, de scélératesses plus fortes les unes que les autres" (below, p. 247). Quite taken aback at first, Diderot regains his composure during the course of this lengthy recital. He then delivers an eloquent rejoinder of such persuasive force that the canon is shaken in his resolve and finally agrees to provide his unworthy brother with a substantial endowment.

When Rivière, curious to know how his victim has fared, pays his next visit to the philosopher's home, he is greeted with the news that the undertaking has been successful. He is subjected also, needless to say, to a sermon on the necessity of personal reform. As the young man is being ushered out he thanks his benefactor for his good offices as well as for this sound advice; but the quality of his gratitude is revealed by his parting words:

Monsieur Diderot ... savez-vous l'histoire du *Formica-leo* ? ... C'est un petit insecte très-industrieux; il creuse dans la terre un trou en forme d'entonnoir, il le couvre à la surface avec un sable fin et léger, il y attire les insectes étourdis, il les prend, il les suce, puis il leur dit : « Monsieur Diderot, j'ai l'honneur de vous souhaiter le bonjour » (below, p. 248).

"Mon père rit comme un fou de cette aventure," says Madame de Vandeul. And she goes on to relate how, some time later, the two meet by chance in a café. (It is this final encounter that is the occasion of *Lui et Moi*.) Diderot, as we might expect, upbraids the younger man for his evil ways; Rivière, equally true to character, shows himself thoroughly impenitent.

This anecdote, if it is a true one, is not difficult to situate in Diderot's life. In the *Paradoxe sur le comédien* we find his own account of the incident,[4] ending with the visit to the canon, and here he refers to the

3 See the preceding note.
4 A.T., VIII, 384–5. Reproduced below in Appendix 3, item 2 (p. 248).

priest as "le théologal."[5] Elsewhere, in a fragment entitled *S'il est plus aisé de faire une belle action qu'une belle page*, Diderot speaks fondly of the eloquence he displayed on the occasion of his visit to "le Théologal de Notre-Dame."[6] The *Almanach Royal*, from 1758 to 1790, lists a Rivière among the canons of Notre-Dame. Beginning in 1759 he is designated as "théologal."

Here are some facts relative to the life of Abbé Rivière, assembled from scattered sources. Jean-François Rivière was born in 1718 in Paris.[7] He entered the clerical state in 1734, was admitted the following year to the degree of *maître ès arts* in the University of Paris,[8] and some time later became a Doctor of Theology at the Sorbonne.[9] In June 1758 he was named abbot of Saint-Chéron in the diocese of Chartres. On the thirtieth of the same month he was appointed Canon of Notre-Dame, and on 3 March 1759 the office of *théologal* was entrusted to him.[10] At this time and for the remainder of his life in Paris he resided next to the cathedral, at the corner of the rue Massillon and the rue Cloître-Notre-Dame. (This house, destroyed in 1903 and rebuilt, was undoubtedly the setting of Diderot's interview with the canon.) He emigrated to Tournai during the Revolution.[11]

If there were still any doubt that this is the *théologal* concerned in our anecdote, it would be dispelled by the evidence of the official list of preachers for the diocese of Paris. This publication shows that, in 1760, the same Chanoine Rivière preached the Lenten sermons before the King.[12] Now these sermons, according to Madame de Vandeul's

5 According to the *Dictionnaire de droit canonique* (ed. R. Naz, Paris, 1935–65, 5 vols.), the ecclesiastic known as "théologal" (in English, "Canon Theologian") is that member of a cathedral chapter of canons, preferably a Doctor of Theology, appointed by the bishop to give public Scripture lessons in the cathedral to which he is attached (III, 568–9).

6 A.T., III, 539. Reproduced below in Appendix 3, item 3 (p. 249).

7 Paris, Archives of the Archevêché, card catalogue assembled by Abbé Paul Pisani, dean of the chapter of Notre-Dame, s.v. "Rivière."

8 Paris, Archives Nationales, T202-12, act of 20 October 1738.

9 *Nouvelles ecclésiastiques*, XXXII (1759), 33.

10 H. Fisquet, *La France pontificale. Diocèse de Chartres* (Paris, n.d.), 498.

11 Pisani card catalogue, s.v. "Rivière." Maurice Tourneux, speculating on the identity of the Rivière brothers (A.T., XVII, 478), cites a reference in Quérard (*La France littéraire*) to a lawyer-author of that name who died at Caen in 1778, and another reference to a certain Rivière from Rouen who had done some writing in the field of theology. Both Paul Vernière (Diderot, *Œuvres esthétiques* [Paris, Garnier, 1959], 333) and Georges Roth (Diderot, *Correspondance*, x, 180) have repeated these false identifications as though they were positive.

12 The *Liste générale de tous les prédicateurs de Paris* (1616–1790), Tome II, gives, under the heading "Liste des prédicateurs du Caresme de cette année 1760, à Paris & aux environs," the following information: "*A Versailles, au Château devant Leurs Majestés*, M. l'Abbé Rivière, Chanoine & Théologal de l'Eglise de Paris" (Bibl. Nat., Rés. 4⁰LK⁷ .6743).

version of the story, were an occasion of bitterness between the canon and his brother. The latter had maliciously claimed authorship of them, thus throwing ridicule on the canon and thwarting his hopes for a bishopric (below, p. 247). This fact definitely identifies our man, and at the same time gives the earliest possible date for the Rivière episode: Lent ended that year on Saturday, 5 April.

The parents of Jean-François Rivière died within a few months of one another, the mother late in 1752 and the father early in 1753. In an act dated 2 June of that year he formally renounced the succession of his father as being "plus onéreuse que profittable."[13] His father had been Louis Rivière, *avocat au parlement*. On 22 June 1753 we find the *acte de partage* of his mother's estate, shared equally by her two children. The co-heir, and apparently the elder of the two brothers, is Louis-Pierre Rivière, *avocat au parlement*.[14]

There are few documents available containing information about Louis-Pierre Rivière. He was born at the earliest in 1714, the marriage of his parents having taken place in September of the preceding year.[15] In September 1736 he took the *serment d'avocat*.[16] Since this required that he have passed his licentiate in law, he was at the very least in his twentieth year at this time.[17] In 1738, after the required two years spent as a *stagiaire*, he was admitted to the bar. In 1739 the name Rivière appears for the first time in the *Almanach Royal* among the *avocats au parlement* who had taken the oath in 1736. There it is found listed every year until 1755 inclusive.

This is the last reference I have been able to find to Louis-Pierre Rivière except in the writings of Diderot. He was no longer practising law at the time of their encounter, for in the dialogue *Lui et Moi* we see Lui attempting to borrow money from Moi in order to "reprendre la robe de palais" (below, p. 243). What happened to Louis-Pierre in 1755? The copy of the *Tableau des Avocats* reserved for the personal

13 Arch. Nat., T202–1, act of 2 June 1753.

14 The principals are referred to as "Mr Louis Pierre Rivière, avocat au Parlement demeurant ordinairement à Versailles, rue des Sœurs, paroisse Saint Louis, étant ce jour à Paris, d'une part, et Mr Louis Jean François Rivière, docteur en théologie de la maison et société de Sorbonne, chanoine de Saint Merry et clerc de la chapelle de la reine, demeurant à Paris, cloître Saint Merry d'autre part, tous les deux seuls et uniques héritiers chacun pour moitié de deffunte dame Margueritte Legalis, à son décès épouse non commune en biens de deffunt Mr Louis Rivière, ancien avocat au Parlement, leur mère ..." Under this act, Louis-Pierre inherited 7800 livres (Arch. Nat., T202-1, act of 22 June 1753).

15 Arch. Nat., T202-12, contract of 10 September 1713.

16 Arch. Nat., x¹ᵃ.9327 (4 September 1736).

17 At that time the university regulations forbade registration to a student before the completion of his sixteenth year. Three years of study in a university, and the licentiate degree, were required for admission to the bar. See Antoine-Gaspar Boucher d'Argis, *Histoire abrégée de l'ordre des Avocats*, in *Règles pour former un avocat* [by Pierre Biarnoy de Merville], nouvelle édition (Paris, 1778), 72–6.

use of the librarian of the Bibliothèque de l'Ordre des Avocats in Paris contains the name Louis-Pierre Rivière from 1738 to 1751. In the volume dated 1751 a contemporary librarian has written the words "a quitté" beside the name.[18] Apparently there was no *Tableau* printed during the exile of the Paris Parlement – volumes are lacking for the years 1752–4 – and that of 1755 no longer bears the name Rivière.[19] We may be certain, however, that Louis-Pierre continued to practise law until 1755, for the fact that the *Almanach Royal* records his name in that year is sufficient proof that he had been in good standing when the Parlement reconvened in November of 1754.[20]

Returning to Madame de Vandeul's anecdote, we are able to affirm that none of the historical facts presented above is at variance with her written account. Moreover, the first part of the story – the visit paid to the canon – is supported in every detail by her father's relation of it in the *Paradoxe sur le comédien* (below, p. 248) ; and the second part, the meeting with Rivière, is confirmed point for point by the satire *Lui et Moi*. We may therefore accept the anecdote as being fundamentally true, except perhaps for the claim that the canon, as a result of Diderot's eloquent presentation of the case, contributed to his brother's support. I have found no proof that this is other than a detail added to the story for effect.

Louis-Pierre Rivière, at the time of the meeting with Diderot that was to assure him a place in literary history, was not exactly a young man as Madame de Vandeul describes him. He was in his middle forties, and had been a practising lawyer for some fifteen years before abandoning the bar for what must have been a life of bohemian freedom. Both Diderot and his daughter affirm that he was an aspiring writer; and the fact that he claimed to have composed his brother's sermons seems to support that possibility.

THE DIALOGUE

With this somewhat clearer picture of Rivière, we may now turn to *Lui et Moi*. The dialogue is introduced by two paragraphs explaining the background and the circumstances of this encounter of Diderot with

18 Paris, Palais de Justice, Bibliothèque de l'Ordre des Avocats. *Nouveau Tableau des Avocats au Parlement* (A Paris, au Palais, chez Paulus-Du-Mesnil), 1751. Unlike the *Almanach Royal*, the *Tableau* gives both the baptismal names and the surname of those listed. The librarian was in the habit of recording deaths and withdrawals beside the names, in the copy of the *Tableau* in which they last appeared.

19 The name Rivière that reappears in the *Almanach Royal* in 1761 under the entry date of 1755 is not that of Louis-Pierre, but of a certain Antoine Rivière (*Nouveau Tableau des Avocats*, 1760).

20 The *Almanach Royal* is always a year behind the *Tableau des Avocats* in adding new names or in removing old ones.

his interlocutor (below, pp. 242–3). Lui, we are told, had previously borrowed money from Moi, then had turned and written a satire against his benefactor. He had had the impudence to read the satire to the *philosophe*, who indulgently suggested certain improvements. The satirist had then ended the interview with an unparalleled piece of insolence which Diderot relates in a footnote: it is the fable of the *formicaleo*, familiar to us from the Rivière anecdote. Now, five or six months later, the two meet at a corner of the rue Mâcon. Lui has apparently reaped the harvest of his misdeeds: he is in pitiable condition, "accablé de misère et de vilaines maladies." He stops the *philosophe* and they chat.

The conversation that follows has a single dominant theme: it is so designed as to bring out the loathing and disgust that Moi feels in the presence of this despicable character. He refuses Lui's request for money and reminds him of his former treachery. The satire that Lui had written, it appears, had been directed against Moi and his friends. Its title was *Les Zélindiens*, and it had been printed by "ce coquin d'Hérissant, qui court après tout ce qu'on écrit contre les encyclopédistes." Lui pretends to know nothing of the satire and invites the *philosophe* into a nearby café, pleading the inclemency of the weather. But Moi refuses. It is obvious to him that no amount of moralizing can reform such a worthless rascal. He suggests ironically that Lui might solve his financial problems by daring to be more consistent with his character. How? Well, for example, if he had a rich father who might be put out of the way ... Lui's answer is a perfect *mot de caractère*: "Je n'ai point de père." Moi, overcome with horror, takes refuge in flight, whilst Lui shouts after him: "Philosophe, écoutez donc, écoutez donc. Vous prenez les choses au tragique."

The scene just described has numerous traits found also in the Rivière anecdote, and we are obliged to conclude that it is a single incident that occasioned both. The café, the threatening weather, the quip about Lui's father, and the "impertinent apologue" of the *formicaleo*, all have their place in Madame de Vandeul's biography.

But there is one remarkable inconsistency: our dialogue makes no mention of the visit to the Chanoine Rivière, which according to the anecdote was the real prelude to this encounter. Instead we are told that Lui had written a satire against Diderot and that this was the occasion of their falling out.

Now the episode concerning the satire, which figures so prominently in *Lui et Moi*, does appear in the *Mémoires* of Madame de Vandeul, but it is treated as a completely separate anecdote having nothing whatever to do with Rivière. And the same story is related by the Encyclopedist himself in a letter to Falconet, once again without mention of

Rivière.[21] Yet the evidence of *Lui et Moi* is unequivocal, so that Maurice Tourneux was able to conclude that the satirist and Rivière were one and the same person (A.T., XVII, 477–8). However, the details given both by Diderot and by his daughter show beyond doubt that it was early in the career of the *philosophe* that the incident concerning the satirist occurred. The two accounts refer to the Duc d'Orléans (1703–52) as still living, which establishes our *terminus ad quem*; and Diderot's statement in the letter to Falconet, "J'habitois alors l'Estrapade,"[22] puts the *terminus a quo* in 1747 at the very earliest.

The episode must, therefore, belong to the period shortly before or after 1750, certainly not later than 1752; and we know that Diderot's encounter with Rivière took place some ten years later. Until 1755 Rivière had been a lawyer in good standing; only after that was he to fall on evil days and become, like the satirist, an impecunious scribbler. We must therefore reject the identification of the satirist with Rivière, and draw the opposite – and much more significant – conclusion: *Lui et Moi* combines the facts of two separate incidents in Diderot's life, and Lui is an amalgam of two distinct individuals.

In all probability the framework of *Lui et Moi* was an actual conversation with Louis-Pierre Rivière. However, Diderot saw fit to introduce into his account of that conversation elements which it did not in fact contain. There is nothing in the dialogue that might not have been said on that occasion with the exception of the part that concerns the satire. In attributing that piece of treachery to Rivière, Diderot shows complete disregard for the facts. But more than this, he gives to the pernicious work a title, *Les Zélindiens*, which it could not possibly have had. Tourneux has pointed out that *Les Zélindiens*, of which he tried in vain to locate a copy, was probably the work of a certain Mademoiselle Fauque.[23] It must have appeared early in 1762, for Grimm reviews the book on 1 June of that year.[24] If it had been a satire on the *philosophes*, Grimm would certainly have mentioned the fact; but he dis-

---

21 These two texts are reproduced below in Appendix 3, items 4 and 5 (pp. 249–50).

22 Below, p. 250. Louis III, Duc d'Orléans, spent the last years of his life in retirement at Sainte-Geneviève. At the time of his death in 1752, Diderot had been living nearby on the rue de la Vieille-Estrapade for four or five years.

23 A.T., XVII, 478. I have been equally unsuccessful in locating a copy of *Les Zélindiens*.

24 *Corr. lit.*, v, 90. Reproduced below in Appendix 3, item 6 (p. 250). Maurice Tourneux, commenting on Grimm's review of *Les Zélindiens* which attributes the book to "Mlle F***," makes the following remarks: "Voilà qui est formel : Grimm a lu la brochure puisqu'il rapporte ce qu'elle contient et qu'il en désigne l'auteur dont l'initiale figure peut-être d'ailleurs sur le titre. D'un autre côté, comment supposer que Diderot pût montrer une telle irritation contre un mauvais petit pamphlet sur les Parisiens, s'il n'avait eu la certitude que l'auteur lui fût connu et qu'il lui avait lu sa satire manuscrite ?" (A.T., XVII, 478).

misses it scornfully as a vapid treatment of Parisian life which no one bothered to read.[25] Whether or not it was Hérissant who published *Les Zélindiens* – we shall perhaps never know – it is evident that Diderot is here merely throwing a barb at one of the persistent enemies of the philosophic party.[26]

These facts allow us to glimpse the manner in which Diderot composed his *Lui et Moi*. The little work is essentially a prose satire in dialogue form, aimed at heaping ignominy upon the mean and vicious of heart. The author, as usual, builds upon an actual occurrence of which he has personal knowledge. In this instance he chooses to combine two striking examples of knavery – the black ingratitude of the satirist who turned his pen against a benefactor, and the cynical perversity shown by Rivière in his fable of the *formica-leo* – to form the character of a self-confessed rogue called Lui.

Not content with this, he goes on to identify Lui with the anti-encyclopedist party – despite the fact that the satire, if there was one, could have had nothing to do with the campaign against the *Encyclopédie* which had left Diderot still embittered in 1762.[27] At one point he raises his sights to aim a volley at contemporary society by suggesting that Lui is capable of writing "une apologie des persécuteurs ou des sangsues de la nation" (below, p. 244). Lui's baseness and impudence are revealed in every word he utters, and the conversation is brought to a close with the ironical proposal that the crime of patricide might prove a satisfactory way of relieving his financial distress.

In the final paragraph the author speaks again in his own name. "L'horreur me saisit. Je m'enfuis." Here the tone of scorn and revulsion that permeates the dialogue, and the deep-rooted antagonism between Lui and Moi that is indicated by the title, find explicit expression in the words: "j'étais bien loin de cet homme que je m'en croyais encore trop près." The moral of the satire is clear: men who are instinctively vicious are beyond hope of any lasting reform, and prudence dictates that the virtuous give them a wide berth.

Let us turn for a moment to the problem of the date of composition of *Lui et Moi*. We have seen that the meeting with Rivière must have

25 Maurice Tourneux gives the names of two other authorities who support this opinion. See below, Appendix 3, item 7 (p. 251).

26 See below, Appendix 2 (p. 245, n. 5).

27 The pamphlet belongs, as we have seen, to a period several years previous to the concerted attacks launched against the *Encyclopédie* by Moreau, Palissot, Chaumeix, et al. Madame de Vandeul calls it "une satire amère de sa personne et de ses ouvrages" (below, p. 250), and her father tells Falconet that it was "une satyre contre les miens et moi" (below, p. 250). Arthur Wilson, in his biography of Diderot, suggests that the satire might have recounted the notorious quarrel which took place in 1751 between Diderot's wife and his mistress, Madame de Puisieux (*Diderot: The*

occurred some time after the spring of 1760. The fact that Diderot, in the dialogue, gives vent to his indignation against the enemies of the *Encyclopédie* in general and against the bookseller Hérissant in particular, indicates that the dialogue belongs in all probability to the period shortly after 1759. The reference to *Les Zélindiens*, which, as has been pointed out, Grimm reviewed in his newsletter of 1 June 1762, gives us a *terminus a quo* that must be fairly accurate. And we might suspect that *Lui et Moi* was written shortly after this time while the title of that eminently obscure work was still fresh in Diderot's mind.

There is another indication that *Lui et Moi* belongs to the summer of 1762. It is the reference in the closing paragraph to Diderot's friend Georges Le Roy. The *philosophe*, expressing his abhorrence of Lui's turpitude, finishes with the words: "M. Le Roy m'a dit qu'il avait beaucoup de pareils. Ma foi, je ne saurais le croire." Now why should Diderot summon the authority of Le Roy, or of anyone else, in support of the commonplace statement that this world is full of *méchants*? It may be, of course, that Le Roy had made such a remark upon hearing this story from his friend. In his post as "Lieutenant des chasses royales et des parcs de Versailles et de Marly" and as author of the article "Instinct" of the *Encyclopédie*, he was well fitted to judge the animalistic conduct of Rivière. But it is also quite likely that this is Diderot's little revenge against Le Roy for his despicable behaviour in July of 1762. The letters to Sophie Volland from 14 July to 28 July tell a story of jealousy and amorous intrigue that upset the d'Holbach household and caused Diderot to go through an agony of suspicion and doubt. Some of his best friends were suspected of trifling with the Baron's lovely wife; but only Le Roy, "le satyre," was known to have made an open bid for the lady's favours. "Et ce Le Roy qui foule au pied toute considération d'honnêteté et qui hazarde impudemment une déclaration à la femme de son ami!" exclaims Diderot, as he tells his mistress how each of the actors in this domestic drama has fallen in his esteem.[28] He did not break with Le Roy, of course; but the latter's treachery towards his generous host d'Holbach was certainly worthy to rank, in Diderot's mind, with the ingratitude shown by his satirist protégé and by Rivière. It may well be that the harrowing experience of that July 1762 incited Diderot to write against such viciousness, and that his indignation took the satirical form of the dialogue *Lui et Moi*.

## *Lui et Moi* AND *Le Neveu de Rameau*

It is impossible to read *Lui et Moi* without being struck by its many

---

*Testing Years, 1713–1759* [New York, Oxford University Press, 1957], 174 n.). For the quarrel itself, see ibid., 118.

28 *Corr.*, ed. Roth, IV, 61 (22 July 1762). See also IV, 52, 65.

similarities to *Le Neveu de Rameau*.[29] The two works are dialogues opening with a short introduction that sets the scene and leads into a conversation between Diderot (Moi) and a real-life acquaintance of his (Lui). In each case Lui is presented as a literary hanger-on, a failure in his chosen profession, and is identified by the author with the enemies of the *Encyclopédie* – perhaps with as little justification in the one case as in the other. In *Le Neveu* the author, attracted by the originality and imitative talents of Rameau while at the same time being repelled by his viciousness, interrupts the conversation at intervals to record his own intimate reactions: "Je ne scavois, moi, si je devois rester ou fuir, rire ou m'indigner" (Fabre, p. 76). In the shorter work the dialogue proceeds without interruption; the author does not resume his role until the final paragraph, in which he indicates the revulsion he feels by taking flight.

These two derelicts – both had borrowed money from the *philosophe* – are accused of inconsistency in their evil ways. Rameau, despite his pretentions to sublimity in wickedness, is "vacillant dans [ses] principes" (Fabre, p. 72). Rivière is "sans caractère"; if he were more consistent he might solve his financial problems by hastening his father's demise (below, p. 245). Moreover, the satirical use of animalism and of the argument based on the "pacte tacite" of Nature, so effective in *Le Neveu de Rameau* (Fabre, pp. 68–71), finds its place in *Lui et Moi*: "Si je fais la sottise de réchauffer un serpent, je ne serai pas surpris qu'il me pique" (below, p. 245). And the same deterministic philosophy rules the ending of the two satires: each despicable hero remains fixed in his character, fated to be what Nature has made him.

*Lui et Moi* was composed, in all probability, towards the end of the summer of 1762. This alone would be sufficient to connect it with *Le Neveu de Rameau*, the first draft of which critics are unanimous in placing in 1761 or 1762. More important, however, is the manner in which this brief satire, a kind of *Neveu de Rameau* in miniature, reveals the author's literary use of real-life experiences. The conversation with Rivière which actually took place between 1760 and 1762 is revised to fit the literary figure Lui, who is a combination of the ungrateful lawyer and the satirist of the early 1750s. What matter if, in reality, the incidents occurred ten years apart and concerned two different men? And what matter if the pamphlet of 1750 is given the title of an obscure book written a decade later? "Mais les circonstances momentanées s'oublient," says Diderot in his article "Encyclopédie"; "la postérité ne voit plus que la folie, le ridicule, le vice et la méchanceté couverts d'ignominie" (A.T., XIV, 466–7).

29 All references to *Le Neveu de Rameau* are to the critical edition by Jean Fabre (Genève, Droz, 1950), cited as Fabre.

This statement, which is Diderot's apology for satire directed against living persons, tells us a great deal about his attitude towards Rivière, Rameau, Palissot, and a host of other targets of his wrath. Posterity, he is sure, will attach to their names as little importance as modern readers accord, for example, to those of Horace's victims. His enemies, therefore, take on symbolic shapes for Diderot – or so he pretends – and thus he feels free not only to name them but also to rearrange the facts concerning them.[30] With the same supreme scorn for their mediocrity he can double Rivière with the satirist, or produce a literary Rameau who, unlike his model, is a pimp and a parasite; represent *Les Zélindiens* as a satire against the *Encyclopédie*, or bring Fréron *fils* (born 1754) into a conversation which appears to have taken place in 1761 (Fabre, pp. 16, 152–3). Future generations will reap the benefits of this artistic selection in the more pointed moral instruction it permits; meanwhile, the author can indulge his contempt for the wicked and the untalented by moving them about like the pawns they are on the chess-board of their literary existence.

*Lui et Moi*, though very brief, is so similar in conception and execution to *Le Neveu de Rameau* that it deserves to be given a place among the works of Diderot that bear the name "Satire." It has, of course, a certain value for his biographers; what is more, it indicates the kind of personal experience that prompted the *philosophe* to write satire. But especially, it reveals to us one of the techniques by which Diderot the satirist strove to achieve universality in the presentation of character while remaining firmly anchored in the reality of everyday experience.

The discovery that his antagonist Lui is endowed with the characteristics of two real-life individuals is perhaps less noteworthy in itself than for the new speculations it suggests. Does it not seem likely that the author of *Le Neveu de Rameau* employed the same procedure in his masterpiece? Is it not possible that the portrait of Rameau-Lui in the longer work was modelled after several of Diderot's contemporaries? These questions will be considered in Part III below.

30 Diderot defends this procedure in a passage added to the article "Pyrrhonienne" of the *Encyclopédie*, where he describes Pierre Bayle as "menteur comme tous les gens d'esprit, qui ne balancent guère à supprimer ou à ajouter une circonstance légère à un fait lorsqu'il en devient plus comique, ou plus intéressant" (A.T., XVI, 490–1).

**PART III**

Anatomy of a classic: *Le Neveu de Rameau*

# 1
# Introduction

With his edition of *Le Neveu de Rameau* in 1950, Jean Fabre opened a new era in the criticism of Diderot's enigmatic dialogue.[1] Since that time his brilliant Introduction and notes to the text have been systematically mined by scholars, with the result that each passing year sees the publication of new insights and fresh points of view that have considerably deepened our understanding of *Le Neveu*. But despite the host of useful commentaries on the work, there is as yet no discernible consensus as to what constitutes its essential unity. Whether from classical concern to conceal his art or from indulgence of his penchant for mystification, Diderot seems to have left no unequivocal guideposts to his thought; and his masterpiece, now universally recognized as such, appears fated to remain forever a battleground for conflicting opinions.

Despite the tendency of recent literary criticism to play down the significance of authorial intention and even to discount it entirely, the present essay is based on the double assumption that Diderot had a single unifying concept in which all the ideas of his dialogue converge, and that a useful service would be rendered to scholarship if this elusive element could be identified. No apology is offered for the second part of this proposition; as to the first, it seems difficult to admit that Diderot, a philosopher who never tired of stressing unity as a prerequisite of artistic beauty, should have been capable of producing a work lacking a coherent pattern of thought. If no significant pattern has emerged, is it not perhaps because the themes so cleverly orchestrated by the author have not been consistently examined in depth? For example, we have an excellent article on the theme of genius;[2] but there has been no attempt to treat the more general question of individuality, which embraces not only genius but also, among other matters, uniqueness of character and

1 All references to *Le Neveu de Rameau* will be to this edition (Geneva, Droz, 1950), cited as Fabre.

2 Otis Fellows, "The Theme of Genius in Diderot's *Neveu de Rameau*," *Diderot Studies*, II, (1952), 168–99.

artistic originality. Similarly, there is reason to believe that the theme of music requires to be studied more closely in relation to the ethical connotations traditionally attached to that word. In short, *Le Neveu de Rameau* gives evidence of being a complicated piece of "poetry," the product of a philosophic mind; only when the ideas it contains have been analyzed in their deeper resonances may we hope that the kinship of the various themes will become apparent. If the unity of the work can be satisfactorily established – and that is the principal concern of this study – there will perhaps be less difficulty in determining the lines along which criticism can most profitably move.

The only known autograph copy of *Le Neveu de Rameau* is preserved in the Pierpont Morgan Library in New York City. It is generally agreed on the basis of internal evidence that the final reworking which this manuscript represents cannot be placed earlier than 1774; and a recent study made of the watermarks on the paper gives reason to believe that it could date from as late as 1783, the year preceding Diderot's death.[3] It is most significant for our understanding of this work that the definitive draft, into which the author incorporated changes and additions made over the course of perhaps twenty years, bears the title "Satyre 2$^{de}$."

The various interpretations of the work – both of form and of content – stem from the different ways in which this title is understood. Everyone admits that *Le Neveu de Rameau* has certain satirical qualities and that the author conceived it at least in part as an instrument of personal vengeance; almost no one believes that any of the ordinary forms of satire is adequate to define it.[4] It has been called a novel, a short story, a "sotie." Most, however, accept the title "Satire" as being a defensible one, maintaining that the admixture of non-satirical elements (the pantomimes, for example, or the long section on music) is consonant with the traditional concept of satire as a medley or miscellany.

The title "Satire" is rather more ambiguous when it is a question of determining who or what is being satirized. The "common sense" view is that Diderot, in naming his two characters "Moi" and "Lui," meant to signify that Moi is his *porte-parole* and that Lui represents a moral position and a style of life that the author abominated.[5] But there are

3 Paul Vernière, "Histoire littéraire et papyrologie : à propos des autographes de Diderot," *Revue d'Histoire Littéraire de la France*, July–September 1966, 418.

4 For the Horatian qualities of *Le Neveu de Rameau*, see Karl Maurer, "Die Satire in der Weise des Horaz als Kunstform von Diderots *Neveu de Rameau*," *Romanische Forschungen*, LXIV (1952), 365–404.

5 A recent proponent of this view is Roland Desné: "Monsieur le Philosophe et le Fieffé Truand," *Europe*, Nos. 405–6 (Jan.–Feb. 1963), 182–98; "Le *Neveu de*

several facts that would seem to argue against this interpretation: first, Lui has by far the more prominent role, as well as being the more memorable of the two characters by virtue of his picturesque language and his rugged individualism; secondly, he frequently expresses ideas that were Diderot's own; and finally, the debate is allowed to end in an inconclusive manner, neither interlocutor having abandoned his position or having been reduced to silence. These are serious reasons for suspecting that the dialogue is not a straightforward contrast of opposing views, and that Moi cannot be identified fully with the author.

In addition to these observations which throw doubt on Diderot's intention in the satire, there have been expressed a number of personal judgments unfavourable to Moi that may or may not be justified by the text. Some see him as insincere and hypocritical, as too dogmatic or too colourless to represent Diderot; others think he is no match for Lui in argumentation, that he defends his position weakly, that he wins some points and loses others, and so forth. Hence a variety of critical opinions, some more plausible than others, making Lui more or less Diderot, making Moi more or less the butt of the satire, interpreting the dialogue as a debate between two sides of the author's character or an exploratory probing of the consequences of immoralism.[6]

It is not the purpose of this study to criticize theories about *Le Neveu de Rameau* but to criticize the work itself; the following pages will therefore refer only incidentally and very infrequently to points of view expressed by others. It should be remarked here, however, that only the "common sense" theory mentioned above seems to respect fully the intention of the author implied by the title "Satire." Does not satire, whether Horatian, Juvenalian, Menippean, or even satire in the broad sense of the term, presuppose on the part of the author, if not a definite moral point of view, at least the recognition of a norm of reason from which the actions of men tend to deviate? It is true, of course, that

*Rameau* dans l'ombre et la lumière du xviiie siècle," *Studies on Voltaire and the Eighteenth Century*, xxv (1963), 493–507; *Diderot et Le Neveu de Rameau. Essai d'explication* (Paris, Centre d'Etudes et de Recherches Marxistes, n.d.). See also M. Desné's Introduction to his edition of *Le Neveu de Rameau* (Paris, Club des Amis du Livre Progressiste, 1963).

6 Studies representative of the various schools of opinion are: Daniel Mornet, "La Véritable Signification du *Neveu de Rameau*," *Revue des Deux Mondes*, 7th per., xl (August 1927), 881–908; Roger Laufer, "Structure et signification du *Neveu de Rameau* de Diderot," *Revue des Sciences Humaines*, n.s., c (1960), 399–413; Lester Crocker, "Le *Neveu de Rameau*, une expérience morale," *Cahiers de l'Association Internationale des Etudes Françaises*, xiii (1961), 133–55. See also Milton F. Seiden, "Jean-François Rameau and Diderot's Neveu," *Diderot Studies*, i (1949), 143–91; *Entretiens sur "Le Neveu de Rameau*," ed. Michèle Duchet and Michel Launay (Paris, Nizet, 1967), 7–28; and Herbert Josephs, *Diderot's Dialogue of Gesture and Language: Le Neveu de Rameau*, 107–15.

partial satires are not uncommon in which the satirical intent is limited
to a single character or a single episode; but if a work merits the title
"Satire," must we not expect that all its components – characters, ideas,
image of society – have been dictated by the satirical posture adopted
by the author? The reason, surely, why the unity of Diderot's dialogue
is still a matter of debate is that the satirical set of mind that presided
over its conception has never been adequately defined.

In the course of this essay I shall try to show that the sardonic view,
if it does not coincide precisely with the "idée artistique" that Jean Fabre
seeks to define (pp. xli–xliii), is at the very least its most important element. Critics such as Georges May and Otis Fellows have indicated their
awareness of this fact by tracing the genesis of *Le Neveu de Rameau* to
a "crise de pessimisme" concerning human nature on the part of Diderot, or to a gnawing doubt as to his own genius.[7] Their analyses give
recognition to the highly personal character that marks all of Diderot's
writings; but, in order fully to grasp the import of the *Satyre 2$^{de}$*, we
must go beyond Diderot the man, full of rancour and a prey to insecurity, to his *alter ego* "Denis le philosophe"; for the pessimism and
self-doubt that gave rise to the all too human invective were sublimated,
at another level, into an ironical world-view that dictated the structure
and content of *Le Neveu de Rameau*, making it perhaps the most successful combination of philosophy and poetry in the literature of the
French Enlightenment.

7 Georges May, *Quatre Visages de Denis Diderot* (Paris, Boivin, 1951), 34–99;
Otis Fellows, "The Theme of Genius in Diderot's *Neveu de Rameau*."

# 2

# Two contemporary influences

## PALISSOT AND *Les Philosophes*

LITERARY critics, beginning with Goethe in 1805, have unanimously recognized in *Le Neveu de Rameau* a satirical reply to the play of Charles Palissot entitled *Les Philosophes*.[1] This comedy, written by a young man already known for the venom of his pen, had little to say in 1760 that had not been said many times already by its author and other opponents of the *parti philosophique*. For its victims, however, *Les Philosophes* was the crowning humiliation by virtue of its being presented, with a certain measure of success, by the actors of the Comédie Française.

It was no new thing for Diderot, of course, to find himself publicly vilified. The preceding few years had seen him caricatured as chief of the "cacouacs," ridiculed for his dramatic theories, and accused of plagiarism. But nothing, surely, had equalled this ultimate indignity: being singled out for portrayal as the hypocritical Dortidius, having his "Jeune homme, prends et lis" repeated mockingly five times in two consecutive scenes,[2] having four of his works held up to derision in the much discussed scene of the *colporteur* (III, 6), and seeing himself and his friends treated, in the sight of all Paris, as "des gens de sac et de

---

1 *Les Philosophes*, comédie, en trois actes, en vers, représentée pour la première fois par les Comédiens François ordinaires du Roi, le 2 mai 1760. Par M. Palissot de Montenoy. Paris, Duchesne, 1760. A conscientious study of the relations between Palissot and the Encyclopedists will be found in Hilde H. Freud, *Palissot and "Les Philosophes,"* *Diderot Studies*, IX (Geneva, Droz, 1967).

2 Act II, Sc. 3 and 4. The words "Jeune homme, prends et lis" had appeared at the beginning of the foreword to Diderot's *De l'interprétation de la nature* (1754). Assézat records the unfavourable reactions of certain readers to this seemingly pompous exhortation (A.T., II, 4). It has never been suggested, I believe, that Diderot is here merely borrowing as an epigraph the words of Plato's Euclides in the *Theaetetus* (143c). Wishing to have read aloud the dialogue on scientific knowledge between Socrates and Theaetetus, Euclides invites his slave to begin: "Boy, take the book and read" ('Αλλά, παῖ, λαβὲ τὸ βιβλίον καὶ λέγε). The fact that Diderot refrained from defending himself against the charge of vanity on this score is not without importance in our estimation of his character.

corde, sans principes, et sans mœurs."[3] How mockingly must the closing lines of the comedy have sounded in the ears of one who was pleased to be called "le philosophe":

Des sages de nos jours nous distinguons les traits:
Nous démasquons les faux, et respectons les vrais!

Already in 1757 Palissot had given Diderot a stinging rebuke by stating, in the final pages of his *Petites Lettres sur de grands philosophes*, that some of his major works were mere slavish imitations or translations of Shaftesbury, Bacon, and Goldoni.[4] Now, in a prefatory Letter published shortly after his play had closed, he took care to point out that the Encyclopedist and his ilk were unworthy of comparison with Voltaire and Montesquieu, the true philosophers of the nation.[5]

If Palissot's comedy, characterized by a contemporary wit as "une feuille de Fréron mise en action," did indeed play a role in the genesis of *Le Neveu de Rameau*, it was a role similar to that played by a spark in an explosion. For Diderot, in his counterattack, did not merely turn back upon his tormentor the well-worn weapons of satire – charges of hypocrisy, viciousness, and mediocrity – as a lesser man might have done. More characteristic of him is what we find in *Le Neveu*: the calm, deliberate exposition, in literary form, of a philosophy of mediocrity and talent, of utility and inutility, of being and seeming, of vice and virtue, that develops with every page until it finally involves the Palissots of every age, and the type of society that spawns them, in a thundering universal condemnation. We must be careful, therefore, not to exaggerate the importance of Palissot the man in our judgment of Diderot's masterpiece. When it has been duly noted that his name appears twenty-three times in the course of the work and that his comedy is mentioned once, there remains little to be said about the "personal vendetta" aspect of the satire, except that Palissot's portrait is given a place of honour in this gallery of mediocrity.

Apart from direct invective against Palissot, it is possible to find in *Le Neveu de Rameau* certain traces of the war of pamphlets that occupied Paris for several months following the presentation of *Les Philosophes*. For example, the frequently repeated charge that Palissot had profited from selling the favours of his wife[6] almost certainly prompted the final scene of *Le Neveu*, in which Lui weeps mock tears over the loss of his "chere moitié": "Elle auroit eu, tot ou tard, le fermier general,

3 D'Alembert, in a letter to Voltaire, 6 May 1760 (Best. 8155).
4 *Petites Lettres sur de grands philosophes*, in *Œuvres*, (Liège, 1778, 7 vols.), II, 148–9.
5 *Lettre de l'auteur de la comédie des Philosophes, au public, pour servir de Préface à la Pièce*, 10–11. This letter was not reproduced in any of Palissot's collected works.
6 The pamphlets hostile to Palissot seldom fail to make the accusation: *Préface*

tout au moins. ... Mais helas je l'ai perdue; et mes esperances de fortune se sont evanouies avec elle. ... Non, non, je ne m'en consolerai jamais" (Fabre, pp. 108–9). We can see also, in Diderot's prolonged description of Bertin in terms of the art of puppetry (Fabre, pp. 47–8), a reflection of the fact that the financier was reputed at the time to be the author of *Les Philosophes de bois, farce pour les marionnettes,* in reality from the pen of Louis Poinsinet de Sivry.[7] And the famous scene at Bertin's dinner table (Fabre, pp. 62–3), one of the most stylistically successful passages in *Le Neveu de Rameau,* does not owe its inspiration only to the classic literary banquets of antiquity: we are obliged to see its immediate source in the satirical engravings entitled *Repas de nos Philosophes* and *Dîner des Philosophes* that had such wide circulation in 1760.[8]

If *Le Neveu de Rameau* owes so much of its material to the literary quarrel that gave it birth, we should not leave the subject of Palissot without first considering the possibility that the form of Diderot's satire might also show the influence of *Les Philosophes.* This is quite likely, since much of the storm raised by this play in 1760 was precisely a question of genre. It will be remembered that Palissot had been censured by friend and foe alike for having used the comic stage to ridicule identifiable living people. Was not comedy, they asked, traditionally concerned with the depiction of vice and folly in a general way, whereas satire was the genre of personal attack?[9] The author of *Les Philosophes* defended himself stoutly by pointing to the example of Aristophanes and the Old Comedy of Athens. Everyone knew that comedy, in its origins, had been

de la Comédie des Philosophes, ou la Vision de Charles Palissot* (Paris, 1760, 20 pp.), 3–4 [by Morellet]; *Les Qu'est-ce?* (Paris, 1760, 32 pp.), 5; *Les Quand* (Paris, 1760, 23 pp.), 18. D'Alembert also, in his letter to Voltaire of 6 May 1760, refers to "Mᵣ Palissot, maquereau de sa femme, & banqueroutier" (Best. 8155).

7 "*Les Philosophes de bois* sont une mauvaise farce qu'on a fait jouer à Passy par les marionnettes. C'est une production du génie de M. Bertin, trésorier des parties casuelles" (Grimm, *Corr. lit.,* IV, 305, 15 October 1760). In *La Comédie satirique au XVIII° siècle* (Paris, Perrin, 1885), Gustave Desnoiresterres tells us: "*Les Philosophes de bois* s'attachaient de préférence à Diderot, qui y était désigné sous le nom de 'M. Fagot,'" and a note explains: "Diderot se vantait un jour d'avoir détruit une forêt de préjugés. 'C'est pour cela, lui répondit-on, que vous nous comptez tant de fagots.' Cela expliquerait le sobriquet sous lequel il est désigné ici" (p. 133).

8 Henry Cohen, *Guide de l'amateur de livres à vignettes du XVIII° siècle* (4° édition, Paris, P. Rouquette, 1880) gives the following details: "On rencontre quelquefois toutes ces pièces réunies avec beaucoup d'autres en un ou deux volumes in -12. Dans les recueils du Temps, on trouve généralement une grande figure pliée, intitulée: 'le Repas de nos Philosophes,' et une jolie vignette que l'on peut attribuer à Eisen" (p. 357).

9 The prevailing opinion had been stated by Diderot himself in the *Entretiens sur le Fils naturel*: "Le principal personnage d'une comédie doit ... représenter un grand nombre d'hommmes. Si, par hasard, on lui donnait une physionomie si particulière, qu'il n'y eût dans la société qu'un seul individu qui lui ressemblât, la comédie retournerait à son enfance, et dégénérerait en satire" (A.T., VII, 138).

satirical, and that Aristophanes had not hesitated to paint a ridiculous picture of Socrates, his contemporary, in *The Clouds*. Palissot, in his Preface, contended that this procedure seemed to be the only manner of dealing with a pernicious sect like that of the *philosophes*: "Il ne restait, pour abattre ce parti puissant, que de l'attaquer par le ridicule aux yeux mêmes du Public assemblé : c'était ramener le théâtre à sa première institution ..."[10] Soon all Paris was speaking of him as a modern Aristophanes.[11]

Such fatuous posturing could scarcely be expected to sit well with Diderot, especially in view of his profound admiration for Aristophanes' victim, Socrates. We know that his fellow-feeling for the persecuted Athenian philosopher, always strong, was to reach the proportions of a veritable cult after the condemnation, in 1759, of the *Encyclopédie*.[12] Aristophanes, on the other hand, he had condemned to the rank of "farceur original" in his *Discours sur la poésie dramatique* (A.T., VII, 319). Under such circumstances it is quite conceivable that the ancient conflict between the comic poet and the philosopher should have had an effect on the Diderot-Palissot confrontation, for if Palissot had adopted the persona of Aristophanes, Diderot as surely identified himself with Socrates. The conflict itself, of course, is not reflected in the subject matter of *Le Neveu de Rameau*, for the name of Aristophanes appears nowhere in its pages. But is it not likely that Palissot's pretence of returning to the satirical origins of comedy should have provoked Diderot to reply in a similar vein? The conscious identification of *Les Philosophes* with the political comedy of antiquity must inevitably have presented itself to the Encyclopedist, already steeped in classical literature and fresh from his research into the dramatic theory of the ancients in 1757 and 1758, as a challenge difficult to ignore. It would be premature at this point of our inquiry to ask whether or not our knowledge of the ancient theatre can help to explain the literary form of *Le Neveu de Rameau*. The question will be raised again in a later chapter.

HELVETIUS AND *De l'esprit*

The search for contemporary sources that might have influenced the composition of *Le Neveu de Rameau* has not paid sufficient attention to the work of Claude-Adrien Helvétius entitled *De l'esprit*. The publi-

10 *Lettre de l'auteur de la comédie des Philosophes, au public*, 8.

11 Grimm, *Corr. lit.*, IV, 241 (1 June 1760); ibid., 275 (15 August 1760); *Les Qu'est-ce?* (1760, 32 pp.), 21–2; *Le Philosophe, ami de tout le monde, ou Conseils désintéressés aux Littérateurs* (A Sophopolis, chez le Pacifique, 1760, 36 pp.), 25–6 [by L. Coste].

12 See Jean Seznec, *Essais sur Diderot et l'Antiquité* (Oxford, Clarendon Press,

cation of this controversial book in the summer of 1758 was a crucial event in the life of Denis Diderot; coming when it did, it was undoubtedly instrumental in the condemnation the following year of the already beleaguered *Encyclopédie,* which hostile contemporaries insisted on seeing as the source-book for the crude materialism of *De l'esprit.*[13] Ironically, the Encyclopedist was accused of having collaborated with Helvétius,[14] whereas we know from his *Réflexions sur le livre De l'esprit,* written shortly after the book's appearance,[15] that he was inimical to many of the ideas contained therein. The *Réflexions,* despite the sympathetic attitude which they manifest toward the author of *De l'esprit,* assert quite bluntly that at least three of its four central statements are false.

When Helvétius persisted in presenting the same notions some fifteen years later in his posthumous *De l'homme* (1773), Diderot felt compelled to write a lengthy refutation of his late friend's fundamental assumptions, the well-known *Réfutation suivie de l'ouvrage d'Helvétius intitulé L'Homme.*[16] Judging from the sincerity and tenacity of the *Réfutation,* it is clear that *De l'homme* had struck a sensitive chord; but why is it that *De l'esprit,* which contained essentially the same material,[17] had not had a similar effect? Why do the *Réflexions* occupy a mere eight pages, whereas the *Réfutation* was to assume book-length proportions? Was Diderot, in 1758, too occupied otherwise? Did he hesitate to refute Helvétius openly for fear of revealing dissension in the philosophic ranks? Or was it only the intervening years, perhaps, that brought full realization of the import of Helvétius' conclusions for his own philosophy?

These questions are, of course, unanswerable. What is important is

1957), 1–22; Raymond Trousson, *Socrate devant Voltaire, Diderot et Rousseau : la Conscience en face du mythe* (Paris, Minard, 1967), 45–65.

13 This whole question is treated by D. W. Smith, *Helvétius: a Study in Persecution* (Oxford, 1965), 140–54.

14 *Corr. lit.,* IV, 80; D. W. Smith, *Helvétius,* 186–9; A. M. Wilson, *Diderot: the Testing Years, 1713–1759,* 312; Virgil Topazio, "Diderot's Supposed Contribution to Helvétius' Works," *Philological Quarterly,* XXXIII (1954), 313–29.

15 A.T., II, 267–74. Diderot's *Réflexions* appeared in Grimm's *Correspondance littéraire* in three parts, on the 15th of each month from August to October 1758. See Jean de Booy, "Inventaire provisoire des contributions de Diderot à la *Correspondance littéraire,*" *Dix-huitième Siècle,* No. 1 (1969), 360.

16 A.T., II, 275–456.

17 D. W. Smith (*Helvétius,* 185–6) affirms the similarity of the two works: "The later work is much fuller, more direct and hard-hitting than *De l'esprit,* since it was published posthumously and abroad, but it contains no ideas fundamentally new to his thought. The difference is entirely one of stress. ... his materialistic epistemology, his sexual ethics, and his views on despotism, religion, education, aesthetics, and economics were expanded and clarified, but the fundamental theories remained the same as those of *De l'esprit.*"

that we should not make the error of measuring the depth of Diderot's disagreement with Helvétius by the brevity of his *Réflexions*. I hope that it will become clear in the course of the following pages that Diderot did in fact react strongly to *De l'esprit*, and that this reaction was to play an important role in shaping the work we know as *Le Neveu de Rameau*.

The first-edition copy of *De l'esprit* owned by Diderot, bearing a number of autograph notes, has been located recently in Leningrad. A preliminary sampling of these notes, published by V. S. Lioublinski, shows that some of them served as a basis for the *Réflexions sur le livre De l'esprit*.[18] "Si peu nombreuses, si courtes que soient ces remarques," Lioublinski concludes, "elles évoquent assez clairement une lecture attentive, intéressée (et critique!)."[19] The few references to *De l'esprit* found in his *Correspondance* tell us little or nothing of his opinion of the work, so that his *Réflexions sur de livre De l'esprit* remain the principal source of information on that matter.

*De l'esprit*, according to the *Réflexions*, will prove to be one of the great books of the century. Diderot praises its high moral tone and the many truths to be found in its pages, while insisting that its general principles are erroneous (A.T., II, 274). Helvétius' reduction of all mental activity to physical sensitivity is treated rather facetiously (II, 267–8); his reduction of all moral activity to the promptings of self-interest and the desire for physical goods is expressly branded as false (II, 271); and his famous paradox of the original equality of minds and the equal educability of all is met with Horace's expression of extreme scepticism: *Credat judaeus Apella* (ibid.).

In spite of the kind words that are reserved for Helvétius' treatment of certain questions such as luxury and despotism, the *Réflexions* reveal clearly the gulf that separates the thinking of the two men. Their differences are such that a detailed analysis of them would take us far beyond the scope of this work; however, the broad lines along which their views diverge can be usefully indicated here.

First, the moral question. Helvétius, with characteristic bluntness, had developed a hedonistic ethics that was consciously mechanistic in character.[20] The immediate motive forces of his moral world are pleasure

18 V. S. Lioublinski, "Sur la trace des livres lus par Diderot," *Europe* (jan.–fév. 1963), 276–90, esp. 283 ff. The book described by Lioublinski has been identified as the "édition cartonnée" published in July 1758 (D. W. Smith, "The Publication of Helvétius's *De l'esprit*, 1758–9," *French Studies*, XVIII [1964], 342).

19 Art. cit., 289.

20 "J'ai cru qu'on devoit traiter la morale comme toutes les autres sciences, &

and pain, and the general law of motion is that of self-interest.[21] Just men can and do exist, according to Helvétius, but their justice is not the result of altruism. Speaking of personal self-interest, he asks: "Quel autre motif pourroit déterminer un homme à des actions généreuses ? Il lui est aussi impossible d'aimer le bien pour le bien, que d'aimer le mal pour le mal."[22]

Diderot's reaction to this last statement is indicated by the fact that these words are underlined in his copy of *De l'esprit*.[23] Helvétius' moral principles were certain to be repugnant to one whose constant and unchanging conception of virtue was that it necessarily involves sacrifice.[24] On the level of practical morality there is radical opposition between Diderot's view and that of the author of *De l'esprit*, who wrote: "L'homme vertueux n'est donc point celui qui sacrifie ses plaisirs, ses habitudes & ses plus fortes passions, à l'intérêt public, puisqu'un tel homme est impossible; mais celui dont la plus forte passion est tellement conforme à l'intérêt général, qu'il est presque toujours nécessité à la vertu" (pp. 374-5).

It is not, however, the descriptive presentation of man's egoism that we find attacked in the *Réflexions*, but rather the normative part of the system. Actions, according to Helvétius, are to be judged solely by their consequences for the common good; and Diderot, going to the heart of the matter, points out that the author's purely utilitarian viewpoint excludes all absolute moral values (A.T., II, 270). He opposes to this his own belief that there is an ontological basis for moral judgment in human nature itself – in the universal similarity of human needs, physical organization, and sensitivity. "C'est, à la vérité, l'intérêt général et particulier qui métamorphose l'idée de juste et d'injuste," Diderot concludes, "mais son essence en est indépendante" (ibid.). This empirical version of Natural Law, which Diderot shared with d'Alembert and d'Holbach, is found so consistently beneath his pen that Ernst Cassirer has called it "the fixed point in Diderot's absolutely flexible and dy-

---

faire une morale comme une physique expérimentale" (*De l'esprit*, i-ii). All subsequent quotations will be from the original "édition cartonnée" (Paris, Durand, 1758).

21 "la douleur & le plaisir des sens font agir & penser les hommes, & sont les seuls contrepoids qui meuvent le monde moral" (*De l'esprit*, 366); "Si l'univers physique est soumis aux loix du mouvement, l'univers moral ne l'est pas moins à celles de l'intérêt" (ibid., 53).

22 *De l'esprit*, 73.

23 See V. Lioublinski's article, p. 287.

24 See A.T., I, 13 (*Discours préliminaire* to his translation of Shaftesbury, 1745); A.T., VII, 69 (*Le Fils naturel*, 1757); A.T., V, 214 (*Eloge de Richardson*, 1760); A.T., III, 288 (*Essai sur les règnes de Claude et de Néron*, 1778-82).

namic philosophy."[25] It is this intimate conviction that underlies all of his thinking about happiness, virtue, utility, and self-interest and forbids our considering him as a proponent of utilitarianism except in a modified sense. The essential point for our purpose is to note that *De l'esprit* brought Diderot face to face with the moral problem of utility in both its egoistic and its universalistic aspects, forcing him once again to clarify his position on this much-debated philosophical question.

Let us turn now to Helvétius' ideas on education and genius. Following Condillac, the author of *De l'esprit* had made the human mind totally passive before experience, and had been able to conclude that any man having his five senses in working order could be brought, through control of his education and environment, to the heights of genius.[26] The pure rationalism of this approach to the problem of man is best exemplified by the paradox of the original equality of minds, an idea which Helvétius later attributed to John Locke.[27] But Locke had modified his earlier statements on this matter in his treatise entitled *Conduct of the Understanding*,[28] and Diderot agrees with the English philosopher in insisting that our judgments concerning the mind must not be based on an abstraction, but on the real individual man as known to science and medicine. His outright rejection of intellectual egalitarianism (*Credat judaeus Apella*) is followed immediately in the *Réflexions* by a series of arguments against Helvétius' conclusions that will be developed more fully in the *Réfutation*. Slight differences among men at birth, says Diderot, are magnified with time; characters are infinitely

25 Comparing Diderot with Voltaire, Cassirer says: "In Diderot, too, belief in the immutable moral nature of man and in a firm principle of justice arising from this nature remains unshakable. And this belief constitutes the fixed point in Diderot's absolutely flexible and dynamic philosophy. When Helvetius in his book *On the Mind* attempted to undermine this belief, when he sought to expose all ostensibly moral impulses as veiled egotism, Diderot expressly raised objections to any such leveling process" (Ernst Cassirer, *The Philosophy of the Enlightenment*, trans. Fritz Koelln and James P. Pettigrove [Boston, Beacon Press, 1955], 246).

26 Helvétius calls physical sensitivity and memory "deux facultés, ou, si je l'ose dire, deux puissances passives ..." (*De l'esprit*, 1–2). Thus: "Il est donc certain que l'inégalité d'esprit, appercue dans les hommes que j'appelle communément bien organisés, ne dépend nullement de l'excellence plus ou moins grande de leur organisation; mais de l'éducation différente qu'ils reçoivent, des circonstances diverses dans lesquelles ils se trouvent ..." (ibid., 438). And again: "L'homme de génie n'est donc que le produit des circonstances dans lesquelles cet homme s'est trouvé. ... J'ai senti ... combien la persuasion où l'on est que le génie & la vertu sont de purs dons de la nature, s'opposoit aux progrès de la science de l'éducation, & favorisoit, à cet égard, la paresse & la négligence" (ibid., 473–4).

27 See Diderot's *Réfutation*, A.T., II, 296–7.

28 The evolution of Locke's ideas concerning natural equality in the *Thoughts Concerning Education* (1693) and the *Conduct of the Understanding* (1704) is outlined by Robert R. Rusk, *The Doctrines of the Great Educators* (London, Macmillan, 1952), 116–20.

varied; one man differs from himself from moment to moment, owing to his succession of mental states; the good or bad condition of the brain, whether due to nature or to accident, is of paramount importance for the mind; finally, if it is the physical organization that distinguishes man from animal, as Helvétius avers, the difference between the genius and the ordinary man should logically be traced to the same cause (A.T., II, 271).

Such was Diderot's reaction to the doctrine of the equality of minds in 1758, some three or four years before he undertook *Le Neveu de Rameau*. Similarly, his attitude to the equal educability of all, deduced from the equality of minds, differs not at all in the *Réflexions* from what we shall find years later in the *Réfutation*. Here, the basic opposition between the two men with regard to the development both of character and of intellect has to do with origins. Helvétius, who chooses to ignore heredity and innate dispositions, considers that the great character and the great mind are made, not born. Neither, therefore, can be called "original" in the etymological sense of the word. For Diderot, on the other hand, the word "original" has a real meaning when applied both to the extraordinary character and to the genius. Neither could have become such had he not been born with certain predispositions.

His *Réflexions*, therefore, conclude the attack on Helvétius' position in this way: "On n'a pas vu la barrière insurmontable qui sépare l'homme que la nature a destiné à quelque fonction, de l'homme qui n'y apporte que du travail, de l'intérêt, de l'attention, des passions" (A.T., II, 271). The words "l'homme que la nature a destiné à quelque fonction" contain implicitly the organicist doctrine of the *Réfutation*, with its appeals to natural dispositions and aptitudes which Helvétius had swept away along with innate ideas and the faculties of the soul. Diderot cannot allow either acts of mind or moral actions to be totally indeterminate at their source, for they are functions of a material organism and will therefore be the expression of its unique properties.

At the risk of oversimplifying, we may consider the Diderot-Helvétius conflict generally in terms of universality and individuality. Helvétius' implicit denial of a moral absolute represents for Diderot a failure to recognize as the root of morality the universality of human nature. On the other hand, in his insistence on the universal perfectibility of reason, Helvétius had ignored the very real limitations imposed on the mind by the individuality of the human organism. The central issues at stake are three: utility, individuality, and equality. These fundamental philosophical problems had often been pondered by Diderot; but his attention was focussed on them again, especially in their ethical ramifications,

when he saw what they had become beneath Helvétius' pen. As he was
to affirm many years later in the *Réfutation* (A.T., II, 316), while agreeing with Helvétius' principles (materialism and sensationalism), he
found himself unable to accept the conclusions of the book *De l'homme*.
The same antagonism towards a mechanistic interpretation of man is
already evident in the *Réflexions* of 1758. When, four years thereafter,
Diderot felt constrained to express himself in the moral genre of satire,
he was led to frame his thoughts in terms of these basic questions of
utility, individuality, and equality. It is impossible to exaggerate the
significance of these ideas for *Le Neveu de Rameau*. Each will be given
special consideration in the chapters that follow.

In the century and a half since the authentic text of *Le Neveu de Rameau* was first published, no document has come to light indicating the
author's intention in this dialogue. Conjectures based on internal evidence have not been wanting; none, however, has found external justification. If it is permissible to speak of "sources" in relation to a masterpiece, there does exist a text that can be considered as a source of *Le
Neveu de Rameau*, and on which a defensible analysis of the work can
be constructed. One would scarcely expect to find such a passage among
the ponderous pages of *De l'esprit*; yet here, overlooked by generations
of critics, lies, I believe, the germ of the "grande idée" that was destined
to produce one of the great works of modern literature.

The last section of *De l'esprit* (*Discours* IV) begins with a lengthy
review of the various uses of the word "esprit." After several chapters
devoted to "l'esprit fin," "l'esprit fort," "le bel esprit," and so forth, we
come to the seventh, entitled "De l'esprit du siecle." These pages are a
surprisingly bitter condemnation of Parisian society, which the author
accuses of sacrificing all values on the altar of brilliant conversation and
the *bon mot*. The usually mild Helvétius, suddenly transformed into
an indignant satirist, lashes out against the spirit of scintillating detrac-
tion and slanderous wit that indulges feelings of envy by disparaging
everything of merit in both the moral and the intellectual order. Fear-
lessly brandishing similes, he compares those guilty of jealous defamation
to "ces plantes viles qui ne germent & ne croissent que sur les ruines des
palais"; carping critics who turn their corrosive sarcasm against all that
appears in print are likened to "ces animaux immondes qu'on rencontre
quelquefois dans les villes, & qui ne s'y promenent que pour en chercher
les égouts." This scathing diatribe concludes on a calmer note. Helvétius admits that those he condemns are not necessarily wicked; but so
great is the urge to shine in conversation that many, because of their
piteous mediocrity, must resort to calumny and slander as the only
means of achieving social recognition. Such is the spirit of the age.

This Juvenalian attack on mediocrity, traditional enough, would have nothing to recommend it to our attention were it not for the final paragraph. Following are the words that Diderot, in 1758, found on pp. 546–7 of his copy of *De l'esprit* :

Je n'ajouterai qu'un mot à ce que j'ai déjà dit de l'esprit du siecle; c'est qu'il est facile de se le représenter sous une image sensible. Qu'on charge, pour cet effet, un peintre habile de faire, par exemple, les portraits allégoriques de l'esprit de quelques-uns des siecles de la Grece, & de l'esprit actuel de notre nation. Dans le premier tableau, ne sera-t-il pas forcé de représenter l'esprit sous la figure d'un homme, qui, l'œil fixe, l'ame absorbée dans de profondes méditations, reste dans quelques-unes des attitudes qu'on donne aux Muses ? Dans le second tableau, ne sera-t-il pas nécessité à peindre l'esprit sous les traits du Dieu de la raillerie, c'est-à-dire, sous la figure d'un homme qui considere tout avec un ris malin & un œil moqueur ? Or, ces deux portraits si différents nous donneroient assez exactement la différence de l'esprit des Grecs au nôtre. Sur quoi j'observerai que, dans chaque siecle, un peintre ingénieux donneroit à l'esprit une physionomie différente; & que la suite allégorique de pareils portraits seroit fort agréable & fort curieuse pour la postérité, qui, d'un coup d'œil, jugeroit de l'estime ou du mépris que, dans chaque siecle, l'on a dû accorder à l'esprit de chaque nation.

Readers familiar with Diderot will have no difficulty in visualizing the reaction that this proposal of Helvétius might have had on the *philosophe*. "Une image sensible"; "portraits allégoriques"; "l'esprit de la Grece"; "la postérité"; in the words of Madame de Vandeul used in another connection, "le quart de tout cela aurait suffi pour intéresser mon père" (A.T., I, xlviii). And the closing sentence, with the words "estime" and "mépris," points directly to the praise and blame that are the basic elements of satire. We are therefore justified, I believe, in tentatively applying to *Le Neveu de Rameau* the contrast outlined in this passage. Following Helvétius' pattern, Lui will incarnate the spirit of the eighteenth century – "un homme qui considere tout avec un ris malin & un œil moqueur" – while Moi, high-minded and pensive, will represent the spirit of Greek philosophy. Let us examine each in turn.

There are many indications throughout *Le Neveu de Rameau* that Lui, however unusual his character, is conceived as a typical product of his age from the point of view of morality. The non-conformism that most critics see in Lui is belied by the words in which he excuses his "idiotismes de métier" : "Je ne m'avilis point en faisant comme tout le monde" (Fabre, p. 35). His vulgar love of money and pleasure is anything but rare: "vous ne vous doutez pas que dans ce moment je repre-

sente la partie la plus importante de la ville et de la cour" (p. 39). He
boasts of practising "des vices ... qui quadrent avec les mœurs de ma
nation" (p. 44), and defends his "impertinences" on the same pretext:
"C'est le sentiment et le langage de toute la société" (p. 55). Finally,
we find the author himself intervening to point out ironically that it is
Lui's unashamed frankness that makes him different from those around
him:

> Voila, en verité, la difference la plus marquée entre mon homme et la plu-
> part de nos entours. Il avouoit les vices qu'il avoit, que les autres ont; mais
> il n'etoit pas hippocrite. Il n'etoit ni plus ni moins abominable qu'eux; il
> etoit seulement plus franc, et plus consequent; et quelquefois profond dans
> sa depravation (p. 93).

It is evident, then, that this portrait, in addition to the air of mocking
cynicism, has been endowed with a native candour that allows Lui, by
exposing his own vices, to implicate the whole of society in his depravity.
Nothing could be clearer than this: Lui is a perfect rendering of the
portrait of "l'esprit du siecle" commissioned by Helvétius.

As for Moi, we must determine whether or not it is possible that he
be a projection of the author beneath the mantle of an ancient philosopher. We are immediately reminded of the *Discours sur la poésie
dramatique*, where Diderot himself proposes that he create a "modèle
idéal" of a philosopher, to serve as his constant standard for judging
the true, the good, and the beautiful (A.T., VII, 393). Is Moi this ideal
model modified, as Diderot suggests, to fit the circumstances – that is,
given flesh in the person of Denis Diderot and placed in eighteenth-
century Paris? Not only is this possible, but it helps to explain the difficulties critics have encountered in attempting to equate Diderot with
his character Moi. The ideal model of the spirit of Greek philosophy
might well be painted, according to Helvétius' formula, "l'œil fixe,
l'ame absorbée dans de profondes méditations"; and no doubt Diderot,
alone on the "banc d'Argenson" or sunk in his armchair at home with
his nightcap pulled over his eyes, might have presented such a spectacle.
It is not thus, however, that posterity imagines the *philosophe* in the
midst of a spirited conversation. Less still can we picture him striking
the attitudes of the nine Muses! But if Moi is an idealized Diderot, a
Diderot who represents all that is noble in ancient Greek thought, pitted
against the folly of his age in the person of Lui, certain ambiguities of the
dialogue disappear.

The problems posed by the character Moi can be resolved if we suppose that Diderot, following Helvétius, was seeking to personify in this
portrait the spirit of Greek philosophy *through several ages*. In this

hypothesis Moi is not a single individual, but a series of masks that change according to the shifts of conversation. Undoubtedly it is not a question of attempting to trace every statement of Moi to a given ancient philosopher. We must remember that Moi is also Diderot, and that the problems raised are those that preoccupied eighteenth-century France. It is rather the *attitudes* – intellectual, moral, and aesthetic – of the great thinkers of antiquity that we should expect to find reflected in the positions taken by Moi in this debate. In all probability the succession of masks adopted will be found to correspond to the broad divisions of the dialogue.

*Le Neveu de Rameau* opens with a prologue (Fabre, pp. 3–6) that sets the scene and introduces the two interlocutors. It is the author who is speaking here, and we should expect him to present himself as having the same traits of character as Moi. He is evidently a man of contemplative spirit ("rêvant sur le banc d'Argenson") who is nonetheless not disdainful of real life, even that lived in the cafés of Paris, yet who is careful to preserve his integrity while studying at close range such bizarre individuals as Jean-François Rameau (p. 5). The dialogue that follows can be divided into four sections. The first (pp. 7–32) deals principally with intellectual topics – genius, truth, education, science; the second (pp. 32–77) is concerned with vice and virtue; the third (pp. 77–89) treats of the aesthetics of music; the fourth (p. 89 to the end) recapitulates, analysing the social forces that are responsible for the decline of intellectual, moral, and artistic values in France.[29]

The Moi of the first section of the dialogue is an intellectual idealist, stoutly defending genius, truth, and science against the attacks of the cynical Lui, and at the same time a practical realist, proposing for his daughter's education a highly utilitarian program of mental and physical training (pp. 9–11, 30–2). He can have only one model in antiquity, the philosopher with whom Diderot was wont to identify himself – Socrates; but a Socrates in holiday mood as befits a Saturnalian setting, who, while appreciating the occasional flashes of insight that a wise man should expect to glean from speaking with a fool, has no illusions that any serious truth will emerge from this conversation. It is perhaps for that reason that there seems to be no consistent attempt made to use the Socratic method in the conduct of the dialogue, though at one point Lui is led through Moi's questions to see that he is contradicting himself in despising great men while desiring to belong to their number (p. 10). Moi, of course, remains Diderot throughout, as is clearly shown by the details of his past and present life that are evoked (pp. 28–30). Socrates

29 The following chapter will attempt to justify these divisions of the dialogue. The reader is asked to accept them meanwhile for the sake of the argument.

is little more than a shadow in the background. Is it deliberately that Diderot (p. 8) has Moi make the ironic proposal of setting the bust of his interlocutor "a coté ... d'un Socrate"? This is the only explicit mention of the Athenian philosopher, except for the praise accorded to his serene acceptance of an unjust death (one of Diderot's favourite enthusiasms) during the debate on genius (pp. 10–11). His shadow appears again when Moi speaks of the nagging wife whom he is obliged to placate (p. 29). Diderot sometimes regretted his inability to imitate Socrates' patient treatment of his ill-tempered Xantippe: "Ah! Socrate! je te ressemble peu," he wrote with reference to Socrates' domestic virtues; "mais du moins tu me fais pleurer d'admiration et de joie."[30] These few details are certainly not probative; the overall picture, nonetheless, does match the pattern that we are seeking to establish.

In the long second section (Fabre, pp. 32–77), Lui discloses with disarming candour the vices, petty and otherwise, of the society that he frequents. The role of Moi is here restricted for the most part to leading on his interlocutor to further revelations and interjecting comments heavy with irony. Familiar themes such as the equivalence of virtue and happiness, the jaded appetites of voluptuaries and the inner contentment of the just (pp. 42–3), show that Diderot is painting himself beneath the mask of Moi. There is, however, an indication that the author is attempting to oppose to the brutal hedonism of Lui an enlightened hedonistic naturalism reminiscent of the doctrine of Epicurus. In the midst of a discussion of pleasure as a way of life, Moi points out the fact that there are pleasures other than carnal. "Je ne meprise pas les plaisirs de sens," he declares (p. 42), as he intones a brief apology of occasional fleshly indulgence from which "une partie de debauche, meme un peu tumultueuse" is not excluded. "Mais ... il m'est infiniment plus doux encor d'avoir secouru le malheureux, d'avoir terminé une affaire epineuse, donné un conseil salutaire, fait une lecture agreable ..." and so forth. The whole passage is pure Diderot, of course, but should nonetheless be compared to the words with which Epicurus is made to expound his ethical position in the *Encyclopédie*: "Nous ne mépriserons point les plaisirs des sens; mais nous ne nous ferons point l'injure à nous-mêmes de comparer l'honnête avec le sensuel."[31]

Diderot considered Epicurus to be the only ancient philosopher whose doctrine managed to strike a happy balance between the physical and the moral imperatives of human nature,[32] and throughout his life

---

30 *Encyclopédie*, art. "Socratique," A.T., XVII, 156.

31 Art. "Epicuréisme," A.T., XIV, 521.

32 The article "Epicuréisme" of the *Encyclopédie* concludes the presentation of Epicurus' moral doctrine with these words of Diderot: "Voilà les points fondamen-

his own moral outlook was to remain close to epicurean naturalism. It is, no doubt, for that reason that he had such strong feelings about the calumniation to which Epicurus had been subjected over the centuries.[33] Not unexpectedly, he was prone to associate this persecution with the cries raised against Helvétius' hedonism in 1758.[34] Shortly after the publication of *De l'esprit*, the Encyclopedist had pointed out in his *Réflexions* that Helvétius had not taken sufficient pains to define the meaning of certain terms which appear in his book;[35] and indeed the failure to do so allowed Palissot to write the most successful passage of his play, the farcical scene in which the servant picks his master's pocket while listening to him expound the theory of self-interest.[36] If this charge of gross egoism was unjust when made against Helvétius, it was doubly so in the case of Diderot, whose own views on self-interest were far more refined and humanistic than those found in *De l'esprit*. We can therefore point to two reasons – a polemical and a personal one – that suggest why he might have adopted the mask of Epicurus in *Le Neveu de Rameau*, where he retaliates by accusing his enemies in their turn of vicious and unprincipled conduct.

In the third section (Fabre, pp. 77–89) Moi does little more than listen to Lui. He takes no positive stand with regard to music, apparently agreeing with Lui's dictum that "un garçon charbonnier parlera toujours mieux de son metier que toute une academie" (p. 82). That he is slightly sceptical concerning Lui's musical theories, however, is evident from his grudging admission: "Il y a de la raison, a peu près, dans tout ce que vous venez de dire" (ibid.). When Lui comes to the practical demonstration of these ideas, the author breaks off his description of the superb musical mime to indicate that he shares Moi's non-committal attitude: "Admirois je ? Oui, j'admirois ! etois je touché de pitié ?

taux de la doctrine d'*Epicure*, le seul d'entre tous les philosophes anciens qui ait su concilier sa morale avec ce qu'il pouvait prendre pour le vrai bonheur de l'homme, et ses préceptes avec les appétits et les besoins de la nature : aussi a-t-il eu et aura-t-il, dans tous les temps, un grand nombre de disciples. On se fait stoïcien, mais on naît *épicurien*" (A.T., XIV., 522).

33 See art. "Epicuréisme," A.T., XIV, 508.

34 In the *Essai sur les règnes de Claude et de Néron*, Diderot draws a direct comparison between the ancient philosopher and the author of *De l'esprit*: "Il paraît que le mot *volupté*, mal entendu, rendit Epicure odieux, ainsi que le mot *intérêt*, aussi mal entendu, excita le murmure des hypocrites et des ignorants contre un philosophe moderne" (A.T., III, 316).

35 A.T., II, 273. See the same thought expressed by Saint-Lambert at the end of his article "Intérêt" of the *Encyclopédie* (A.T., XV, 231–2). Are these words perhaps an addition by Diderot?

36 *Les Philosophes*, II, 1. "Le seul trait théâtral," says Grimm, "le moment où le valet vole son maître en conséquence de sa morale, ce trait est tiré de *Timon le misanthrope*" (*Corr. lit.*, 1 June 1760, IV, 239). The play *Timon* is by Delisle (1722).

j'etois touché de pitié; mais une teinte de ridicule etoit fondue dans ces sentimens, et les denaturoit" (p. 84). This reticence would seem to register moral rather than aesthetic disapproval, and is perhaps designed to warn the reader not to allow himself to fall under the spell of mere technical skill.

Although the author-narrator states clearly that he shares Moi's reluctance to side with Lui, some critics still insist that Moi is here being presented in a bad light. If, however, Moi represents the spirit of Greek philosophy, his disdain for the antics of Lui could reflect a judgment made in accordance with the view, universally held among the Greeks, that certain types of music and pantomime have undesirable effects on the character of those exposed to them. There is not a shred of evidence in the dialogue to support this conjecture; but it does allow us to fit the section on music into the overall pattern, and helps to clarify a particularly difficult passage. The question will be raised again in a later chapter, when we come to speak of ethos and harmony.

The final section (Fabre, pp. 89 ff.) is, as I have said, a recapitulation of some of the ideas found in the three previous parts. Moi opens with a question that relates musical taste, the subject of the third part, back to the problem of morality discussed in the second: "Comment se fait il qu'avec un tact aussi fin, une si grande sensibilité pour les beautés de l'art musical, vous soiez aussi aveugle sur les belles choses en morale, aussi insensible aux charmes de la vertu ?" (p. 89). Lui, in his own inimitable way, lays the blame on the "maudite molecule" that he inherited from his father and on the education that he received, both of which have left him ill equipped to meet society on its own terms ("L'or est tout; et le reste, sans or, n'est rien" – p. 92) without having to play the parasite and the buffoon. His idea of a good education, of course, is "celle qui conduit a toutes sortes de jouissances, sans peril, et sans inconvenient" (p. 96). Next, Moi probes into the relationship of musical taste to genius: "Cher Rameau, parlons musique, et dites moi comment il est arrivé qu'avec la facilité de sentir, de retenir et de rendre les plus beaux endroits des grands maitres; avec l'enthousiasme qu'ils vous inspirent et que vous transmettez aux autres, vous n'aiez rien fait qui vaille" (p. 96). Here again Lui excuses himself, this time accusing fate of having shaped him in a bizarre mould and having refused him the talents necessary to produce a great work (pp. 96–8). Other reasons too are offered for his lack of success: the pettiness and insipidity of social life in Paris tend to stifle artistic inspiration; and enforced poverty obliges artists to become fawning hypocrites living on the bounty of vulgar and immoral financiers (pp. 98–104). The first fifteen pages of this section, then, are less expository than they are analytical. It is Lui who provides the analysis of his own situation as well as of the socio-logical conditions by which he has been determined. Moi, the "accou-cheur" (another allusion to Socrates – p. 98), presides over the operation with persistent questions and sharp thrusts of irony.

In thus bringing together at the end the major themes of genius, morality, and music, Diderot underlines the fact that Lui is the typical offspring of an age marked by intellectual, moral, and artistic bank-ruptcy. This is the point to which the whole satire has been leading. Lui's nihilistic cynicism, which is that of the society that created him, is now contrasted with the cynicism of righteous indignation that Moi adopts at this point. Having defended intellectual idealism in the first section and enlightened hedonism in the second, Moi now dons the mask of Diogenes the Cynic.

Diderot had frequently identified himself with Diogenes, especially in the Cynic's fierce desire to be independent.[37] In his article "Cyniques" he had praised Diogenes and his sect, admiring their espousal of poverty and hardship in witness to the vanity of their age, and sympathizing with, if not approving, the deliberate flouting of decency by which they sought to shock the world into a realization of its artificiality.[38] The false cynics of antiquity, on the other hand, he had condemned as "une populace de brigands travestis en philosophes."[39] In the dialogue, Moi recommends that Lui seek the freedom that artistic creation requires by adopting the independence of Diogenes (p. 106); but the musician mocks his suggestions, pleading that it is impossible to do without the material comforts that, unfortunately, only subservience can procure. This prompts the final satirical word of Diderot-Moi to Lui and to the fools and knaves of this world whom he represents. The image that he draws of the self-sufficient Cynic retiring to his tub to masturbate ("Je veux mourir si cela ne vaudroit mieux que de ramper, de s'avilir, et se

37 See the letter to Sophie Volland, 19 August 1762 (*Corr.*, ed. Roth, IV, 112), and M. Fabre's note to *Le Neveu de Rameau* (p. 240, n. 326). No biographer, as far as I am aware, has pointed out the distinctly cynical flavour of Diderot's famous cry "Terre! terre!" that heralded the completion of the *Encyclopédie* (to Sophie Volland, 18 August 1765, *Corr.*, ed. Roth, V, 91). According to Diogenes Laertius (VI, 38), Diogenes the Cynic gave voice to a similar sentiment one day when listening to a lengthy scroll being read aloud. Seeing a blank space appear, he cried: "Cheer up, men, I see land!"

38 A.T., XIV, 252–67, esp. 253 and 254.

39 Ibid., 267. There can be little doubt that Diderot, in *Le Neveu de Rameau*, has in mind a comparison of his own age with the corrupt world of antiquity described in the same article, p. 255: "L'ignorance des beaux-arts et le mépris des décences furent l'origine du discrédit où la secte tomba dans les siècles suivants. Tout ce qu'il y avait, dans les villes de la Grèce et de l'Italie, de bouffons, d'impudents, de men-diants, de parasites, de gloutons et de fainéants ... prit effrontément le nom de *cyniques*."

prostituer") is not meant to be prescriptive; it symbolizes the total rejection, not of human society as such, but of the society of eighteenth-century Paris which the conversation with Lui has shown to be beyond redemption.

The above exposition may appear satisfactory to some, perhaps less so to others. In its support, it might be well to point out that we are dealing here with an author who prided himself on imitating the great thinkers of antiquity[40] and with a work which has long been considered a deliberate mystification.[41] Ought we really to be surprised to find him adopting the literary procedure described above? It is undeniable, of course, that some of the details we have remarked are little more than fleeting impressions. But aside from these textual indications, there would seem to be solid reasons why Diderot, shortly after the condemnation of the *Encyclopédie*, might have chosen to depict himself in the guise of the three ancient philosophers who had been most persecuted and reviled. And the likelihood is even stronger following the success of Palissot's play *Les Philosophes*. We know, moreover, the favour in which he held eclecticism in philosophy; and it is not difficult to see our division of the dialogue reflected in his description of the Eclectic in the *Essai sur les règnes de Claude et de Néron*: "raisonnant avec So-crate, doutant avec Carnéade, luttant contre la nature avec Zénon, et cherchant à s'y conformer avec Epicure, ou à s'élever au-dessus d'elle avec Diogène" (A.T., III, 28).

Whatever the case may be, the identification of the character Moi with a series of ancient philosophers is not essential to the thesis that *Le Neveu de Rameau* is a literary confrontation between the folly of the age and the spirit of Greek philosophy. Diderot had certainly read Helvétius' text where this suggestion is found. There is nothing in the dialogue to invalidate such an interpretation; there is much to substantiate it. Further confirmation will be forthcoming as our inquiry proceeds.

---

40 There was, in Diderot's mind, an intimate relationship between his own admiration for the moral and intellectual heroes of the past and the glory which he expected to receive from future ages: "Nous existons dans le passé par la mémoire des grands hommes que nous imitons; dans le présent où nous recevons les honneurs qu'ils ont obtenus ou mérités; dans l'avenir, par la certitude qu'il parlera de nous comme nous parlons d'eux" (letter to Falconet, 29 December 1766, *Corr.*, ed. Roth, VI, 376).

41 Diderot's most explicit statement regarding concealment in art is found in his *Réflexions*, where he complains that *De l'esprit* is too laboriously methodical: "D'ailleurs, l'appareil de la méthode ressemble à l'échafaud qu'on laisserait toujours subsister après que le bâtiment est élevé. C'est une chose nécessaire pour travailler, mais qu'on ne doit plus apercevoir quand l'ouvrage est fini" (A.T., II, 272-3).

# 3

# Utility, turpitude, beauty

THE seemingly gratuitous division of *Le Neveu de Rameau* given in the preceding chapter (p. 51) requires some justification. We are faced here with a peculiar problem. If Diderot is following in this work the example of his favourite satirist, Horace, it is conceivable that he might have adopted the "pot-pourri" formula originally implied in the word *satura*; on the other hand, although he condemned the abuse of method in his *Réflexions sur le livre De l'esprit*, he recommended in the same passage that every author have in the back of his mind what he called "un ordre sourd."[1] We are justified, therefore, in looking for a formula such as the one I have proposed. The fact that those who have grappled with this question have each found a different schema could perhaps be taken to mean that the "pot-pourri" solution must be the correct one.[2] It could mean also, however, that there is an element of mystification involved in the structure of the work that has not as yet been detected.

It is with this last possibility in mind that I have proposed the tentative division of the dialogue proper (everything following the prologue) into four parts: (1) intellectual questions, Fabre, pp. 7–32; (2) moral questions, pp. 32–77; (3) aesthetic questions, pp. 77–89; (4) satirical recapitulation, pp. 89 to the end.[3] It would be too easy, of course, to

---

1 A.T., II, 273: "Si tout ce que l'auteur [Helvétius] a écrit eût été entassé comme pêle-mêle, qu'il n'y eût eu que dans l'esprit de l'auteur un ordre sourd, son livre eût été infiniment plus agréable, et, sans le paraître, infiniment plus dangereux ..."

2 See *Entretiens sur "Le Neveu de Rameau,"* ed. M. Duchet and M. Launay, 22–3.

3 The break on p. 32 follows a moment during which Moi apparently allows his mind to wander. When Lui calls him back to reality ("A quoi revez vous?"), Moi abandons the intellectual question (science) of which they have been speaking to introduce an ethical one (teaching music without knowing even the rudiments of it). On p. 77 there occurs a similar transition. Moi is once again distracted, this time by the problems posed by the "grand criminel." Lui is solicitous: "Qu'avez vous? est ce que vous vous trouvez mal?" (p. 76). After a moment of silence (p. 77), Moi brings up the question of the aesthetic value of the latest melodies. The musical section ends when Lui pauses for refreshment (p. 89); the recapitulation picks up the

see in the first three parts the famous trinity of true, good, and beautiful that Lui invokes (p. 82), and with which Diderot himself was constantly preoccupied. A brief examination suffices to show that, although the section on aesthetic questions is consistently concerned with beauty, there is very little about good (except by contrast) in the second section, and the question of truth occupies only a few lines in the first (pp. 9–10). I would suggest that the problem is centred in the first twenty-five pages, and that the difficulty in determining the order that the author had in mind arises from the fact that the particular viewpoint from which all the questions in this section are considered has never been taken into account. I am referring to the viewpoint of utility. When we examine the dialogue in this perspective, it immediately becomes apparent that the ideas expressed here are an extension of the author's disagreement with Helvétius over the utilitarian problem.

*Le Neveu de Rameau* attacks philosophical matters in a down-to-earth, most un-metaphysical fashion. Whereas Socrates might have asked "What is genius?", the approach here is rather more practical; from Lui's opening question, "A quoi bon la mediocrité ..." (Fabre, p. 7), we are led into a ten-page discussion of the advantages and disadvantages of genius. The influence of Helvétius can be seen in this manner of dealing with the question of genius, for it is from the point of view of utility that he had considered the matter in *De l'esprit*. The general public, he said at the beginning of his second *Discours,* having no way of measuring the intellectual brilliance required by artists and thinkers to excel in their various domains, can accord the title "homme d'esprit" only to those who have created or discovered something of practical value to mankind. As Diderot put it in the *Réflexions,* summing up Helvétius' doctrine: "Selon lui, l'intérêt général est la mesure de l'estime que nous faisons de l'esprit, et non la difficulté de l'objet ou l'étendue des lumières" (A.T., II, 269). Helvétius, after drawing a rather bizarre comparison between Ninon de l'Enclos and Aristotle in this regard, proceeded to illustrate his thought with an example that is of some interest for *Le Neveu de Rameau*:

En effet, si les combinaisons du jeu des échecs sont infinies, si l'on n'y peut exceller sans en faire un grand nombre; pourquoi le public ne donne-t-il pas aux grands joueurs d'échecs le titre de grands esprits ? C'est que leurs idées ne lui sont utiles ni comme agréables ni comme instructives, & qu'il n'a par conséquent nul intérêt de les estimer : or l'intérêt préside à tous nos jugements.[4]

This passage indicates clearly that the subject of chess with which

earlier themes of morals and genius and discusses them in relation to music (pp. 89 ff., 96 ff.).
    4 Disc. II, Ch. I (orig. ed., 45–6).

our dialogue opens (p. 7) leads logically into the question of genius, but genius seen especially from the viewpoint of its utility; and it is around this central notion that the debate revolves. Lui shows himself to be what we should call today an egoistic utilitarian, measuring himself against a universalistic utilitarian in the person of Moi. Gifted people, says Lui with reference to his famous uncle, "ne sont bons qu'a une chose. Passé cela, rien" (p. 9). The egoism that often characterizes men of genius is, he admits, the philosophy of life that he himself follows systematically; but the system depends on keeping the number of egoists to a minimum: "Entre nous, il faut leur ressembler de tout point; mais ne pas desirer que la graine en soit commune" (ibid.). The genius, moreover, who by definition is a seeker after truth, poses a serious threat to a world in which folly is king and the vast multitude satisfied with the regime. It is even possible, he adds, to demonstrate from history that truth is often harmful, untruth useful. He can only conclude that the world would be a better place if budding geniuses were ruthlessly suppressed (ibid.).

Moi, in reply to this impertinence, takes his stand on a broader conception of utility. He maintains that the genius, however bizarre his conduct may seem and however much at variance he may be with the laws of his society, will be considered by future ages as a benefactor of the human race. In the course of time, truth will always prove to be of greater utility than falsehood (p. 10). Often a man of genius such as Racine will be lacking in the fundamental virtues of humanity; but his contribution as a member of society must be measured, not by ordinary standards, but by the long-range effects: "Mais pesez le mal et le bien. Dans mille ans d'ici, il fera verser des larmes; il sera l'admiration des hommes, dans toutes les contrées de la terre."[5]

5 Fabre, 13. Diderot had been much impressed by Helvétius' remarks on this subject, and it is only after the publication of *De l'esprit* that the idea appears in his writings. He applies it to Plato and Bacon in his article "Platonisme" (A.T., XVI, 314), written some time after October 1759 (*Corr.*, ed. Roth, II, 309), and from then on it appears constantly in his works. In Disc. IV, Ch. VIII of *De l'esprit*, Helvétius had excused the bizarre character of the man of genius. Addressing himself to mediocre persons who criticize the faults of great men, he says: "Un homme de génie, eût-il des vices, est encore plus estimable que vous. En effet, on sert sa patrie, ou par l'innocence de ses mœurs & les exemples de vertu qu'on y donne, ou par les lumieres qu'on y répand. De ces deux manieres de servir sa patrie, la derniere, qui, sans contredit, appartient plus directement au génie, est, en même temps, celle qui procure le plus d'avantages au public. Les exemples de vertu que donne un particulier ne sont guere utiles qu'au petit nombre de ceux qui composent sa société : au contraire, les lumieres nouvelles, que ce même particulier répandra sur les arts & les sciences, sont des bienfaits pour l'univers" (orig. ed., 554–5). When Diderot goes on to show (Fabre, 14) that it is often the personal faults of men of genius that are responsible for the merits of their works ("Si vous jettez de l'eau froide sur la tete de Greuze, vous eteindrez peut etre son talent avec sa vanité"), he is following what Helvétius says regarding Fontenelle in Disc. IV, Ch. XIV (orig. ed., 597–9).

Lui, however, fixed in his egoism, is not to be converted. Socrates'
death undergone for the sake of an ideal arouses in him only contempt:
"Le voilà bien avancé!" (p. 11). If Lui shows preference for uninspired
and uninspiring bourgeois mediocrity, it is because this way of life is
useful for attaining pleasures of all kinds (pp. 12–13); if he envies his
uncle's success in the world of music, it is for similar selfish reasons (pp.
15–17). It is in vain that Moi appeals to an ideal order: "Songeons au
bien de notre espece" (p. 14); Lui's viewpoint remains immutably
egocentric: "Le meilleur ordre des choses, a mon avis, est celui ou j'en
devois etre; et foin du plus parfait des mondes, si je n'en suis pas"
(ibid.).

The discussion of genius terminates at p. 17 with the lines clearly
drawn between the two interlocutors. Their differing views concerning
utility, now well established, will be less explicitly contrasted in the following pages as the form of the work passes from reasoned argument
to narration and action. Lui's dismissal from the Bertin household, occasioned by an unexpected upsurge of common sense, shows that that
reputedly widespread quality can be the reverse of useful: "J'ai tout
perdu pour avoir eu le sens commun, une fois, une seule fois en ma vie"
(p. 19). A serious fault in a fool – his master had made no mystery of
the fact that in some societies common sense is positively unwelcome:
"Cela veut avoir du sens, de la raison, je crois! Tirez. Nous avons de
ces qualités la, de reste" (ibid.). Moi, of course, is all compassion on
hearing this sad tale, and hastens to suggest a formula of apology that
will effect a reconciliation with the mistress of the house: "Pardon,
madame! pardon! je suis un indigne, un infame. Ce fut un malheureux
instant; car vous scavez que je ne suis pas sujet a avoir du sens commun,
et je vous promets de n'en avoir de ma vie" (p. 20). The irony of this
situation needs no comment.[6]

A similar type of irony is employed in the following scene. The conversation threatens momentarily to turn to a purely moral topic when
Lui sets out to prove that he has known the honest sentiment of self-
reproach. He begins with a masterly display of the art of seduction (pp.
22–3), then goes on to explain that somehow, for all his expertise, he
has failed to turn this natural talent to effect, and for this he reproaches
himself bitterly. It becomes clear at this point that we are dealing in
reality with an ironic treatment of the utility of natural talent: Lui

6 It is only in the following section, where the question of the utility of common
sense arises again, that Moi abandons his irony. To Lui's question, "Et n'est ce pas
pour avoir eu du sens commun et de la franchise un moment, que je ne scais ou aller
souper ce soir?", he replies: "Hé non, c'est pour n'en avoir pas toujours eu. C'est
pour n'avoir pas senti de bonne heure qu'il falloit d'abord se faire une ressource
independante de la servitude" (pp. 43–4).

defines the sentiment of self-reproach as "ce tourment de la conscience qui nait de l'inutilité des dons que le Ciel nous a departis" (p. 24). Moi, needless to say, would scarcely have numbered seduction among the useful arts, and would have had quite another definition of "le mepris de soi meme."

A short passage follows (pp. 24–5) in which Moi's moral indignation is met by a further display of cynicism on the part of Lui. Then abruptly, in the middle of a paragraph (p. 26, top), we pass to a demonstration of the effectiveness of hard work in overcoming natural disabilities. There is perhaps some relationship, especially in the mind of a fool, between the corruption of death of which Lui has been speaking (p. 25) and the stiffness of his wrists, which, he proudly affirms, only strenuous effort was able to remedy. As proof of his success, Lui performs on an imaginary violin and is pleased when Moi manifests his admiration: "Cela va, ce me semble; cela resonne a peu pres, comme les autres" (p. 27). There follows an inspired imitation of a harpsichord player, with a further expression of self-congratulation: "Ces passages enharmoniques dont le cher oncle a fait tant de train, ce n'est pas la mer a boire, nous nous en tirons" (p. 28). Our debate on genius has now turned into a practical illustration of the relative value of inspiration and exercise in the mastery of an art.

The transition from musicianship to musical instruction is a natural one, and we find ourselves immediately engaged in a discussion of utility in education. The debate, it seems, is to centre around the distinction between pleasing talents and useful ones. Lui opens by declaring that Moi's young daughter should have begun her musical education at the age of four; but the father questions the practical value of this discipline, "une etude qui occupe si longtems et qui sert si peu" (p. 30). According to Moi's way of thinking, nothing could be more useful for life than perfection of the rational faculty. Lui, the parasite and fool, is of the contrary opinion: "Et laissez la deraisonner, tant qu'elle voudra. Pourvu qu'elle soit jolie, amusante et coquette" (ibid.). This proposal does not satisfy Moi, who would limit lessons in singing and dancing to their benefits for speech and carriage, and in music to learning the rudiments of harmony. The time thus saved could be devoted to "de la grammaire, de la fable, de l'histoire, de la geographie, un peu de dessein [sic], et beaucoup de morale" (p. 31). But in Lui's view, this program does not prepare a child for life in the real world, rather the opposite: "Combien il me seroit facile de vous prouver l'inutilité de toutes ces connoissances la, dans un monde tel que le notre; que dis je l'inutilité, peut etre le danger" (ibid.). Once again, as with the question of genius, the two interlocutors think along totally divergent lines on the subject of utility.

Lui ends the discussion of education by linking it with the section that preceded. Only those, he says, are really capable of instructing others in a given discipline who have spent their lives in patient study, such as his uncle in music and d'Alembert in mathematics. On this point at least, he and Moi are in agreement. The latter, as is fitting in a dialogue between a fool and a wise man, manifests surprise at Lui's perspicacity: "O fou, archifou, m'ecriai je, comment se fait-il que dans ta mauvaise tete, il se trouve des idées si justes, pêle mele, avec tant d'extravagances" (p. 32). This exclamation is perhaps intended to prepare the reader for an even more profound statement from the foolish musician: he compares his own scattered bits of wisdom with the isolated gleanings of physical science, "une goutte d'eau prise avec la pointe d'une aiguille dans le vaste ocean; un grain detaché de la chaine des Alpes" (ibid.). Lui's expression of scientific pessimism would seem to be little more than a paraphrase of what the Encyclopedist himself had said in *De l'interprétation de la nature* concerning the insufficiency of human reason and the infinite variety of natural phenomena (A.T., II, 13); but Diderot's observations had not undermined his optimism about the future of the physical sciences, which would continue to flourish, he believed, as long as their usefulness to mankind remained evident: "l'utile circonscrit tout ... J'accorde des siècles à cette étude, parce que la sphère de son utilité est infiniment plus étendue que celle d'aucune science abstraite, et qu'elle est, sans contredit, la base de nos véritables connaissances" (ibid.). It is for this reason, as M. Fabre's note indicates (p. 165), that Moi is able to characterize Lui's judgment on the futility of science as "plus specieux que solide" (p. 32).

Diderot's considerations on the utility of genius, truth, common sense, talent, education, and science are completed at p. 32, and the transition is made to topics of a purely moral nature. The question of utility, however, has a general relationship even here, from several points of view: traditionally, libertines and cynics had stressed the inutility of virtue and the utility of vice; parasites and satirists had always been referred to as drones and wasps in contrast to socially productive citizens. Diderot's personal ideal of a useful life, which was that of all the great figures of the Enlightenment, is best illustrated by his relentless efforts to complete the *Encyclopédie* in the face of opposition, and he visualized his great dictionary as preserving the fruits of human progress "afin ... que nos neveux, devenant plus instruits, deviennent en même temps plus vertueux et plus heureux; et que nous ne mourions pas sans avoir bien mérité du genre humain" (A.T., XIV, 415). It is in this context that we must see the treatment of moral questions in the second section of the dialogue. The Palissots, the Bertins, the Frérons, and all those who live off society rather than living for it, meet their judgment here. They are all implicated in the biting irony with which Moi praises Lui's ambition to become wealthy and his dreams of the licence and debauchery this would permit: "Vous vivriez la d'une maniere bien honorable pour l'espece humaine, bien utile a vos concitoyens; bien glorieuse pour vous" (p. 39). This is the only explicit appeal to social utility in the second section, which is principally concerned with displaying the moral turpitude of Palissot and the "menagerie."

Having examined the role played by utility in the first section of *Le Neveu de Rameau*, we may now return to the problem with which we began – the overall structure of the dialogue. Our division of the work into prologue and four parts is certainly defensible from internal evidence, and it would seem that the series intellectual-moral-aesthetic that we found in the first three parts does have a certain logical consistency. It would be more satisfying, of course, if there were some external model that would coincide with these divisions. But we have seen that it is impossible to apply to this schema the true-good-beautiful model of philosophy; and the same may be said of the *utile-dulce* model of literary criticism, though all these elements are present throughout the work.

There are, however, two further possibilities to consider, and these perhaps come closer to representing what Diderot had in mind. Aristotle, in a well-known passage of the *Rhetoric*, divides that science into three branches according as it deals with what is useful or harmful, what is just or unjust, what is fair or ugly.[7] These rhetorical categories, in the order given them by Aristotle, would seem to coincide generally with the divisions we have found in *Le Neveu de Rameau*. We can add to this a similar scheme which must surely have attracted Diderot's attention because it is a statement of what Horace, his favourite Latin poet, learned from Homer, his favourite poet of all time. According to Horace, the works of Homer teach us

quid sit pulchrum, quid turpe, quid utile, quid non.[8]

Did Diderot simply reverse two of the terms of this series, to give us a satirical view of what is useful, what is foul, what is beautiful, what is not? The question cannot be answered with any degree of certainty; it would seem, nonetheless, that the three sections of the dialogue between the prologue and the recapitulation correspond to the pattern given by Horace: utility, turpitude, beauty.

7 *Rhet.*i.iii.5.          8 *Ep.*i.ii.3.

# 4

# Individuality, diversity, scepticism

THE words "variété" and "diversité" that are found in the opening lines of the *Satire première* (below, p. 226) set the tone of that work, and announce the perspective in which Diderot will develop therein his thoughts concerning character and language. In *Le Neveu de Rameau*, a similar function is performed by the newly coined expression "individualité naturelle" that appears in the prologue (Fabre, p. 5). After introducing Jean-François Rameau as "un des plus bizarres personnages de ce pais ou Dieu n'en a pas laissé manquer," the author explains that a person such as this, who has retained his radical singularity of character, is able by his very presence to break through the shell of dull uniformity imposed on social man by education and manners: "S'il en paroit un dans une compagnie, c'est un grain de levain qui fermente et qui restitue a chacun une portion de son individualité naturelle." Now, individuality and diversity are the two faces of a single reality; if each man is unique, then all men are diverse. Both of these ideas have a satirical function in *Le Neveu de Rameau*. The individuality of Lui will be the principal instrument of personal satire ("Il secoue, il agite; il fait approuver ou blamer; il fait sortir la verité ...") ; the diversity between Moi and Lui will be used to raise the satire to a universal level.

The conviction that every man is diverse from every other was one of the constants of Diderot's thought; it was implied by his philosophical position and confirmed by observation and introspection. Let us simply recall in this connection the affinity of his philosophy with Lucretian atomism, his belief in the heterogeneity of matter,[1] his frequent references to the law of indiscernibles – "les deux grains de sable de Leibnitz"[2] – and his interest in the problem of personal identity;[3] it is little

---

1 See his *Principes philosophiques sur la matière et le mouvement* (A.T., II, 64–70), and Marx W. Wartofsky, "Diderot and the Development of Materialist Monism," *Diderot Studies*, II (1952), 279–329.

2 Cf. art. "Leibnitzianisme" (A.T., XV, 456) ; *Eloge de Richardson* (A.T., V, 221) ; *De l'interprétation de la nature* (A.T., II, 55) ; *Salon de 1767* (A.T., XI, 136), etc. See also Yvon Belaval, "Note sur Diderot et Leibniz," *Revue des Sciences Humaines*, n.s. CXII (1963), 435–51.

3 The chapter entitled "Of Identity and Diversity" that appeared in the second

wonder, with this background, that he was fascinated by the moral aspects of individuality, especially in its extreme forms – the genius, the "grand criminel," the monster, the "original." It need scarcely be added that his whole approach to these questions was coloured by consciousness of his own singularity and his strong personal drive for self-realization. But the intuition of his own individuality and identity through time was complicated by his scientific evolutionism on the one hand, and by his experience of man's moral inconsistency on the other. If we can say that no two individuals are alike, it is equally true to say that each individual differs from himself from one moment to the next. How, then, is he one?

The unity of the individual organism posed one of the major problems that Diderot encountered in his attempt to construct a coherent materialist philosophy of man. What constitutes the self of which I am conscious? Where does it reside? How does it maintain its identity in face of the constantly changing material form? These questions, some of which had preoccupied him as early as *Les Bijoux indiscrets*,[4] were given extensive consideration in *Le Rêve de d'Alembert*. There is no need here to examine that work, and the function it gives to the brain and to memory in the development of self-consciousness and the sentiment of personal identity.[5] Suffice it to say that the self, in Diderot's philosophy, results from the physical constitution and is determined by it, as well as by every vicissitude that the organism undergoes. When he speaks of the individual, therefore, he means the sum of a series of material determinations – natural tendencies plus experiences. Each man is a distinct entity, rigorously determined to be what he is here and now: the ultimate term of a chain of cause and effect stretching back to eternity. Although subject to constant change, he constitutes at any given moment a unity, an integral whole, the single and necessary cause of the action of that moment:

Est-ce qu'on veut, de soi ? La volonté naît toujours de quelque motif intérieur ou extérieur, de quelque impression présente, de quelque réminiscence du passé, de quelque passion, de quelque projet dans l'avenir. Après cela je

edition of Locke's *Essay on Human Understanding* (Bk. ii, Ch. xxvii) was the first extensive treatment of the problem in modern philosophy. Personal identity soon became a hotly debated issue among the British empiricists, and Diderot was no stranger to this quarrel. *Le Rêve de d'Alembert* represents, in part, his attempt to find a solution. For Locke's contribution, see Henry E. Allison, "Locke's Theory of Personal Identity: a Re-examination," *Journal of the History of Ideas*, xxvii (1966), 41–58.

4 See Otis Fellows, "Metaphysics and the *Bijoux indiscrets*: Diderot's Debt to Prior," *Studies on Voltaire and the Eighteenth Century*, lvi (1967), 509–40.

5 For a brief treatment of this question, see Jean Mayer, *Diderot, homme de science* (Rennes, Imprimerie Bretonne, 1959), 237–43.

ne vous dirai de la liberté qu'un mot, c'est que la dernière de nos actions est
l'effet nécessaire d'une cause une : nous, très-compliquée, mais une (A.T.,
II, 175).

It is in the context of his determinism, therefore, that we must see
Diderot's repeated insistence on his own individuality and that of others.
With reference to Rousseau's first *Discours* he says: "Rousseau fit ce
qu'il devait faire, parce qu'il était lui. Je n'aurais rien fait, ou j'aurais
fait tout autre chose, parce que j'aurais été moi."[6] Determinism leads
to indulgence for the shortcomings of others, as he tells Falconet: "Si
je ne m'impatiente pas, c'est qu'il faut que vous soyez vous, et que je
sois moi."[7] And he complains of his friends' importunity in a letter to
Sophie Volland: "Ces gens là ne veulent pas que je sois moi."[8] Each
man, he assures us, develops his talents "comme soi et non comme un
autre."[9] The principal reason why Newton made his great discoveries
was that "il était lui."[10] In *Jacques le fataliste*, the servant inquires
petulantly of his master: "Puis-je n'être pas moi? Et étant moi, puis-je
faire autrement que moi ? Puis-je être moi et un autre ?"[11] However
strong our sentiment of personal freedom, the forces of determinism and
flux are inescapable: "Tout s'est fait en nous parce que nous sommes
nous, toujours nous, et pas une minute les mêmes."[12]

Diderot's determinism, of course, did not exclude the possibility that
the individual might be subject to modification – if not in his nature,
at least in his actions.[13] It is with satirical intent, therefore, that in *Le
Neveu de Rameau* he has Lui continually affirm his individuality, excus-
ing his vicious tendencies by an appeal to the necessity of being true to
his nature. Whatever forces he may believe to be responsible for his
present condition – the company of wicked men or the influence of the
"maudite molecule paternelle" – Lui is doomed, like a tragic hero of
antiquity, to remain what fate and circumstances have made him. And
he accepts his condition with cynical equanimity, even revels in it: "Le
point important est que vous et moi nous soions, et que nous soions vous
et moi" (Fabre, p. 14); "Il faut que Rameau soit ce qu'il est" (p. 46);
"Je suis moi et je reste ce que je suis" (p. 60); "N'est il pas vrai que je
suis toujours le meme ?" (p. 109). Not only Lui, but all the members
of Bertin's "menagerie" are presented as victims of cosmic determinism:

6 A.T., II, 285 (*Réfutation d'Helvétius*).
7 5 August 1766 (*Corr.*, ed. Roth, VI, 252).
8 15 November 1768 (*Corr.*, ed. Roth, VIII, 223).
9 A.T., II, 346 (*Réfutation d'Helvétius*).
10 Ibid., 376.
11 A.T., VI, 15.
12 A.T., II, 373 (*Réfutation d'Helvétius*).
13 Diderot's article "Malfaisant" (A.T., XVI, 57) contains the best summation of
his constant opinion on this matter. Cf. A.T., II, 296 (*Réfutation d'Helvétius*).

nature made them vile and mediocre, and they cannot be other than they are. In the bitterest satirical passage of the whole work, Rameau explains the "pacte tacite," or nature's law of consequences. As surely as debauchery will ruin the health, he tells Moi, as surely as a tiger will tear an imprudent hand thrust into its cage, just as surely Palissot and the other "especes" may be expected to visit all manner of evil on those foolish enough to associate with them (pp. 68–71). To wish that they were otherwise would be to impugn the order established by nature.

The type of satire that presents men as instinctively and irremediably evil is not uncommon – examples can be found in Molière, La Bruyère, and Voltaire.[14] That aspect of *Le Neveu de Rameau*, however, in no way exhausts the uses of Lui's individuality, for the *diversity* which the term implies has possibilities at quite another satirical level. Some critics have seen in Moi and Lui two men, one of whom has a moral sense, the other, none; but however true that may be, Diderot was too subtle to limit himself to a contrast between virtue and vice. *Le Neveu de Rameau* is not a morality play, but an ironical essay in human communication. The two interlocutors see life from such divergent viewpoints that meaningful discourse between them is a downright impossibility.

It is only when Diderot's satire is seen in this light that its real significance for its author becomes clear. The wave of pessimism that swept over the *philosophe* during the years 1760–2 may well have been responsible for the rather jaundiced view of human nature that we find in his satire, as Georges May's carefully documented study points out;[15] but if his faith in the goodness of man was temporarily shaken by the condemnation of the *Encyclopédie* in 1759, much more important for his personal life was the depressing suspicion that he was a voice crying in the wilderness to men who would not or could not hear. For Diderot, the *Encyclopédie* was the great instrument of enlightenment; faced with persecution from without his group and desertion from within, his decision to continue the work was made in spite of the gravest reasons for doubting the possibility of educating his own generation. This form of scepticism is already apparent in the bitter complaint made to Voltaire on 19 February 1758:

Il faut travailler; il faut être utile; on doit compte de ses talents, etc. – *Etre utile aux hommes* ? Est-il bien sûr qu'on fasse autre chose que les amuser, et qu'il y ait grande différence entre le philosophe et le joueur de flûte ? Ils

14 Molière, *Le Misanthrope*, 173–8; La Bruyère, *Les Caractères*, xi, 1; Voltaire, *Candide*, Ch. xxi *in fine*.
15 Georges May, *Quatre Visages de Denis Diderot*, chapter entitled "Diderot pessimiste" (pp. 34–99). See, by the same author, the article "L'Angoisse de l'échec et la genèse du *Neveu de Rameau*," *Diderot Studies*, iii (1961), 285–307.

écoutent l'un et l'autre avec plaisir ou dédain, et demeurent ce qu'ils sont. Les Athéniens n'ont jamais été plus méchants qu'au tems de Socrate, et ils ne doivent peut-être à son existence qu'un crime de plus (*Corr.*, ed. Roth, II, 39).

It is easy to understand how the following years might have deepened this searing doubt that tended to undermine the fundamental optimism of the Enlightenment movement. The courage to complete the crushing task that devolved upon the editor-in-chief of the *Encyclopédie* after 1759 was drawn largely from his profound belief in the benefits he was bringing to future generations. It is from this period that the appeal to posterity becomes a psychological necessity for Diderot, and we may consider the letters to Falconet of 1765–6 not only as an act of faith in future glory, but also as an expression of scepticism concerning the present outcome of the battle between light and darkness, between wisdom and folly, in which he had played such a difficult and ill-rewarded role.

I have used the words "scepticism" and "doubt" in describing Diderot's state of mind during these years because "pessimism," as a diagnosis, fails to penetrate to the root of the problem. However frequently he may have succumbed to black moods in which human nature appeared to him as irredeemable, the Encyclopedist remained convinced that the struggle between truth and falsehood was in momentary jeopardy not only because of the power of evil in the hearts of men, but also because of the weakness of truth's principal weapon, language. Like Bacon, Leibniz, and many another before him, he dreamed of the possibility of perfecting language as an instrument of philosophic communication; but the linguistic scepticism that was inseparable from eighteenth-century empiricism returned continually to haunt him. Not that Diderot was a sceptic in any strict sense of the term – a recent study by Jerome Schwartz has clearly shown that this aspect of his philosophical development was limited to the early years of his career;[16] however, a certain mistrust of language as a means of communication finds expression in most of his major writings, and especially, as we shall see, in *Le Neveu de Rameau*.

The fact that he had hopes for the creation of a perfect philosophical language is sufficient proof that linguistic scepticism was for Diderot little more than a pretext for moralizing. A letter to Falconet dated July 1767 is optimistic, even enthusiastic, concerning the possibility of compiling a dictionary that would satisfy the requirements of modernity and the critical spirit, and that might serve as a basis for international com-

16 Jerome Schwartz, *Diderot and Montaigne: the* Essais *and the Shaping of Diderot's Humanism* (Genève, Droz, 1966), 60–85.

munication among scholars (*Corr.*, ed. Roth, VII, 88–91). Here, as always, it is sensationalism that dictates his theory of language; and, like a good nominalist, he wants all words that cannot be related to a sense image to be considered "vuides de sens" (ibid., 89). This is his constant view concerning language; but whenever he is particularly preoccupied with the diversity of men, his nominalism shades into scepticism, as the following quotations show: "A proprement parler, les sensations d'un homme sont incommunicables à un autre, parce qu'elles sont diverses. Si les signes sont communs, c'est par disette."[17] "Et par la raison seule qu'aucun homme ne ressemble parfaitement à un autre, nous n'entendons jamais précisément, nous ne sommes jamais précisément entendus; il y a du plus ou du moins en tout : notre discours est toujours en deçà ou au delà de la sensation."[18] "Combien les hommes sont peu d'accord ? Combien ils s'accorderoient moins encore si la langue suffisoit à toute la variété de leurs sensations; mais heureusement elle est pauvre; et en sentant tout diversement, ils parlent a peu près de même."[19]

It is undoubtedly Diderot the moralist who is speaking in these passages, and no attempt is made to pursue the question further. But there was one occasion that we know of, in 1758, when Diderot the philosopher found himself face to face with the practical consequences of the sceptical temptation in such a way that he was obliged to make a thorough re-examination of his theory of knowledge and communication; and his thoughts at that time, carefully preserved, provide us with the most revealing self-portrait to be found in his works. The closing pages of the *Discours sur la poésie dramatique* show him, in the person of his *alter ego* Ariste, analysing the problem of universals as it affects the philosopher, the literary artist, and the critic. The lines in which Ariste sets up the elements of the problem are of such importance for our purpose that they deserve to be quoted at length:

Il n'y a peut-être pas, dans l'espèce humaine entière, deux individus qui aient quelque ressemblance approchée. L'organisation générale, les sens, la figure extérieure, les viscères, ont leur variété. Les fibres, les muscles, les solides, les fluides, ont leur variété. L'esprit, l'imagination, la mémoire, les idées, les vérités, les préjugés, les aliments, les exercices, les connaissances, les états, l'éducation, les goûts, la fortune, les talents, ont leur variété. Les objets, les climats, les mœurs, les lois, les coutumes, les usages, les gouvernements, les religions, ont leur variété. Comment serait-il donc possible que

---

17 A.T., II, 325 (*Réfutation d'Helvétius*). Cf. ibid., 279.
18 A.T., II, 180–1 (*Rêve de d'Alembert*).
19 Herbert Dieckmann, *Inventaire*, 199. See also 213, 214.

deux hommes eussent précisément un même goût, ou les mêmes notions du vrai, du bon et du beau ? La différence de la vie et la variété des événements suffiraient seules pour en mettre dans les jugements (A.T., VII, 391).

Having reviewed the internal and external causes of diversity among men, Ariste goes on to consider how the life of each individual is a process of continual change, with the result that no man can be perfectly consistent with himself in matters of taste and judgment. The doubts that arise from these observations are then framed in a series of questions:

L'homme est-il donc condamné à n'être d'accord ni avec ses semblables, ni avec lui-même, sur les seuls objets qu'il lui importe de connaître, la vérité, la bonté, la beauté ? Sont-ce là des choses locales, momentanées et arbitraires, des mots vides de sens ? N'y a-t-il rien qui soit tel ? Une chose est-elle vraie, bonne et belle, quand elle me le paraît ? Et toutes nos disputes sur le goût se résoudraient-elles enfin à cette proposition : nous sommes, vous et moi, deux êtres différents; et moi-même, je ne suis jamais dans un instant ce que j'étais dans un autre ? (A.T., VII, 391–2).

The solution that Ariste proposes to these questions – the construction of a "modèle idéal" to serve as a permanent standard of taste and judgment – is well known; its significance has been carefully analysed by Jacques Chouillet in an article that should be required reading for every student of Diderot's works.[20] The only comment that need be added here is that there seems to be a close connection between this section of the *Discours sur la poésie dramatique* and Diderot's reading of *De l'esprit*.

Helvétius' book, it will be remembered, appeared in July 1758. In the following month, or shortly thereafter, Diderot must have put the finishing touches on his essay on dramatic poetry – the manuscript was delivered to the printer in September.[21] The paragraph just quoted which details with Rabelaisian exhaustiveness the causes of dissimilarity among men almost certainly reflects Diderot's reaction to Helvétius' theory of the original equality of minds. We have seen in Chapter 2 the thoughts inspired by that reaction as they are recorded in the *Réflexions sur le livre De l'esprit*, at least partly written during those summer months. Driven by Helvétius to a forceful reaffirmation of the natural diversity of men, the *philosophe* could scarcely have avoided reflecting

20 Jacques Chouillet, "Le Mythe d'Ariste, ou Diderot en face de lui-même," *Revue d'Histoire Littéraire de la France*, LXIV (1964), 565–88.
21 For the chronology of the preparation of this work and of *Le Père de famille*, which were published together, see Diderot, *Œuvres esthétiques*, ed. Paul Vernière, 179–82.

on the sceptical consequences of such a position. Everything indicates that the meditations of Ariste, however idealized, are the account of a crisis experienced by Diderot himself, a crisis which involved the reaction to Helvétius, the resultant encounter with scepticism, and finally a retreat to the middle ground between empiricism and idealism represented by the "modèle idéal." Certainly the closing pages of the *Discours sur la poésie dramatique*, which are in no way anticipated by what precedes them, could easily have been prompted by such a fortuitous event as the publication of a provocative book. It would seem that *De l'esprit* appeared at just the opportune moment to furnish Diderot's treatise on the drama with a very personal and very striking conclusion.

The above discussion shows clearly, I believe, that Diderot was well aware of the dangers of subjectivity and scepticism inevitable in an empirical system, and that his whole being cried out for certitude. Nothing better expresses this intimate need than his words to Madame Riccoboni in November 1758: "Dans les mœurs et dans les arts, il n'y a de bien et de mal pour moi, que ce qui l'est en tous temps et partout. Je veux que ma morale et mon goût soient éternels" (*Corr.*, ed. Roth, II, 95). Always somewhat inimical to philosophical scepticism in its extreme forms,[22] he nonetheless admits to adopting the Pyrrhonist's mask from time to time as a weapon against prejudice, while recognizing that Pyrrhonism is "une arme également propre à écarter le mensonge et à blesser la vérité."[23] When the fancy struck him, he even liked to view the world from the standpoint of the solipsist, as he confesses in an interesting letter to Falconet:

Mon ami, ne rétrécissons pas notre existence; ne circonscrivons point la sphère de nos jouissances. Regardez y bien; tout se passe en nous. Nous sommes où nous pensons être; ni les tems ni les distances n'y font rien. A présent, vous êtes à côté de moi. Je vous vois; je vous entretiens; je vous aime. ... Car après tout, qu'il y ait hors de nous quelque chose ou rien, c'est toujours nous que nous apercevons, et nous n'apercevons jamais que nous. Nous sommes l'univers entier. Vrai ou faux, j'aime ce système qui m'identifie avec tout ce qui m'est cher. Je sçais bien m'en départir dans l'occasion.[24]

We should not be surprised, in view of this, to see him donning the sceptic's mask for satirical purposes in *Le Neveu de Rameau*.

22 See, for example, the articles on the history of philosophy, "Mosaïque et Chrétienne" (A.T., XVI, 122), and "Pyrrhonienne ou Sceptique" (A.T., XVI, 483, 491–2). As for solipsism, Diderot recognized the folly of the position but also the difficulty of refuting it. See A.T., I, 304–5 (*Lettre sur les aveugles*).

23 *Encyclopédie*, art. "Pythagorisme," A.T., XVI, 514.

24 Letter of 29 December 1766 (*Corr.*, ed. Roth, VI, 376).

Philosophy, Epictetus tells us, begins with "a recognition of the conflict between the opinions of men, and a search for the origins of that conflict."[25] No one, I am sure, can fail to see the conflict of opinions in *Le Neveu de Rameau*; the difficulty in interpreting the work lies in the fact that, as a dialectical inquiry into the causes of disagreement, it seems to be an exercise in futility. Whatever turn the conversation takes, it almost invariably leads to an impasse; and the dialogue ends on a most inconclusive note. Whenever Moi has exhausted his fund of arguments, he resorts to irony; Lui, in the same situation, takes refuge in epithets; neither yields an inch, and the contest appears to finish in a draw.

Yet the author, whenever he intervenes, takes the side of Moi against Lui; how, then, did he so badly mismanage the dialogue that some readers consider Moi to be defending a vulnerable position? Are we assisting at an experiment in moral chemistry that fails to precipitate the expected truth? Or is Diderot deliberately presenting strength and weakness on both sides, and thereby counselling suspension of judgment?

Although both these solutions have been supported by some critics, there is a third that can be defended without doing violence either to the text or to the author's psychology. From what we have seen in the preceding pages, does it not seem more likely that we have in *Le Neveu de Rameau* an ironical use of linguistic scepticism, paralleling the use of determinism as a satirical weapon in the parts of the dialogue that are concerned with strictly moral topics? In that hypothesis, the disagreement between the two interlocutors can have only one cause: it arises from the fact that they are totally dissimilar. The argument reaches a stalemate precisely because Moi is Moi and Lui is Lui, and the language of one is not the language of the other. If the dialectic seems to yield no truth, it is because the author intended the truth to spring from the irony of the confrontation. His faith in reason and in the possibility of knowledge puts him firmly on the side of Moi; but despite his belief in the educability of man, he sardonically makes Lui impervious to rational argument. Lui speaks with the voice of egoism and animality, Moi with that of altruism and rationality. And Diderot, with satirical intent, conceals himself behind the mask of scepticism – but not of philosophical scepticism. The attitude he assumes is not despair of arriving at truth, but despair of communicating truth to those who are determined not to understand.

It would be tedious to cite all the passages that point to this conclusion; a few examples will suffice for illustration. Besides Moi's ironical comments that indicate a failure of communication (Fabre, pp. 38, 39,

25 Epictetus, *Disc*.II.xi.13.

50, 53, 58), there are numerous instances of mutual incomprehension where the irony is simply implied. Early in the discussion, Lui sets out to justify his stated preference for the happiness of bourgeois mediocrity (p. 12); Moi breaks into laughter when Lui's words reveal what he has in mind: the gross sensual indulgence that a comfortable fortune might afford. A few pages later, Moi encourages the musician to explain what he means by the expression "mepris de soi" (p. 22), only to learn that this sentiment, for Lui, arises from his failure to exploit all his natural talents for vice (p. 24). Again, Moi's edification at hearing that Lui studies the great moralists lasts only until it becomes apparent that he uses Molière and La Bruyère as manuals of the art of hypocrisy (pp. 59–61). Finally, Lui expresses envy for Moi's command of language; not, however, for the sake of truth, but in order to advance his fortune more quickly through lying and flattery (p. 94).

If irony is the means by which the author most frequently signals the breakdown in communication, there are several occasions on which he makes it explicit. When, for example, the musician fails to comprehend Moi's version of happiness, he is told: "Je vois, mon cher, que vous ignorez ce que c'est, et que vous n'etes pas meme fait pour l'apprendre" (p. 46). Lui himself is well aware of the problems involved in language, especially when one is speaking to a "visionnaire"; his frank avowal of viciousness is immediately nullified by the comment: "Quand je dis vicieux, c'est pour parler votre langue; car si nous venions a nous expliquer, il pourroit arriver que vous appellassiez vice ce que j'apelle vertu, et vertu ce que j'apelle vice" (p. 62). Again, when Lui defines a good education as "celle qui conduit a toutes sortes de jouissances, sans peril, et sans inconvenient," the philosopher makes it clear that these words have a different meaning for him: "Peu s'en faut que je ne sois de votre avis; mais gardons nous de nous expliquer" (p. 96). And on the pretext of professing his ignorance of musical terminology, he sarcastically underlines the same point: "Quand je prononce le mot chant, je n'ai pas des notions plus nettes que vous, et la pluspart de vos semblables, quand ils disent, reputation, blame, honneur, vice, vertu, pudeur, decence, honte, ridicule" (pp. 77–8).

Many other texts could be adduced to show that *Le Neveu de Rameau* was intended as a satirical comment on the futility of casting pearls before swine, of bearing light to those who prefer darkness. In this interpretation, which nothing in the satire belies, it is possible to consider Diderot's masterpiece as forming part of a trilogy on communication – the first two parts being the *Lettre sur les aveugles* and the *Lettre sur les sourds et muets*. This time, however, it is a question not of physical, but of moral and intellectual deficiencies; and Diderot's approach is not experimental but satirical. The earlier works were marked by a buoyant optimism in the progress of knowledge; *Le Neveu de Rameau*, on the other hand, is an expression of the author's bitterness and disappointment at the stubborn resistance of his generation to the process of enlightenment.

Yet the very existence of this satire is proof that Diderot, far from despairing, still entertained hopes for the betterment of mankind. *Le Neveu de Rameau*, despite the apparent pessimism of some of its pages, has nothing of the outraged vituperation usually associated with Juvenal. The Saturnalian setting, the engaging qualities of Rameau the "fieffé truand," the indirectness of the "confessional" form the satire takes, the occasional traits of Horatian self-mockery, and even the constant appeal to determinism, all conspire to lend to the work an air of mock seriousness by which we are assured that the author has lost neither his zest for life nor the serenity of the philosophic mind. Indeed, a further dimension is added to the satire when it is seen to rise above the goals of recrimination and personal vengeance to a level approaching the comic. On this level, the mask of the sceptic becomes the mask of the spirit of comedy, Diderot's favourite disguise. "Dans la grande comédie, la comédie à laquelle je reviens toujours, celle du monde ... "; if these words of the *Paradoxe sur le comédien* (A.T., VIII, 348) find their justification in *Jacques le fataliste*, they are equally applicable to *Le Neveu de Rameau*. In a letter dated 27 July 1762, Diderot ironically imagines himself as the comic spirit looking down amusedly on the world of men:

Oh ! que ce monde-cy seroit une bonne comédie, si l'on n'y faisoit pas un rôle; si l'on existoit par exemple dans quelque point de l'espace, dans cet intervalle des orbes célestes où sommeillent les dieux d'Epicure, bien loin, bien loin, d'où l'on ne vît ce globe sur lequel nous trottons si fièrement gros tout au plus que comme une citrouille, et d'où l'on observât, avec le télescope, la multitude infinie des allures diverses de tous ces pucerons à deux pieds qu'on appelle des hommes.[26]

If the author plays a role in *Le Neveu de Rameau*, it is surely that of the spirit of comedy watching, with huge delight, the futile attempts of men to communicate by word and gesture. "Rira bien qui rira le dernier" (p. 109). Although Lui was confident that he would have the last laugh, there was one, Diderot knew, whose cosmic laughter would continue rolling long after his was stilled.

26 To Sophie Volland (*Corr.*, ed. Roth, IV, 71). These thoughts, which express Diderot's reaction to Rousseau's *Profession de foi du vicaire savoyard*, recall a similar passage in Erasmus, *The Praise of Folly*, XLVIII *in fine*.

# 5

# Mediocrity, inconsistency, inequality

ALTHOUGH the theme of genius occupies an important number of pages in *Le Neveu de Rameau*, it is properly confined to two sections of the dialogue, one at the beginning (Fabre, pp. 7–17), and another near the end (pp. 96–103). We have seen how this theme is used to highlight the author's ideas on utility. It has a further function as one of the elements of the satire: it serves to bring out the mediocrity of the foolish musician, and by implication, that of Palissot and his friends.

The conversation opens with a discussion of the talents of chess-players and actors. Lui, in words that paraphrase those of La Bruyère,[1] condemns mediocrity in chess as well as in poetry, eloquence, music, "et autres fadaises comme cela" (p. 7). In the pages that follow, we are surprised to learn that his scorn for mediocrity is more than matched by his contempt for genius. It is evident that the author's intention in the conduct of the dialogue is to show Lui in flagrant contradiction with himself. Moi defends genius against Lui's repeated attacks, pointing out that his disparagement of great men is hardly consistent with his desire to achieve glory himself (p. 10). Lui is finally brought to admit that it is his own mediocrity as a musician, and his resultant envy, that lie at the root of his hatred of genius: "Je suis envieux ... Oui, oui, je suis mediocre et faché" (p. 15).

The next time that the question of genius arises, it is Moi who introduces it in the form of a question: Why, despite your musical gifts, have you produced no work of value? (p. 96). In reply, Lui mimes an artist in the throes of inspiration; but the muse fails to appear, and he collapses in mock despair: "je suis un sot, un sot, un sot" (p. 98). Lack of inspiration, however, is only one of the reasons for his failure. Everything has conspired against him: the dull banality of the people he frequents; his lack of courage; the refusal of nature to provide him with

1 "Il y a de certaines choses dont la médiocrité est insupportable : la poésie, la musique, la peinture, le discours public" (*Les Caractères*, I, 7). Cf. Horace, *Ars poet.*, 366–84; Boileau, *Art poét.*, IV, 29–40.

talent equal to that of his father; poverty, and the impossibility of conquering it without becoming the parasite of a vile wretch such as the Jew of Utrecht, or worse, of a man like Bertin (pp. 97–103).

It should be pointed out that Diderot had different purposes in mind in introducing these two passages on genius and mediocrity. The first, which concludes with a confession of envy on the part of Lui, is a preparation for the unmasking of Palissot and the "menagerie" as a pack of envious parasites (p. 57), and as such it serves the end of purely personal satire; the second passage, on the other hand, aims at a sociological explanation of mediocrity which, humorous in itself, gives a further satirical dimension to the dialogue.

We need not dwell at any great length on the social implications of *Le Neveu de Rameau,* for it has long been recognized that the portrayal of Rameau as a parasite dependent on the financier Bertin raises the satire from purely personal invective to an attack on the social forces in France that had fostered mediocrity in the arts. As early as 1755, in the *Encyclopédie,* Diderot had written a burning indictment of the social system and especially of what he calls "la protection mal placée," which forces men of talent either to accept subservience to the wealthy or suffer persecution.[2] Nowhere did he state his thoughts on this matter more forcefully than in his *Satire contre le luxe à la manière de Perse.*[3] This brief diatribe exposes, in tones of exasperation, the great harm wrought by false luxury and ostentatious wealth: artistic genius is stifled by the vulgar taste and corrupt morals of the opulent and by the willing acceptance of mediocrity on the part of the envious multitude. Stern moralist that he is, Diderot goes on to point out the effect that the race for riches has upon the moral fibre of the nation: "Au moment où l'on put arriver à tout avec de l'or, on voulut avoir de l'or; et le mérite, qui ne conduisait à rien, ne fut rien" (A.T., XI, 90). Thus the ideal of society became "Soyons, ou paraissons riches" (XI, 91). In such an atmosphere there is no longer any incentive for study or education, minds are incapable of rising above the grossly material to a conception of great and noble things, and the arts languish. "Si les mœurs sont corrompues, croyez-vous que le goût puisse rester pur? Non, non, cela ne se peut; et si vous le croyez, c'est que vous ignorez l'effet de la vertu sur les beaux-arts" (XI, 92).

2 Art. "Eclectisme," A.T., XIV, 349.
3 A.T., XI, 89–94. Editors of Diderot's *Salons,* from Naigeon to Jean Seznec, have inserted this short piece in the *Salon de 1767* immediately following a discussion of the effects of luxury on the fine arts that takes the form of a dialogue between Grimm and Diderot (XI, 84–9). There is no doubt that the two passages are related; but the fact that many of the ideas are expressed in practically identical terms would seem to argue that the *Satire contre le luxe* was intended by the author to be a separate work.

These thoughts, and the satirical spirit in which they are expressed, have their parallel in *Le Neveu de Rameau*. The author's presentation of Rameau as a failure, whatever other motives might have inspired it, was certainly aimed at underscoring the unfavourable situation of the arts in French society. In reply to Moi's question why he has never produced a great musical work (Fabre, p. 97), Lui blames first the shallow preoccupations of Parisians: "Mais le moyen de sentir, de s'elever, de penser, de peindre fortement, en frequentant avec des gens, tels que ceux qu'il faut voir pour vivre" (p. 98). Other sociological reasons for his mediocrity are evident in the story of his life. His first experience of parasitism was with the Jew of Utrecht, "opulent et dissipateur"; but this was an expedient that even the most vile could not support for long. "Alors je me separai de lui. Je revins ici. Quoi faire ? car il falloit perir de misere, ou faire quelque chose" (p. 102). The possibilities were not too brilliant: wandering actor? mountebank? street-singer? These were finally rejected in favour of "le geste d'un doigt dirigé vers sa bouche entrouverte" – unashamed beggary. "Et puis pensez grandement; faites de belles choses, au milieu d'une pareille détresse" (ibid.). But the low point had not yet been reached; the final stage of decadence was to join the Bertin household: "De cascade en cascade, j'etois tombé la" (ibid.).

By means of this comic saga Diderot condemns patrons, parasites, and public for their petty vices and their lamentable mediocrity which have sapped the talent of the nation. There is no attempt, however, to point to a solution of this social problem. Rameau has simply bowed to necessity, respecting the values of those around him, values which he feels obliged to pass on to his young son: "De l'or, de l'or. L'or est tout; et le reste, sans or, n'est rien" (Fabre, p. 92). Cynically complying with his role as parasite and fool, he pretends to consider his talents as the means of restoring the balance of nature upset by the piracy of the financiers: "Je les aidois a restituer, moi, et une foule d'autres qu'ils emploioient comme moi" (p. 37). Diderot, in the *Salon de 1767*, is equally ironical, praising the mediocre artists and others who pander to the corrupt taste of those grown fat at the expense of the nation: "ce sont ces gens-là qui nous vengent. C'est la vermine qui ronge et détruit nos vampires, et qui reverse goutte à goutte le sang dont ils nous ont épuisés."[4]

4 A.T., XI, 88. The idea is found in Saint-Evremond, *Sentiment d'un honnête courtisan sur la vertu rigide*: "Ceux qui prennent avec violence pour répandre avec profusion sont excusables. Leur dépense est comme une espèce de restitution; les dépouillés semblent rentrer en quelque part de leur bien quand la magnificence expose à leurs yeux ce que la force avait arraché à leurs mains" (*Œuvres*, 1705 ed., 2 vols., I, 431). Cited by André Morize, *L'Apologie du luxe au dix-huitième siècle et le Mondain de Voltaire* (Paris, Didier, 1909), 37.

The fact that there exists in *Le Neveu de Rameau* a level of satire that goes beyond the purely personal to involve the whole of eighteenth-century society is further justification of the thesis that Lui is representative of the folly of his age. This process of generalization is of the utmost importance for our understanding of Diderot's mind, for we shall see that his classical training will not permit him to stop there. The next step in the process is universalization; but how does a literary artist raise to the universal level a genre so immersed in present reality as is the genre of satire? The most obvious expedient would be the use of allegory. Related to this would be the procedure of identifying the here-and-now conditions of the world with those of previous ages. Each of these possibilities will be examined in a later chapter.

The use of mediocrity in *Le Neveu de Rameau* is not limited to the contrast that we have noted between genius on the one hand and lack of talent on the other. This aspect of the satire is exhausted in a very few pages; far more important for Diderot's purpose is mediocrity considered from the moral point of view, that is, inconsistency of action. This, as we shall see, is the principal moral trait given to Lui; and, for the sake of contrast, the author brings in the "grand criminel," the man whose actions flow from a totally unified character. This fascinating personage, who is in reality the moral counterpart of the genius, has attracted considerable attention from critics;[5] the result has been that the inconsistent man, represented by Lui, has never been adequately examined. The task is not a simple one because, in dealing with commonplaces such as human inconsistency and unity of character, the question of sources is problematical. The fact, however, that the "grand criminel" became prominent in Diderot's works only shortly before he undertook *Le Neveu de Rameau* should make us suspect that his attention was drawn sharply to this subject at about that time. Once again, we are led to Helvétius and *De l'esprit*.

It will be remembered that Diderot, while disagreeing with the fundamental moral doctrine of *De l'esprit*, nonetheless considered the author to have expressed therein a number of valuable insights, "une infinité de vérités de détail" (A.T., II, 274). Certainly the Encyclopedist did not take Helvétius' psychology seriously; however, in his diffuse, rambling description of man, the author of *De l'esprit* had not failed to make many penetrating statements that might have appealed to the moralist in Diderot. We must not look on Diderot's reaction to Helvétius as being entirely negative; he was to remain indebted to the book *De*

5 See Pierre Hermand, *Les Idées morales de Diderot* (Paris, Presses Universitaires de France, 1923), 108–10; Jean Thomas, *L'Humanisme de Diderot* (2e éd., Paris, "Les Belles-Lettres," 1938), 129–30; Yvon Belaval, *L'Esthétique sans paradoxe de Diderot* (Paris, Gallimard, 1950), 72–3.

*l'esprit* for certain of his ideas, and especially for the particular manner in which he chose to express them.

There is one theme to which Helvétius keeps returning constantly in his investigation of the mind – that of genius and mediocrity. Refusing to accept natural aptitude as a limiting factor in human perfectibility, he sees the man of genius as one whose dominant passion is the desire for glory. So strong is this motivation that the genius is led to direct his power of attention exclusively towards a single object, and he attains excellence in the field in which he concentrates his efforts.[6] The long hours of reflection to which the genius must devote his early years often prevent him from assimilating the everyday information that is taken for granted as common knowledge; he therefore appears stupid and ignorant to ordinary men.[7] But if mediocre persons find fault with men of genius, such a judgment is conditioned by their very mediocrity – they are not endowed with what Helvétius calls "ce principe de vie & de passions qui produit également les grands vices, les grandes vertus & les grands talents."[8]

Helvétius, like Diderot himself, laid great importance on the passions in his analysis of human nature. For him, passion is the direct expression of physical sensitivity, and he considers it to be the source of all that can be called vice and virtue in man. Passions may differ in degree of intensity, and this is the basis of the distinction he makes between two kinds of virtue – active and passive. Passive virtue is the attribute of that numerous class of people called "honnêtes"; having no strong passions of any kind, they remain meekly in the path of virtue through sheer sloth. Active virtue, on the other hand, is achieved only by that rare individual whose desire for glory is so powerful that he is led to sacrifice all his other passions to it, performing acts that win him public esteem by the fact that they contribute to the common good of society.[9]

It is evident from this that the man of great virtue is merely a moral version of the man of great intellect; and the family resemblance is shared by their ugly cousin, the genius in evil. Under certain historical circumstances, Helvétius says, the only way to achieve renown is through

6 Speaking of the desire for glory, he says: "Ce desir enfin est l'ame de l'homme de génie : il est la source de ses ridicules & de ses succès; succès qu'il ne doit ordinairement qu'à l'opiniâtreté avec laquelle il se concentre dans un seul genre. Une science suffit pour remplir toute la capacité d'une ame : aussi n'est-il pas & ne peut-il y avoir de génie universel" (Disc. IV, Ch. I, orig. ed., 480–2).

7 "La science des choses communes est la science des gens médiocres; & quelquefois l'homme de génie est, à cet égard, d'une ignorance grossiere. Ardent à s'élancer jusqu'aux premiers principes de l'art ou de la science qu'il cultive ... il néglige toute autre espece de connoissance. Sort-il du sentier lumineux que lui trace le génie? il tombe dans mille erreurs; & Newton commente l'*Apocalypse*" (Disc. IV, Ch. VIII, orig. ed., 552).

8 Ibid., 554.

9 Helvétius expose ces idées in Disc. III, Ch. XVI (orig. ed., 368–9).

acts of ruthlessness and cruelty. In such an age, men who might otherwise have been heroes of virtue will indulge their passion for glory with
the same singleness of purpose, stopping at nothing to attain their goal:

[Les ambitieux de gloire] ne peuvent jamais être que de grands criminels;
parce que les grands crimes, par la supériorité des talents nécessaires pour
les exécuter & le grand prix attaché au succès, peuvent seuls en imposer
assez à l'imagination des hommes, pour ravir leur admiration; admiration
fondée en eux sur un desir intérieur & secret de ressembler à ces illustres
coupables. Tout homme amoureux de la gloire est donc incapable de tous
les petits crimes. Si cette passion fait des Cromwel [*sic*], elle ne fait jamais
des Cartouche.[10]

There are, however, few men capable of the sustained attention necessary to commit great crimes or perform outstanding acts of virtue; and
even those who succeed are subject, at times, to the inconstancy that is
the lot of the multitude. The human heart is a prey to many contrary
passions, some favourable to the good of society, others unfavourable
to it. Normally we judge a man virtuous or vicious by his dominant
passion, according as it is either useful or harmful to the general interest;[11] but this is a simplification of the reality: "L'homme absolument
conséquent n'existe point encore; & c'est pourquoi rien de parfait sur
la terre, ni dans le vice, ni dans la vertu."[12]

It is surely no coincidence that when these ideas begin appearing in
Diderot's works, the hero in evil is linked with the notions of unity,
energy, and passion, and associated with mediocrity and inconsistency.
The first example is the famous statement about the weathercock: "La
tête d'un Langrois est sur ses épaules comme un coq d'église au haut
d'un clocher."[13] Diderot immediately goes on to say that, having
achieved a certain stability over the years, he himself is constant in his
tastes, especially in his appreciation of the identity of unity with beauty:
"Un tout est beau lorsqu'il est un. En ce cens, Cromwell est beau, et
Scipion aussi, et Médée, et Aria, et César, et Brutus."[14] At about that

---

10 Ibid., 370. Cf. Disc. iv, Ch. xiii (orig. ed., 590): "Ce n'est pas qu'on ne puisse,
à beaucoup d'intrigue, unir beaucoup d'élévation d'ame. Qu'à l'exemple de Cromwel
[*sic*], un homme veuille monter au trône : la puissance, l'éclat de la couronne, & les
plaisirs attachés à l'empire, peuvent sans doute à ses yeux ennoblir la bassesse de ses
menées, puisqu'ils effacent déjà l'horreur de ses crimes aux yeux de la postérité qui
le place au rang des plus grands hommes : mais que, par une infinité d'intrigues, un
homme cherche à s'élever à ces petits postes qui ne peuvent jamais lui mériter, s'il
est cité dans l'histoire, que le nom de coquin ou de friponneau, je dis qu'un pareil
homme se rend méprisable, non seulement aux yeux des gens honnêtes, mais encore
à ceux des gens éclairés. Il faut être un petit homme pour désirer de petites choses."
11 Disc. iii, Ch. xvi (orig. ed., 370–2).
12 Disc. ii, Ch. ii (orig. ed., 49).
13 To Sophie Volland, 11 August 1759 (*Corr.*, ed. Roth, ii, 207).
14 Ibid., 208.

time, Sophie Volland was reading, apparently with enjoyment, Helvétius' book *De l'esprit*.[15]

It is a full year later that the "grand criminel" appears again, still in the company of the mediocre man:

Au reste, un coup d'œil sur les inconséquences et les contradictions des hommes, et l'on voit que la plupart naissent moitié sots et moitié fous. Sans caractère comme sans physionomie, ils ne sont décidés ni pour le vice ni pour la vertu. Ils ne sçavent ni immoler les autres ni se sacrifier; et soit qu'ils fassent le bien, soit qu'ils fassent le mal, ils sont malheureux et j'en ai pitié.[16]

The next paragraph begins: "Ces idées tiennent à d'autres que j'établissois hier à table ... "; and the familiar theme is repeated: "Si les méchants n'avoient pas cette énergie dans le crime, les bons n'auroient pas la même énergie dans la vertu." The question of the aesthetic value of crime continued to preoccupy Diderot, as a letter dated 14-15 October 1760 indicates.[17] The moral aspect of the question also posed a problem: is the "grand criminel" a literary figure only, or does nature produce such individuals? In December of the same year he tells of spending an evening with Helvétius during which he undertook to defend human nature in this regard:

Nous nous sommes arraché le blanc des yeux, Helvétius, Saurin et moi, hier au soir. Ils prétendoient qu'il y avoit des hommes qui n'avoient aucun sentiment honnête, ni aucune idée de l'immoralité. ... Je voulois qu'un homme qui préféroit son intérêt propre au bien public sentît plus ou moins qu'on pouvoit faire mieux et qu'il s'estimât moins de n'avoir pas la force de se sacrifier.[18]

Finally, in July 1762, the whole doctrine finds expression in a letter to Sophie Volland:

Tout ce que la passion inspire, je le pardonne. Il n'y a que les inconséquences qui me choquent. Et puis, vous le sçavez, j'ai de tout tems été l'apologiste des passions fortes. Elles seules m'émeuvent. ... Si les actions atroces qui déshonorent notre nature sont commises par elles, c'est par elles aussi qu'on est porté aux tentatives merveilleuses qui la relèvent. L'homme médiocre vit et meurt comme la brute. Il n'a rien fait qui le distinguât pendant qu'il vivoit. Il ne reste de lui rien dont on parle, quand il n'est plus. ... D'ailleurs les suites de la méchanceté passent avec le méchant; celles de la bonté restent. Comme je disois une fois à Uranie, s'il faut opter entre

15 "Je souhaite que la lecture de *l'Esprit* continue de vous plaire" (30 October 1759, *Corr.*, ed. Roth, II, 308).

16 Letter to Sophie Volland, 30 September 1760 (*Corr.*, ed. Roth, III, 97-8).

17 To Sophie Volland, *Corr.*, ed. Roth, III, 141.

18 To Sophie Volland, 1 December 1760 (*Corr.*, ed. Roth, III, 281). Cf. ibid., IV, 210 (31 October 1762) and IV, 220 (11 November 1762), where the same idea is expressed.

Racine méchant époux, méchant père, ami faux et poëte sublime, et Racine
bon père, bon époux, bon ami et plat honnête homme, je m'en tiens au
premier. De Racine méchant, que reste-t-il? Rien. De Racine homme de
génie, l'ouvrage est éternel.[19]

This passage is sufficient to establish the relationship in Diderot's
mind between the immoral genius ("Racine méchant"), the genius in
evil ("le grand criminel") and the inconsistent man ("l'homme médiocre"). We may now concentrate our attention on the last-named,
who is least familiar to readers of Diderot yet by far the most important
for Le Neveu de Rameau. Pierre Mesnard has attempted to show that
Diderot, between 1761 and 1775, became aware of the existence of a
certain type of individual whom modern characterology calls "amorphe," and that he chose Jean-François Rameau, the very incarnation
of the type, as a model for Lui in his satire.[20] There are many points of
M. Mesnard's analysis that are undeniably correct; it is unfortunate
that the method applied led to a distortion of the conclusions.

The fact is that there was a well-defined character-type recognized
by moralists in the eighteenth century, similar to the "amorphe," but
referred to as "l'homme sans caractère."[21] La Bruyère describes him
simply as "fade;"[22] Vauvenargues says of him: "Les traits de son âme
sont faibles, légers, changeants;"[23] the Dictionnaire de Trévoux (art.
"Caractère") goes much farther: "Un homme sans caractère est alternativement honnête homme ou fripon sans qu'on puisse jamais le deviner";
and d'Alembert, who obviously had the Jesuit writer's text before him
when composing the corresponding article for the Encyclopédie, gives
a full-length portrait:

19 31 July 1762 (Corr., ed. Roth, IV, 81). It is an exaggeration to say with Jean
Thomas (L'Humanisme de Diderot, 130–1) that this theory of the long-range
benefits to humanity of "Racine méchant" upset Diderot's moral system. A post
factum judgment of this kind is not prescriptive, and he remained convinced that
one's personal happiness is founded on virtue. He is merely echoing Helvétius'
opinion that the public disregards the evil in the lives of great men. This is stated
more than once in De l'esprit: "C'est uniquement par ses talents qu'un homme
privé peut se rendre utile & recommandable à sa nation. Qu'importe au public la
probité d'un particulier? cette probité ne lui est de presqu' aucune utilité. Aussi
juge-t-il les vivants comme la postérité juge les morts : elle ne s'informe point si
Juvenal étoit méchant, Ovide débauché, Annibal cruel, Lucrece impie, Horace
libertin, Auguste dissimulé, & César la femme de tous les maris : c'est uniquement
leurs talents qu'elle juge" (Disc. II, Ch. VI, orig. ed., 81–2).

20 Pierre Mesnard, Le Cas Diderot. Etude de caractérologie littéraire (Paris,
Presses Universitaires de France, 1952), 189–211.

21 René Le Senne gives the modern sense in his Traité de caractérologie (Paris,
Presses Universitaires de France, 1949), 10: "On accuse d'être 'sans caractère' un
homme, qui, au sens psychologique, a bien un caractère, mais au sens moral, manque
de l'originalité qu'on lui voudrait, 'n'est pas un caractère'."

22 Les Caractères, V, 1. Cf. ibid., XI, 147.

23 Introduction à la connaissance de l'esprit humain, XVI, "Du caractère,"
Œuvres, ed. D.-L. Gilbert (Paris, 1857, 2 vols.), I, 24.

Rien n'est plus dangereux dans la société qu'un homme sans *caractère*, c'est à dire dont l'âme n'a aucune disposition plus habituelle qu'une autre. On se fie à l'homme vertueux; on se défie du fripon. L'homme sans *caractère* est alternativement l'un et l'autre, sans qu'on puisse le deviner, et ne peut être regardé ni comme ami, ni comme ennemi; c'est une espèce d'anti-amphibie, s'il est permis de s'exprimer de la sorte, qui n'est bon à vivre dans aucun élément.[24]

The character-type described by d'Alembert in this passage is familiar to us from Diderot's letter of September 1760, quoted above (p. 81). There, he put the majority of mankind in that category: "Sans caractère comme sans physionomie, ils ne sont décidés ni pour le vice ni pour la vertu." In September 1761, a letter to Sophie Volland distinguishes between "les gens de bien" and "la foule, qui est alternativement bonne et mauvaise" (*Corr.*, ed. Roth, III, 319). A year later, we find him passing judgment on Clairet, Sophie's personal maid: "Il faut que Clairet soit une fille sans caractère, bonne ou mauvaise, selon le vent qui souffle, et j'en suis fâché."[25] And in the *Salon de 1763* we find the following remark concerning the Marquis de Marigny's rather bizarre taste in painting: "Si un homme qui fait bien aujourd'hui et mal demain est un homme sans caractère ou sans principes, que faut-il dire du goût de celui qui associe dans un même cabinet des choses si disparates ?" (A.T., X, 163).

Human inconsistency, of course, is one of the oldest problems of moral philosophy. For the Stoics, the rationality of the universe, guaranteed by the Logos, is reflected in the individual whose life is directed by a single harmonious principle. This is the ideal of consistency (*homologia*; in Latin, *convenientia*), which is the quality essential to true virtue, and consequently, to happiness.[26] The virtuous life is therefore identical with life according to nature and with life according to reason.[27] The doctrine of consistency with nature is summed up by Arnold (*Roman Stoicism*, 282) as follows:

Because virtue is one thing and not many, it makes a man's life one consistent whole, and stands in sharp contrast to the changing and undecided ways of the crowd. Virtue is therefore frequently defined as consistency in life, an even steady course of action,[28] self-consistency,[29] a principle in

24 *Encyclopédie*, art. "Caractère (en morale)," II, 666.
25 To Sophie Volland, 17 October 1762 (*Corr.*, ed. Roth, IV, 200).
26 See E. Vernon Arnold, *Roman Stoicism* (Cambridge, at the University Press, 1911), 71–2. Cf. Cicero, *De finibus*, III.vi.21.
27 Cicero, *De finibus*, III.ix.31: "convenienter naturae vivere"; Seneca, *Ep.*, L, 8: "virtus secundum naturam est; vitia inimica et infesta sunt." See Arnold, *Roman Stoicism*, 282, n. 58.
28 Seneca, *Ep.*, XXXI, 8: "perfecta virtus aequalitas [est] ac tenor vitae per omnia consonans sibi." This note and the three following are Arnold's.
29 Ibid., XXXV, 4: "ante omnia hoc cura, ut constes tibi."

agreement with its applications.[30] The opposite of virtue is the unending restlessness and indecision of the man in the crowd.[31]

This is the classical background of Diderot's notions of mediocrity and unity of character, which were given, as we have seen, a distinctive orientation by Helvétius and eighteenth-century determinism.

We may now turn to *Le Neveu de Rameau* and its more immediate source, the satires of Horace. Critics have not failed to point out the relationship between Diderot's satire and Horace's *Sat*.II.vii from which the epigraph "Vertumnis, quotquot sunt, natus iniquis" (v. 14) is drawn. Diderot's borrowings from Horace extend to both form and content. It is generally agreed that the confrontation between the fool and the philosopher partakes of the Saturnalian atmosphere of *Sat*.II.vii. Lui's frankness, which plays such an important role in the unmasking of Diderot's enemies, undoubtedly has its model in the freedom of speech granted to slaves during the Roman festival and used so effectively by Davus in preaching his lengthy Stoic sermon to his master Horace. As for the content, E. R. Curtius is of the opinion that "the basic theme – contrast between the fool, enslaved by want, necessities, lusts, and passions, and the self-sufficient and therefore only free man, the sage – is identical in the two works."[32] Herbert Dieckmann has rightly objected that this theme is not central to *Le Neveu de Rameau*.[33] The difficulty here is that Curtius stated the matter badly. The two Stoic paradoxes, "every slave is a fool" and "only the sage is free," are devices employed by Horace to develop the satire's main topic, which is the importance of rational control. Niall Rudd, in a recent authoritative work on Horace, explains it in this way: "The control in question ... is that which ought to be exercised by the reason over irrational desires. When such control is wanting, the unruly desires gain the upper hand and the true self becomes enslaved. This, says Davus, is what has happened to Horace. Therefore, except for his legal status, the master is in no way superior to the slave."[34]

When Horace is read in this light, it becomes evident that Diderot is indeed indebted to the Roman satirist for the central theme of *Le Neveu de Rameau*. The basic opposition between Moi and Lui lies in

30 Ibid., LXXIV, 30: "virtus convenientia constat: omnia opera eius cum ipsa concordant et congruunt."

31 Ibid., XII, 16–17: "[stultitia] semper incipit vivere: quam foeda [est] hominum levitas cottidie nova vitae fundamenta ponentium, novas spes in exitu incohantium! quid est turpius quam senex vivere incipiens?"

32 Ernst Robert Curtius, *European Literature and the Latin Middle Ages*, trans. Willard R. Trask (New York, Pantheon Books, 1953), 582.

33 "The Relationship Between Diderot's *Satire I* and *Satire II*," 25.

34 Niall Rudd, *The Satires of Horace* (Cambridge, at the University Press, 1966), 189–90.

this, that the philosopher leads a virtuous life under the control of reason whereas the musician is a fool in the Stoic sense, swayed this way and that by his passions for lack of a guiding principle. We must not think, however, that Moi is to be identified with the wise man of Stoicism; the passing reference to the self-sufficient philosopher towards the end of Diderot's satire (Fabre, p. 106) is meant to be taken lightly, for it is in the Horatian tradition to scoff at the self-righteous Stoic sage. Neither must we think that Lui's character is modelled only after that of the Stoic fool; we shall see that he is much more than that. It is nonetheless certain that Diderot seriously intended Moi to represent the consistent follower of rational nature, as opposed to the inconsistent man who follows nature's irrational promptings.

It is lack of rational control that makes Lui the very model of inconsistency. As the epigraph indicates, he was born under the influence of Vertumnus, the god of the changing seasons, and this puts him in the class of men described by Davus in the opening lines of *Sat.*II.vii. Davus begins by contrasting two types of character: "Some men persist in their love of vice and stick to their purpose; the greater number waver, now aiming at the right, at times giving way to evil."[35] The Kiessling-Heinze edition of Horace (*ad loc.*) points out that this is a reference to the Stoic doctrine of the wavering crowd (the *phauloi*), who, Davus indicates (v. 19), are in a worse case than those who follow their vices consistently. It is easy to see how Diderot related these types to "le grand criminel" and "l'homme sans caractère." Persistence in vice, as a theme, does not reappear in Horace's works; but Diderot, with the aid of Helvétius, saw the possibilities of the idea for satire. The admiration expressed by Lui for the "grand criminel" is one of the devices by which Diderot brings out Rameau's fundamental ineffectualness. When he boasts of having raised parasitism to a fine art, Lui is merely being true to his type as found in ancient comedy; but Diderot goes on, with devastating irony, to show him and Palissot struggling, yet failing, to emulate the "grand criminel" and attain a degree of depravity that will place them above the mire of moral mediocrity. This is one of the most original and most effective parts of the satire.[36]

Even a cursory glance at the text of *Le Neveu de Rameau* suffices to

35 "Pars hominum vitiis gaudet constanter et urget
      propositum; pars multa natat, modo recta capessens,
      interdum pravis obnoxia" (vv. 6–8, trans. Fairclough).

36 The irony can be considered, in a way, to be directed also against Helvétius. The author of *De l'esprit*, in the passage quoted above (p. 80), had said that the admiration of the multitude for the "grand criminel" was based on a secret desire to emulate him. Diderot, on the other hand, developed a theory of the sublime in literature that would explain the attraction of such characters. He would never admit, except ironically, that aesthetic admiration was an indication of moral approval.

show that Diderot carried out the intention, implied in the epigraph, of painting Lui as a man of inconstant character. This is the first moral trait mentioned by the author in introducing Lui: "Rien ne dissemble plus de lui que lui meme."[37] There follows the well-known description reminiscent of Priscus in Horace's *Sat*.II.vii: "Quelquefois, il est maigre et have ... Le mois suivant, il est gras et replet ... Aujourdhuy, en linge sale, en culote dechirée ... Demain, poudré, chaussé, frisé ... " (Fabre, p. 4). This bizarre individual, who condemns both mediocrity (p. 7) and genius (p. 10), is advised by Moi of his inconsistency: "Vous ne serez jamais heureux, si le pour et le contre vous afflige egalement. Il faudroit prendre son parti, et y demeurer attaché."[38] But despite his admission that it is foolish to rebel against Nature's established order (p. 15), the thought of great men arouses him to impotent rage: "J'ai donc eté, je suis donc faché d'etre mediocre. Oui, oui, je suis mediocre et faché" (ibid.). He insists pathetically on his dignity as a human being, but confesses that this sentiment is anything but constant in him: "Cela se reveille a propos de bottes. Oui, a propos de bottes; car il y a d'autres jours ou il ne m'en couteroit rien pour etre vil tant qu'on voudroit ... " (p. 21). Bravely demonstrating his mastery of the art of seduction, he recognizes that nothing stands in the way of a successful career as a procurer – "Mais ces heureuses dispositions apparemment ne duroient pas; car jusqu'a present, je n'ai pu faire un certain chemin" (p. 24).

Moi persists in pointing out Lui's basic instability: "en depit du role miserable, abject, vil, abominable que vous faites, je crois qu'au fond, vous avez l'ame delicate."[39] But his foolish interlocutor will admit only to an occasional qualm of conscience: "Je suis a vos yeux un etre tres abject, tres meprisable, et je le suis aussi quelquefois aux miens; mais rarement. Je me felicite plus souvent de mes vices que je ne m'en blame. Vous etes plus constant dans votre mepris" (pp. 71–2). Lui's frank avowal of his vicious tendencies is aimed at achieving in the eyes of Moi the stature of a monster of evil: "On crache sur un petit filou; mais on ne peut refuser une sorte de consideration a un grand criminel. ... On

37 Fabre, 4. It has frequently been pointed out that this is an almost literal translation of Horace's description of the unpredictable singer Tigellius in *Sat*.I.iii.18–19: "nil fuit umquam sic impar sibi" ("Never was a creature so inconsistent" – Fairclough).

38 Fabre, 10. Cf. Epictetus: "No man is able to make progress when he is facing both ways" (IV.ii.4).

39 Fabre, p. 56. This statement of Moi is not meant to be ironical, for Diderot was persuaded that no man is totally evil. This is clear from his letter to Sophie Volland of 31 October 1762: "c'est que la nature a laissé dans l'âme des méchants une petite place qui n'est pas tout à fait pourrie, qui vit, qui est douloureuse, et où de tems en tems ils sont frappés" (*Corr.*, ed. Roth, IV, 210).

prise en tout l'unité de caractere" (p. 72). Moi, however, is not deceived: "Mais cette estimable unité de caractere, vous ne l'avez pas encore. Je vous trouve de tems en tems vacillant dans vos principes" (ibid.). Lui modestly grants that he has been surpassed in malignity by three people: Bouret, Palissot, and the renegade of Avignon (ibid.); but he steadfastly refuses to put himself on the level of the mediocre "especes," whom he professes to scorn as "egalement gauches dans le bien et dans le mal" (p. 90). Finally, the author intervenes to settle the matter. Lui, he says, is no better and no worse than the majority of his contemporaries: "Il n'etoit ni plus ni moins abominable qu'eux; il etoit seulement plus franc, et plus consequent; et quelquefois profond dans sa depravation" (p. 93).

The mediocrity of the common man expressed in this passage was a moral topic to which Diderot frequently returned throughout his life, especially, perhaps, because he felt that Helvétius' failure to take this factor into account had rendered his theory of education totally unrealistic:

Il est un phénomène, constant dans la nature, auquel Helvétius n'a pas fait attention, c'est que les âmes fortes sont rares, que la nature ne fait presque que des êtres communs ... Quelle que soit l'éducation publique ou particulière ... la multitude ne vous montrera qu'un mélange de bonté et de méchanceté.[40]

It is this contempt for the pettiness and inconstancy of the generality of men, somewhat exaggerated for the purposes of satire, that dictated the characterization of Lui as morally, and therefore artistically, mediocre. Unlike Moi, who incarnates the ideal of consistency and rational control (*convenientia*), Lui is fated to lead an aimless existence that precludes his ever becoming either a successful musician or a useful member of society. The exigencies of literary presentation required that he be given a certain relief; but for all his singularity, he is one of the crowd when considered from the moral point of view – the crowd that will continue to go its uncertain way despite encyclopaedias, bourgeois dramas, and, indeed, despite satire and irony aimed at its correction.

The questions that we have been considering in this chapter and in the previous one are similar in that they involve paired opposites that are reducible to elemental philosophical ideas. The opposition between unity of character and inconsistency is in reality the fundamental notion of "one and many" as it pertains to a given individual; the opposition between individuality and diversity, treated in Chapter 4, is an aspect

40 A.T., II, 393 (*Réfutation d'Helvétius*).

of the fundamental notion of "same and other" applied to the individual as a member of society. Related to both of these, and no less important, is another pair of opposites that is properly a relation of quantity: equality and inequality.

We have, in effect, dealt with one form of "inequality" in our analysis of inconsistency earlier in this chapter.[41] It was pointed out there that Diderot, in borrowing from Horace, modelled Lui after the two inconsistent characters of the satires – Priscus ($Sat$.ii.vii.8–14) and Tigellius ($Sat$.i.iii.1–19). In each of these descriptions there is a reference to "inequality." Of Priscus, Horace says "Vixit inaequalis" (v. 10 – "He lived an uneven life") ; of Tigellius, "Nil aequale homini fuit illi" (v. 9 – "There was nothing consistent in the fellow"). E. R. Curtius refers to this moral defect as "inaequalitas,"[42] which corresponds to the French "inégalité." Diderot, as we have seen, made Lui *inégal* by nature; and he knew well, by way of contrast, how to give to Moi the virtue essential to the "vir bonus" of antiquity – *aequabilitas* – which implies both steadiness of character and philosophical serenity.[43]

"Equality" and "inequality" used in this sense are aspects of a much broader motif; the two terms have a variety of other connotations, many of which lie behind the principal topics of the satire. Hegel was the first to catch a glimpse of the importance of these ideas for the dialogue, but he did not proceed beyond their purely social significance.[44] Much more remains to be said; indeed, it is no exaggeration to state that the equality-inequality opposition was employed by Diderot as a kind of "basse fondamentale" to which all the themes of his satire are related in harmonic proportion.

First, let us consider the literary framework into which he fitted his dialogue. The Roman Saturnalia, which took place yearly during a three-day period in December, commemorated the golden age of Saturn when, according to tradition, all men were equal. For the duration of the feast, all forms of social inequality were suspended. Horace's $Sat$.ii.vii

41 Current English does not normally use the words "equality" and "inequality" to mean "moral consistency" and "moral inconsistency." Quotation marks will be employed whenever they are given that sense.

42 *European Literature*, 581–2. Word unknown in classical Latin.

43 Cicero, *De off.*, i, xxvi: "Praeclaraque est aequabilitas in omni vita et idem semper vultus eademque frons, ut de Socrate ... accepimus" ("But it is a fine thing to keep an unruffled temper, an unchanging mien, and the same cast of countenance in every condition of life; this, history tells us, was characteristic of Socrates ...").
Trans. Miller. See also *Tusc. disp.*, ii, 65: "Nihil enim potest esse aequabile quod non a certa ratione proficiscatur" ("For nothing can keep the same level unless it starts with fixed principle"). Trans. King.

44 See Jean Hyppolite, *Genèse et structure de la "Phénoménologie de l'esprit" de Hegel* (Paris Aubier, 1946), 180–4, 398–404; and Roland Mortier, *Diderot en Allemagne* (Paris, Presses Universitaires de France, 1954), 281–8.

shows the slave Davus taking advantage of his short-lived freedom to berate his master for indulging in petty vices; Lucian's *Saturnalia* has the poor writing a letter to the king, requesting that they be allowed to sit at the tables of the rich during the festival. In *Le Neveu de Rameau*, the fool is temporarily accepted by the philosopher on terms of intellectual equality and given licence to expound his views on life: "Je n'estime pas ces originaux la; d'autres en font leurs connoissances familieres, meme leurs amis. Ils m'arrêtent une fois l'an ... " (Fabre, p. 5).

The Saturnalia theme, therefore, implies questions that had preoccupied both Diderot and Rousseau around 1754 – the natural equality of men and the inequality imposed by society. There is no need here to enter into the details of these problems, for they have received competent attention elsewhere.[45] It is sufficient for our purpose to point out that the ideas of social equality and inequality have resonances throughout *Le Neveu de Rameau* in every mention of poverty and luxury, of parasitism and patronage, of slavery and freedom. No one, I think, except those for whom literary criticism is a political game, will exaggerate the revolutionary tendencies of the inequality theme. Diderot's main concern here is the degradation of the arts; the villain of the piece is not luxury as such but the false luxury that he thought to be inescapably connected with the venality of offices as practised in his day. His *Satire contre de luxe*, where these ideas are most fully treated, is the surest guide for judging this aspect of *Le Neveu de Rameau*.[46]

Most important for the overall interpretation of the dialogue is the form of inequality that we considered in Chapter 4 under the name of "diversity." We have seen the influence of Helvétius in this regard, and I need only indicate here that the words "inégalité" and "inégal" occur countless times throughout *De l'esprit*, especially in the third *Discours*, where the author sets out to prove that "la grande inégalité d'esprit des hommes" (p. 252) is the effect of education rather than of natural

---

45 See George R. Havens, "Diderot, Rousseau, and the *Discours sur l'inégalité*," *Diderot Studies*, III (1961), 219–62; and Jacques Proust, *Diderot et l'Encyclopédie*, 2e éd. (Paris, A. Colin, 1967), 366–74. A comprehensive treatment of the problem is found in Sanford A. Lakoff, *Equality in Political Philosophy* (Cambridge, Mass., Harvard University Press, 1964), esp. 89–125.

46 A.T., XI, 89–94. See also A.T., II, 417–21 (*Réfutation d'Helvétius*). If the *Satire contre le luxe* shows evidence of the influence of physiocratic theory, *Le Neveu de Rameau* reflects rather Diderot's reading of *De l'esprit*. In his chapter on luxury, Helvétius wrote: "Le luxe n'est donc pas nuisible comme luxe, mais simplement comme l'effet d'une grande disproportion entre les richesses des citoyens. Aussi le luxe n'est-il jamais extrême, lorsque le partage des richesses n'est pas trop inégal; il s'augmente à mesure qu'elles se rassemblent en un plus petit nombre de mains; il parvient enfin à son dernier période, lorsque la nation se partage en deux classes, dont l'une abonde en superfluités, & l'autre manque du nécessaire" (Disc. I, Ch. III, orig. ed., 18–19). Cf. Fabre, 103–4.

endowment. His doctrine, which the *Journal de Trévoux* immediately dubbed "ce système d'égalité naturelle entre les Esprits,"[47] ran directly counter to Diderot's thinking on the matter. For the latter it is nature that makes men unequal, and education that imposes uniformity (Fabre, p. 5).

Diderot was well aware of the importance of his disagreement with Helvétius, and the *Réfutation* bears eloquent witness to this fact. Frank E. Manuel, who has traced the historical development of these conflicting ideas in the thought of Cabanis, de Bonald, and Saint-Simon, brings out the significance of the equality-inequality opposition for any theory of man and the seriousness of its implications for politics, sociology, and education.[48] Eighteenth-century egalitarianism in all its forms was repugnant to Diderot not only because it was based on an unscientific physiology and a false conception of human psychology, but also because of its foreseeable consequences in the political order. His personal involvement in the problem of equality, intensified by his differences with Rousseau and Helvétius, conferred on *Le Neveu de Rameau* the depth of thought and feeling that every reader can sense in the work. Of such stuff, and only of such stuff, is great literature made.

It is interesting to note that Diderot uses the word "inégalité" only once during the course of the dialogue. As Lui begins his story of the "renegat d'Avignon," Moi remarks: "Je reve a l'inegalité de votre ton; tantot haut, tantot bas" (Fabre, p. 74). This reminds us immediately of Horace's portrayal in *Sat*.i.iii of the inconstant Tigellius, who, we are told, would chant "Io Bacche!" continuously throughout a banquet "now with the highest voice and now with one responding to the lowest pitch to the tetrachord."[49]

Inconsistency of character is probably not the only trait that Diderot borrowed from Tigellius in creating his literary Rameau. This bizarre individual had the honour of being Horace's *bête noire*,[50] perhaps because he had publicly criticized the poet's verse, and he is attacked frequently in Book i of the *Satires* in a manner that is reminiscent of Diderot's running commentary on Palissot throughout *Le Neveu de*

---

47 November 1758, 2828.

48 Frank E. Manuel, "From Equality to Organicism," *Journal of the History of Ideas*, XVII (1956), 54–69. The article opens with these words: "One of the crucial developments in modern intellectual history is the reversal from the eighteenth-century view of men as more or less equal, or at least similar, in nature and hence in rights, to the early nineteenth-century emphasis upon human uniqueness, diversity, dissimilarity, culminating in theories of inequality and organicism."

49 "modo summa / voce, modo hac, resonat quae chordis quattuor ima" (vv. 7–8). Trans. Fairclough.

50 There were probably two Tigellii, one of whom Horace refers to as Hermogenes. The scholiasts thought they were one and the same man; from the time of Dacier,

*Rameau.* In addition to being a singer, Horace's Tigellius was a music-master in a girls' school,[51] a bohemian,[52] and a crony of literary hacks.[53] It is difficult to judge from the evidence which characteristics of Lui belonged to Jean-François Rameau and which ones were modelled after Horace's portrait of Tigellius. In all likelihood, Lui's "inequality" had a real foundation in the character of Diderot's erratic contemporary.

The identification of Lui with Tigellius does not exhaust the influence of *Sat.*I.iii. If Diderot can be said to have built his dialogue around the equality-inequality motif, it is almost certain that this satire of Horace suggested to him the use of such a procedure. Niall Rudd has pointed out that Horace here adopts as his leit-motif the idea of equality. The introduction (vv. 1–19), he says, deals with lack of *aequabilitas*, i.e., inconsistency; vv. 25–75 treat of *aequitas* or fairness; and vv. 76–98 criticize the Stoic doctrine that all sins are equal.[54] Horace, as Professor Rudd shows, beginning with the "inequality" of Tigellius, plays with the word "aequus" ("equal," "equitable"), ringing all the changes on the notions of equality, inequality, iniquity, justice, and balance.[55] In a similar way, Diderot used this poetic technique to exploit the manifold resonances of the basic relationship of equality to inequality.

If the execution of such a plan called for a literary artist, its conception required a philosophic mind. It is interesting to see that mind at work, some years before, constructing a theory of beauty which can perhaps help to explain the appeal of his masterpiece. In the *Principes généraux d'acoustique*, we read:

Le plaisir, en général, consiste dans la perception des rapports. Ce principe a lieu en poésie, en peinture, en architecture, en morale, dans tous les arts et dans toutes les sciences. ... Or, de tous les rapports, le plus simple, c'est celui d'égalité ... (A.T., IX, 104).

The conception of aesthetic appreciation as "la perception des rapports" would seem to be consistent with the use of binary oppositions that we have noted in Diderot's satire. And it should be added that both the theory and the practice reflect the polarity that is so characteristic of his thought.

---

most scholars make the distinction. I am assuming here that Diderot was a "unitarian" rather than a "separatist," terms employed by Niall Rudd in his summary of the question, *The Satires of Horace*, 292, n. 15.

51 *Sat.*I.x.90–1.  52 *Sat.*I.ii.1–4.
53 Ibid., 78–80.  54 *The Satires of Horace*, 5–8.
55 *Aequale* (v. 9); *impar* (19); *aequo* (52); *iniquam* (67); *aequum* (69); *compenset* (70); *trutina* (72); *aequum* (74); *ponderibus modulisque* (78); *paria* (96); *justi ... aequi* (98); *iniusti* (111); *justo ... iniquum* (113); *aequas* (118); *pares* (121).

# 6

# Plato, Rousseau, music

THE textual analysis presented in the three preceding chapters has allowed us to isolate certain aspects of what can perhaps best be described as Diderot's satirical posture in relation to *Le Neveu de Rameau*. We have seen, among other things, that the question of utility or expediency, considered from opposing points of view, plays a major role in the first part of the satire (Ch. 3); that the difficulty of communication between Moi and Lui suggests a pessimistic attitude on the part of the author with regard to the educability of men to virtue (Ch. 4); and that unity of character in the *grand criminel* is contrasted with the moral inconsistency of the multitude of mankind whom Lui seems to represent (Ch. 5).

Having made these observations, tentative though they may be, we are now in a position to explore further the implications of Chapter 2, where it was shown that there are solid reasons for seeing Lui and Moi as representing, respectively, the folly of the eighteenth century and the wisdom of Greek philosophy. This interpretation implies, of course, that Diderot must have identified himself with Moi and with the ethical doctrines for which he stands. In consequence of this, and in view of the fact that our satire was undoubtedly provoked by Palissot's scurrilous attack in *Les Philosophes*, it is possible to conceive of Diderot's reply as being not only a vindication of philosophy, but also a sort of *apologia pro vita sua* in the tradition of Plato's *Apology* for Socrates.

In our earlier attempt to verify the hypothesis, suggested by *De l'esprit*, that Moi represents the spirit of Greek philosophy, we found it impossible to draw from the text more than a few details pointing in that direction; at the same time, there appeared to be no evidence showing such an interpretation to be untenable. Now, in the absence of probative textual support, one ought normally to seek corroboration of an hypothesis in evidence exterior to the text. In the case of *Le Neveu de Rameau*, however, we are confronted with one of those rare works that seem to have been born in a vacuum; its very existence, as far as we know, goes unmentioned until 1798, and scholars have searched in vain for clues contemporary with its composition that might help to explain it. We are obliged, therefore, to go farther afield and consider an area of investigation suggested by the hypothesis itself: is *Le Neveu de Rameau* perhaps based on some model in the literature of antiquity? If it could be shown that Diderot owed his central inspiration to some ancient source, we should no doubt find ourselves immeasurably closer to a definition of the spirit in which he wrote his masterpiece.

Although, on the face of it, the odds against making such a discovery are extremely high, we are not left entirely without resources. Knowing as we do Diderot's fondness for Plato and his tendency to identify himself with Socrates, the obvious place to begin our search would seem to be the Socratic dialogues; certainly, no philosopher among the ancients would be more likely to represent for him the spirit of Greek thought than would the Sage of Athens! Our starting-point, then, is clearly indicated; but what method of procedure are we to follow in examining this immense body of literature? What element or elements should we look for in the ancient dialogues that might conceivably have served as a source for *Le Neveu de Rameau*? A random comparison of parallel themes in Diderot and Plato appears to offer little hope of arriving at useful conclusions, for our satire concerns itself with a bewildering multiplicity of subjects, many of them commonplaces in ancient literature. We should be well advised, therefore, to concentrate our attention first on the broad patterns of form and thought, leaving aside for the present questions of detail. The difficulty that confronts us here, of course, is that it is next to impossible to make a general statement about the form and thought of *Le Neveu de Rameau* with any degree of confidence.

There is, nonetheless, one thing that we can assert with little fear of contradiction concerning *Le Neveu de Rameau*: Diderot's satire is basically a dialogue between a moral idealist and a nihilist. Thus far, most would agree, we are on fairly safe ground. Now, is there any instance in the Platonic corpus in which Socrates finds himself matched against a proponent of immoralism? We can, in fact, point to two such instances: his debate with Callicles in the *Gorgias* (481b ff.) and his dispute with the sophist Thrasymachus in the first book of the *Republic* (336b ff.).

Once our attention is drawn to these humorous portraits of Callicles and Thrasymachus, we recall how they stand out as superb examples of Plato's art. The vigorous individuality and forthrightness of character of these two opponents of Socrates come through with a realism and a dramatic intensity that place them incontestably in the ancestral line of literary libertines that gave birth to Diderot's "fieffé truand." A closer examination reveals that the resemblance goes much deeper than a purely literary affinity: Lui of Diderot's dialogue seems to make his own the attitudes to life of Plato's two immoralists, who, despite certain differences in the presentation of their character, are both rugged individualists firmly entrenched in the ethical position that we have called egoistic utilitarianism. In each case they are made to expose their views with regard to the same question of practical morality: whether the just man or the unjust leads the happier life. Callicles and Thrasymachus are bent on convincing their interlocutor Socrates that might makes right, and that the strong man who overreaches his weaker neighbour is the happier of the two. Ultimately they are reduced to silence by the subtle dialectic of the Athenian philosopher.

The extent to which Diderot drew on these two portraits for *Le Neveu de Rameau* can be shown only by a detailed comparison. In addition to the text of the *Gorgias* (481b ff.) and that of the first book of the *Republic* (336b ff.), we must include in our consideration the opening section of *Republic* II (357a–367e) in which Glaucon and Adeimantus restate the opinions of Thrasymachus with the intention of eliciting from Socrates a more convincing demonstration of his position.[1]

### FRANKNESS, FREEDOM OF SPEECH

The native frankness of Lui (Fabre, pp. 4, 24, 56), of such importance for the exposure of vice in Diderot's satire, has, as we have seen, an obvious connection with the Saturnalia theme of Horace's *Sat.*II.vii. It is this quality, as the author remarks, that sets Lui apart from the majority of his contemporaries: his open espousal of grossly materialistic values contains "beaucoup de ces choses qu'on pense, d'apres les quelles on se conduit; mais qu'on ne dit pas" (p. 93). Callicles too is endowed with frankness of speech (*parrhesia*), for which he twice receives ironical praise from Socrates (*Gorgias*, 487ab, 492d). On the second occasion (492d), after a blunt avowal of immoralism on the part of his interlocutor, Socrates points out that Callicles is "now stating in clear terms what the rest of the world think indeed, but are loth to say."

### THE RIDICULOUS PHILOSOPHER

Throughout *Le Neveu de Rameau*, Lui is lavish in heaping scorn on philosophy and its practitioners. Socrates, for him, was "un particulier

---

1 Except as otherwise noted, all translations of Plato in this chapter are taken from the Loeb Classical Library editions: *The Republic*, trans. Paul Shorey, 2 vols. (London, Heinemann, 1930) and *Gorgias*, trans. W. R. M. Lamb (London, Heinemann, 1946).

audacieux et bizarre" (Fabre, p. 11); the pretended freedom of the Cynic Diogenes is merely a pious myth: "Et ou est cet animal la? S'il n'a rien il souffre; s'il ne sollicite rien, il n'obtiendra rien, et il souffrira toujours" (p. 106); and "Monsieur le philosophe," in his detachment from material things, is nothing more than a "visionnaire" (p. 46). Although willing to admit that he himself is an "impertinent raisonneur," Lui is satisfied to remain as he is: "Je n'entends pas grand chose a tout ce que vous me debitez la. C'est apparemment de la philosophie; je vous previens que je ne m'en mele pas" (p. 15). The idea that virtue is essential to happiness strikes him as an "étrange vision" that betrays "un certain tour d'esprit romanesque ... une ame singuliere, un gout particulier" (p. 39). This is one form of singularity that tempts him not at all: "Imaginez l'univers sage et philosophe; convenez qu'il seroit diablement triste" (p. 40). Moreover, he bitterly resents the criticism levelled by philosophers at his way of life; his fond dreams of wealth are accompanied by the delicious prospect of avenging himself on hypocrites who preach virtue: "nous en donnerons sur dos et ventre a tous ces petits Catons, comme vous, qui nous meprisent par envie; dont la modestie est le manteau de l'orgueil, et dont la sobrieté est la loi du besoin" (p. 39).

However eloquent may be Lui's denunciation of philosophy, it can scarcely match the magnificent tirade of Callicles in the *Gorgias* (484c–486d). Philosophy, he declares, is quite acceptable for boys, but on reaching man's estate one should seek higher things. The pursuit of philosophy beyond the proper time of life leaves one ignorant of what a man of the world must know – the laws of the City, the language of society, the pleasures and desires and characters of men. The philosopher, indeed, cuts a ridiculous figure in the world of politics as well as in business; he is both ludicrous and unmanly, similar to an adult imitating a lisping child. He is, moreover, unable to speak out like a freeman, for he has spent his time dealing with foolish trifles and neglecting the truly liberating things of this life. The self-control that philosophy recommends, says Callicles in a later passage (491d–492b), is practised only by fools and simpletons who praise temperance and blame its opposite because they are too weak to indulge their desires. Happiness, in truth, lies only in licentiousness and pleasures of all kinds; those who declare that they are free from want and therefore happy are clearly content with an existence befitting a corpse or a stone (492e).

THE "GRAND CRIMINEL"

We have seen above (Ch. 5) the importance for *Le Neveu de Rameau* of the hero in evil. "On crache sur un petit filou," says Lui; "mais on ne peut refuser une sorte de consideration a un grand criminel" (Fabre, p. 72). If Diderot was inspired by Helvétius' remarks on this subject, it was not without being aware of the debt Helvétius owed to Plato. Thrasymachus, in the *Republic*, having argued that justice is the advantage of the stronger (338c), points out that by "the stronger" he means the man who has power to overreach on a large scale, and not the petty thief or swindler who practises partial forms of injustice (343e–344b). The totally unjust man – the tyrant – is Thrasymachus' ideal; and he asserts that all who hear of a tyrant's having successfully enslaved an entire nation pronounce such a man happy and blessed (344bc). Injustice perpetrated on a sufficiently impressive scale is therefore "a stronger, freer, and more masterful thing than justice" (344c).

This opinion of Thrasymachus is in accord with that of Callicles in the *Gorgias*. The latter also pretends that it is right for the stronger to have advantage over the weaker; conventional justice, for him, is merely an invention of inferior people who, by enshrining their version of justice in the laws, seek to remain on an equal footing with the strong (483bc). Callicles has nothing but admiration for the man of great force who can enslave a whole people to his will; the picture that he paints of his hero arising from the slavery of conventional morality is truly terrifying: "he shakes off all that we have taught him, bursts his bonds and breaks free; he tramples underfoot our codes and juggleries, our charms and 'laws,' which are all against nature; our slave rises in revolt and shows himself our master, and there dawns the full light of natural justice" (484a). Thus does a tyrant attain to the pinnacle of freedom and happiness that only all-prevailing force can secure (492c).

### NATURE AND CONVENTION

The argument of Callicles in favour of injustice, expounded at length at *Gorgias* 482e ff., is based on the distinction between "nature" and "convention" – a distinction that is a commonplace of Greek, and indeed of all western, thought. The same framework is employed by Glaucon in *Republic* II, in his attempt to arrive at a true definition of justice and law (358e ff.). The question raised by these two passages has always divided political and ethical thinkers, and especially those of the eighteenth century: is justice innate in the heart of man or is morality a pure convention? It is, I think, unnecessary to stress the fact that we are here at the heart of the ethical problems posed by *Le Neveu de Rameau*, in which "individualité naturelle" is expressly opposed, on the very threshold of the dialogue, to "cette fastidieuse uniformité que notre education, nos conventions de société, nos bienseances d'usage ont introduite" (Fabre, p. 5). Since the antithesis of nature and convention has much broader implications than are apparent on the surface, we had best reserve treatment of the matter for a later chapter. It is sufficient here to indicate that the nature-convention opposition would seem to be one of the important links in the chain that binds Diderot's satire to the *Gorgias* and the *Republic* of Plato.

### VICE AND VIRTUE INTERCHANGED

One of the major problems of communication arises when two interlocutors employ words in different, and even in contrary, senses. Socrates points this out to Callicles at the beginning of their debate: "Callicles, if men had not certain feelings, each common to one sort of people, but each of us had a feeling peculiar to himself and apart from the rest, it would not be easy for him to indicate his own impression to his neighbour" (*Gorgias*, 481cd). Callicles, indeed, does not venture beyond a relative application of moral terms, calling justice and temperance "bad and disgraceful" when they are found in a tyrant (492b). Thrasymachus, however, in the *Republic*, flatly approves of injustice, which he deems to be wise discretion, while mocking justice as being nothing more than simplicity of heart (348c). He makes no objection (though perhaps only for the sake of the argument) when Socrates accuses him of putting "injustice under the head of virtue and wisdom, and justice in the opposite class" (348e). As for Diderot's immoralist, we may say that he takes up a position close to that of Thrasymachus when he explicitly warns against giving his words their conventional interpretation: "si nous venions a nous expliquer, il pourroit arriver que vous appellassiez vice ce que j'apelle vertu, et vertu ce que j'apelle vice" (Fabre, p. 62). It has already been pointed out that Diderot, like Socrates, is concerned about the failure of communication that such an abuse of language entails.

### INTERNAL DISCORD

We have examined in Chapter 5 the moral inconsistency of Diderot's Protean hero, whose lack of rational control forbids his attaining the unity of character of the "grand criminel" and whose lack of virtue denies him the "aequabilitas" of the philosopher. This is a theme that recurs constantly in Plato and notably in the two works that concern us here.

In the *Gorgias*, Socrates praises philosophy for giving consistency to his thought. Without her, he would be like a lyre discordant and out of tune, having "internal discord and contradiction in my own single self" (482c), as indeed Callicles will be all his life in discord with Callicles unless he is able to refute Socrates' philosophical position on justice (482b). The *Republic*, on the other hand, stresses the moral dimension of the question. Here, Socrates proceeds against Thrasymachus by showing that the success of any common endeavour in a society requires that justice, and therefore oneness of mind, reign among the participants; injustice, contrariwise, is divisive, sowing hatred and strife and thereby crippling any effective action (351c–e). The same situation obtains, he avers, in the case of a single individual; the unjust man is divided, lacking in self-agreement and an enemy to himself as well as to the just (352a). It is clear that in these passages we find the double ideal of virtue and rational control that, in *Le Neveu de Rameau*, is the measure of Lui's failure both as a man and as an artist.

These, then, are the main lines of convergence between *Le Neveu de Rameau* and the passages from Plato that we have been considering. Certain aspects of form and thought undoubtedly correspond in many instances, so much so that we can, I think, refer unhesitatingly to Plato as a "source" of Diderot's dialogue. It is evident, however, that this comparison has added little to what we already knew of *Le Neveu de Rameau*, either in regard to specific details or to its overall interpretation. The complexity of the work cannot, certainly, be reduced to a debate on justice and happiness similar to that found in Plato; neither may we presume that Diderot's intention in his satire was in any way comparable to that of the ancient philosopher. Plato has Thrasymachus and Callicles reduced to silence by their interlocutor Socrates, whereas Diderot's irrepressible immoralist swaggers off the stage at the end, none the wiser for his conversation with Moi. This alone is sufficient to give us pause and to forbid our arriving at hasty conclusions.

If our examination of ancient literature seems thus far to have yielded rather meagre results, it is nonetheless true that the field has narrowed considerably, for we have at least succeeded in justifying the suspicion that Socrates and Plato are not altogether strangers to the origin of Diderot's thought. Infinitely more important, as it will appear, is the fact that our investigations have brought us face to face with that monumental creation, the *Republic*, part of which has now been shown to have served as a model for our satire.

When we consider the subject matter of the *Republic*, we are reminded that Plato's quest for a definition of justice in the first two books led him to expound on a host of topics – music, education, artistic creation, imitation, appearance and reality – all of which he attempted to integrate into a complete psychology of man. Comparing these with some of the principal matters treated in Diderot's dialogue – music, education, genius, pantomime, hypocrisy – we are bound to acknowledge that similarities of such a striking nature can scarcely be the result of chance. And, indeed, if Diderot drew principally on any single "source" for his satire, the *Republic* is certainly one of the few works of western literature rich enough to have nourished an offspring of the stature of *Le Neveu de Rameau*.

As we proceed, it will become apparent that the resemblances noted above are not merely superficial ones, and, in fact, that a comprehensive explanation of *Le Neveu de Rameau* is possible if we examine the work against the background of Plato's thought, especially that of his *Republic*. I am not, of course, speaking of parallel passages, although there are some of these; it is rather a question of Diderot's having so thoroughly assimilated and made his own the ideas of the Greek philosopher that the masterpiece of the one inspired the masterpiece of the other. *Le Neveu de Rameau*, for all its striking originality, is one of the great achievements of literary mimesis; in every line it presupposes Plato and can be understood only in the light of his doctrine.

Our first concern will be to examine a number of direct parallels between the *Republic* and *Le Neveu de Rameau*, sufficient to establish their intimate relationship. We shall then be in a position to suggest a possible identification of the two interlocutors and to formulate an exploratory general statement as to the author's purpose in the dialogue. When this has been done, there will still remain many important questions, the answers to which must be matter for surmise. A subsequent chapter will be devoted to these questions, proposing conjectural solutions and indicating directions that might prove fruitful for future research.

If Diderot was powerfully attracted to the writings of Plato, it was not because of any sympathy he might have felt for Platonic metaphysics. Rather, like many a modern scholar, he saw in the Greek philosopher a man of high ideals who lived his adult life in a post-war era of cultural decay and who, turning away from politics which had brought him nothing but disillusionment, applied his noble mind to diagnosing the ills that beset his nation's culture.[2] Plato, indeed, was no idle dreamer but a hard-headed, practical moralist; his *Republic* must have appeared

2 This sentence paraphrases a statement from John Wild's Preface to his perceptive study entitled *Plato's Theory of Man: an Introduction to the Realistic Philosophy of Culture* (Cambridge, Mass., Harvard University Press, 1946), v.

to an eighteenth-century thinker as a mosaic of brilliant paradoxes by means of which the inner workings of the human psyche were exposed with consummate skill. Politics, as Rousseau had pointed out, is only a secondary concern of the *Republic*;[3] it is the theory of man which it contains that is truly sublime, and only therein shall we find the basis of the affinity between its author and his Encyclopedist admirer.

Plato's *Republic* had a special appeal for Diderot at the period of his great pessimistic crisis of 1759–62, for he found in the ancient work both a justification of philosophy (against Palissot and *Les Philosophes*) and the basis for an explanation, on the moral and psychological level, of the cultural decline of his age – a decline which he was prone to hold responsible for the popular success of such productions as that of Palissot, for the failure on the part of the public to appreciate *Le Père de famille*, and for the hostile reception afforded by many of his contemporaries to the *Encyclopédie*. He felt the need to give satirical expression to his disgust and disappointment; and the comprehensive picture of man and society in the *Republic* made that work an ideal frame wherein to set a truly philosophic satire – one in which the ephemeral issues and personal attacks inseparable from the satiric genre would serve principally as the point of departure for a universal statement concerning human life. The *Republic* furnished him, moreover, with a reference point to which he might relate many of the ideas currently preoccupying him: utilitarianism, determinism, inequality, genius, music, education, luxury, mimesis, and the sublime.

Among the myriad questions that arise in the course of the *Republic*, let us single out one which figures prominently there as well as in all the works of Plato: the question of *unity*. How is a man one and not many? How is a City one and not many? How is virtue one and not many? The *Republic* gives us Plato's answer to these questions from a psychological and a sociological standpoint. The ideal of unity – unity in the arts and crafts, in society, in the human soul – permeates the work from end to end; and the famous search for justice, which occupies the first four books, is crowned by the discovery that justice is the virtue which enables an organism (a City or a soul) to function as a unified whole. Injustice, on the other hand, is found to be a condition of inner disunity, dissension, and fragmentation.

In developing his theory of justice, Plato introduces an idea that we have already had occasion to discuss in our treatment of Helvétius'

3 "Ce n'est point un ouvrage de politique, comme le pensent ceux qui ne jugent des livres que par leurs titres. C'est le plus beau traité d'éducation qu'on ait jamais fait" (*Emile, ou De l'éducation*, in *Œuvres complètes* [Paris, Gallimard, 1959–    ], iv, 250). Cited henceforth as Pléiade ed.

theory of education – namely, the all-importance of natural aptitudes in the human constitution. Like Diderot after him, the Greek philosopher sees each individual as destined by nature to do one thing well. Thus, "to do one's own" ($τὸ τὰ αὑτοῦ πράττειν$) has for him the basic meaning of "doing the task for which one is fitted." Diderot sometimes takes over this expression, translating it "être à sa chose,"[4] a much more literal rendering of Plato's thought than we find in the "cultiver notre jardin" for which Voltaire is justly famous.[5] In *Le Neveu de Rameau*, Lui makes fun of this principle: "A votre avis, la societé ne seroit-elle pas fort amusante, si chacun y etoit a sa chose ?" (Fabre, p. 41).

"Doing one's own" is of greater interest to Plato for its moral than for its economic significance, as will appear shortly. Nonetheless, it is with the arts and trades that he begins, showing that since men are diverse in their natures, one is more apt for one task, one for another (370b). The specialization of labour that is required for the efficient functioning of society is therefore an outgrowth of this connatural differentiation (370b–d); and Socrates, in planning the first stage of his City, very casually assigns each class of men to the task appropriate to their nature – farmers, carpenters, smiths, shepherds, weavers, cobblers, traders, shopkeepers, and so forth (370c–371e). There can be little doubt that Diderot had this passage in mind when he put the following words in the mouth of Lui: "Perchez vous sur l'epicycle de Mercure, et de la distribuez, si cela vous convient, et a l'imitation de Reaumur, lui la classe des mouches en couturieres, arpenteuses, faucheuses, vous, l'espece des hommes, en hommes menuisiers, charpentiers, coureurs, danseurs, chanteurs, c'est votre affaire" (Fabre, p. 103). It is interesting to note how the allusion to Socrates and the *Republic* is deliberately obscured by the mention of Réaumur and by the addition of singers and dancers to the brief catalogue of trades.

Building on the notion of innate aptitudes and of "doing one's own," Plato moves into the sphere of social organization, his intention being to develop the analogy he has drawn (368e) between a political entity

4 Like Plato, Diderot associates these words with the knowledge of a craft or trade proper to one who practises it. The traveller learns a great deal of general information by questioning the craftsmen of a foreign country such as Holland, "où chacun est à sa chose et n'est qu'à sa chose ..." (*Voyage de Hollande*, A.T., XVII, 367). The *Satire première*, written at about the same time, stresses the moral benefits of such specialization: "Heureuse la société où chacun seroit à sa chose, et ne seroit qu'à sa chose !" (below, p. 233).

5 This association is made by George Lamb, the translator of Henri-Irénée Marrou's *Histoire de l'éducation dans l'Antiquité* (Paris, 1948). At the end of his chapter on Plato (Pt. I, Ch. II) Marrou writes: "Le Sage ... passera sa vie 'à s'occuper de ses propres affaires' ..." (4th ed., 120). The translation reads: "The Wise Man shall spend his life 'cultivating his own garden' ..." (*A History of Education in Antiquity* [London, Sheed and Ward, 1956], 78).

and a human soul. The three social classes of the City (rulers, soldiers, producers) form a natural hierarchy, he says, as do the three parts of the soul (reason, spirited element, appetitive element). In both the political and the moral order, it is the dynamic, voluntary submission of the lower to the higher that he calls temperance or self-control. Justice, which presupposes temperance, consists in each of the three classes in a City – and each of the three parts in the case of the soul – "doing its own" (427e–443c). The just and temperate man, in whom the three faculties actively co-operate according to their due order and proportion, will therefore be one man and not many (443e). Moral justice, Plato concludes, can be characterized as the harmony and health of the soul; injustice, on the contrary, is discord and disease (443c–444e).

Before continuing this brief sketch of Plato's psychology in the *Republic*, let us pause for a moment to consider two aspects of it that might apply to *Le Neveu de Rameau*. It has already been pointed out that Lui's inconsistency of action arises from his lack of unity – that unity of character he so much admires in the "grand criminel" (Fabre, p. 72). Born under the sign of Vertumnus, the god of the changing seasons, it is his peculiar characteristic to be many men rather than one. Consequently, he can be said to correspond to Plato's notion of the man who is deficient in temperance or self-control. Because self-control (*sophrosyne*), for Plato, consists in the rule of reason over the lower faculties, it is frequently found in his writings in direct opposition to *aphrosyne* (folly).[6] We have every reason, therefore, to see in Moi and Lui, who are presented by the author as a philosopher and a fool, examples of the *sophron* soul and the *aphron* soul much as they are contrasted by Socrates in his refutation of Callicles (*Gorgias*, 507a). Now folly (*aphrosyne*) is more than a mere foible, implying as it does lack of self-control; and, since self-control is for Plato a necessary (though not a sufficient) condition of justice, anyone who lacks it is not only intemperate but also unjust. Socrates makes this clear at *Gorgias* 507a, where he states that the *sophron* soul is good (*agathe*) and the *aphron* soul is bad (*kake*).

Thus far, there is no difficulty in applying Plato's psychology to *Le Neveu de Rameau*, where we have Moi presented as the temperate, virtuous philosopher and Lui as the intemperate, vicious fool. These observations are, of course, elementary, and are intended merely to show that there is a parallel development here. Much more important

6 See Helen North's invaluable work entitled *Sophrosyne: Self-knowledge and Self-restraint in Greek Literature* (Ithaca, N.Y., Cornell University Press, 1966), 3, 18, 131, 159, 193.

is the fact that, still following Plato, we may characterize Moi as a harmonious soul, Lui as a discordant one. The musical implications of this doctrine will be pursued later in the present chapter.

We may now proceed to follow Plato into Books VIII and IX of the *Republic*, where he brings to a conclusion his investigation of the question whether the just man or the unjust man is happier. Time and again he has pointed out the seriousness and all-importance of this inquiry: "it is no ordinary matter that we are discussing, but the right conduct of life" (352d); "do you think it is a small matter that you are attempting to determine and not the entire conduct of life that for each of us would make living most worth while?" (344de); "our inquiry concerns the greatest of all things, the good (*agathos*) life or the bad (*kakos*) life" (578c). Here again, as in Books II–IV, we find the political order serving as an analogy for the moral order: in this instance, we are taken step by step through the progressive political deterioration of a City, and parallel with this, the gradual moral corruption of a human soul, both City and soul reaching their lowest point of degradation in the establishment of a tyrannical regime. In our consideration of this section of the *Republic*, we shall concentrate our attention on three individuals who helped to shape Diderot's thought in *Le Neveu de Rameau*: the democratic man, the tyrannical man, and the tyrant.

The process of moral decay is a gradual one, and is presented by Plato as though each downward step corresponded to a generation. The aristocratic father, who stands for the ideal of justice and temperance, has a timocratic son; he in turn engenders an oligarchical son, who becomes the father of a democratic son. Each stage of decline is accompanied by a new renunciation of rational control. The first son, having handed over the government of his soul to its spirited element, becomes covetous of honour (550b); the second, having relegated both reason and spirit to the position of slaves, submits his soul to the domination of avarice (553cd); the third, the democratic man, goes a step farther and completely relinquishes control, his actions being henceforth directed by the promptings of his chaotic desires. Like the political regime which he represents, "a delightful form of government, anarchic and motley, assigning a kind of equality indiscriminately to equals and unequals alike" (558c), the democratic man esteems all pleasures equally good:

"And does he not," said I, "also live out his life in this fashion, day by day indulging the appetite of the day, now wine-bibbing and abandoning himself to the lascivious pleasing of the flute and again drinking only water and dieting; and at one time exercising his body, and sometimes idling and neglecting all things, and at another time seeming to occupy himself with philosophy. And frequently he goes in for politics and bounces up and says and does whatever enters his head. And if military men excite his emulation, thither he rushes, and if moneyed men, to that he turns, and there is no order or compulsion in his existence, but he calls this life of his the life of pleasure and freedom and happiness and cleaves to it to the end." "That is a perfect description," he said, "of a devotee of equality" (561c–e).

This portrait, like those of Priscus and Trebatius in Horace's two satires, might well have served as a model for Diderot's Lui. It should be remarked, however, that neither in Horace nor in Plato do we find any trait that goes beyond the simple depiction of inconsistency and folly (in the benign sense). If we would fill out the picture of Lui as we know him – parasite, wastrel, go-between, "ame de boue" – we must descend one step lower to Plato's tyrannical man, son of a democratic father (572d). Educated in the parental philosophy of egalitarianism and seduced by ambitious companions, he falls under the tyranny of a ruling passion that "purges him of sobriety" (573b) and gives free rein to a host of insatiable and unruly desires. Although men of this stamp are potentially capable of any crime, however heinous, they will normally confine themselves to petty misdeeds (*kaka smikra*) : "Oh, they just steal, break into houses, cut purses, strip men of their garments, plunder temples, and kidnap, and if they are fluent speakers they become sycophants and bear false witness and take bribes" (575b). If once they become numerous in a state, one of their number may turn into an actual tyrant, rising up to enslave his native land (575c); but that is not the ordinary lot of the tyrannical man:

they associate with flatterers, who are ready to do anything to serve them, or, if they themselves want something, they themselves fawn and shrink from no contortion or abasement in protest of their friendship, though, once the object gained, they sing another tune. ... Throughout their lives, then, they never know what it is to be the friends of anybody. They are always either masters or slaves, but the tyrannical nature never tastes freedom or true friendship (575e–576a).

It is possible, with the aid of this portrait, to locate Diderot's Lui in the descending scale of moral turpitude outlined by Plato: he is essentially a democratic soul with strong tendencies toward the tyrannical. His creator makes this clear when he informs us that Lui is no more abominable than the majority of his contemporaries, "seulement plus franc, et plus consequent; et quelquefois profond dans sa depravation" (Fabre, p. 93). But the contagion of moral decline does not stop there;

we need only look at Lui's young son, schooled in his father's principles, to be assured of a further degeneration: "Je tremblois de ce que deviendroit son enfant sous un pareil maitre" (ibid.). Such a boy, once he is a full-fledged tyrannical man, will be destined like his father to be the slave of his passions and to wallow in moral mediocrity – unless (to follow out Plato's thought) some stroke of ill fortune should give him the opportunity to seize power and become the greatest of criminals, an actual tyrant who "while unable to control himself, attempts to rule over others" (579c). This, in Plato's view, would make him the most miserable, the most enslaved, and the unhappiest of men, for there is no condition of human life less desirable than that of complete injustice (579d–580c).

We must not, however, confuse Plato's great criminal, the tyrant, with the "grand criminel" whom Lui professes to admire, for that would be to miss the point of Diderot's irony. Like most of his ilk, Lui can never rise to greatness, even greatness in crime. So far from conceiving grandiose schemes, he is incapable of imagining anything more sublime in evil than a Bouret, a Palissot, a "renegat d'Avignon," and he takes pride in having attained, in his own estimation, the rank immediately below these illustrious heroes (Fabre, p. 72). Such mediocrity is explained in Plato's *Republic* on more than one occasion: only great souls, we are told, can produce acts of great virtue or of great vice whereas small, weak natures accomplish nothing of significance (vi, 491e, 495b). Lui, ill-endowed in this regard, pursues his pitiful destiny, unable either to rise above the level of parasite in society or to create anything of merit in the field of music. For, despite the authority with which he expounds his musical theories, he readily admits to being "bien subalterne en musique" (p. 94) ; as for his ethical system, to which he modestly grants a certain superiority, he is equally inept, as Moi points out, in reducing it to practice: "Il faut entre bien maladroit, quand on n'est pas riche, et que l'on se permet tout pour le devenir" (p. 95).

The "grand criminel" finds a place in *Le Neveu de Rameau* less for his own sake than as a means of accentuating the ineffectualness of Lui. Diderot is not interested in portraying Plato's tyrant – in appearance free and happy while in reality the most enslaved and unhappiest of men – but is satisfied to have the description of him given in the *Republic* serve as a backdrop, grimly suggesting the ugliness concealed beneath the gay façade that Lui presents to the world. In the same way we can divine, behind the character named Moi, the presence of Plato's just philosopher who enjoys true freedom and properly human happiness, the fruits of a life lived in accordance with reason (580b ff.). He is the "true musician," Plato tells us, and will always be found "attuning the

harmonies of his body for the sake of the concord of his soul" (591d).
While allowing due importance to the "pleasures of necessity" (581e),
the wise man keeps strict control over the "many headed beast" of
appetite (588c). His gaze is fixed on the upper regions where his soul
finds real and lasting pleasure, unlike the common multitude who seek
their satisfaction in lower things: "with eyes ever bent upon the earth
and heads bowed down over their tables, they feast like cattle, grazing
and copulating, ever greedy for more of these delights; and in their greed
kicking and butting one another with horns and hooves of iron they
slay one another in sateless avidity ..." (586ab). Both Plato and Diderot
(Fabre, p. 57) are fond of using animalism to bring out the baseness
and inhumanity of the "unexamined life."

There are good reasons, then, for believing that Diderot might be
attempting in his dialogue to put before our eyes living proof of Plato's
central thesis in the *Republic*: that the just man has a better and happier
life than the unjust. He is not, however, writing a philosophical treatise
closing with *quod erat demonstrandum*; even a Plato had failed to con-
vince the world that one's personal interest is best served by being just,
and Diderot was well aware that such a proposition is not susceptible
of rational proof. Neither is he writing a tragedy – the proper vehicle
for characters as sublime as the tyrant or the sage described by Plato –
but a satire, and is consequently obliged to reduce somewhat the proportions of his heroes. It must be remembered in judging these literary
creations that any diminution of the tyrant, who represents mediocrity
gone mad, can result only in a "pauvre diable"; the ideal of the sage,
on the other hand, can be scaled down with dignity and can even gain
in credibility thereby. Plato himself takes care to lace his description of
the wise man with humour, especially in his elaborate proof that the
sage enjoys 729 times as much real pleasure as the tyrant (587b–588a);
and Diderot, as I have already remarked, does not fail to employ at
times the self-mockery of which Horace was the great master.

This is a crucial point in the interpretation of *Le Neveu de Rameau*,
for the character of Moi has come in for much undeserved criticism
that has raised doubts as to the possible identification of "Monsieur le
philosophe" with the author. If Moi admits his partiality to an occasional bout of debauchery of the "wine, women and song" variety
(Fabre, p. 42), we need not for that reason accuse him of hypocrisy or
lasciviousness; the great Socrates, after all, was not loath to engage in
friendly drinking parties (*symposia*), and Plato's philosopher considers
a sober man to be one who has "neither starved nor indulged to reple-
tion his appetitive part" (571de). Nor may we charge Moi with over-
weening pride for a statement such as "Je parle mal. Je ne scais que dire

la verité" (Fabre, p. 94) ; this is merely an echo of Socrates in the *Ion*, who compares himself with inspired poets in the same ironic terms: "I am a common man, who only speak the truth."[7] There is nothing, in fact, that forbids our identifying Moi with Socrates at one level and with Diderot at another. We cannot, however, make a more positive statement than this without further support. If Plato's treatment of the virtue-happiness equivalence has been useful for our understanding of the individual psychology that guided the creation of Lui and Moi, we may well find, on a broader scale, that the analysis of the obstacles to social reform found in Books v and vi of the *Republic* can help us to define more closely what must have been the attitude of the Encyclopedist toward his own century that prompted the bitter satire of *Le Neveu de Rameau*.

In Book v (to 471c) Plato describes the social and political organization of the ideal City, then goes on to consider the role to be played by philosophy in the state. Philosophers, of course, must be kings, or kings philosophers, before any real reforms can be instituted (473cd), and the philosophic nature suited to the "royal art" of government is accordingly subjected to an intense scrutiny (v, 474b–vi, 487a). We need not linger over this aspect of the question; suffice it to say that the philosopher is shown to combine all the intellectual and moral virtues that bespeak true nobility of soul. What is important for our purpose is the analysis of society that follows, in which the evils besetting mankind are attributed to the widespread hostility toward philosophy and the rule of reason. The ideal state, Plato tells us, will never be realized until philosophy is accorded the honour it deserves and reason regulates the actions of men. Unfortunately, there seems to be little hope that philosophy can be rehabilitated: the few real philosophers are reputed to be useless dreamers; most of those who might have become philosophers have been corrupted and have turned to other pursuits; and many of those who proclaim themselves philosophers are charlatans unworthy of the name.

First, Plato defends philosophy against the charge of inutility. In the famous image of the ship (of state) seized by ignorant sailors from the "useless star-gazer" who is its rightful pilot (488a ff.), he stresses the fact that if philosophers are useless in politics it is only because the public refuses to make use of them.

Secondly, he considers the question why the majority of men endowed by nature with a philosophic spirit almost inevitably turn bad, and even become great criminals. Their outstanding natural gifts, of course, put them in the way of serious temptation; but more important in their

7 *Ion*, 532e. Trans. Benjamin Jowett.

downfall is the noxious atmosphere created by the ignorant public, that "great sophist" whose raucous praise or blame sets the standard of public morals and education, reducing all values to the level of its own depraved taste (491d ff.). Few can resist this corrupting influence, especially when so-called educators – the sophists – sacrifice to the "great and powerful beast" of public opinion, teaching as "good" and "bad" the shifting whims and preferences of the motley multitude; poets, craftsmen, politicians, all alike are obliged to give the public what it demands. Philosophy, it seems, is impossible for the multitude, and any true philosopher is therefore fated to meet with censure on every side. "From this point of view," asks Socrates, "do you see any salvation that will suffer the born philosopher to abide in the pursuit and persevere to the end?" (494a).

Thirdly, when philosophy is abandoned by those who might have become society's noblest and most useful members, a crowd of men unfit for culture rush in to fill the void, ambitious weaklings whose souls have been crabbed and twisted by the practice of illiberal crafts and trades (495c–e). Such as these, espousing philosophy, produce nothing but the misbegotten sophisms that pass for knowledge in a perverse and ignorant world (496a). It is they, and not the true philosophers, who are responsible for the low esteem in which philosophy is held.

This section of the *Republic*, even in brief summary, can be seen to contain many of the unspoken assumptions and judgments that must lie behind *Le Neveu de Rameau*. And indeed, does it not seem likely that the Diderot who lived through the years 1757–62 should have seen his century through the eyes of Plato? The condemnation of the *Encyclopédie*, the desertion of his erstwhile collaborators, his break with Rousseau turned "anti-philosophe," the success of *Les Philosophes* and the failure of *Le Père de famille* – these are only some of the incidents, all of them worthy of fourth-century Athens, that undermined his native optimism and caused him to doubt, momentarily, that the forces of enlightenment would prevail. No one need be astonished, then, to find that the black colours used by Plato to paint the life of his times should have flowed over into *Le Neveu de Rameau*.

It must not be forgotten, however, that we are dealing here with a work entitled "Satire" and therefore, presumably, designed as a corrective – if not for the age in which it was written, at least for posterity. This satire, moreover, was composed by a man who strove mightily during those same years to complete the *Encyclopédie* in the firm conviction that he was contributing to human enlightenment. These facts do not argue in favour of total pessimism. There is undoubtedly reason for stating that Diderot, who identified strongly with Socrates, tended also to identify the spirit of his age with the spirit of Athens so sardonically depicted in the *Republic*.[8] But, if we accept this proposition, we are obliged to give equal credence to its corollary: that he shared with Plato the optimism with which the Greek philosopher concludes this section of his dialogue. Although offering no immediate hope for the reform of society and counselling the philosopher to abstain from politics and to keep himself unspotted by the world (496de), Plato nonetheless envisions a time when the tiny remnant of true philosophers may be able to persuade the multitude that its scorn for philosophy is unjustified (498d–500c). Some day, in some state, philosophy may find herself allied with political power and prove that the realization of his ideal City is not an impossibility (502a–c). Having said this, he proceeds in Book VII (the Myth of the Cave) to make a profession of faith in human reason (however restricted it may be to the few) that is nothing short of sublime.

Hope for the future, then, is combined in Plato with a bitterly pessimistic view of the immediate present; and this, we know, must have been also the attitude of Diderot towards his own century. The author of a satire cannot, of course, make an explicit profession of optimism such as we find in Plato's dialogue; but, this alone excepted, *Le Neveu de Rameau* either states or implies on the part of the author an orientation of thought that coincides perfectly with that of the Greek philosopher. There is every justification for supposing that Book VI of the *Republic*, in which Plato analyses the ills of Athenian society, is the model to which Diderot would instinctively have turned, had he set out to paint a satirical picture of the spirit of Greek philosophy at grips with the spirit of the age. That he did so in fact is in no way proven; nonetheless, the likelihood of this influence adds strength to the link we are forging between Plato and *Le Neveu de Rameau*.

One of the most intriguing facets of *Le Neveu de Rameau* is the sustained comparison it presents between art and morality. The clearest statement of this preoccupation is found towards the end of the dialogue, where the serious-minded Moi, after witnessing the admirable operatic mime by which Lui illustrates his musical theories, brings the conversation back to his favourite subject, morals: "Comment se fait il qu'avec un tact aussi fin, une si grande sensibilité pour les beautés de l'art musical, vous soyez aussi aveugle sur les belles choses en morale, aussi insensible aux charmes de la vertu?" (Fabre, p. 89). Lui obligingly suggests

8 Grimm, in the *Corr. lit.* of 1 August 1762 (v, 134), quotes Diderot as follows: "Socrate, au moment de sa mort, était regardé à Athènes comme on nous regarde à Paris."

several factors that might help to explain his moral obtuseness – environment, heredity, education – but none of these is settled upon conclusively and the discussion moves on to other topics. The same parallel between morals and music appears many times throughout the dialogue: "Il s'entendoit mieux en bonne musique qu'en bonnes mœurs" (p. 76); "Je suis pourtant bien subalterne en musique, et bien superieur en morale" (p. 94). This theme, moreover, is matched by the analogy everywhere implied between the art of pantomime and the art of hypocrisy, each a species of imitation in its own realm. Similarly, questions touching on both ethics and art appear in the section on the poet-genius who is a wicked man (p. 12) and also in that concerning the aesthetic value of great crimes (p. 76).

These observations allow us to make two further comments regarding the possibility of Platonic influence on the composition of *Le Neveu de Rameau*. First, the analogy that we have noted between morality and the arts is a quite familiar one to readers of Plato, for there is nothing more characteristic of Socratic ethics than the invariable comparison between moral virtue and the "know-how" displayed in carpentry, flute-playing, or other arts and trades. The fact that Diderot employs a similar procedure proves nothing, of course, except that his satire can be said to have a certain affinity to Plato's dialogues in this regard. Secondly, and much more significant, is the peculiar combination of themes in *Le Neveu de Rameau*: music, education, and imitation. We are reminded that Plato's theory of primary education in the *Republic* is built around the concepts of music (*mousike*) and imitation (*mimesis*). This association, however speculative, is worthy of being pursued further.

Before we attack this complicated subject, it is necessary to digress for a moment in order to introduce a new element that will subsequently be shown to have a close connection with Plato. It has to do primarily with the sections of *Le Neveu de Rameau* that treat of education. These, it would seem, have a role in the dialogue which has never been fully understood for the simple reason that the irony permeating them has concealed their real significance.

The topic of education is broached early in the dialogue with reference to the teaching of Moi's eight-year-old daughter (Fabre, pp. 30–1). After stating briefly his conception of the aims of education – development of the rational faculty and of moral courage – Moi goes on to propose, apparently in all seriousness, a program for the little girl's instruction: "de la grammaire, de la fable, de l'histoire, de la geographie, un peu de dessein [*sic*], et beaucoup de morale" (p. 31). No critic, to my knowledge, has noticed that this is nothing more than a list of the subjects which Rousseau, in *Emile*, proclaimed must *not* be taught to young children![9] Immediately our perspective is broadened; if Diderot's satire marks the author's hostility to prevailing educational theories, we must number Jean-Jacques among his opponents. But even more important is the reaction of Lui to this proposal: "Combien il me seroit facile de vous prouver l'inutilité de toutes ces connoissances la, dans un monde tel que le notre; que dis je l'inutilité, peut etre le danger." Rousseau, of course, had criticized the traditional subjects as useless, and, like Plato before him, had condemned the teaching of fables as dangerous.[10] This is a firm indication that Rousseau, along with Palissot and Jean-François Rameau (and how many others?), is concealed beneath the figure of Lui.

That Diderot should have utilized the character Lui to release his venom against Rousseau need scarcely surprise us. The suspicion that such might be the case has undoubtedly crossed the minds of many readers of *Le Neveu de Rameau*, only to be dismissed for lack of any substantial evidence. The first thing to note is that the satire directed at Rousseau's pedagogical theories seems to be restricted to those elements which lend themselves most readily to parody. The distortion that results from this procedure is necessarily unfair to the author of *Emile*, in much the same way as *Candide* was unfair to Leibniz. Broadly speaking, Lui can be said to represent a "naturist" approach to education. Sceptical concerning the benefits of giving positive instruction to his son, he prefers to let nature take its course; but he is not quite as convinced as was Rousseau of the goodness of natural dispositions: "Je n'y fais rien a present. Je le laisse venir. Je l'examine. Il est deja gourmand, patelin, filou, paresseux, menteur. Je crains bien qu'il ne chasse de race" (p. 90). Nonetheless, he does not totally neglect the child. The famous mime scene in which he instructs his young son in the value of money (p. 92) can be seen as a burlesque of moral education through imitation: the implanting of certain "vertus de singe" which, according to Rousseau, will lay the groundwork for future acts of benevolence on the part of Emile.[11] As for Moi's daughter, Lui believes that her education should be limited to developing her talents to please: "Et laissez la deraisonner, tant qu'elle voudra. Pourvu qu'elle soit jolie, amusante et coquette"

9 Rousseau does stress the importance of free-hand drawing for Emile, but it must not be taught as an art (*Œuvres*, Pléiade ed., IV, 397). He dismisses grammar (pp. 293–4), fables (pp. 352–7), history (pp. 348–50), geography (p. 347), and moral instruction (pp. 303, 317–24).

10 There are few of the traditional studies that Rousseau does not number among "les inutilités de l'éducation" (ibid., 346). All verbal instruction before the age of reason results in bogus knowledge and is therefore dangerous (ibid., 350).

11 Ibid., 339–40. Diderot's text also recalls a passage from Horace's *Ars poetica* (vv. 325–32).

(p. 30). Rousseau, of course, had posed as one of the first principles of female education that "la femme est faite spécialement pour plaire à l'homme."[12] This parody, while it renders Rousseau's doctrine almost unrecognizable, is sufficiently clear to assure us that Diderot had Jean-Jacques in mind when composing the sections of the dialogue that deal with the instruction of children. The text, however, is very sparse, and allows us no more than to draw the broad lines of division between a "naturist" and an "intellectualist" approach to education.

Rousseau, then, was one of several contemporaries of Diderot who contributed certain personal traits to the literary mask that is Lui. The extent of his contribution will be examined in the following chapter; we must limit ourselves here to establishing, through him, a new link between *Le Neveu de Rameau* and Plato. We know, of course, that Rousseau had made a cult of his admiration for the author of the *Republic* and the *Laws*, and in the opening pages of *Emile* he had advanced the opinion that Plato's masterpiece was "le plus beau traité d'éducation qu'on ait jamais fait."[13] This was not mere lip-service paid to an ideal, for there are many details of his own treatise on education that are adapted from the *Republic*, such, for example, as the attack on fables already mentioned and the concept of early education as a form of play.[14] But, however Platonic Rousseau may have thought himself to be, he was consciously and resolutely un-Socratic: that is, his whole doctrine runs counter to the intellectualist current of Greek thought. This is not to say, of course, that reason plays an insignificant role in his theory of man; indeed, it is the contrary that is true. But his moral doctrine, as Robert Derathé well shows, was "aux antipodes de l'intellectualisme."[15] Indeed, if anything is consistently affirmed in Rousseau's writings, it is that reason cannot be the sole basis of the moral life. His scepticism in this regard springs from two deeply-held convictions: that reason, formed in society, is necessarily conditioned by society's prejudices;[16] and that a cognitive power alone cannot lead to action.[17] Hence his insistence on the necessity of an innate, intuitive "sentiment intérieur" by which reason is rectified; hence also the importance he

12 *Emile*, Pléiade ed., IV, 693.
13 Ibid., 250.
14 Ibid., 352 ff., 344. The influence of Plato on Rousseau's educational theories is stressed repeatedly by Charles W. Hendel, *Jean-Jacques Rousseau, Moralist* (London, Oxford University Press, 1934, 2 vols.), II, 75–123.
15 Robert Derathé, *Le Rationalisme de J.-J. Rousseau* (Paris, Presses Universitaires de France, 1948), 93. Cf. ibid., 75, 82, 88.
16 Against Diderot's doctrine of conscience as the voice of practical reason, Rousseau wrote in the first draft of the *Contrat social*: "Mais cette voix n'est, dit-on, formée que par l'habitude de juger et de sentir dans le sein de la société et selon ses loix, elle ne peut donc servir à les établir ..." (*Œuvres*, Pléiade ed., III, 287).
17 R. Derathé, *Le Rationalisme de J.-J. Rousseau*, 91–2.

gives to the dynamism of will.[18] It is significant that his first avowal of moral innatism – the doctrine of "pitié" in the *Discours sur l'inégalité* – was accompanied by an explicit statement that Socratic intellectualism is an impracticable ideal for the majority of men: "Quoi qu'il puisse appartenir à Socrate, et aux Esprits de sa trempe, d'acquerir de la vertu par raison, il y a longtems que le Genre-humain ne seroit plus, si sa conservation n'eût dépendu que des raisonnemens de ceux qui le composent."[19]

Diderot, on the other hand, having rejected Shaftesbury's "moral sentiment" theory in the article "Beau" of the *Encyclopédie*,[20] tended in the years that followed to adopt a modified form of intellectualism with its accompanying psychological determinism. The article "Droit naturel," in which he attempts to establish justice and natural right on an empirical basis, moves clearly in that direction. Apart from the naturalist foundation on which it is built, the doctrine propounded in this article is not far removed from the traditional rationalist theory of natural law: it makes reason the necessary ground of all moral action and conscience a pure act of understanding.[21] But it is clear from the distinction that the author draws between "la liberté" and "le volontaire" – admitting the first and denying the second (A.T., XIV, 297) – that he has already swung in the direction of intellectualism. We are *not* free, it seems, to disobey the dictates of reason, but we *are* free to reason or not to reason; and the "raisonneur violent" whose passions blind him to his obligations in justice is precisely "celui qui ne veut pas raisonner."[22]

Like other rational optimists of his century, Diderot adopted as his own the paradoxical virtue-happiness formula – not on rational grounds, but as one of those "vérités de sentiments" which he says have a greater hold on us than do logically demonstrated truths.[23] Accordingly, he liked to believe (with Socrates) that all vice is simply ignorance of

18 Ibid., 62–73, 112–25.
19 *Œuvres*, Pléiade ed., III, 156–7.
20 A.T., X, 20–5. He affirms that our ideas of beauty, order, proportion, etc., are experimental "comme toutes les autres" (p. 25). Cf., in the same context, the *Salon de 1767*: "Tout est expérimental en nous" (A.T., XI, 25).
21 "il faut raisonner en tout, parce que l'homme n'est pas seulement un animal, mais un animal qui raisonne" (A.T., XIV, 298) ; "la volonté générale est dans chaque individu un acte pur de l'entendement qui raisonne dans le silence des passions sur ce que l'homme peut exiger de son semblable, et sur ce que son semblable est en droit d'exiger de lui" (ibid., 300).
22 "celui qui ne veut pas raisonner, renonçant à la qualité d'homme, doit être traité comme un être dénaturé" (A.T., XIV, 301).
23 Letter to Falconet, 15 February 1766: "Les vérités de sentiments sont plus inébranlables dans notre âme que les vérités de démonstration rigoureuse, quoiqu'il soit souvent impossible de satisfaire pleinement l'esprit sur les premières" (*Corr.*, ed. Roth, VI, 98).

where one's true happiness lies, whether it be the wilful ignorance of
the egoist who is "méchant par système" or the ignorance of the multitude that results in faulty calculation of benefits.[24] The *méchant* is one
of nature's sports who suffers from a congenital malformation; he is so
"malheureusement né" that he is totally incapable of finding happiness
in virtuous living.[25] The vast majority of men, however, are not vicious
by nature; the shortsightedness that leads them to grasp immediate
advantage at the expense of their neighbour's rights is the result of their
being corrupted by bad laws, bad education, and the degenerate state
of public morals.[26] The combined deficiencies of these three forces –
law, education, and *mœurs* – may frequently have persuaded Diderot
that moral progress is an improbable dream; but he never doubted that,
if social reform *was* possible, it could come about only through enlightenment. He had no illusions about the goodness of nature, which for
him was neither good nor bad but merely necessary. Both personal
self-interest and sociability were natural and necessary to man; but so
also was reason, the instrument through which he believed it possible
to bring individualistic utilitarian drives into harmony with the general
interest.[27]

If Rousseau took a strong stand against this theory of enlightened
self-interest, it was because neither enlightenment nor self-interest posed
the same problems for him as for Diderot. According to Rousseau reason
does not provide a sufficient basis for morality, and it fails to do so
through both excess and defect. On the side of excess he puts the abuse
of reason that gives rise to prideful dogmatism; this, he says, is much
more pernicious in its effects than is ignorance, which commonly proves
to be more useful than harmful.[28] On the other hand, he sees reason as
inadequate because it is simply incommensurate with the task. Even

24 Diderot wrote the following in a letter to Sophie Volland, 22 September 1761:
"L'ignorance est la mère de toutes nos erreurs. ... Les lumières sont un bien dont on
peut abuser, sans doute. L'ignorance et la stupidité, compagnes de l'injustice, de
l'erreur, et de la superstition, sont toujours des maux" (*Corr.*, ed. Roth, III, 312–13).
25 "Mais quoi! est-ce que la pratique de la vertu n'est pas un sûr moyen d'être
heureux? ... Non, parbleu, il y a tel homme si malheureusement né, si violemment
entraîné par l'avarice, l'ambition, l'amour désordonné des femmes, que je le condam-
nerais au malheur si je lui prescrivais une lutte continuelle contre sa passion
dominante" (A.T., VI, 438). Robert Mauzi places this previously undated statement
in 1769 (*L'Idée du bonheur dans la littérature et la pensée française au XVIIIe
siècle*, 3rd ed. [Paris, A. Colin, 1967], 99, n. 3).
26 Letter to Sophie Volland, November 1760: "Non, chère amie, la nature ne
nous a pas faits méchants; c'est la mauvaise éducation, le mauvais exemple, la
mauvaise législation qui nous corrompent. Si c'est là une erreur, du moins je suis
bien aise de la trouver au fond de mon cœur, et je serois bien fâché que l'expérience
ou la réflexion me détrompât jamais" (*Corr.*, ed. Roth, III, 226).
27 For Diderot's position on these questions in relation to that of Rousseau, see
Jacques Proust's indispensable study in *Diderot et l'Encyclopédie*, 2nd ed., 359–99.
28 Letter to Voltaire, 7 September 1755: "Recherchons la prémière source de

when rightly formed it is powerless by itself to subdue passion, which can be countered effectively only by a force of the same nature.[29] This pessimism with regard to reason has enormous consequences of a practical nature because of Rousseau's conviction that self-interest stands so directly opposed to the general interest that it is chimerical to think of bringing them into harmony.[30] The only solution for society is to effect an absolute *unity* between them, and this imposes the necessity of radical reforms. Justice must be defined not by reason but by the general will expressed in law;[31] and education must become a form of conditioning that will mould a child into a citizen.[32]

In these doctrines, both of which are found in Rousseau's article "Economie politique," Diderot recognized two elements that he considered both false and dangerous: the idea that justice is pure convention,[33] and the implication that man has somehow to be denatured before he can be made to fit into society.[34] He and Rousseau, even before their break, were poles apart on these questions. Whereas for Diderot education and good government were the fruit of enlightenment, for Rousseau they were both absorbed into the utilitarian art of politics.

The opposition between these two thinkers has been reduced to its simplest elements in order not to take us too far from our original subject, Plato. Even this brief analysis suffices to show that, if *Le Neveu de*

tous les désordres de la société : Nous trouverons que tous les maux des hommes leur viennent de l'erreur bien plus que de l'ignorance, et que ce que nous ne savons point nous nuit beaucoup moins que ce que nous croyons savoir" (*Correspondance complète de Rousseau*, ed. R. A. Leigh [Geneva, Institut et Musée Voltaire, 1965–  ]), iii, 166. Cited henceforth as *Corr.*, ed. Leigh. For a just evaluation of Rousseau's well-known tendency to praise ignorance, see Robert Derathé, *Le Rationalisme de J.-J. Rousseau*, 170.

29 See Derathé, ibid., 91–3.

30 First draft of the *Contrat social* (against Diderot) : "loin que l'intérêt particulier s'allie au bien général, ils s'excluent l'un l'autre dans l'ordre naturel des choses, et les loix sociales sont un joug que chacun veut bien imposer aux autres, mais non pas s'en charger lui même" (*Œuvres*, Pléiade ed., iii, 284).

31 *Encyclopédie*, art. "Economie politique," in *Œuvres*, Pléiade ed., iii, 245: "Le corps politique est donc aussi un être moral qui a une volonté; et cette volonté générale, qui tend toûjours à la conservation et au bien-être du tout et de chaque partie, et qui est la source des lois, est pour tous les membres de l'état par rapport à eux et à lui, la regle du juste et de l'injuste ..."

32 Ibid., 259–62. Cf. *Emile*, in *Œuvres*, Pléiade ed., iv, 249: "Les bonnes institutions sociales sont celles qui savent le mieux dénaturer l'homme, lui ôter son existence absolue pour lui en donner une relative, et transporter le *moi* dans l'unité commune; en sorte que chaque particulier ne se croye plus un, mais partie de l'unité, et ne soit plus sensible que dans le tout." The same idea is repeated in the *Contrat social*, Bk. ii, Ch. 7 (*Œuvres*, Pléiade ed., iii, 381).

33 Lester G. Crocker contrasts the views of Rousseau and Diderot on this subject, "The Priority of Justice or Law," *Yale French Studies*, No. 28 (1961–2), 34–42.

34 On this question, see Lester G. Crocker, *Rousseau's Social Contract: an Interpretive Essay* (Cleveland, Case Western Reserve University Press, 1968), 9–17.

*Rameau* is indeed a confrontation between Socratism and anti-Socratism, Rousseau would not be altogether miscast in the role of adversary. As we have seen, his rejection of reasoned benevolence in the *Discours sur l'inégalité* took the form of a criticism of Socratic intellectualism; moreover, despite his frequent borrowings from Plato's *Republic*, he denied what is perhaps the central moral teaching of that work when he made convention the basis of justice; and in the case of his educational theories, while he stressed the Spartan features that Plato had introduced as a corrective into his propaedeutic training, he was not at all influenced by the fact that "Plato built his system of education on a fundamental belief in truth, and on the conquest of truth by rational knowledge."[35] On all of these important matters Diderot took a firm stand on the side of Plato and against Rousseau, who must have appeared to him to be using Plato for his own ends contrary to the spirit of the ancient author.

This judgment can be given further support if we consider *Le Neveu de Rameau* from yet another angle. It was shown earlier that Socrates' debates with the immoralists Callicles and Thrasymachus served as background for certain aspects of the satire; should not the entrance of Rousseau on the scene lead us to suspect that the great enemies of Plato's Socrates – the sophists – have also been granted a share in the honours? Of all the terms of abuse hurled at Rousseau throughout the 1750s when his reputation was at its lowest ebb, the word "sophiste" was one of those most frequently employed by his critics. As one controversial work after another flowed from his pen, many were persuaded that there was no paradox too bizarre for Jean-Jacques to defend and it was commonly held that he was an insincere notoriety seeker skilled in the art of sophistry.[36] After his break with the Encyclopedists, they too seized upon the name "sophist" to designate their former ally.[37] It is not difficult to understand, under these circumstances, that Diderot-Socrates should have envisaged his quarrel with the "sophist" Rousseau in terms of the ancient enmity recorded in so many of Plato's dialogues. Not only did he know those dialogues well, but he was inclined to exaggerate the

35 H.-I. Marrou, *A History of Education in Antiquity*, 66.

36 See Samuel S. B. Taylor, "Rousseau's Contemporary Reputation in France," *Studies on Voltaire and the Eighteenth Century*, xxvii (1963), 1545–74. Summarizing the early period of Rousseau's career, Professor Taylor writes: "A standard vocabulary emerged, to caption this paradoxical polemic figure, and it became the fashion to refer to Rousseau in such terms as: *Diogène, charlatan, apôtre de l'ignorance, esprit de contradiction, homme paradoxe, cynique, sophiste, misanthrope* etc." (p. 1552).

37 Grimm's review of the *Lettre à M. d'Alembert sur les spectacles* (1 December 1758) declares that "M. Rousseau est né avec tous les talents d'un sophiste" (*Corr. lit.*, iv, 54). Thenceforth, Rousseau became "le sophiste" for the Encyclopedists. Cf. ibid., iv, 342, 344, 346; vi, 179; Diderot, *Corr.*, ed. Roth, i, 235, 257; ii, 144; a.t., ii, 292, 412; vi, 354.

importance given by Plato to the Socrates-sophist dispute; a comment found in the article "Beau" expresses regret that Plato had been less interested in expounding truth in his written works than in unmasking the sophists.[38] It seems perfectly natural, therefore, were he to have occasion to write a satire against a "sophist," that he should turn to Plato as a guide.

It is only when we look into Plato's dialogue entitled *The Sophist* that we discover the full significance for our satire of the parallel between Rousseau and those popular teachers so roundly condemned by Plato. The main charge laid against the sophists is that their willingness to dispute on any subject deceives their hearers into thinking that the art of sophistry alone can make men universally wise (*Soph.*, 232a). Of course, it is no more possible to know all things than it is to create all things (233a); but the sophist, like the painter skilled in imitation, produces in his audience by the art of words the illusion that he has mastered universal knowledge (233d–234c). He is a kind of juggler, an imitator whose business is not truth but entertainment (235a). The sophist should properly be classed with the practitioners of the mimetic art – those who ape the voice or figure of other persons (267a). But there are mimics who know what they imitate and others who do not; the sophist belongs to the latter group (267bc). Not only is he ignorant, but he is conscious of his ignorance. He makes a great show before the public of being a philosopher, knowing all the while in his heart that he does not know the true nature of virtue and justice (267c–268d).

It is evident from these passages of *The Sophist* that Diderot had good reason, if he chose to draw a caricature of the "sophist" Rousseau, to depict him in the guise of a pantomimic performer. Nor is this the only link between the citizen of Geneva and Plato that might have inspired such a procedure. Jean-Jacques was well aware that his *Lettre à M. d'Alembert sur les spectacles* (1758), in which he defended Geneva's moral purity against the corrupting influence of the histrionic art, stood in a long line of writings against the theatre stretching back to Plato's *Republic*. It was perhaps for this reason that he hesitated to publish the chapter entitled "De l'imitation théâtrale" which he wrote as part of his letter to d'Alembert, and which he admitted to be little more than a paraphrase of Plato's tenth book.[39] Is it possible that Di-

38 A.T., X, 23: "Il suit de ce qui précède, que Platon s'étant moins proposé d'enseigner la vérité à ses disciples, que de désabuser ses concitoyens sur le compte des sophistes, nous offre dans ses ouvrages, à chaque ligne, des exemples du *beau*, nous montre très-bien ce que ce n'est point, mais ne nous dit rien de ce que c'est."

39 In *Œuvres complètes* (Paris, Hachette, 1909, 13 vols.), I, 358–70. The "Avertissement" tells us: "Ce petit écrit n'est qu'une espèce d'extraits de divers endroits où Platon traite de l'imitation théâtrale. ... L'occasion de ce travail fut la *Lettre à M. d'Alembert sur les Spectacles*; mais, n'ayant pu commodément l'y faire entrer, je le mis à part pour être employé ailleurs, ou tout à fait supprimé."

derot overlooked the parallel between these two stern philosophers who saw fit to banish theatrical representations from their respective republics? We know, at any rate, that he sent a copy of the *Lettre à d'Alembert* to Sophie Volland in 1759 with the words: "Voilà, ma tendre et solide amie, l'ouvrage du grand sophiste."[40] It was, of course, a bitter blow to Diderot when Rousseau publicly condemned all spectacle as harmful just at the moment when the *philosophe* was launching a campaign to reform the theatre as an instrument of enlightenment and an effective means of purifying public morals. Must we conclude that he was equally incensed at Plato's attack on dramatic poetry, as indeed many critics in every age have been? Or did he interpret Plato in such a way that he could agree with him in principle, while at the same time taking exception to Rousseau's position as an exaggeration of Plato? This second solution would seem to be the more acceptable in view of the fact that Diderot thought highly of Plato's theory of imitation, as the *Salon de 1767* well shows (A.T., XI, 3–18); and he was prone to excuse Plato's rejection of Homer on the grounds that the author of the *Republic* (he thought) was not hostile to poetry as such, but to poetry as bad theology.[41] Whatever Diderot's attitude to Plato may have been in this regard, we may rest assured of one thing: that if *Le Neveu de Rameau* is a satire aimed at Rousseau, there is every reason why Plato and his imitation theory should figure prominently therein.

We may now return to the problem with which we began: education in its relation to mimesis and music. The section of the *Republic* where these matters are discussed (II, 376c – III, 412b) is one of the best-known passages in Plato's work, so that there is no need to enter here into any great detail.[42] The central question for our purpose is the doctrine of mimesis as it applies to *mousike* (poetry, music, and dancing) and *paideia* (education). It should be pointed out that the term *mimesis*, for Plato, covers not only every aspect of composition and representation in the "musical" and other arts, but also the identification or assimilation by which an individual *psyche* tends to become – or to become

---

40 *Corr.*, ed. Roth, II, 144 (2 June 1759).

41 Letter to Falconet, 15 February 1766: "Ce n'est point à Homère comme poëte que Platon et d'autres hommes sages ont refusé leur hommage; c'est à Homère comme théologien" (*Corr.*, ed. Roth, VI, 77).

42 Useful essays on this much-treated subject are those of Werner Jaeger, *Paideia: the Ideals of Greek Culture*, trans. Gilbert Highet (New York, Oxford University Press, 1943, 3 vols.), III, 211–30; H.-I. Marrou, *A History of Education in Antiquity*, 61–78; R. L. Nettleship, *Lectures on the Republic of Plato* (London, Macmillan, 1937), 77–130, and *The Theory of Education in Plato's Republic* (London, Oxford University Press, 1935); Warren Anderson, *Ethos and Education in Greek Music* (Cambridge, Mass., Harvard University Press, 1966).

like – the persons or things (whether real or artistically represented) that it contacts through sight or hearing.[43] Mimesis, then, is the process that underlies both artistic creation and moral development.

It is on this analogy between artistic and ethical mimesis that Plato bases his doctrine of *mousike* and its role in education. He states explicitly that his argument rests upon the "division of labour" principle: that nature determines the one task for which each man is fitted. Whoever, therefore, tries his hand at a multiplicity of things will surely fail to achieve renown in any of them (394e). This judgment is supported, we are told, by the experience of mimetic artists: no one can succeed in both tragedy and comedy, either as poet or as actor (395ab). Similarly, on the moral level, no man can imitate well more than one style of life (395b). Each must choose to imitate that which is appropriate to his nature – and for future Guardians, that means whatever is brave, pious, sober, and free (395c). The good man, and the poet who would serve his community well, will discriminate carefully between what is worthy of imitation and what is not (395c–396d). The more debased (*phaulos*) a man is, the more he will be inclined to imitate just anything and everything, even "claps of thunder, and the noise of wind and hail and axles and pulleys, and the notes of trumpets and flutes and pan-pipes, and the sounds of all instruments, and the cries of dogs, sheep and birds ..." (397a). The manifold forms of expression employed by such entertainers, although ensuring their popularity with children and the multitude, are quite unsuited to a City in which men are not multiform but simple (397c–e). With all due respect to their pleasing qualities, those who possess such varied talents and are able to imitate all things must be ejected gently but firmly from the ideal republic (397e–398a).

The reason for Plato's distrust of pantomime, poetic or other, does not become altogether clear until the following section (398c–403c) where he puts aside the discussion of poetry to consider the question of mimesis in instrumental music. He strictly limits the use of musical modes (*harmoniai*), approving only those having a moral character (*ethos*) suitable to freemen who are temperate and courageous (398c–399c). As for musical instruments, he banishes from the ideal City those which are "many-stringed" and "pan-harmonic" (399cd), comparing them to the over-refined dishes for which Sicilian cookery was famous

---

43 Recent studies of mimesis are found in H. Koller, *Die Mimesis in der Antike: Nachahmung, Darstellung, Ausdruck* (Berne, A. Francke, 1954); W. J. Verdenius, *Mimesis. Plato's Doctrine of Artistic Imitation and its Meaning to Us* (Leiden, E. J. Brill, 1949); Eric A. Havelock, *Preface to Plato* (Cambridge, Mass., Harvard University Press, 1963), 20–35. For the eighteenth century, especially in England, see John D. Boyd, s.j., *The Function of Mimesis and its Decline* (Cambridge, Mass., Harvard University Press, 1968).

(404d). Similarly, the choice of rhythms is restricted to those which are fit to express a brave and orderly style of life, avoiding over-great variety and complexity (399e–400a) as well as everything that smacks of illiberality, insolence, or madness (400b).

These passages leave no doubt as to Plato's central preoccupation in the section he devotes to *mousike*. One of the best-known authorities on the *Republic*, R. L. Nettleship, puts it this way: "It is not difficult to see the leading idea which runs through Plato's criticisms of music and of the artistic and literary work of his time. It is that of simplicity as opposed to complexity."[44] This concern of Plato's is a moral rather than an aesthetic one: he makes it clear at 404e that in music, intricacy (*poikilia*) begets licentiousness whereas simplicity engenders temperance. It is for this reason especially that he considered the complexity introduced into fourth-century musical instruments to be a most unwelcome innovation; and he was equally opposed to the variegated rhythms of every sort which his age had produced (399e). The principle operative here is the one we saw applied in the doctrine of the virtues, where the harmony and unity of the just soul were contrasted with the discord and fragmentation of the unjust. It is not complexity as such that Plato abhorred, but the confusion resulting from the absence of any ordering principle. To quote Nettleship again: "Plato's objections to mere indiscriminate imitation of human life arise from the feeling that such indiscriminateness implies that no principle of good or bad in human life is recognized."[45] The rational principle (*Logos*) that renders the world intelligible is fundamental to Plato's concept of ethical and artistic mimesis. It is the aim of early education to surround the child with an atmosphere of true beauty and grace (400d ff.) so that his soul will be brought insensibly into accord with "beautiful reason" (401d).

Before returning to *Le Neveu de Rameau*, we should do well to examine briefly the relationship between the doctrine contained in Book III of the *Republic* and Plato's attack on democracy in Book VIII. It is interesting to note that, in describing democracy as "the most beautiful of polities ... diversified with every type of character" (557c) where one seeking an ideal form of government can "select the model that pleases him, as if in a bazaar of constitutions" (557d), he uses again and again (esp. 557bc, 561e) the ironic words *poikilia* ("excessive variety") and *pantodapos* ("of every sort") which appear repeatedly in his condemnation of complexity in music and universality in imitation.[46] It would seem that multiplicity uncontrolled is the great enemy

44 R. L. Nettleship, *Lectures on Plato's Republic*, 109.
45 Ibid.
46 *Pantodapos* (397c, 398a, 399e); *poikilia* (404d, 404e); *poikilos* (399e). For Plato's ironic use of *pantodapos*, see Shorey's note to *Rep.*, 557b (Loeb Library ed., II, 286).

for Plato in the political sphere as well as in morality and in artistic creation. Political confusion, moral licentiousness, artistic licence – these are the fruits reaped by society when the great king, Reason, abdicates his throne.

Our examination of the doctrines set forth in the *Republic* has been restricted to a few essential notions which can be related without difficulty to *Le Neveu de Rameau*. Chief among these is Plato's deep-seated conviction that human life must reflect the order and beauty of the cosmos, and that this is possible only when the multiple phenomena of experience have been subjected to rational control. It is from this ground that he launches his attack on the forces of unreason – sophistry, poetry, democracy – that engender chaos and turmoil by inverting human existence and placing society under the rule of its non-philosophic element. The same idea lies beneath the criticism of society found in *Le Neveu de Rameau*; but the similarity of inspiration is disguised by the techniques employed in the later work. Whereas Plato had proceeded mainly by way of argumentation, Diderot sets out to make us *see*, through mimesis, the helter-skelter saturnalian confusion of a world ruled by impulse and chance. It is the universe of comedy that he paints for us, replete with the spirit of the harlequinade: a music-hall stage with its garish variety, featuring clownish antics and phantasmagoric illusion, the mechanical gestures of marionettes and the versatile mockery of mimes, the improvised wit of Italian comedy and the parody of *vaudeville* song, the artistic jumble of the *opéra-comique* and the burlesque of the *parade* – all is there in the figure of Lui, including Pathos awaiting her cue in the wings.

No one, I am sure, will dispute the fact that pandemonium reigns throughout *Le Neveu de Rameau*. The temptation is great to condemn this apparent disorder as lack of artistry, and more than one critic has been content so to conclude. Perhaps the most telling argument in support of the suggestion that Plato influenced the conception of the work is that it makes such a judgment unnecessary, for the parallel with the *Republic* not only provides artistic justification for the *pot-pourri* technique but also furnishes an explanation of its underlying satirical meaning.

Further evidence of Platonic influence is afforded by the identification (at least in part) of Lui with Jean-Jacques Rousseau. If Rousseau was nicknamed "le sophiste" in the public writings of Diderot and Grimm, their private papers designate him also as "le fou;"[47] and these two

47 See, for example, Madame d'Epinay's pseudo-memoirs, revised by Diderot and Grimm around 1770 with the intention of showing Rousseau in an unfavourable light: *Histoire de Madame de Montbrillant*, ed. Georges Roth (Paris, Gallimard, 1951, 3 vols.), III, 141, 178, 183, 186, 194, 198, 203, 332.

traits, seen through the prism of the Socratic dialogues, seem to have guided the author in his creation of the scatter-brained pantomime called Lui. In addition to these (supposed) characteristics, there are several historical facts about Rousseau that lead us, through Plato, to *Le Neveu de Rameau*. Had Jean-Jacques not written treatises on the major themes of the *Republic* – music, education, theatrical imitation, politics? Was he not a fervent egalitarian in the manner of Plato's democratic man? Did he not, like the Athenian democrats of old, pride himself on his freedom of speech – that *parrhesia* of which Plato speaks so witheringly in the *Republic* (557b)? And does it not therefore seem likely that Plato might have furnished the background against which Diderot was to draw a caricature of his famous friend?

We have now reached a point, I believe, where it may be taken as substantially proven that Plato and his *Republic* were present to Diderot's mind when he composed *Le Neveu de Rameau*. The outlines of his plan are still somewhat vague, and we must attempt to bring them into sharper focus. Our discussion in this final section will still have much to do with Plato and will be centred around the question of music. It is here especially that we must not forget the presence of Jean-Jacques Rousseau in the background – Jean-Jacques, leading polemicist of the "Querelle des Bouffons" and sworn enemy of the great Rameau, composer of a comic opera and author of the articles on music in the *Encyclopédie*, whose first contacts with the young Denis Diderot blossomed into friendship in the warmth of their mutual love of music.

The spirit of comic opera that breathes through *Le Neveu de Rameau* is redolent of that exciting twenty-month period (1 August 1752 to 7 March 1754) when a troupe of Italian actors, invading Paris with their light-hearted *opera buffa*, divided audiences of the Opéra into two playfully hostile camps busily engaged in a war of pamphlets over the relative merits of French and Italian music.[48] Some of the participants, of course, took the "Querelle des Bouffons" quite seriously; the Encyclopedists, generally, did not. With great gusto they took up cudgels on behalf of the Italians and proved abundantly that even sober-minded philosophers can have their lighter moments. Rousseau too managed to

48 A useful study of the "Querelle" is that of Louisette Richebourg, *Contribution à l'histoire de la "Querelle des Bouffons"* (Paris, Nizet et Bastard, 1937). For a more general picture, see Alfred R. Oliver, *The Encyclopedists as Critics of Music* (New York, Columbia University Press, 1947). Bibliographical information is given by Donald S. Grout at the end of his article "Opéra bouffe et Opéra-comique" in the *Encyclopédie de la Pléiade, Histoire de la musique* (Paris, Gallimard, 1960–3, 2 vols.), II, 5–25. Diderot's personal contributions to the literature of the quarrel are found in A.T., XII, 143–70.

inject a tone of gaiety into his contributions to the debate – but as usual he went too far. So far, in fact, that he made a host of enemies, among them the recognized dean of French music, Jean-Philippe Rameau. The needlessly outspoken criticisms contained in Rousseau's famous *Lettre sur la musique française* (1753) provoked in Rameau a reaction that was typical of the man: "Etoit-ce à la Musique Françoise qu'on en vouloit, ou au Musicien François?"[49] In his opinion – and he was not altogether wrong – the disparagement of French music by the *philosophes* was in reality an attack on himself; and he was not one to forgive an injury.

This was the unpleasant side of the "Querelle des Bouffons"; and the animosities generated during those years were not allowed to die with the departure of the *bouffons* in 1754. As late as 1759 d'Alembert reviewed certain aspects of the affair in his essay *De la liberté de la musique*;[50] in 1761 the French public was treated to a reassertion of Rousseau's musical theories in *La Nouvelle Héloïse*;[51] and between these two literary events, after a three-year cessation of hostilities, Rameau resumed his fulminations against the "errors" he descried in the articles on music in the *Encyclopédie*, now officially suppressed. It was d'Alembert, this time, who felt the wrath of the great composer, and he was not slow in springing to his own defence. Rameau, of course, replied. The dispute continued hot and heavy into the summer of 1762.[52]

Diderot, meanwhile, remained quietly on the sidelines. He had always refrained from entering into personal controversy with Rameau, although he had taken responsibility, along with d'Alembert, for the openly antagonistic "Avertissement des Editeurs" which introduced the sixth volume of the *Encyclopédie*. As for the issues of the "Querelle" itself, while believing that the French had much to learn from the Italians, he had every hope that the lyric theatre could be perfected in France; his discussion of the matter in the *Entretiens sur le Fils naturel*

49 *Réponse de M. Rameau à MM. les éditeurs de l'Encyclopédie sur leur dernier avertissement* (London, 1757), 27. The "avertissement" referred to is that of the sixth volume of the *Encyclopédie*.

50 In *Mélanges de littérature, d'histoire, et de philosophie* (nouv. éd., Amsterdam, 1773, 5 vols.), IV, 383–462.

51 Part I, Letter 48 and Part II, Letter 23 (*Œuvres*, Pléiade ed., II, 131 ff., 280 ff.).

52 The *Lettre à M. d'Alembert sur ses opinions en musique insérées dans les articles* Fondamental *et* Gamme *de l'Encyclopédie* (1760) was followed by two letters in the *Mercure* (April and July 1761) replying to d'Alembert's article in the earlier April issue of that journal. D'Alembert's "Discours préliminaire" to the second edition of his *Elémens de musique*, published early in 1762, provoked two further answers, the *Lettre de M. Rameau aux philosophes* (*Année littéraire*, July 1762) and the *Lettre aux philosophes, concernant le corps sonore et la sympathie des tons* (*Journal de Trévoux*, August 1762).

(A.T., VII, 156 ff.) leaves no doubt on that score. During the "Querelle" he had adopted a conciliatory attitude, and his role as peacemaker must be considered as an indication that, however zestfully he had entered into the controversy, he was aware of the merits and the shortcomings of both French and Italian music. Consequently, it is difficult to admit that the musical content of *Le Neveu de Rameau* was intended to be a late contribution to the debate.

How, then, are we to evaluate the function of music in the satire? Is it just one theme among others, a pretext for conversation? Perhaps. But many critics consider it to be much more than that, and some have even suggested that music is the very soul of the work. If we presume for the moment that such is the case, it must mean that music has a function with respect to the structure of the dialogue, or to its moral significance, possibly to both. In attacking this problem, there is no need for us to go over the ground already covered by those who have studied the musical content as such.[53] Their direct approach, while usefully clarifying certain details, seems to have yielded little for our overall understanding of the satire. We must therefore approach the question obliquely, seeking the solution not in the ideas expressed in the work but in their relation to an outside source. Once again, we must turn for assistance to the Socratic dialogues of Plato.

If Diderot was searching for a vehicle which would enable him to answer his critics and condemn his century while at the same time giving universal significance to his ideas, he could have wished for nothing more appropriate than Plato's theory of harmony. It is, of course, principally owing to the Greek philosopher that no other word in modern languages is richer in overtones – political, ethical, and aesthetic – than is the word "harmony." And, in relation to our dialogue, it must not be forgotten that "harmony," in the eighteenth century, was practically synonymous with "Rameau."

There is much evidence to indicate that the meaning of Diderot's masterpiece can be found only in musical harmony and in the ethical notions related to it in Greek thought.[54] As we saw above, Plato con-

---

53 Pierre Trahard, *Les Maîtres de la sensibilité française au XVIIIᵉ siècle (1715–1789)* (Paris, Boivin, 1931–3, 4 vols.), II, 254–64; Jean-Pierre Barricelli, "Music and the Structure of Diderot's *Le Neveu de Rameau*," *Criticism*, V (1963), 95–111; Jean-Yves Pouilloux, "L'Esthétique dans le *Neveu de Rameau*," *La Pensée*, no. 129 (October 1966), 73–90.

54 A few recent works on this subject are: Evanghélos Moutsopoulos, *La Musique dans l'œuvre de Platon* (Paris, Presses Universitaires de France, 1959); Warren D. Anderson, *Ethos and Education in Greek Music*; Leo Spitzer, *Classical and Christian Ideas of World Harmony* (Baltimore, The Johns Hopkins Press, 1963); Edward A. Lippman, *Musical Thought in Ancient Greece* (New York, Columbia University Press, 1964); Curt Sachs, *The Rise of Music in the Ancient World, East and West* (New York, W. W. Norton, 1943).

sidered *mousike* to be essentially mimetic in character, and the stringent regulations which he lays down in the *Republic* and the *Laws* for the control of artistic expression reflect his sober judgment that only the imitation of what is noble and worthy can be properly admissible to an ideal state. Books III and X of the *Republic* stress the fact that imitation in the arts is positively harmful unless it springs from a rationally ordered nature and is restricted to those things of which the artist has genuine knowledge. In the *Laws* Plato points out that there are rhythms fit only for slaves, and others suitable for free men (669c); there are dances comely and dignified which are acceptable, and others ludicrous and comic which are to be proscribed (814e–815d). In these stern doctrines of Plato we find a reasonable explanation of why Moi in Diderot's satire, if he represents the spirit of Greek philosophy, should have reacted so negatively to Lui's musical theories and to his pantomime (Fabre, pp. 82, 84). Is not the disdain shown by Moi in the musical section of the work precisely the attitude that we should expect Plato to take if confronted by Jean-François Rameau?

Many seeming ambiguities of Diderot's dialogue disappear when examined in the light of Greek musical theory. Plato, while placing great importance on rhythm and harmony as an essential part of human life, was always careful to subordinate the cultivation of music to the pursuit of values which he considered more worthy. Throughout his works he returns constantly to the idea that pleasure of the ear is vastly inferior to the contemplation of intelligible beauty to which philosophy aspires. Diderot was well aware of this preoccupation of Plato and made special note of it in the article "Platonisme" of the *Encyclopédie*: "Il s'en manquait beaucoup qu'il méprisât l'astronomie et la musique; mais la perfection de l'entendement et la pratique de la vertu étaient toujours le dernier terme auquel il les rapportait" (A.T., XVI, 323). There exists in Plato's work, then, a well-defined tendency to depreciate music, or rather, to judge music according to a rational and ethical standard. In the *Timaeus*, for example, where Plato sets forth his ideas concerning the harmonious structure of the World Soul and of the human soul, we are told that harmony was given to man by the Muses, not for irrational pleasure, but for the sake of interior order and the concord of the soul with itself (47c–e). On a less exalted level we have the criticism in *Republic* V of false philosophers – lovers of sounds and sights – who are avid enthusiasts for choral presentations and spectacles of all kinds, but who are incapable of transcending the multiplicity of sense impressions to attain to an appreciation of beauty in and for itself (475d ff.). These dilettanti are contrasted with genuine philosophers whose passion it is to see the truth (475e).

It is only when we consider *Le Neveu de Rameau* against the background of these doctrines that the author's meaning becomes apparent. Diderot's treatment of music (Fabre, pp. 77–89) is little more than a repetition of what had been said many times by the Encyclopedists during the "Querelle des Bouffons," especially by Rousseau; this section has a special function in the dialogue which we shall examine shortly. It is not, however, the discussion of musical questions that defines the musical meaning of the satire, but the ethos of music as expressed by the characterization. The comparison of French with Italian music is one thing; the comparison of music (*mousike*) with philosophy is another – and it is this that underlies the whole work. The satirical attitude adopted by Diderot can best be defined by two famous statements of Plato's Socrates which sum up his constant teaching concerning music: first, that harmony of soul is the truest music (*Rep.*, 591d); and secondly, that philosophy is the supreme music (*Phaedo*, 61a). Virtue and true knowledge, the attributes of Moi, are opposed to the vicious habits and false opinions of Lui; the musical setting implies the harmony of the one and the discord of the other. Moi is the man of understanding who, Plato tells us, strives to maintain harmony between the spirited and the rational elements of his nature (*Rep.*, 591cd); he is the "true musician" whose words and deeds are in accord (*Laches*, 188d). Lui, on the other hand, lacks harmony of soul and is therefore intemperate, foolish, and undisciplined (*Gorgias*, 504b). This contrast is implied in every word and gesture of the two characters, and the reader is left to draw his own conclusions.

These few general observations concerning the orientation of Diderot's thought in *Le Neveu de Rameau* have completed the groundwork for the construction of a theory which will furnish an explanation of the overall meaning of the satire. It is toward this goal that the whole of the present chapter has been directed, for Plato and his *Republic* are essential pieces of the puzzle and only through them can we arrive at an understanding of our dialogue. Returning, then, to the third book of the *Republic*, let us examine what seems to have been the raw material out of which Diderot was to spin his masterpiece. Nothing is more fascinating or more illuminating than to follow his thought processes as he moves from the original elements to the finished literary creation. *Le Neveu de Rameau* is, as many have guessed, a deliberate mystification. With a source as well known as the *Republic*, the author felt obliged to cover his traces carefully. But not so carefully that they would be totally obliterated.

The first thing to remark is the manner in which Diderot identified the eighteenth-century situation – the quarrel between French and

Italian music – with a similar musical dispute in antiquity to which Plato was no stranger. In the *Republic* (III, 398c–399c) Plato examines the various musical "harmonies,"[55] each of which was traditionally recognized as possessing a certain ethical character (*ethos*). He excludes from his state as unfit for the education of the young Guardians both the Lydian and the Ionian harmonies, which are described as "relaxed." The Phrygian and the Dorian harmonies are retained because of their particular ethos: the former can inculcate courage in time of war and adversity, the latter is the strain of temperance and freedom. In thus justifying the acceptance of both the indigenous Hellenic harmony (Dorian) and the foreign harmony imported from Asia Minor (Phrygian), Plato adopts an attitude comparable to that of Diderot during the "Querelle des Bouffons." The Dorian and the Phrygian harmonies had been traditionally as much opposed as were French and Italian music in 1752, and in both quarrels there was inevitably an element of national pride.[56] In the case of ancient music the opposition of the two harmonies, celebrated in myth and fable, took the form of a musical contest in which the flute,[57] of Phrygian origin, was matched against the Greek lyre. It is to be noted that Plato, while admitting the Phrygian harmony into his state because of its utility in time of war, at the same time rejected the flute, which is the instrument most closely associated with that harmony. The reason for this inconsistency, no doubt, is that the flute had become extremely complicated in his time; and Plato, as we know, was much opposed to complexity.[58] He therefore condemns the flute, calling it metaphorically the most "many-stringed" of instruments and, indeed, the model after which all other pan-harmonic instruments had been patterned (399d).

Plato's text in the *Republic* must be supplemented by Aristotle's prescriptions for musical education in the *Politics* (VIII, 1339a, 3 ff.) if

55 For lack of a better English word, I shall use "harmony" to refer to the Dorian and other *harmoniai*, which have nothing to do with harmony as we know it but are rather of the nature of melodic patterns. On this problem, see Curt Sachs, *The Rise of Music in the Ancient World*, 216–38.

56 The espousal of the cause of Italian music by the Encyclopedists was considered by many of their contemporaries to be unpatriotic. The irony of this judgment is indicated by the title of d'Alembert's essay *De la liberté de la musique* (1759) as well as by his opening words: "Il y a chez toutes les Nations deux choses qu'on doit respecter, la Religion & le Gouvernement; en France on y ajoute une troisième, la Musique du pays" (*Mélanges*, 1773 ed., IV, 383).

57 I shall use the word "flute" for the aulos because that was the practice of Diderot and other eighteenth-century writers. The standard work on the aulos is that of Kathleen Schlesinger, *The Greek Aulos* (London, Methuen, 1939). All pertinent material is found in E. Moutsopoulos, *La Musique dans l'œuvre de Platon*, 81–96.

58 See Warren D. Anderson, *Ethos and Education in Greek Music*, 64–74, 98–108, and E. Moutsopoulos, *La Musique dans l'œuvre de Platon*, 81–96.

we are to see the basic elements with which Diderot was working. The flute, says Aristotle, is not a moralizing but an exciting influence. He repeats the ancient idea that flute-players are unable to accompany their music with words [as can one playing the lyre], and concludes that the irrational character of the flutist's art can have no useful role in educating the young (1341a, 5). Plato, he claims, was inconsistent in banishing the flute from his state while retaining the Phrygian harmony, for both of them are effective in stirring religious and other enthusiasms such as are associated with Bacchic festivals (1342a, 8–9).

Both Plato (399e) and Aristotle (1341b, 8) support their conclusions about the relative merits of flute and lyre by invoking an ancient myth that is one of the commonplaces of musical literature – a myth which was to become a favourite subject of poets and artists through the ages. The most common version of the story is this: Athene, goddess of arts and science, was the first to discover the musical possibilities of a certain type of reed, which she fashioned into a flute. She learned, however, upon examining the reflection of her face in a stream, that the effort required to blow on the instrument had distorted her features. She angrily threw the flute away and laid a curse on him who would find it. Marsyas, a satyr, picked up the flute, learned to use it, and became so proud of his musical skill that he challenged Apollo, the god of harmony, to a contest. The nine Muses were named judges of the competition and their verdict favoured Apollo. The satyr was punished for his temerity by being bound to a pine tree and flayed alive.[59]

It was natural that Diderot should have been attracted by a story such as this, for he and his friends, during the "Querelle des Bouffons," had chosen to express their ideas almost exclusively under the form of satirical allegory.[60] In Le Neveu de Rameau, where he amused himself by transporting the musical dispute of his century back into ancient Greece, he adopted the myth of Apollo and Marsyas as a framework for his thought. Some critics, following Nietzsche, have used the terms "Apollonian" and "Dionysian" with respect to Moi and Lui without ever suspecting how close they were to the truth. For beneath this conversation in an eighteenth-century Parisian café lies the contest of Apollo

59 See the article "Marsyas" in W. H. Roscher (ed.), Ausführliches Lexikon der griechischen und römischen Mythologie (Leipzig, 1884–1921, 10 vols.), II², cols. 2439–60. Among painters who treated the Marsyas myth, either the contest or the flaying, Wilmon Brewer, in his Ovid's Metamorphoses in European Culture (France-town, N.H., Marshall Jones, 1941, 3 vols.), lists Rubens, Jordaens, Perugino, Correggio, Raphael, Biliverti, Domenichino, Guido Reni, Barbiere, and Ribera (II, 44).

60 Grimm's Petit Prophète de Boehmischbroda (1753) set the tone. Many of the pamphlets, which amounted to over sixty in all, have been described by Louisette Richebourg, Contribution à l'histoire de la "Querelle des Bouffons," 46–83.

with the satyr Marsyas, man's reasonable nature in combat with his passionate nature, the harmony of the lyre matched against the wild irrational strains of the flute. Moi is an incarnation of the god of philosophy and light, the protector of the arts; Lui is an untamed thing, half man half beast, living on the fringe of human society.

It is not difficult to show that Marsyas must have served as a model for Lui, for Diderot permitted himself to leave a clue here and there throughout his text. The most significant passage is one which is well known, but which must be read with the fable in mind:

Quand la nature fit Leo, Vinci, Pergolese, Douni, elle sourit. Elle prit un air imposant et grave, en formant le cher oncle Rameau ... Quand elle fagota son neveu, elle fit la grimace et puis la grimace, et puis la grimace encore; et disant ces mots, il faisoit toutes sortes de grimaces du visage; c'etoit le mepris, le dedain, l'ironie; et il sembloit paitrir entre ses doigts un morceau de pâte, et sourire aux formes ridicules qu'il lui donnoit. Cela fait, il jetta la pagode heteroclite loin de lui; et il dit: C'est ainsi qu'elle me fit et me jetta, a coté d'autres pagodes ... (Fabre, pp. 96–7).

The distorting mirror has done its work well, but we immediately discern, beneath this comic description, the goddess Athene fashioning the flute, grimacing, and throwing it away.

It is interesting to see the way in which Diderot chose to mark the path that his mind was taking. The only obvious reference to Lui as a satyr is in the opening lines, where there is a passing mention of his "ventre de Silene" (Fabre, p. 8). Silenus, of course, was the pot-bellied father of satyrs. And near the end of the dialogue we are told by the author that Lui was one of those (along with Rabelais and Abbé Galiani) who had furnished him with a number of ridiculous masks which he fitted to certain grave gentlemen of his acquaintance (Fabre, p. 105). One of these masks is that of a satyr. Another most obscure allusion is found in the passage where Lui speaks of his situation as a parasite of the wealthy Jew of Utrecht. He refers to his spendthrift patron as "le tonneau des Danaïdes" (p. 100), and depicts himself crouched beneath the bottomless barrel ("sous le tonneau percé") waiting to catch a few drops of sustenance. We are reminded of Diderot's *Salon de 1761* in which he describes a painting by Amédée Van Loo entitled "Les Satyres," representing a family of satyrs. The father satyr has pierced two holes in a cask, and his two goat-footed children, lying beside the cask, have their mouths open to receive the wine. "Est-ce que l'idée de ce tonneau percé par l'autre satyre; ces jets de vin qui tombent dans la bouche de ses petits enfants étendus à terre sur la paille ... ne vous plaît pas ?" (A.T., x, 127).

There is one further detail linking Lui with the satyr Marsyas, although it seems scarcely likely at first sight that the author should have buried a clue as deeply as this one is buried. Yet only in the light of the fable can we explain a difficult passage and absolve Diderot of faulty workmanship. I am referring to the passage mentioned in an earlier chapter in which Lui suddenly breaks off what he has been saying about the equality of all men in death to launch into a description of how he managed to overcome the stiffness of his wrists (Fabre, p. 26; cf. p. 99). There is no strictly logical connection between death and the stiffness of one's wrists, and it is puzzling to find such an awkward passage in a work in which the transitions are normally handled in masterly fashion. If, however, Lui is a metamorphosed Marsyas, the transition is easily explained. The flaying of Marsyas was a much more frequently treated subject in art than was the contest with Apollo because of the possibilities it presented for anatomical study; and the usual depiction of Marsyas, wrists bound together and arms stretched high, was familiar to all lovers of art ...[61]

Turning now to the character Moi, we find no details such as those we have mentioned to show that he is to be identified with the god Apollo. This is not surprising, for Diderot, while keeping Apollo in the back of his mind, seems to have established another identification, one which is much more fitting and more meaningful for the dialogue. In Plato's *Symposium* there is a well-known passage which Diderot esteemed highly as a model of literary composition and which he proposed to artists as an example of the fact that Plato is as worthy of imitation as is Homer.[62] Toward the end of the banquet (*symposion*), Alcibiades arrives on the scene in a rather drunken state and proceeds to deliver an encomium of Socrates in which he expansively pays tribute to the power of philosophy over the minds of men. Having drawn a striking comparison between Socrates and the race of Sileni, he goes on to state that there is a way in which the Athenian philosopher bears a special resemblance to the satyr Marsyas (215ab). Addressing himself directly to Socrates who is reclining at table, he enlarges on his theme:

Are you not a piper [*auletes*]? Why, yes, and a far more marvellous one than

---

61 Probably a late interpolation, the vivid description given by Lui of the manipulation of his wrists, tendons, and fingers might have been inspired by Demarteau's engraving of the tortured Marsyas on which Diderot reported briefly in the *Salon de 1767*. See Jean Seznec's edition of the *Salons* (Oxford, Clarendon Press, 1957–67, 4 vols.), III, 334 and plate 102.

62 *Encyclopédie*, art. "Composition (en peinture)," A.T., XIV, 203–4. This passage, which occupies a whole page in the A.T. edition, is highly praised by Naigeon in a note quoted by Assézat in connection with the article "Platonisme" (A.T., XVI, 315).

the satyr. His lips indeed had power to entrance mankind by means of instruments; a thing still possible to-day for anyone who can pipe his tunes ... You differ from him in one point only – that you produce the same effect with simple prose [*logos*] unaided by instruments.[63]

This quotation is of the utmost importance for *Le Neveu de Rameau*, for it allows us to identify a third level of meaning concealed beneath what is ostensibly a conversation between Diderot and Jean-François Rameau. At the lowest level we have Marsyas and Apollo engaged in a musical contest: *the flute against the lyre*. Then the satyr again, this time matched with Socrates: *the flute against philosophy*. And finally Jean-Jacques Rousseau – creature of the woods, force of nature – measuring himself with Diderot: *rhetoric against philosophy*.

This last statement, since it is based partly on inference, cannot be allowed to pass without some explanation. What connection is there between the music of Marsyas and the rhetoric of Rousseau? Let us begin with Marsyas. The power of music to charm the souls of men is one of the oldest and most widespread themes of folklore; and Marsyas, although less well known than Orpheus, stands with him as a prototype of the spellbinding musician. One of the sources of this tradition in antiquity is Plato's *Symposium*, where, as we have seen, tribute is paid by Alcibiades to the enchanting virtue of the satyr's flute. In the context, however, the praise bestowed on Marsyas is meant to bring out the fact that philosophy is an art "far more marvellous" than that of music.

We know from other sources what is Plato's constant attitude toward the pleasing arts such as flute-playing: they have only apparent value – entertainment value – suitable to captivate an audience of children or the ignorant multitude.[64] It will be remembered that he expressed such an opinion with regard to the pantomime-poet of *Republic* III (397d); and it is precisely the same criticism that we find levelled against the sophists in *Republic* VI (493b–d), against poets in *Republic* X (607e–608b) and against flute-players, poets, and rhetoricians in the *Gorgias* (463a ff.; 510d ff.). All these performers, we are told, seek to flatter and please their hearers, making no distinction between what is good

63 *Symposium*, 215bc. Translation by W. R. M. Lamb in the Loeb Classical Library edition (London, Heinemann, 1925).

64 In *Le Neveu de Rameau*, after the brilliant mime scene which has attracted the attention of all in the café (Fabre, 82–6), Lui returns to a discussion of musical theory. The author, intervening, comments on the reaction of the on-lookers (p. 87): "Tandis qu'il me parloit ainsi, la foule qui nous environnoit, ou n'entendant rien ou prenant peu d'interet a ce qu'il disoit, parce qu'en general l'enfant comme l'homme, et l'homme comme l'enfant aime mieux s'amuser que s'instruire, s'etoit retirée ..." It is surely no coincidence that Plato had made his observation about childish amusements (*Rep.*, 397d) immediately after the great mime scene at 397a quoted above, p. 119.

or bad, useful or harmful, so long as the audience is gratified (*Gorgias*, 502b).

Of all those who fall under Plato's censure, it is the sophist-rhetorician who receives the sternest rebuke. Plato does make a distinction between sophists and rhetoricians, but "they are so nearly related that sophists and orators are jumbled up as having the same field and dealing with the same subjects, and neither can they tell what to make of each other, nor the world at large what to make of them" (*Gorgias*, 465d). Everything that is said about rhetoric in the *Gorgias*, then, can be taken as applying equally to sophistry. Rhetoric is condemned because its practitioners are charlatans. Like a cook who would usurp the role of doctor and deceive foolish people into thinking that appetizing dishes are those most conducive to health, the rhetorician ministers to the souls of men by flattering their tastes, with no thought for what is best (464b ff.). Rhetoric is not an art (*techne*) but an empirical technique, that is, one which cannot justify its methods on rational grounds. "I," says Socrates, "refuse to give the name of art to anything that is irrational" (465a). Plato leaves no doubt about his opinion of rhetoric and sophistry, for it sounds like a refrain throughout this long passage of the *Gorgias* (463a ff.) : these so-called arts are nothing but forms of flattery.

The significance of all this for *Le Neveu de Rameau* can scarcely be exaggerated. First, it answers a question which has always puzzled readers of Diderot's dialogue: if the author intended to satirize Lui, why did he endow him with such attractive qualities? In the light of Alcibiades' speech and of Plato's dispraise of the "flattering" arts, we see that it is the very attractiveness of Lui's talent that drives home the point Diderot is trying to make: a versatile performer can dazzle the ignorant and foolish crowd, whereas only the few are able to appreciate the true utility of philosophy. Secondly, Rousseau's role in the dialogue becomes clear – Rousseau, of whom Diderot wrote the following evaluation in the *Réfutation d'Helvétius*:

Jean-Jacques est tellement né pour le sophisme, que la défense de la vérité s'évanouit entre ses mains; on dirait que sa conviction étouffe son talent. Proposez-lui deux moyens dont l'un péremptoire, mais didactique, sentencieux et sec; l'autre précaire, mais propre à mettre en jeu son imagination et la vôtre, à fournir des images intéressantes et fortes, des mouvements violents, des tableaux pathétiques, des expressions figurées, à étonner l'esprit, à émouvoir le cœur, à soulever le flot des passions; c'est à celui-ci qu'il s'arrêtera ... Je le sais par expérience. Il se soucie bien plus d'être éloquent que vrai, disert que démonstratif, brillant que logicien, de vous éblouir que de vous éclairer (A.T., II, 292).

Time and again we find Diderot and Grimm paying similar tribute to the gift of eloquence with which nature had endowed Jean-Jacques Rousseau – a gift which they believed was being put into the service of unreason.[65] We may be sure, therefore, that the furious satire of *Le Neveu de Rameau* was not prompted by personal spite alone. Diderot's resentment was undoubtedly intensified by the frustration he felt, after years of laborious study and plodding drudgery devoted to the *Encyclopédie*, at seeing Rousseau's untaught genius and colourful pen build a few paltry paradoxes into an international reputation almost overnight; and there must also have been fear that this apostle of unreason was able, with a few bold flourishes, to do serious injury to the work of enlightenment to which he, Diderot, had given his life. Little wonder, then, that in the brief period (1760–2) during which *La Nouvelle Héloïse, Emile,* and *Du contrat social* made Rousseau's name a household word throughout Europe, Diderot should have experienced a deepening of that pessimism which he had expressed a few years before in a letter to Voltaire already quoted:

*Etre utile aux hommes?* Est-il bien sûr qu'on fasse autre chose que les amuser, et qu'il y ait grande différence entre le philosophe et le joueur de flûte? Ils écoutent l'un et l'autre avec plaisir ou dédain, et demeurent ce qu'ils sont. Les Athéniens n'ont jamais été plus méchants qu'au tems de Socrate, et ils ne doivent peut-être à son existence qu'un crime de plus.[66]

Resentment, jealousy, pessimism, fear. These can perhaps define the emotional state which produces satire of a certain kind – but not *Le Neveu de Rameau*. Diderot was well aware that the expression of uncontrolled emotion can result in nothing but mediocrity; did he not, a few years later, write a treatise entitled *Paradoxe sur le comédien* in order to prove that very point? He also knew that the spirit with which a satirist must be imbued, if he is to move his readers to sympathy, is neither jealousy nor resentment but righteous indignation. Now, how does one go about expressing righteous indignation in an artistic manner? It would seem that the best way to inform oneself about any passion or emotion, a way proven by the experience of writers through the centuries, is to see how Aristotle defines it in the *Rhetoric*. Diderot was quite familiar with the *Rhetoric*, and perhaps years before had taken mental note of the brief passage in which Aristotle gives an interesting example of this emotion. We feel righteous indignation (*nemesis*), says

---

65 Grimm, *Corr. lit.*, iv, 54, 100, 343. Diderot, *Corr.*, ed. Roth, ii, 145, viii, 107; A.T., ii, 317, 412.

66 19 February 1758. *Corr.*, ed. Roth, ii, 39.

Aristotle, "in any case where an inferior contends with his superior; a musician, for instance, with a just man, because justice is better than music."[67]

There is good reason to believe that these few simple words provided Diderot with the original pattern for his masterpiece. Not only do they tell us a great deal about his manner of working but they also corroborate the interpretation at which we arrived through studying Plato.

Both the passage from Aristotle's *Rhetoric* and the speech of Alcibiades from the *Symposium* indicate that Diderot, in creating the character Moi, had uppermost in his mind the intention of presenting an idealized picture of the just philosopher. The Marsyas-Apollo myth, of course, remains an essential part of his plan; but we cannot charge him with the temerity of painting himself under the guise of Apollo, the god of light – despite the fact that Grimm, who was undoubtedly privy to the secret of *Le Neveu de Rameau*, did not hesitate so to honour him in 1763.[68] Unlike Plato, who had employed myth in his dialogues as a means of expressing the inexpressible, Diderot used the Marsyas-Apollo myth to serve the purpose of literary mystification. Its main function, however, is that of an allegory giving substance and universality to his thought. And indeed, if his satire was intended to be a confrontation of the spirit of Greek philosophy with the spirit of a dissolute age, the myth of Apollo and Marsyas communicates admirably the author's message: philosophy is the true music, the most beautiful music; but the frivolous world prefers the pipes of Pan.

Analyses such as the above are always more satisfying when corroborated by evidence exterior to the text. In this case we are fortunate to have proof that the Marsyas-Apollo myth has an intimate connection with the "Querelle des Bouffons." Here is what Grimm reported to his subscribers on 15 August 1753, when the quarrel was at its height:

67 *Rhetoric*, II.9.11. Cope's commentary paraphrases slightly in order to include the idea contained in the preceding sentence: "(Chiefly in the *same* art, profession, or pursuit), or if not in the same, any case whatsoever of competition of inferior with superior (understand $\dot{\alpha}\mu\varphi\iota\sigma\beta\eta\tau\bar{\eta}$) ; of a musician, for instance, with a just man ('ut si musicus cum iusto viro *de dignitate* contendat.' Victorius) ; because justice is better than music." The commentary continues: "The claims of the two are unequal, of which the inferior ought to be sensible" (*The Rhetoric of Aristotle*, ed. E. M. Cope, revised by J. E. Sandys [Cambridge University Press, 1877, 3 vols.], II, 118–19).

68 "Ce philosophe, grand poëte, grand peintre, grand sculpteur, grand musicien, artiste mécanicien, artisan, sans jamais avoir fait ni de vers, ni de tableaux, ni de musique, ni de statue, ni de machine, ressemble à cet homme extraordinaire dont l'antiquité fabuleuse a fait son dieu Apollon" (*Corr. lit.*, 1 October 1763, v, 395).

Inscription pour la nouvelle toile qu'on suppose qu'on doit faire au théâtre de l'Opéra:

HIC MARSYAS APOLLINEM.

Cette inscription est de M. Diderot. On l'a mise depuis en ces vers:

O Pergolèse inimitable,
Quand notre orchestre impitoyable
T'immole sous son lourd violon,
Je crois qu'au rebours de la fable
Marsyas écorche Apollon.[69]

This playful inscription was Diderot's last contribution to the "Querelle des Bouffons." It is worth remarking that the verses (not composed by Diderot) apply the fable to the heavy-handed manner in which the French orchestra (Marsyas) interpreted Pergolesi's score, not to the relative merits of French and Italian music. But the inscription itself, we may be sure, refers to the triumph of Italian *opera buffa* (Marsyas) over serious French opera (Apollo).

This distinction is of considerable importance for our interpretation of *Le Neveu de Rameau*. By reversing the traditional outcome of the musical contest in his inscription for the curtain of the Opéra, Diderot was pointing out in a humorous way that the Italian *bouffons* had succeeded in giving Rameau and his school a much-needed lesson in music as "imitation of nature." But the humour of the inscription is dependent upon the incongruity of this reversal; the myth itself is a static form in which the triumph of Apollo is a foregone conclusion, for any contest between a god and a satyr is an unequal trial of strength. In his choice of the myth, therefore, Diderot implied the essential superiority of serious opera over the comic genre. We must be careful to take this into account in applying the Marsyas-Apollo myth to our dialogue, where the issues involved go far beyond those of a frivolous musical controversy. The author's central preoccupation in *Le Neveu de Rameau* is the opposition of enlightenment to enthusiasm; and this time it is Apollo, the god whom Socrates served so faithfully (*Phaedo*, 85b), who wins out over the irrational forces of nature represented by Marsyas-Lui.

69 *Corr. lit.*, II, 272. Reprinted in A.T., XII, 141–2.

# 7

# The caricature of Jean-Jacques Rousseau

ONE of the major problems posed by *Le Neveu de Rameau* is the origin of the creative force that guided the execution of this unusual work. Is it really possible, critics have asked themselves, that resentment towards a third-rate author like Charles Palissot should have inspired a satire of such extraordinary richness and power? What is more, can we honestly believe that for twenty years of his life Diderot came back constantly to retouch the portrait of an insignificant musician like Jean-François Rameau? These anomalies have led scholars to fathom the soul of Diderot the satirist in the effort to uncover other secret sources of his motivation. Thus far, no fully satisfactory explanation has been found; but if it could be shown, as suggested in the previous chapter, that the character Lui is in large part a caricature of Jean-Jacques Rousseau, no doubt would remain that the cause is indeed commensurate with the effect. It will be the purpose of the present chapter to bring to light whatever evidence can be found to support this contention.

Let it be understood from the outset that the identification of Lui with Rousseau is in no way incompatible with the well-attested fact that Jean-François Rameau is, as the author assures us (Fabre, p. 6), the model of the portrait.[1] But Diderot, insofar as we know, had no serious reason to paint a malicious picture of Rameau's nephew,[2] whereas his hostility to Jean-Jacques was of such an intensely passionate nature that one critic has remarked with astonishment the absence of the latter's

[1] See Milton F. Seiden, "Jean-François Rameau and Diderot's Neveu," *Diderot Studies*, I (1949), 143–91.

[2] It is possible that Diderot was not amused by Fréron's description of one of the pieces contained in Jean-François Rameau's *Nouvelles Pièces de clavecin*: "Mais le plus piquant de tous ces morceaux, c'est le Menuet intitulé l'*Encyclopédique*, avec une autre dénomination de *Menuet intra ou ultramontain. L'Encyclopédique* est assez bisarre de caractère; il finit par une chûte grotesque & qui fait du fracas" (*Année littéraire*, October 1757, Tome VII, 47). However, this is scarcely enough to rank Rameau among the enemies of the *Encyclopédie*!

name from the catalogue of those attacked in *Le Neveu de Rameau.*[3] It is not unreasonable to propose, therefore, that Lui might have been conceived principally as a caricature of Rousseau whilst Rameau was chosen as the ostensible model, not for purposes of personal satire but for the sake of the "bouffon" motif that is essential to the dialogue.

That Rameau is not the only model is already well established; even apart from Lui's literary antecedents, we have seen that at least one of his traits must have been borrowed from Charles Palissot (above, pp. 40–1). Furthermore, it is not difficult to recognize in him certain characteristics of still another enemy of Diderot, Charles Duclos.[4] Everything, in fact, indicates that Lui is a composite creation inspired, at least to some extent, by a variety of historical individuals; and this conclusion is strengthened by the fact that the author, as we saw in Part II, employed the same technique elsewhere in the summer of 1762: he combined the traits of two other acquaintances of his in forging the character of Rivière-Lui in the satire entitled *Lui et Moi* (above, p. 27). The suggestion, then, that Jean-Jacques Rousseau is one of several contemporaries of Diderot concealed beneath Lui's leering mask should occasion no surprise, especially when we recall that the fundamental requirement of Lui's nature is that he be, as Plato would say, many men rather than one.

INCONSISTENCY

The epigraph which Diderot affixed to his dialogue – "Vertumnis, quotquot sunt, natus iniquis" – serves not only to epitomize the character of Lui but also to evoke in the mind of the reader the *inaequalis-iniquus* theme from Horace.[5] Our analysis in Chapter 5 demonstrated the importance of the "inequality" motif; and it should be pointed out here

3 Jean Fabre, "Deux Frères ennemis : Diderot et Jean-Jacques," *Diderot Studies,* III (1961), 191.

4 Duclos, under the name of "Desbarres," shares with Rousseau the role of villain in Madame d'Epinay's *Histoire de Madame de Montbrillant* as revised by Diderot and Grimm. This literary portrait, which the editor Georges Roth describes as caricature "poussée à la charge" (II, 599–600 n.), gives special prominence to one trait of the real Duclos, his outrageous "franchise" (II, 88, 102, 132, 288; see the editor's note at II, 110 and II, 547–8). "Desbarres" has one physical characteristic that reminds us of Lui: his extraordinarily powerful lungs (II, 401, 405; cf. Fabre, pp. 4, 49, 83), as well as the vulgar habit of drinking two or three glasses of beer in rapid succession (II, 98, 124; cf. Fabre, pp. 88, 89). These idiosyncracies, like the famous "coupure imperceptible à la lèvre inférieure" (A.T., V, 277), are evidence that Diderot's method of realistic portraiture is at work in both cases.

5 "Pour le thème (inaequalis-iniquus), le mouvement, le choix des détails même, cette pochade d'Horace [*Sat.* II. vii. 8–14] a fourni à Diderot le canevas d'un portrait-charge de Rameau" (Fabre, p. 111, n. 1).

that *inégalité* in the moral sense of the word was the most striking trait that Rousseau, the great opponent of other forms of inequality, shared with the inconsistent musician of our satire.

Nothing, indeed, was more characteristic of Jean-Jacques than the instability of temperament which he himself and all his biographers have brought to our attention.[6] Contemporary testimony concerning the "man of contradictions" is unanimous on this point; and both Grimm and Diderot, long familiar with the inconstancy of Rousseau's nature, do not hesitate to describe him as "sans caractère."[7] Especially noteworthy is a remark made by Diderot in July 1762 concerning the author of *Emile*: "Rien ne tient dans ses idées. C'est un homme excessif, qui est ballotté de l'athéisme au baptême des cloches. Qui sçait où il s'arrêtera?"[8] One can easily imagine the strain that such changeableness must have put upon their relationship, a strain that is perhaps reflected in a deeply sensitive observation found in Diderot's article "*Inégal (Gramm.)*" of the *Encyclopédie*, where he illustrates the moral connotations of that word: "Il est d'un caractère *inégal*; le commerce des personnes *inégales* est très-incommode; elles vous ramenent sans cesse sur vous-mêmes, & l'on se tourmente à chercher en soi le motif du changement qu'on apperçoit en elles" (VIII, 695).

Rousseau, then, much more than Diderot, was a weathercock, a harlequin, a creature of constantly shifting moods; and we need only glance at the three-page description which he gives of himself in *Le Persifleur* – that abortive imitation of Addison's first issue of the *Spectator* – to recognize it as a full-length portrait of Diderot's chameleon-like Lui. The opening lines set the tone of the passage:

Quand Boileau a dit de l'homme en général qu'il changeoit du blanc au noir, il a croqué mon portrait en deux mots; en qualité d'individu, il l'eut

6 Jean Starobinski, *Jean-Jacques Rousseau. La Transparence et l'obstacle* (Paris, Plon, 1958), 58–70; Ronald Grimsley, *Jean-Jacques Rousseau, a Study in Self-awareness* (Cardiff, University of Wales Press, 1961), 15ff. See especially Marcel Raymond, "J.-J. Rousseau. Deux aspects de sa vie intérieure (intermittances et permanence du 'Moi')," *Annales J.-J. Rousseau*, XXIX (1941–2), 5–57; Virgil W. Topazio, "Rousseau, Man of Contradictions," *Studies on Voltaire and the Eighteenth Century*, XVIII (1961), 77–93; Basil Munteano, "Les 'Contradictions' de J.-J Rousseau," in *Jean-Jacques Rousseau et son œuvre; problèmes et recherches* ("Actes et Colloques," 2. Paris, Klincksieck, 1964), 95–111.

7 *Histoire de Madame de Montbrillant*, III, 352: "C'est un homme sans caractère, et cette race se multiplie tous les jours davantage." The person referred to is "René" (Rousseau). Diderot, complaining of his friend Grimm's actions in a letter to Madame d'Epinay, makes this distinction between Rousseau and Grimm: "Il y a cette différence que l'un est sans caractère, et que Grimm en a un" (*Corr.*, ed. Roth, VIII, 214. November 1768).

8 Letter to Sophie Volland, 25 July 1762 (*Corr.*, ed. Roth, IV, 72).

rendu plus précis s'il y eut ajouté touttes les autres couleurs avec les nuances intermédiaires. Rien n'est si dissemblable à moi que moi-même ... Quelquefois je suis un dur et feroce misantrope, en d'autres momens, j'entre en extase au milieu des charmes de la societé et des délices de l'amour. Tantôt je suis austére et dévot ... mais je deviens bientot un franc libertin ... En un mot, un protée, un Caméléon, une femme sont des êtres moins changeans que moi.[9]

The facetious style of this article has deceived no one; it depicts Rousseau as he actually was and as he describes himself on many a later occasion.[10] Two observations should be made with regard to this portrait: first, that Diderot was undoubtedly familiar with it;[11] and secondly, that the expression "Rien n'est si dissemblable à moi que moi-même" parallels the description of Lui in *Le Neveu de Rameau*: "Rien ne dissemble plus de lui que lui meme."[12] It has already been indicated that these words paraphrase Horace's comment on Trebatius in *Sat*.i.iii. 18–19: "Nil fuit umquam sic impar sibi."

This allusion to Horace's Trebatius would seem to establish a direct link between the portrait of *Le Persifleur* and that of *Le Neveu de Rameau*. Indeed, it is difficult to accept as mere coincidence the fact that these two intimate friends, each with the same literary model in mind, should have chosen to portray a Protean character – Rousseau describing himself, and Diderot depicting an old acquaintance of his (Fabre, p. 5: "Je connoissois celui cy de longue main"). We can, however, admit the influence of Rousseau's self-portrait upon the author of our dialogue without thereby concluding that Lui is intended to represent Rousseau. Such a conclusion is more than ever a possibility; but the question must remain open until further substantiation is found.

9 *Œuvres*, Pléiade ed., I, 1108. The image with which Rousseau concludes his portrait is especially striking: "Je suis sujet ... à deux dispositions principales qui changent assés constamment de 8 en 8 jours et que j'appelle mes ames hebdomadaires, par l'une je me trouve sagement fou, par l'autre follement sage ..." (p. 1110).

10 Especially in *Rousseau juge de Jean-Jacques*, from which the following quotation is drawn: "Voulez-vous donc connoitre à fond sa conduite et ses mœurs? Etudiez bien ses inclinations et ses gouts; cette connoissance vous donnera l'autre parfaitement; car jamais homme ne se conduisit moins sur des principes et des régles, et ne suivit plus aveuglément ses penchans. Prudence, raison, précaution, prevoyance; tout cela ne sont pour lui que des mots sans effet. Quand il est tenté, il succombe; quand il ne l'est pas, il reste dans sa langueur. Par là vous voyez que sa conduite doit être inégale et sautillante, quelques instans impétueuse, et presque toujours molle ou nulle" (*Œuvres*, Pléiade ed., I, 811–12). See also ibid., 795, 817–18.

11 Rousseau sent these pages to Diderot, along with a covering letter, towards the end of 1747. See Rousseau's *Correspondance*, ed. Leigh, II, 104–7.

12 Fabre, p. 4. M. Fabre points out this parallel in his article "Deux Frères ennemis," p. 160, n. 1.

A PARASITE DISGRACED

Although *Le Neveu de Rameau* cannot be said to possess a plot in any real sense of the word, it is true that the conversation between the interlocutors is centred with classical care around a single incident, narrated by Lui, that had precipitated a sudden change of fortune in the life of the parasite musician – namely, his dismissal from the house of the financier Bertin, where he had been prostituting his talents in exchange for bed and board (Fabre, pp. 17–21, 62–5). This section of the satire, with its wealth of realistic detail, seems more than any other to have been taken from life; and the known fact that Bertin had been a benefactor of Jean-François Rameau lends credibility to the supposition that Diderot is here relating in burlesque style an incident that is substantially true. In his discussion of this aspect of the satire, however, Rudolf Schlösser suggests another possibility: that Diderot created this scene in retaliation for a vaguely similar episode, wholly fictitious, which Palissot had inserted into his play *Les Philosophes*.[13] There is room for doubt, then, as to the historicity of the story told by Lui; and this doubt justifies the formulation of yet another hypothesis: that the real-life incident lying behind the mock-heroic narration of Lui's disgrace is the expulsion of the "parasite" Rousseau from the Hermitage in December 1757.

The "Hermitage Affair" has been the subject of numerous studies,[14] so that there is no need to mention here more than the few details relevant to our purpose. Jean-Jacques, as Diderot was to point out years later, "fréquentait volontiers chez les fermiers généraux" (A.T., III, 96). Early in his career he had served as personal secretary in the home of Madame Dupin, daughter of the financier Samuel Bernard and wife of a *fermier général*; from April 1756 to December 1757 he enjoyed the hospitality of Madame d'Epinay, whose husband also was a tax-farmer. Concerned for his independence, Rousseau insisted on paying the wages of the gardener at Madame d'Epinay's Hermitage, which he occupied along with Thérèse and her mother; he insisted also on earning what he could by copying music.

Like Madame de Tencin before her, Madame d'Epinay referred

13 Rudolf Schlösser, *Rameaus Neffe. Studien und Untersuchungen zur Einführung in Goethes Uebersetzung des Diderotschen Dialogs (Forschungen zur neueren Litteraturgeschichte*, xv. Berlin, Duncker, 1900), 65–6.

14 In addition to the standard biographies of the two men, see Henri Guillemin, "Les Affaires de l'Ermitage (1756–1757). Examen critique des documents," *Annales J.-J. Rousseau*, xxix (1941–2), 59–258; and by the same author, *Un Homme, deux ombres* (Geneva, 1943). More recent studies have tended to judge Diderot less severely than does M. Guillemin; see Jean Fabre, "Deux Frères ennemis," pp. 196 ff.

affectionately to the habitués of her home as "mes ours"; and Jean-Jacques was her "premier ours." Alexandre Deleyre wrote to him in July 1756: "Assurés de mes respects Madame d'Epinay pour qui j'ai toute l'estime qu'elle a pour son premier Ours. Dites-lui que j'espere augmenter sa ménagerie un jour."[15] But the apostle of liberty soon grew impatient with life in the "ménagerie": "Laissez moi être ce que m'a fait la nature," he wrote to Madame d'Houdetot in October 1757, "et non pas ce que tous ces gens là veulent que je sois, Un ours de parade que l'on méne en laisse, un petit parasite, un vil complaisant."[16] The collar was chafing and the "bear" was eager to be off. Harassed by what he considered to be importunate and humiliating demands, he penned a furious note to Madame d'Epinay: "L'amitié est éteinte entre nous, Madame ..." – requesting nonetheless a few lines farther on that he be allowed to remain at the Hermitage over the winter.[17] Her refusal was curt and definitive.[18] A letter from Rousseau to Sophie d'Houdetot suggests what a blow this dismissal was to his pride: "je sens que vous devez souffrir à chaque quart d'heure que vôtre ami passe dans une maison dont on le chasse."[19] A few days later he is already installed elsewhere; the deep bitterness he felt is recorded in these lines sent to his former hostess: "Rien n'est si simple, madame, et si nécessaire que de sortir de votre maison quand vous n'approuvez pas que j'y reste. Sur votre refus de consentir que je passasse à l'Hermitage le reste de l'hiver, je l'ai donc quitté le quinze décembre."[20]

This painful episode, in burlesque dress, could well have provided the central story-line of *Le Neveu de Rameau*. Lui loses his place in the Bertin "menagerie" (Fabre, p. 57) as punishment for a vulgar remark he had made in Italian (p. 63) – a language which Rousseau knew well.[21] His expulsion (p. 19) goes hard with him, and Moi ironically suggests a reconciliation with the mistress of the house, Mademoiselle Hus: "Je me jetterois aux piés de la divinité. Je me colerois la face contre terre, et sans me relever, je lui dirois d'une voix basse et sanglotante: Pardon, madame! pardon! ..." (p. 20). As these words are being spoken, Lui acts out the scene with an imaginary Mademoiselle Hus, then writhes at the thought of humiliating himself before "une guenon

---

15 Rousseau's *Corr.*, ed. Leigh, IV, 21 (3 July 1756).
16 Ibid., 318 (29 October 1757).        17 Ibid., 372 (23 November 1757).
18 Ibid., 379–80 (1 December 1757).      19 Ibid., 388 (10 December 1757).
20 Ibid., 391–2 (17 December 1757).
21 Rousseau's Italian vocabulary was usually more refined than that employed by Lui; however, Diderot had probably listened more than once to his friend's Venetian adventures related, as in *Confessions* VII, with the occasional use of vernacular colouring. Cf. *Œuvres*, Pléiade ed., I, 317, where Rousseau is led against his will to the abode of "la Padoana" out of a sense of shame, "per non parer troppo coglione."

... une miserable petite histrione que les sifflets du parterre ne cessent de poursuivre" (p. 21). These amusing lines can be interpreted as alluding to an incident that Diderot had recorded in his *Tablettes* as one of the "sept scélératesses" of Jean-Jacques Rousseau: "Il accusoit cette dame [Madame d'Epinay] d'être la plus noire des femmes dans le tems même qu'il se prosternoit à ses genoux, et que, les larmes aux yeux, il lui demandoit pardon de tous les torts qu'il avoit avec elle."[22] Lui is equally ungrateful to his erstwhile benefactors, scrupling not at all to spread malicious gossip about them (pp. 67–8, 71); and this, we know, was precisely the kind of revelation that Diderot and his friends feared that Rousseau would make concerning them in his *Confessions*.[23]

It should be remarked that the dismissal of Lui from the Bertin household is more than just an amusing story; in fact, this episode is absolutely essential to the "confession" type of satire chosen by the author whereby he is permitted to put the denunciation of his enemies in the mouth of a former member of the opposite camp who, in a burst of candour brought on by his expulsion, gives an authoritative account of their vileness and depravity. This technique, we may be certain, formed part of the original plan of the satire as it took shape in Diderot's mind; and there is reason to believe that Jean-Jacques was no stranger to its conception. At the height of the tempest stirred up by *Emile* – especially by the *Profession de foi du vicaire savoyard* wherein Rousseau managed to insult atheists and Christians alike – Diderot wrote the following lines in a letter to Sophie Volland dated 18 July 1762:

Non, mon amie, l'affaire de Rousseau ne se suivra pas. Il a pour lui les dévots. Il doit l'intérêt qu'ils prennent à lui au mal qu'il dit des philosophes. ... Ils espèrent toujours qu'il se convertira; ils ne doutent point qu'un transfuge de notre camp ne doive tôt ou tard passer dans le leur; ou c'est du moins le prétexte dont ils s'enveloppent pour le protéger sans rougir (*Corr.*, ed. Roth, IV, 55).

This statement, however unsound it may have been as prophecy, contains the germ of an idea which, given the benefit of an imaginative twist, could conceivably have produced the master plan of *Le Neveu de Rameau*. The "deserter" will remain the same – Jean-Jacques Rousseau – but will receive his punishment by being portrayed in the motley of a fool; and Diderot's other enemies will be castigated by a clever reversal of plot whereby the fool betrays *their* secrets to a sympathetic but scornful representative of the *philosophes*.

---

22 *Diderot Studies*, III (1961), 314.

23 Diderot lived in constant fear that Rousseau would publish his *Confessions*. Jean Fabre discusses this aspect of the affair in his article "Deux Frères ennemis," pp. 193–6. See also A.T., III, 94–5 (*Essai sur les règnes de Claude et de Néron*).

ROUSSEAU THE "CYNIC"

The most bitterly cynical pages of *Le Neveu de Rameau* are those in which Lui bluntly dismisses as "vanités" the sacred duties of patriotism, friendship, gratitude, and paternal solicitude (Fabre, pp. 40–1). This passage, with its burlesque use of the theme "all is vanity" from the Book of Ecclesiastes, can easily be construed as a reply in kind to Jean-Jacques Rousseau, who had publicly insulted Diderot with a quotation from Ecclesiasticus in the Preface to his *Lettre à M. d'Alembert sur les spectacles*.[24] If this is so, we would seem to be dealing with a parody of Rousseau conceived as a cynic and a parasite; and indeed, the opinions expressed by Lui in these two pages are such that they might, in a spirit of malevolence, be attributed to Jean-Jacques.

First, patriotism. Lui proclaims: "Il n'y a plus de patrie" (Fabre, p. 40). And Rousseau, in *Emile*: "où il n'y a plus de patrie il ne peut plus y avoir de citoyens. Ces deux mots, patrie et citoyen, doivent être effacés des langues modernes."[25] Lui continues: "Je ne vois d'un pole à l'autre que des tyrans et des esclaves." And we read in *Emile*, a few pages farther on: "L'homme civil nait, vit et meurt dans l'esclavage ..."[26]

Next, friendship and gratitude. The cynical attitude manifested by Lui toward friendship ("Est-ce qu'on a des amis? Quand on en auroit, faudroit-il en faire des ingrats ?") is that attributed to Rousseau by his former friends after their break. Diderot, in the *Tablettes*, records his version of their association: "de toutes les marques d'amitié qu'on peut donner à un homme, il n'y en a aucune qu'il n'ait reçue de moi, et il ne m'en a jamais donné aucune."[27] As for gratitude on Rousseau's part, Diderot makes the following comment: "il disoit qu'il haïssoit tous ceux qui l'obligeoient, et il l'a bien fait voir."[28] And Grimm, in September

---

24 See the critical edition by M. Fuchs (Geneva, Droz, 1948), 9; and Anatole Feugère, "Pourquoi Rousseau a remanié la Préface de la *Lettre à d'Alembert*," *Annales J.-J. Rousseau*, xx (1931), 127–62.

25 *Emile*, Pléiade ed., iv, 250.

26 Ibid., 253. Cf. *Du contrat social*, Pléiade, ed., iii, 351: "L'homme est né libre, et par-tout il est dans les fers."

27 *Tablettes*, in *Diderot Studies*, iii (1961), 316. Cf. Rousseau's letter to Diderot, 23 or 24 March 1757: "Je ne veux que de l'amitié, et c'est la seule chose qu'on me refuse. Ingrat, je ne t'ai point rendu de Service, mais je t'ai aimé ..." (*Corr.*, ed. Leigh, iv, 195). For Rousseau's views on friendship, see *Œuvres*, Pléiade ed., i, 1432–4.

28 *Tablettes*, in *Diderot Studies*, iii (1961), 318. The *Essai sur les règnes de Claude et de Néron* contains the following observation: "Ce qu'il [Rousseau] a écrit à M. de Malesherbes, il me l'a dit vingt fois : 'Je me sens le cœur ingrat; je hais les bienfaiteurs, parce que le bienfait exige de la reconnaissance, que la reconnaissance est un devoir; et que le devoir m'est insupportable'" (A.T., iii, 98). In his letter to Malesherbes of 4 January 1762, Rousseau had blamed his "indomptable esprit de liberté" and his "paresse" for the fact that he found the slightest social obligations unbearable: "Voila pourquoi, quoique le commerce ordinaire des hommes me soit

1762, criticizes severely the "apologie des ingrats" found in *Emile*,[29] where Rousseau had written: "L'ingratitude seroit plus rare, si les bienfaits à usure étoient moins communs. ... L'ingratitude n'est pas dans le cœur de l'homme; mais l'interêt y est : il y a moins d'obligés ingrats, que de bienfaiteurs intéressés. ... Le cœur ne reçoit de loix que de lui-même; en voulant l'enchaîner on le dégage, on l'enchaîne en le laissant libre. ... jamais un vrai bienfait ne fit d'ingrat."[30] Much less subtle is Lui's judgment of gratitude in *Le Neveu de Rameau*: "La reconnoissance est un fardeau; et tout fardeau est fait pour etre secoué" (Fabre, p. 40).

Finally, paternal solicitude. "Veiller à l'education de ses enfants? ... Vanité. C'est l'affaire d'un precepteur" (p. 40). If this is meant to be an allusion to *Emile*, it is an unfair one; Rousseau had expressly stated that fathers should look after the upbringing of their children and that the engagement of a tutor for Emile is an unwelcome expedient.[31] But the real issue could well lie elsewhere. Lui's total disregard for the welfare of his progeny, affirmed repeatedly on p. 41, reminds us of Rousseau's abandonment of his own children – a badly kept secret which he tells us he had early confided to certain intimate friends, including Denis Diderot.[32]


## MUSIC

If the object of this section were simply to demonstrate that Lui's musical theories correspond to those of Jean-Jacques Rousseau, it would suffice to quote the succinct and unequivocal statement by Jean Fabre concerning the pages of *Le Neveu de Rameau* that deal with questions of music: "Rameau ne développe aucune théorie qu'on ne puisse retrouver dans le *Dictionnaire de musique*, tant calomnié, de Rousseau" (p. 218, n. 248). This, taken by itself, seems to give considerable weight to the hypothesis that Lui is a caricature of Jean-Jacques; but we cannot pass over in silence the fact that, because Rousseau's ideas on music are commonly considered to be those of Diderot himself, critics have felt justified in drawing the conclusion that the character Lui is a self-portrait of the author. Which of these two interpretations is the more

odieux, l'intime amitié m'est si chere, parce qu'il n'y a plus de devoirs pour elle. On suit son cœur et tout est fait. Voila encore pourquoy j'ai toujours tant redouté les bienfaits. Car tout bienfait exige reconnoissance; et je me sens le cœur ingrat par cela seul que la reconnoissance est un devoir" (*Œuvres*, Pléiade ed., I, 1132).

29 *Corr. lit.*, 1 September 1762, v, 151: "Ce que je voudrais encore effacer du livre de l'Education, c'est cette étrange apologie des ingrats; M. Rousseau prétend qu'il n'y en a point."

30 *Emile*, Pléiade ed., IV, 521-2.

31 Ibid., 263.                                      32 *Confessions*, Pléiade ed., I, 357.

likely? No answer can be given to this question until we have reviewed the part played by the Encyclopedists in the "Querelle des Bouffons" of 1752–4.

It was during these years, as we know, that the relations between Diderot and Rousseau began to deteriorate.[33] Shortly after the first performance of *Le Devin du village* at Fontainebleau (18 October 1752), they had quarrelled over Rousseau's refusal to take the steps required to obtain the pension which had been promised him.[34] This first dispute was undoubtedly patched over quite readily; but the breach had scarcely had time to heal when Rousseau published his Preface to *Narcisse* (late January 1753), wherein he revealed for the first time the anti-philosophic tendency of his thought.[35] This public show of independence was not calculated to please the editor-in-chief of the *Encyclopédie*; it can only have added fuel to the fire.[36] Meanwhile, during these first months of 1753, the two friends seem to have been engaged in a disagreement over two other questions, closely interrelated: the upcoming première of *Le Devin du village* in Paris, and the relative virtues of French and Italian music.

First, Rousseau's *intermède*. *Le Devin* opened in Paris at the Opéra (1 March 1753) to enthusiastic applause. Its success was immediate, bringing to the proud author-composer new titles of esteem and renown. But the price of glory must needs be paid; it was from this moment that Jean-Jacques noted the first signs of coldness on the part of Diderot and Grimm, who, he declares, could not forgive him for having earned widespread acclaim in a genre for which they themselves had no talent.[37] This accusation of envy is generally regarded as unfounded, for Diderot, it is said, gave the highest praise to the musical qualities of *Le Devin* in his brief allegory entitled *Les Trois Chapitres* (A.T,, XII, 157–70). Jean Guéhenno, for example, evaluates the matter as follows: "Cette fiction [*Les Trois Chapitres*] donnait à Diderot les moyens du plus admirable

33 On 14 March 1757, Diderot expressed his annoyance at Rousseau's conduct in the "Hermitage affair" with these words: "il faut bien que je me venge de tout le mal que vous me faites depuis quatre ans" (*Corr.*, ed. Roth, I, 234–5).

34 According to Rousseau, this quarrel took place on 21 October (*Confessions*, Pléiade ed., I, 381).

35 "dans la Préface qui est un de mes bons écrits, je commençai de mettre à découvert mes principes un peu plus que je n'avois fait jusqu'alors" (*Confessions*, Pléiade ed., I, 388). In this Preface (*Œuvres*, Pléiade ed., II, 959–74), Jean-Jacques cynically insults philosophy, decries the doctrine of enlightened self-interest, and praises Spartan egalitarianism.

36 Grimm, speaking of Rousseau's "préface outrée," seems to resent the fact that its publication was completely gratuitous: "Cette préface, qu'il fit imprimer sans aucun sujet, n'est pas trop bonne ... si vous en exceptez quelques pages dignes de M. de Montesquieu" (*Corr. lit.*, 15 February 1754, II, 322).

37 *Confessions*, Pléiade ed., I, 386–7.

et du plus sensible compte rendu du *Devin* qu'on ait jamais écrit. Si Jean-Jacques ne fut pas content, c'est qu'il était insatiable. Ainsi les compères s'aidaient-ils les uns les autres, autant qu'ils le pouvaient."[38] This judgment is accurate up to a point; but it ignores a most important fact – that the purpose of *Les Trois Chapitres* was less to laud the merits of *Le Devin* than to criticize the *divertissement* ("Scène VIII et dernière"), complete with ballet, pantomime, and *vaudeville*, which Rousseau had added to his operetta for its Parisian première.[39]

It is Rousseau who tells us most of what we know concerning this little work of Diderot's. He informs us in a note found among his papers that *Les Trois Chapitres, ou la Vision de la nuit du mardi-gras au mercredi des cendres*[40] was composed on the occasion of his *divertissement* (*not* on the occasion of the *intermède* of which it is part), and that Diderot had it printed but not published.[41] It was therefore neither a pamphlet in the "Querelle des Bouffons" nor, as M. Guéhenno believes, a public manifestation of support for a fellow Encyclopedist. If we consult the text itself, we find that Diderot follows the "prophetic vision" technique popularized by Grimm in his *Petit Prophète de Boehmischbroda*, which had appeared early in February 1753.[42] But, whereas Grimm's prophet-hero had suffered through the performance of a boring French opera, Diderot shows his "little prophet" delighted, on his second trip to Paris, with the music of *Le Devin du village*. Delighted with everything, that is, except the final scene. Just before the *divertissement*

38 Jean Guéhenno, *Jean-Jacques*, nouvelle édition (Paris, Gallimard, 1962, 2 vols.), I, 274. The editors of the Pléiade edition of the *Confessions* concur in this opinion (I, 1450, n. 5 to p. 386).

39 In his *Dictionnaire de musique*, s.v. "Fête," Rousseau writes: "Divertissement de chant et de danse qu'on introduit dans un acte d'opéra, et qui interrompt ou suspend toujours l'action. ... La différence qu'on assigne à l'Opéra entre les mots de *fête* et de *divertissement* est que le premier s'applique plus particulièrement aux tragédies, et le second aux ballets" (*Œuvres*, Hachette ed., VII, 118). The text of *Le Devin du village* is given in *Œuvres*, Pléiade ed., II, 1093–1114. For the composition of the *divertissement*, see *Rousseau juge de Jean-Jacques*, Pléiade ed., I, 870 n.

40 The subtitle reminds us of that Shrove Tuesday (6 March 1753) when, for the second time in three days, *Le Devin du village* was performed at Bellevue by Madame de Pompadour and other members of the court.

41 Rousseau's note on *Les Trois Chapitres* is reproduced in *Corr.*, ed. Leigh, II, 229: "Ce petit Ecrit, qui est une espèce de continuation du petit Prophête, fut fait par M. Diderot à l'occasion du Divertissement du Devin du village, qui n'étoit pas composé quand la Piéce fut donnée à Fontainebleau, et qui n'y fut ajoûté que quand elle fut donnée à Paris. Ce divertissement, d'abord moins goûté que les Scénes, fut ensuite un très grand succés. Les trois Chapitres furent imprimés, mais il en fut tiré très peu d'exemplaires, et ils n'ont jamais été publiés; de Sorte que c'est un Ouvrage encore absolument neuf." Assézat describes the pamphlet as follows: "36 pages in-8º, *S. l. s. d.*, et sans nom d'imprimeur" (A.T., XII, 140).

42 Grimm's little work, dated 25 January 1753, was published by Maurice Tourneux in *Corr. lit.*, XVI, 313–36.

is to begin, the little prophet is taken by the hair of his head and wafted away from the theatre. He must not be allowed to remain, says the "Voice" of his vision, lest he become angry and lest his talent for composing music be contaminated by what is to follow, "car la joie n'y est pas" (A.T., XII, 165). Thus concludes the second of the "three chapters"; in the third, Diderot rewrites the *divertissement* according to his own taste. His version (in contrast to that composed by Rousseau, of course) is marked by "le bon sens et l'honnêteté" (A.T., XII, 170).

This final chapter leaves no doubt as to the ambivalence of Diderot's sentiments with regard to *Le Devin du village*.[43] And indeed, we have a statement in his own words as to the import for him of *Les Trois Chapitres*. In his *Entretiens sur le Fils naturel* (1757), after a brief lecture by Dorval on the subject of ballet in the theatre, Diderot-Moi makes the following observation: "Je vous avoue que je ne vous entends qu'à moitié, et que je ne vous entendrais point du tout, sans une feuille volante qui parut il y a quelques années. L'auteur, mécontent du ballet qui termine le *Devin du village*, en proposait un autre, et je me trompe fort, ou ses idées ne sont pas éloignées des vôtres."[44] In view of this, and of what we know of the relations between Diderot and Rousseau, there is every reason to believe that the *philosophe* would have tried to persuade the author of *Le Devin* to adopt his suggestions for the *divertissement*. If so, it was in vain; for Jean-Jacques, who refused to be governed by others' opinions,[45] was to show himself adamant in his rejection of all proposals to modify his *intermède*. When the musical score was published sometime in March, many were offended by the disdainful petulance of the "avertissement" with which he saw fit to preface it.[46] Was Diderot among those at whom the "avertissement" was aimed? When the *philosophe* received his complimentary copy from the author,[47] did he react by writing *Les Trois Chapitres*? We cannot be certain about these things. We do know, however, that he objected so strongly to

---

43 His mixed feelings are indicated also by the subtitle – *La Vision de la nuit du mardi-gras au mercredi des cendres* – with its suggestion of a passage from joy to sorrow.

44 A.T., VII, 158. Editors of the *Entretiens* seem to have overlooked this reference to *Les Trois Chapitres*.

45 This was especially true in the case of Diderot, who tended to be domineering. All of their disputes, says Rousseau, followed the same pattern, "lui me prescrivant ce qu'il prétendoit que je devois faire, et moi m'en défendant, parce que je croyois ne le devoir pas" (*Confessions*, Pléiade ed., I, 381).

46 In the "avertissement" Rousseau spurns all the improvements suggested by his friends because, he says, "n'ayant fait cet ouvrage que pour mon amusement, son vrai succés est de me plaire : Or personne ne sait mieux que moi comment il doit être pour me plaire le plus" (*Œuvres*, Pléiade ed., II, 1096).

47 See A. J. Freer, "L'Exemplaire du *Devin du village* offert par Rousseau à Diderot," *Revue d'Histoire Littéraire de la France*, July–September 1966, pp. 401–8.

Rousseau's *divertissement* that he took the pains to have his pamphlet printed and distributed among a few friends. It is perhaps fortunate that he had the prudence not to make it public.

Further evidence that all may not have been well between Diderot and Rousseau in 1753 is found in the *Lettre sur la musique française*, published in late November of that year. No one, to be sure, could condone the harsh and abusive criticism of French music which marks the conclusion of this letter,[48] and Grimm undoubtedly spoke for Diderot as well as for himself when he wrote: "On peut dire qu'en général les gens sensés n'approuvent point le ton de la lettre de M. Rousseau. Quand on a de bonnes raisons à dire, on ne doit pas employer les invectives."[49] But it is the section of Rousseau's letter leading up to his notorious concluding paragraph that holds the greatest interest for us. There, in the course of several pages, Jean-Jacques gives a scathing analysis of the musical inadequacies he descried in Lully's opera *Armide*. The reason why he singled out this particular musical composition as the object of his attack on French music is explained in his opening remarks: he was complying (though only partially) with the wishes of the author of an anonymous pamphlet who had suggested that the musical quarrel might be settled in a rational way if someone skilled in music were to make a detailed comparison of a scene from Lully's *Armide* and a similar scene from *Sesostri, re d'Egitto* by Terradellas.[50] We know, of course, that the author of the pamphlet, entitled *Au Petit Prophète de Boehmisch-broda, au Grand Prophète Monet*, was Denis Diderot.

It seems probable at first sight that Diderot's pamphlet and Rousseau's letter were the result of a concerted plan engineered by the Encyclopedists, with Diderot setting the stage on which his friend was to perform; but a close inspection of the pamphlet indicates that the answer is not quite so simple as that. This brief work, which occupies only five pages in the Assézat-Tourneux edition, appears to have been Diderot's

48 "Je crois avoir fait voir qu'il n'y a ni mesure ni mélodie dans la musique françoise, parce que la langue n'en est pas susceptible; que le chant françois n'est qu'un aboiement continuel, insupportable à toute oreille non prévenue; que l'harmonie est brute, sans expression, et sentant uniquement son remplissage d'écolier; que les airs françois ne sont point des airs; que le récitatif françois n'est point du récitatif. D'où je conclus que les François n'ont point de musique et n'en peuvent avoir, ou que, si jamais ils en ont une, ce sera tant pis pour eux" (*Œuvres*, Hachette ed., vi, 197–8).

49 *Corr. lit.*, ii, 313 (1 January 1754).

50 "je ne tenterai pas ... le parallèle qui a été proposé cet hiver, dans un écrit adressé au petit Prophète et à ses adversaires, de deux morceaux de musique, l'un italien et l'autre françois, qui y sont indiqués. La scène italienne ... étant peu connue à Paris, peu de gens pourroient suivre la comparaison ... Mais, quant à la scène françoise, j'en crayonnerai volontiers l'analyse ..." (*Œuvres*, Hachette, ed., vi, 193).

first contribution to the "Querelle."[51] He begins by castigating both camps – the Queen's Corner and the King's Corner, as they were called – for the viciousness and the frivolity of their recriminations. Then, giving recognition to the fact that any clash between two such diverse genres as French serious opera and Italian *opera buffa* was bound to generate more heat than light, he proposes a technical comparison of the two *tragic* operas of Lully and Terradellas, in the hope that, whatever the result of the inquiry, "les raisons succéderont aux personnalités, le sens commun à l'épigramme, et la lumière aux *prophéties*" (A.T., XII, 155). Thereupon follows a most interesting paragraph that gives every sign of having been composed with Jean-Jacques in view:

Si du milieu du parterre, d'où j'élève ma voix, j'étais assez heureux pour être écouté des deux Coins et que la dispute s'engageât avec les armes que je propose, peut-être y prendrais-je quelque part. Je communiquerais sans vanité et sans prétention ce que je puis avoir de connaissance de la langue italienne, de la mienne, de la musique et des beaux-arts. Je dirais ma pensée quand je la croirais juste, tout prêt à rendre grâce à celui qui me démontrerait qu'elle ne l'est pas. Eh! qu'avons-nous de mieux à faire que de chercher la vérité et que d'aimer celui qui nous l'enseigne? S'il a de la dureté dans le caractère, comme il arrive quelquefois, pardonnons-lui ce défaut quand il nous en dédommagera par des observations sensées et par des vues profondes. La nature ne nous présente la plus belle des fleurs qu'environnée d'épines, et le plus délicieux des fruits qu'hérissé de feuilles aiguës. Ceci est une leçon que je me fais d'avance à moi-même, afin que si quelqu'un se croit offensé par cet écrit et me répond avec aigreur, rien ne m'empêche de profiter de ses raisons (A.T., XII, 155).

These lines, full of sweet reasonableness and not-so-sweet mockery, have sometimes been taken as alluding to "le jaloux Rameau" whose name Diderot had invoked on the previous page. But Rameau, although known for his difficult character, had not yet joined the fray and could scarcely have been offended by this conciliatory pamphlet.[52] Rousseau,

51 A.T., XII, 152–6. There are two indications that the author is a newcomer to the "Querelle des Bouffons." The first is found in the epigraph, "Semper ego auditor tantum?" (p. 152); these are the opening words of Juvenal's first Satire. The second indication, even more explicit, is contained in the opening sentence of the long paragraph quoted below.

52 Diderot's pamphlet, dated 21 February 1753, appeared more than a year before Rameau's first contribution to the "Querelle" (his *Observations sur notre instinct pour la musique et son principe*, 1754). The time element, and also the fact that Diderot published his little work anonymously, would seem to preclude the possibility that the paragraph in question was introduced, as some have said, in order to avoid making enemies of Rameau and his partisans. Indeed, these lines can most readily be explained as directed at someone who knew the author's identity and who

on the other hand, had already written his *Lettre sur la musique française* except for the pages devoted to *Armide*.[53] We may safely presume that Diderot, the "Aristarque sévère et judicieux," had discussed the inflammatory letter with his friend and that his intervention here was an attempt to bring Rousseau around to a reasonable position; indeed, he seems to be chiding Jean-Jacques for the acrimonious tone of his previous writings while at the same time challenging him to prove the superiority of Italian music by scientific demonstration.

Once more, however, Rousseau refused to follow Diderot's suggestions. In the *Lettre sur la musique française*, when it was finally completed, he chose to ignore entirely the Italian opera by Terradellas; he took pains to season his criticisms of *Armide* with heavy irony; he added a sarcastic footnote (undoubtedly aimed at Diderot) in which he complains of "ces modérés conciliateurs [qui] ne voudroient pas de goûts exclusifs";[54] he expressed his irritation by the unbridled language with which the letter ends; and in the second edition, which appeared before the end of the year, he maliciously supported his attack on the French language by an appeal to what Diderot himself had said in the *Lettre sur les sourds et muets*.[55] Everything, indeed, seems to justify our concluding that a certain bitterness marked the relationship of the two men during the "Querelle des Bouffons."

But, however much the question of music was involved in the growing estrangement of these two friends, we have still to explain how Rousseau and the "Querelle des Bouffons" fit into the overall pattern

might have been expected to make a vigorous reply. The fact that Rousseau did reply – and vigorously – to the pamphlet would seem to put the matter beyond doubt.

53 The "avertissement" of the first edition bears a piece of information that does not appear in the second: "Cette lettre, à peu de lignes près, est écrite depuis plus d'un an." Cited by Louis J. Courtois, *Chronologie critique de la vie et des œuvres de Jean-Jacques Rousseau*, in *Annales J.-J. Rousseau*, xv (1923), 73, n. 2. This means that the *Lettre sur la musique française* was on the point of completion before the end of 1752. Diderot's pamphlet, in which he suggests the comparison of *Armide* and *Sesostri*, was written several months later.

54 "Plusieurs condamnent l'exclusion totale que les amateurs de musique donnent sans balancer à la musique françoise : ces modérés conciliateurs ne voudroient pas de goûts exclusifs, comme si l'amour des bonnes choses devoit faire aimer les mauvaises" (*Œuvres*, Hachette ed., vi, 176, n. 3).

55 Ibid., 169, n. 1. See the critical edition of the *Lettre sur les sourds et muets* by Paul H. Meyer (*Diderot Studies*, vii [1965]). Diderot, in affirming the superiority of the French language in clarity and precision of expression, had stated that certain other languages are to be preferred "dans les chaires & sur les théâtres" (p. 67). In the final paragraph, however, he manifests his warm appreciation of the literary qualities of his native tongue (p. 89). Rousseau, in his note, refers specifically to the "Additions" of Diderot's letter (ed. Meyer, pp. 90–121). There, the French language is characterized as "naturellement uniforme & tardive," whereas a language more suited for the art of persuasion would be "variée, abondante, impétueuse, pleine d'images & d'inversions" (p. 110).

of *Le Neveu de Rameau*. Is it not true that the main thrust of the satire is directed against those who conspired to bring about the downfall of the *Encyclopédie*? And do we not tend to think of the "Querelle" as a rather pleasant interlude in the ideological struggle having little or no connection with events which we know helped to arouse Diderot's resentment, such as the publication of Palissot's *Petites Lettres sur de grands philosophes* or the persistent attacks by Fréron in the *Année littéraire*? Why, then, does the dispute over French and Italian music play such an important role in the dialogue? Does its presence there have anything to do with Diderot's hostility toward Jean-Jacques Rousseau?

The answer is a simple one, and it is supplied by no less an authority than the co-editor of the *Encyclopédie*, Jean d'Alembert. Surveying in 1759 some of the aspects of the "Querelle," d'Alembert informs us that Rousseau's tactless intervention in the dispute had far greater significance than it is usually given; the *Lettre sur la musique française*, he avers, was the initial spark that ignited the flames of public indignation against the philosophic party.[56] This observation is most enlightening, for it suggests that Diderot, like d'Alembert, must have tended to blame Rousseau for having set on foot the movement that was destined to culminate in the suppression of the *Encyclopédie*. If such was the case, we may be sure that his exasperation at Rousseau's imprudent tirade against French music was not lessened by the fact that he himself had vainly counselled moderation.

It would seem, then, that the animosity between Rousseau and Diderot occasioned by the "Querelle des Bouffons" had really little to do with the issues of the "Querelle." On these, the two men were in substantial agreement. Along with Grimm and d'Alembert, they both held for an expressionistic theory of musical "imitation"; they were of one mind also on the artificiality of French music and on the superior musical qualities of the Italian language. But Rousseau, as we know, was inclined to be an extremist, even a fanatic, on every issue on which he took a stand; it was this characteristic lack of moderation, not his ideas on music, that kindled the wrath of the *philosophe*. This observation is of major importance for our interpretation of *Le Neveu de Rameau*, for, if Diderot did indeed draw a caricature of Jean-Jacques

56 *De la liberté de la musique*, in *Mélanges* (1773 ed.), IV, 390: "L'Encyclopédie, dont les principaux Auteurs avoient le malheur de penser comme M. Rousseau, & la témérité de le dire, ne fut pas epargnée dans ces circonstances; ce fut comme la premiere étincelle de l'embrasement général, qui en gagnant de proche en proche, a depuis échauffé tant d'esprits contre cet ouvrage. On représenta les Auteurs comme une société formée pour détruire à la fois la Religion, l'autorité, les mœurs & la Musique."

in his satire – and who can doubt that, in his eyes, the author of the *Lettre sur la musique française* was richly deserving of that honour – we might expect that the enthusiastic temperament of the real-life model would be given special attention.

Returning now to our original problem – the identification of Lui – let us consider whether our discussion of the "Querelle des Bouffons" can help to bring us closer to a solution. The first thing to remark is that there is no question in Diderot's satire of a debate on the subject of music; as soon as the topic is broached the dialogue turns into a monologue delivered by Lui, the self-acknowledged expert on matters musical. Moi, pleading ignorance (Fabre, p. 77), remains silent; occasionally he interrupts the flow of Lui's eloquence to pose a modest question (pp. 79, 86) or to signify that he shares the views of the speaker (p. 82). The ideas expressed, though colourfully presented, are most disappointing; they are those that had been developed *ad nauseam* by the Encyclopedists in the 1750s. Fortunately, the exposition of musical theory is redeemed by the superb mime scene in which Lui illustrates what he has been saying about music and musicians (pp. 82–5).

What, we may ask, is the function of the six pages (exclusive of the pantomime) devoted to questions of music? Everywhere else, Diderot's dialogue is marked by the severest economy; yet here we have a lengthy, one-sided reiteration of banalities that lacks both the freshness of novelty and the spice of polemic. Artistically, this is inexcusable unless it has a special purpose; but that purpose is not explained by any of the current theories. If Lui is intended to be a portrait of Jean-François Rameau, who is not known to have played any significant role in the "Querelle des Bouffons," a few lines would have sufficed to sketch in his views on music. If, on the other hand, Diderot is painting himself beneath the figure of Lui, he can have no other object in this section than to satirize himself as an irrepressible babbler. It is highly unlikely that he thought of himself in those terms.

There are, however, excellent reasons why the author of *Le Neveu de Rameau* should have wished to caricature Jean-Jacques in the guise of an enthusiastic musician; and the text of the satire seems to indicate that this is precisely what he did. The caricature is a masterpiece in itself. A few deft strokes are enough to fill in the general outline: the word "animal" is added to the commonplace "cri de la passion," "cri de l'homme passionné" (Fabre, pp. 86, 87); a slight exaggeration is given to Rousseau's attack on the French language, characterized here as "roide, sourde, lourde, pesante, pedantesque et monotone" (p. 81). But it is the fanaticism with which Jean-Jacques defended his views that we should expect to be given high relief; and when we see Lui begin his monologue rather academically with a definition of the word "chant" (p. 78), then warm to his subject, making sweeping pronouncements with supreme self-confidence and reinforcing his opinions with bursts of vigorous sarcasm; when we see him gradually reaching a state of exaltation, gesticulating wildly, foaming at the mouth, then suddenly caught up by the demon of music and flung into a vertiginous pantomime that reaches the heights of Bacchanalian frenzy, we can justifiably conclude that the disapproval registered by Moi (p. 84) reflects not only the attitude of a Socrates in the presence of a satyr but also the reaction of Diderot to that buffoon of the musical world, Jean-Jacques Rousseau.

### DETAILS OF A LITERARY PORTRAIT

The many points of similarity that critics have remarked between the real Jean-François Rameau and Lui of our dialogue make it impossible to deny that Diderot intended to depict at least certain physical features of this singular personage with a high degree of fidelity. A glance at the documents assembled by M. Fabre in the Appendix of his edition of *Le Neveu de Rameau* (pp. 243–54) leaves the reader in amazement at the skill with which the author succeeded in capturing the essential traits of the younger Rameau as he is described by his closest friends. But the brilliance of this artistic triumph must not be allowed to blind us to the fact that our knowledge of the historical individual is meagre in comparison with the wealth of detail concerning Lui to be found in Diderot's satire. Therefore, however closely Rameau's nephew resembles the portrait, it remains quite possible that the portrait is more unlike than it is like Rameau's nephew, especially in its moral dimensions. We can be certain that at least some of the sentiments and ideas lent to Lui were either imagined by the author in the interests of universality or borrowed from other contemporaries for purposes of satire; but no one has yet determined to what extent Diderot saw fit to depart from the intellectual and moral idiosyncracies displayed by the living model.

If there is no certainty as to the overall veracity of the portrait, neither is it entirely clear why Diderot chose Jean-François Rameau as the ostensible hero (or anti-hero) of his satire. All, of course, are in agreement that he would naturally have been attracted by the literary possibilities offered by a character of such striking originality. But is this all that we can affirm? Some would go farther, maintaining that there must have existed between the author and his model a certain spiritual affinity, and that the self-knowledge arising from contact with the down-at-heel musician found expression in the (supposed) self-portraiture of the dialogue. This assumption, however, is dependent upon an interpretation of the work that is not universally accepted. For those who find the "Diderot-Lui" theory implausible, there remains another possibility: that Diderot chose to depict Jean-François Rameau for the simple reason that the latter was a living parody of another "original," Jean-Jacques Rousseau. This hypothesis assumes that there are some traits which, at least in Diderot's view, the two men had in common, but that the portrayal of Rameau is subservient to the caricature of Jean-Jacques. We have already seen evidence to show that Lui, who espouses all of Rousseau's theories on music, has also been endowed with two outstanding characteristics – inconsistency and cynicism – that could have been modelled upon similar traits manifested by Jean-Jacques. We may now turn our attention to the finer details of the portrait.

*Ambition*

Despite his acknowledged mediocrity, Lui is haunted by dreams of the greatness that would be his if he could turn out musical compositions with the same skill as his famous uncle: "l'on te diroit le matin que tu es un grand homme; tu lirois dans l'histoire des *Trois siecles* que tu es un grand homme; tu serois convaincu le soir que tu es un grand homme; et le grand homme, Rameau le neveu, s'endormiroit au doux murmure de l'eloge qui retentiroit dans son oreille ..."[57] But alas! the dreams will never be realized; it is, after all, too much to expect that a man should measure up to his great forbears: "Et le nom que je porte donc? Rameau! s'appeler Rameau, cela est gênant" (p. 99).

Since caricature is not bound by the rules of strict logic, this could well be a barb aimed at Rousseau's fierce ambition and his resultant indignation whenever it was implied that he was "le petit Rousseau" in comparison with the poet Jean-Baptiste. "Quelques auteurs se tuent d'appeler le Poete Rousseau le grand Rousseau durant ma vie," wrote Jean-Jacques in 1755 or 1756. "Quand je serai mort le Poete Rousseau sera un grand Poete. Mais il ne sera plus le grand Rousseau."[58] Diderot was perhaps thinking especially of Jean-Jacques when he made the following reflection in September 1762: "j'aimerois mieux n'avoir point

57 Fabre, pp. 16–17. The reference to the *Trois siècles de la littérature française* (1772) of Sabatier de Castres is Diderot's little revenge for the hostile article devoted to him in this critical dictionary of authors. If our interpretation of the dialogue is correct, there is additional irony in putting the reference in the mouth of Rousseau-Lui, for the article on Jean-Jacques is extravagant in its praise of his originality and the sublimity of his style.

58 *Mon Portrait*, in *Œuvres*, Pléiade ed., I, 1129.

de nom du tout, que de n'être qu'un petit homme et porter un grand nom."[59]

## Envy

The discussion of genius in the first part of the dialogue (Fabre, pp. 7–17) culminates in the admission by Lui that he scorns men of genius because he is envious of their success: "Je n'en ai jamais entendu louer un seul que son eloge ne m'ait fait secrettement enrager. Je suis envieux. Lors que j'apprends de leur vie privée quelque trait qui les degrade, je l'écoute avec plaisir. Cela nous rapproche. J'en supporte plus aisement ma mediocrité. ... Oui, oui, je suis mediocre et faché" (Fabre, p. 15).

The envious rage that fills Lui's soul has its parellel in the portrait of René-Rousseau given in the *Histoire de Madame de Montbrillant*. The passage in question (III, 170) was undoubtedly reworked by Diderot: "Il est dévoré d'envie. Il enrage quand il paraît quelque chose de beau qui n'est pas de lui."[60]

## Originality

In the opening pages of his prologue, Diderot informs us that Lui, "un des plus bizarres personnages de ce pais ou Dieu n'en a pas laissé manquer" (Fabre, p. 4), is so unusual a character that he merits close attention if only for the sake of curiosity. The stress placed on his "originalité" (p. 4), is reinforced by classifying him among "ces originaux la" (p. 5) whose company may sometimes prove useful to the observant moralist. This introduction arouses in the reader expectations that are amply fulfilled as the dialogue unfolds; we find no difficulty in accepting Lui's judgment of himself when he affirms: "Je suis rare dans mon espece, oui, tres rare" (p. 65).

How many times must Diderot have heard words similar to these from the lips of Jean-Jacques Rousseau! Nothing, indeed, is more frequently attested in the *Confessions* than the author's profound conviction that he is unique among men. "Je sens mon cœur et je connois les hommes," he tells us on the very first page. "Je ne suis fait comme aucun

---

59 Letter to Sophie Volland, 16 September 1762 (*Corr.*, ed. Roth, IV, 151). His real opinion of Rousseau, however, is rather that found in the *Réfutation d'Helvétius*: "Quelle que soit la révolution qui se fasse dans les esprits, jamais Rousseau ne tombera dans la classe des auteurs méprisés. Il sera parmi les littérateurs ce que sont parmi les peintres les mauvais dessinateurs, grands coloristes" (A.T., II, 412).

60 These words are put in the mouth of Madame Garnier (Madame Diderot). It must be remembered that Rousseau, in a passage of *Emile*, had confessed to having an envious nature: "Ce qu'il y avoit en moi de plus difficile à détruire étoit une orgueilleuse misanthropie, une certaine aigreur contre les riches et les heureux du monde, comme s'ils l'eussent été à mes dépends et que leur prétendu bonheur eût été usurpé sur le mien" (Pléiade ed., IV, 564).

de ceux que j'ai vus; j'ose croire n'être fait comme aucun de ceux qui existent."[61] Although he thought of himself as an "original," it was not in the pejorative sense of that word. His peculiar behaviour, he confesses, undoubtedly gave to him "l'air le plus bizarre et le plus fou dans le public et surtout parmi mes connoissances"; but he defends himself stoutly against the charge of singularity: "On m'a imputé de vouloir être original et faire autrement que les autres. En vérité je ne songeois guére à faire ni comme les autres ni autrement qu'eux. Je desirois sincerement de faire ce qui étoit bien."[62] Today we are prone to accept Rousseau's good faith in this matter; his contemporaries, however, were almost unanimous in judging otherwise.

## The Music-master

Lui, recalling his younger days, entertains Moi with a rollicking account of his experiences as a teacher of music (Fabre, pp. 32–5). He frankly admits that at that time he knew nothing about the subject, with the result that his pupils profited not at all from his instruction (p. 32). But the intervening years have brought changes; his lessons are now improved to the point where they are at least passably good. "La basse fondamentale du cher oncle a bien simplifié tout cela" (p. 37). At present, his is an honest profession – though not practised without a certain artifice, for he is obliged to give to his clients the impression that he is much sought after: "Dans une heure d'ici, il faut que je sois la; dans deux heures, chez madame la duchesse une telle. Je suis attendu a diner chez une belle marquise; et au sortir de la, c'est un concert chez Mr le baron de Bacq, rue neuve des Petits Champs" (p. 35).

Jean-Jacques too, as a young man, had pursued the same career and had made similar progress. At Lausanne, in the summer of 1730, he had undertaken to teach music despite the fact that he could not read a single note. His pupils, he assures us, "ne devinrent pas de grands croque-notes";[63] and, unfortunately, they were few. But the following winter, in Neuchâtel, his new profession proved more lucrative. "J'apprenois insensiblement la musique en l'enseignant."[64] In 1732, after a year spent in a clerical occupation, he began devoting all his time to giving music lessons at Chambéry. It was only after October 1733, at which time a month-long illness gave him the leisure to "devour" Ra-

---

61 *Confessions*, in *Œuvres*, Pléiade ed., I, 5.

62 Ibid., 56. Cf. *Rousseau juge de Jean-Jacques*, ibid., 850. The cruellest parody of Rousseau the "original" had been the portrait of "Le Philosophe" in the eighth scene of Palissot's one-act comedy entitled *Le Cercle, ou les Originaux* (*Œuvres*, Liège ed., II, 41–7).

63 *Confessions*, Pléiade ed., I, 150.

64 Ibid., 153.

meau's *Traité de l'harmonie*, that music became an all-absorbing passion with him.[65] Thereafter, his success as a music-master was enormous:

j'eus bientôt plus d'écoliéres qu'il ne m'en falloit pour remplacer ma paye de secretaire. ... me voila tout à coup jetté parmi le beau monde, admis, recherché dans les meilleures maisons; par tout un accueil gracieux, caressant, un air de fête : d'aimables Demoiselles bien parées m'attendent, me reçoivent avec empressement ... on chante, on cause, on rit, on s'amuse; je ne sors de là que pour aller ailleurs en faire autant ...[66]

## Some Minor Details

There are a number of other passages in *Le Neveu de Rameau* which indicate that Diderot, in his depiction of Lui, borrowed certain traits from Jean-Jacques Rousseau. Before we undertake the examination of those passages, two precautionary remarks should be made: first, that our evaluation of the data must make allowance for the distortion and exaggeration that are proper to literary caricature; and secondly, that we must banish any preconceptions we may have concerning the element of time. Although a close study of the text shows that the satire was begun in 1761 or 1762, we know that the author returned to his manuscript several times over a lengthy period to make interpolations of one kind or another.[67] No care was taken in these revisions to avoid anachronisms; real-life incidents that actually took place some years apart are treated as if they were contemporaneous. There is every reason to suppose, therefore, that the same disdain for strict chronology marked the creation of the character Lui. If the "Rousseau-Lui" hypothesis is correct, we shall no doubt find that Lui is not modelled after Rousseau as we know him at any given period of his life, but is a burlesque composite of all that Jean-Jacques had been from his earliest youth until the end of his association with Diderot.

Let us begin with the setting of the dialogue. The scene opens in the Café de la Régence. Lui detaches himself from the group of idlers with whom he has been watching the progress of a chess match and strikes up a conversation with Moi. As they speak, the afternoon draws on; finally, Lui terminates the interview and hurries off to the Opéra. We are given the impression, from his familiarity with both chess and music, that his time is largely divided between the cafés and the theatres. And we are reminded that Rousseau, during his early years in Paris, used to

65 Ibid., 184.
66 Ibid., 188.
67 See Rudolf Schlösser, *Rameaus Neffe*, 11–29. To this basic study of the chronology of the dialogue should be added that found in *Entretiens sur "Le Neveu de Rameau,"* ed. M. Duchet and M. Launay, 137–72.

spend his afternoons in similar fashion while waiting for fortune to come his way.[68]

Turning to the portrait itself, we find that there are constant parallels between the character and habits of Lui and those of the citizen of Geneva. The mock-heroic wanderings of the parasite musician seem modelled after those of Rousseau's peripatetic youth: "J'ai voyagé en Boheme, en Allemagne, en Suisse, en Hollande, en Flandres; au diable, au verd" (Fabre, p. 100). His early ambitions, too, resemble those of Jean-Jacques: "Je n'avois pas quinze ans lorsque je me dis, pour la premiere fois : Qu'as tu, Rameau? tu reves. Et a quoi reves tu? que tu voudrois bien avoir fait ou faire quelque chose qui excitat l'admiration de l'univers. Hé, oui; il n'y a qu'a souffler et remuer les doigts."[69] But, like Rousseau, Lui has experienced moments of self-doubt of which Moi takes care to remind him: "Mais j'ai vu un temps que vous vous deseseperiez de n'etre qu'un homme commun."[70] Such fits of despair are balanced at times by Lui's recognition that his great natural gifts could easily make his fortune as a procurer (pp. 22–4), and the poor wretch takes heart: "Alors je me sentois du courage, l'ame elevée; l'esprit subtil, et capable de tout" (p. 24); soon, however, his high resolve dwindles away to nothingness: "Mais ces heureuses dispositions apparemment ne duroient pas; car jusqu'a present, je n'ai pu faire un certain chemin" (ibid.). Thus he alternates, as did Rousseau, between bursts of exalted confidence and periods of deep despondency.[71] Yet, despite his acknowledgement of failure, Lui manifests a spirit of stubborn independence

68 In the *Confessions*, Rousseau describes how he employed "ce court et précieux intervalle qui me restoit encore avant d'être forcé de mendier mon pain"; his mornings were given to memorizing poetry in the Luxembourg Gardens, his afternoons to other weighty matters: "J'avois un autre expédient non moins solide dans les Echecs auxquels je consacrois réguliérement chez Maugis les après-midi des jours que je n'allois pas au spectacle. Je fis là connoissance avec M. de Légal, avec M. Husson, avec Philidor, avec tous les grands joueurs d'echecs de ce tems-là, et n'en devins pas plus habile" (*Œuvres*, Pléiade ed., I, 288).

69 Fabre, p. 99. Rousseau was not yet sixteen years old when he set out from Geneva to conquer the world: "Libre et maitre de moi-même, je croyois pouvoir tout faire, atteindre à tout : je n'avois qu'à m'élancer pour m'élever et voler dans les airs. J'entrois avec sécurité dans le vaste espace du monde; mon mérite alloit le remplir ... en me montrant j'allois occuper de moi l'univers ..." (*Confessions*, Pléiade ed., I, 45). Several years later, convinced of his talent for music, he has similar dreams: "j'allois devenir un homme célébre, un Orphée moderne dont les sons devoient attirer tout l'argent du Perou" (ibid., 207).

70 Fabre, p. 10. After learning of the success of his first *Discours*, Jean-Jacques lost his former feeling of insecurity: "Cette faveur du public nullement briguée et pour un Auteur inconnu, me donna la prémiére assurance véritable de mon talent dont malgré le sentiment interne j'avois toujours douté jusqu'alors" (*Confessions*, Pléiade ed., I, 363).

71 In *Rousseau juge de Jean-Jacques* we read the following self-evaluation: "Il n'y a rien de grand, de beau, de genereux dont par élans il ne soit capable; mais il se lasse bien vite, et retombe aussi-tot dans son inertie : c'est en vain que les actions nobles et belles sont quelques instans dans son courage, la paresse et la timidité qui

typical also of Rousseau: "Chacun a la sienne [sa dignité]; je veux bien oublier la mienne, mais a ma discretion, et non a l'ordre d'autrui. Faut-il qu'on puisse me dire : rampe, et que je sois obligé de ramper?"[72] Such a noble attitude is eminently befitting both the offspring of "Mr Rameau, apoticaire de Dijon, qui est un homme de bien et qui n'a jamais fléchi le genou devant qui que ce soit" (p. 21) and the son of that proud republican of Geneva, the watchmaker and sometime dancing-master Isaac Rousseau.

The closer we approach the portrait of Lui, the more we are struck by his resemblance to Jean-Jacques Rousseau – that is, to Rousseau as he was or as Diderot was pleased to remember him. One of Lui's outstanding characteristics is his frankness of speech (Fabre, pp. 24, 56, 93); and Rousseau, whose polemical writings soon earned him a reputation for unvarnished bluntness, was able as early as 1753 to appeal to his "franchise ordinaire" in the *Lettre sur la musique française.*[73] This trait, of course, was part of his republican heritage, and he took care to endow Saint-Preux with "la franchise suisse" of which he himself was so proud.[74] Again, Lui's admission that he frequents prostitutes (p. 8) recalls the Venetian adventures recorded in the *Confessions* as well as Diderot's accusation that Rousseau "ne haïssait pas les courtisanes" (A.T., III, 96). There are times, too, when Lui is made to repeat statements made by Jean-Jacques, and in the same trenchant tones; compare, for example, his condemnation of the unequal distribution of nature's commodities (pp. 103–4: "Que diable d'oeconomie, des hommes qui regorgent de tout, tandis que d'autres qui ont un estomac importun comme eux, et pas de quoi mettre sous la dent") with the ringing conclusion of Rousseau's *Discours sur l'inégalité*: "il est manifestement contre la Loi de Nature ... qu'une poignée des gens regorge de superfluités, tandis que la multitude affamée manque du nécessaire."[75]

---

succedent bientôt le retiennent, l'aneantissent, et voila comment avec des sentimens quelquefois élevés et grands, il fut toujours petit et nul par sa conduite" (*Œuvres*, Pléiade ed., I, 811).

72 Fabre, p. 47. Cf. *Rousseau juge de Jean-Jacques*: "Le travail ne lui coûte rien pourvu qu'il le fasse à son heure et non pas à celle d'autrui. Il porte sans peine le joug de la nécessité des choses, mais non celui de la volonté des hommes" (*Œuvres*, Pléiade ed., I, 845); also Rousseau's letter to Malesherbes, 4 January 1762: "l'espece de bonheur qu'il me faut, n'est pas tant de faire ce que je veux, que de ne pas faire ce que je ne veux pas" (ibid., 1132).

73 *Œuvres*, Hachette ed., VI, 168.

74 *La Nouvelle Héloïse*, Pléiade ed., II, 295. It is Emile, however, who most resembles Lui: "Il vous dira le mal qu'il a fait ou celui qu'il pense tout aussi librement que le bien, sans s'embarrasser en aucune sorte de l'effet que fera sur vous ce qu'il aura dit; il usera de la parole dans toute la simplicité de sa prémiére institution" (Pléiade ed., IV, 420). Cf. ibid., 363, 511, 642, 666, 804.

75 In *Œuvres*, Pléiade ed., III, 194.

When we find Lui cheerfully insisting that he is "un paresseux,"[76] we are reminded of the fact that Jean-Jacques, who was constantly stressing the same trait in himself,[77] speaks in his last letter to Diderot of "moi dont le souverain bien consiste dans la paresse et l'oisiveté ..."[78] And if Lui glories in the title "vaurien" (pp. 44, 76, 90), so too does Rousseau when he recounts the story of his early life.[79] Lui, moreover, is a "man of contradictions" like Jean-Jacques. He neglects his son (p. 41) though he loves him dearly (p. 90); he tyrannizes over his wife (p. 29) while obeying her every whim (p. 41); he has never learned anything (p. 9) but holds strong views on education (p. 90); he defends lying (p. 9) and practises innumerable vices, yet worships truth and goodness (p. 82). Finally, given the many points of resemblance that we have remarked, it is perhaps not too fanciful to recognize the countenance of Rousseau in the facial features with which Lui is endowed: "J'ai le front grand et ridé; l'œil ardent; le nez saillant; les joues larges; le sourcil noir et fourni; la bouche bien fendue; la levre rebordée; et la face quarrée."[80] Be that as it may, there seems to be evidence a-plenty that Diderot modelled Lui after the man whom he had known intimately for fifteen years and whose life story was an open book to him long before it became an open book for the whole world.

DIDEROT AND *Emile*

One of the principal difficulties encountered in tracing the genesis of *Le Neveu de Rameau* is the fact that most of the matters discussed in the dialogue – music, genius, science, determinism, and so forth – are commonplace topics that cannot be associated with any particular stage in the development of Diderot's thinking. We should normally be in-

76 Fabre, p. 18. This vice, which Lui's friends recognize in him (ibid.), seems to have been passed on to his son (p. 90).

77 See especially *Rousseau juge de Jean-Jacques*, Pléiade ed., I, 845–7.

78 *Corr.*, ed. Leigh, v, 48 (2 March 1758).

79 *Confessions*, Pléiade ed., I, 39, 91.

80 Fabre, p. 8. No great weight can be given to this conjecture, although it is no more hazardous than the frequently repeated suggestion that Diderot himself is the model of the portrait. We should compare our text with the description of René-Rousseau found in Madame d'Epinay's *Histoire de Madame de Montbrillant* (I, 520): "Il a le teint fort brun, et des yeux pleins de feu animent sa physionomie"; and we ought also to take into account a portrait of Jean-Jacques by the same lady in the *Mercure de France* (April 1756): "Son teint est brun, ses sourcils et ses cheveux noirs, sa bouche, ni grande ni petite, est très bien bordée et d'un très beau coloris" (cited in *Œuvres*, Pléiade ed., I, 1471, n. 1 to p. 411). We must remember, however, that we are dealing with a caricature. It is quite possible that Diderot, in describing Rousseau's essential features, amused himself by adding the high, wrinkled forehead and the broad cheeks typical of a mask of comedy.

clined to extend such a list of commonplaces to include education; in this case, however, there are excellent historical reasons for giving that subject a place of special importance.

Although interest in educational questions had been increasing noticeably in France since about 1750, we can point to 1762 as the year in which education became the topic of the hour. The month of April brought the closure of all schools directed by the Jesuits; in May came the publication of Rousseau's *Emile*. These two events alone produced a veritable flood of educational literature.[81] Beginning in July, shortly after his reading of *Emile*, Diderot manifests a growing preoccupation with his eight-year-old daughter's instruction.[82] In August he undertakes the task of making extensive revisions in a manuscript on public education (not his own work) which he will see through the press some four or five months later.[83] And over the course of the summer, with some collaboration on his part, the *Correspondance littéraire* devotes more than twenty-five pages (in the printed edition) to Rousseau and his *Emile*.[84] In view of the prominence given to the question of education in *Le Neveu de Rameau*, it is not unreasonable to suppose that the satire might have received its general orientation during those months of 1762 when education was uppermost in Diderot's mind.

This is not to suggest, of course, that Diderot began to compose *Le Neveu de Rameau* in 1762; we are forced to agree that the evidence adduced by Rudolph Schlösser in his careful study points convincingly to 1761 as the year of its inception.[85] However, we must beware of concluding more than the facts will allow. While Schlösser's opinion – that the greater part of the dialogue was completed in 1761 – commands a certain respect, it should not be forgotten that he has proven one thing only: that the work we know as *Le Neveu de Rameau* existed in some rudimentary form as early as that year. Nothing more than this can be

---

81 The *Corr. lit.* of 15 December 1762 (v, 196), perhaps written by Diderot during Grimm's temporary absence from Paris, reports as follows: "Le Parlement ayant ôté aux jésuites l'institution de la jeunesse, et M. Rousseau ayant publié sur l'éducation un ouvrage qui a fait beaucoup de bruit, la manie de cette année est d'écrire sur l'éducation, et les brochures et feuilles sur cette matière sont innombrables."

82 Diderot had read *Emile* by July 18 (*Corr.*, ed. Roth, iv, 55). Shortly thereafter, and for the next several months, he speaks constantly in his letters of his daughter's education: ibid., 74, 86, 108–10, 146, 156, 166, 171, 188, 190, 202–3.

83 Ibid., 108. On the book *De l'éducation publique*, frequently attributed to Diderot during his lifetime, see M. Roth's note (iv, 234) and Roland Mortier, "The 'Philosophes' and Public Education," *Yale French Studies*, No. 40 (1968), 67–70.

84 *Corr. lit.*, 1 June 1762 (v, 91); 15 June (v, 99–106); 1 July (v, 111–17); 15 July (v, 121–30); 1 August (v, 134–8); 1 September (v, 148–54).

85 *Rameaus Neffe*, 11–29. Schlösser concludes (p. 29) that the satire was well-nigh completed, except for later interpolations, by the end of 1761.

stated with certainty. Despite this fact, it has generally been taken for granted in our century that the overall artistic conception of the dialogue – whatever it may be – belongs to the year 1761; the result has been that attempts to analyse Diderot's psychological motivation have usually tended to pay close attention only to that year and to those immediately preceding.

Let us rid ourselves once for all of this prejudice and, thus purified, return to our hypothesis – namely, that the educational controversy of 1762 might have altered radically the direction that Diderot's mind had been taking, perhaps furnishing him with an ideal plan for the literary expression of ideas and pent-up feelings that he had tried with little success for some months past to commit to paper. If we glance ahead to that summer of 1762; if we imagine the Encyclopedist suddenly inspired to take up the brief dialogue with which he had been toying and reshape it according to a new overall conception; if we look for an event that might have awakened in him the genius of satire, an event that is somehow related to education, we are led inevitably to the publication of Rousseau's *Emile*.

If the pedagogical doctrines expounded by Rousseau had appeared sufficiently dangerous to Diderot, we may be sure that he would have reacted, as he was to do in the case of Helvétius, by writing a formal refutation of them. No such refutation is to be found among his works, but this does not mean that *Emile* failed to provoke a response on his part. It is certain, in fact, judging from the articles of the *Correspondance littéraire* of 1 August and 1 September 1762, that Diderot did take strong exception to Rousseau's book – less, however, to the ideas on education that it contained than to those parts of it that were aimed at denouncing the principles and ideals of the *philosophes*.[86] In Diderot's eyes, the author of *Emile* must have been guilty of the same crimes that Palissot had committed in staging *Les Philosophes*: a savage assault on the philosophy of the Encyclopedists and a public impugnment of their moral integrity. Surely, no existing hell was hot enough to punish such

86 The article of 1 August (v, 132–8) will be referred to several times hereafter. It records a discussion which had taken place at a kind of war-council called by the *philosophes* to determine their official attitude towards *Emile*. Grimm and Diderot were the chief participants; the third party present, "un docteur qui était là et qui aimait à raisonner" (p. 135), was probably d'Holbach (see *Corr.*, ed. Roth, IV, 55).

The article of 1 September (v, 148–54), although drawn up by Grimm, betrays Diderot's guiding hand throughout. He contributes an anecdote to illustrate a point (p. 151); and the final lines, which speak of the importance for a man's life of the moment of his conception, were undoubtedly written or inspired by one who, like Diderot, had recently read the first chapter of Sterne's *Tristram Shandy* (see *Corr.*, ed. Roth, IV, 189, n. 5).

misdeeds; a new *Inferno* had to be created where justice might be done.

The suggestion that Rousseau's treatise on education played a key role in the genesis of *Le Neveu de Rameau* requires justification at the broadest level, that of motivation, before we proceed to a textual comparison of the two works. Our first task, therefore, will be to seek out the reasons why *Emile* should have inspired the particular form of satirical expression that we find in Diderot's dialogue. In so doing, we may pass over in silence the greater part of what Rousseau has to say against materialist philosophy; although he devotes an important section of the *Profession de foi du vicaire savoyard* (Book IV) to a criticism of the doctrines of d'Holbach, Helvétius, and Diderot, his remarks contain little that is new.[87] Most pertinent to our subject are three passages, closely grouped together in Book IV, that deserve special consideration because of their highly personal or their highly emotional nature. On these we shall concentrate our attention.

## Socratism and anti-Socratism

The first passage is the well-known one in which Rousseau draws a lengthy comparison between the life of Socrates and that of Christ – to the great disadvantage of the Athenian philosopher.[88] With the benefit of Raymond Trousson's skilful study of the Socratic legend as it affected the lives of Rousseau and Diderot,[89] we are able to appreciate the effect which these lines must have had upon the Encyclopedist. For one with Diderot's intense, sincere desire to be a modern Socrates, for one who venerated as he did the moral sublimity and profound humanity of his ancient model, for one who saw in Socrates not only the sage and the martyr but also "l'ancêtre des philosophes, symbole du triomphe des lumières, et le saint qu'il fallait à la nouvelle Eglise,"[90] the public disavowal by Rousseau of his former hero could be interpreted in only one way – as the defiant gesture of a traitor to the cause of Enlightenment.

It is indeed ironical, under these circumstances, that the tendency of

87 See especially the Pléiade ed., IV, pp. 577–80, 584–7, 598–602.

88 "Quels préjugés, quel aveuglement ne faut-il point avoir pour oser comparer le fils de Sophronisque au fils de Marie? Quelle distance de l'un à l'autre! Socrate mourant sans douleur, sans ignominie, soutint aisément jusqu'au bout son personage, et si cette facile mort n'eût honoré sa vie on douteroit si Socrate avec tout son esprit fut autre chose qu'un sophiste. Il inventa, dit-on, la morale. ... Avant qu'il eut défini la vertu la Grèce abondoit en hommes vertueux" (ibid., 626). The encomium of Jesus that follows the downgrading of Socrates, however sincere it may be, is of a piece with what precedes; as Jean Seznec remarks: "Socrate n'est donc pas, après tout, le héros de Rousseau, peut-être justement parce qu'il est celui des philosophes : c'est *contre* eux qu'il exalte Jésus" (*Essais sur Diderot et l'Antiquité*, 7).

89 *Socrate devant Voltaire, Diderot et Rousseau*, 45–124.

90 Ibid., 102.

Rousseau's contemporaries to see in him another Socrates was never so pronounced as it became after the publication of *Emile* and the resulting persecution of its author. M. Trousson points out the incongruity of this situation:

Sans nul doute, le parallèle Rousseau-Socrate atteint en 1762 sa plus haute intensité. On peut imaginer la réaction des philosophes : comme l'indiquait M. Seznec, Socrate était leur héros, leur patron, leur ancêtre; eux seuls avaient le droit de s'identifier expressément avec lui. Ce privilège, même leurs ennemis le leur reconnaissaient. Mais Jean-Jacques parut, et du jour au lendemain, ce fut lui, le vrai Socrate du siècle.[91]

Even Diderot himself follows the current trend; in a conversation reported by Grimm on 1 August 1762, we find the Encyclopedist drawing a parallel between the "martyrdom" of Jean-Jacques and that of Socrates.[92] However, we must not be misled by this show of generosity. Grimm's article, which is essentially a reply to *Emile*, takes great care to obviate any suspicion that the criticism of Rousseau might spring from personal spite; to this end, he represents Diderot in the guise of an imperturbable sage who, although his genius has been misunderstood and reviled, enjoys nonetheless the serenity of a simple, candid soul unspoiled by the lure of worldly goods or of vainglory.[93] The "sage" magnanimously confers on Rousseau, "qu'il avait tendrement aimé, et dont il n'avait pas à se louer," the honour of being compared with Socrates (as a condition contrary to fact, of course, for Jean-Jacques had not stayed to drink the cup of hemlock prepared for him[94]); but the context clearly indicates that the Rousseau-Socrates parallel is merely the excuse for a lengthy discourse on the Socratic destiny of the *philosophes*.[95] Diderot is not praising Rousseau in these lines, but is using him to further the cause of the party.

91 Ibid., 80. Jean Seznec makes the following observation concerning Diderot: "Toute réflexion qui tend à dénigrer son modèle antique l'affecte, semble-t-il, personnellement" (*Essais sur Diderot et l'Antiquité*, p. 14); he supports this statement with several examples of Diderot's extreme sensitivity to any criticism of Socrates.

92 *Corr. lit.*, v, 134–5.

93 Ibid., 132–4. This lengthy panegyric should be studied closely by those who find it difficult to believe that Moi of *Le Neveu de Rameau* resembles Diderot's image of himself.

94 "Socrate a bu la ciguë; Rousseau *aurait pu* être flétri et conduit aux galères" (ibid., 134). And farther on: "La postérité a vengé Socrate opprimé ... Ce n'est pas Rousseau qui *aurait été* déshonoré, c'est le siècle et le pays qui *auraient vu* porter cet inique jugement" (pp. 134–5). Italics mine.

95 "Socrate, au moment de sa mort, était regardé à Athènes comme on nous regarde à Paris. Ses mœurs étaient attaquées; sa vie calomniée : c'était au moins un esprit turbulent et dangereux qui osait parler librement des dieux; c'était, dans l'opinion du peuple, un homme pour qui rien n'était sacré, parce qu'il ne tenait pour sacré que la vertu et la loi. Mes amis, puissions-nous en tout ressembler à Socrate, comme sa réputation ressemblait à la nôtre au moment de son supplice!" (p. 134).

It is entirely possible, therefore, that at the same moment as Grimm's reply to Rousseau was being prepared, Diderot was busy expressing his real sentiments regarding Jean-Jacques by painting him as the very incarnation of anti-Socratism in *Le Neveu de Rameau*. Not only does Lui resemble Rousseau in his scorn for philosophy, but also, like the author of *Emile*, he disparages the virtues of Socrates (Fabre, p. 11) while at the same time directing his hero-worship towards other models – Bouret and the renegade of Avignon (p. 72) – who are as unworthy as was Christ (in the eyes of a *philosophe*) to be compared with the Sage of Athens. And facing Lui, serene and confident, stands Moi – a modern Socrates who bears a striking likeness to the sage described by Grimm in the article cited above. Indeed, it must be admitted that the literary roles of Lui and Moi match perfectly the real-life roles played by Rousseau and Diderot in the year 1762.

### Reason versus Enthusiasm

We may now consider our second passage, the long footnote that Rousseau placed at the end of the *Profession de foi*.[96] This note is nothing less than a diatribe against the "parti philosophiste,"[97] and its aim is to show that, whereas religion has proved useful to mankind, atheistic philosophy is positively harmful. Rousseau admits that religious fanaticism is a great evil; but, he declares, however misdirected fanaticism may be, it has the virtue of being essentially a high-minded, selfless passion. On the other hand, the "philosophy" of his day tends to reduce human aspirations to the petty confines of self-interest:

le fanatisme, quoique sanguinaire et cruel, est pourtant une passion grande et forte qui élève le cœur de l'homme, qui lui fait mépriser la mort, qui lui donne un ressort prodigieux et qu'il ne faut que mieux diriger pour en tirer les plus sublimes vertus; au lieu que l'irréligion et en général l'esprit raisoneur et philosophique attache à la vie, effémine, avilit les ames, concentre toutes les passions dans la bassesse de l'intérêt particulier, dans l'abjection du *moi* humain, et sape ainsi à petit bruit les vrais fondemens de toute societé ...[98]

He then goes on to point out that godless philosophy is more destructive than the bloodiest of wars; not only are the *philosophes* totally indifferent to the real good of mankind, but their teachings undermine public morals by sowing the seeds of egoism. He concludes: "Ainsi le fanatisme, quoique plus funeste dans ses effets immédiats que ce qu'on

96 *Emile*, Pléiade ed., IV, 632–5.

97 In giving the history of this neologism, P.-M. Masson observes: "En commençant sa note par ce mot de pamphlétaire, Rousseau en marque tout de suite le ton" (*La Profession de foi du vicaire savoyard de Jean-Jacques Rousseau*, édition critique [Fribourg-Paris, 1914], 451, n. 5).

98 *Emile*, Pléiade ed., IV, 632–3 n.

appelle aujourdui l'esprit philosophique, l'est beaucoup moins dans ses consequences."[99]

These sentiments of Rousseau could only have infuriated Diderot and Grimm; in their conversation of 1 August 1762 it is the latter who takes up the defence of reason against the spirit of enthusiasm:

> Que voulez-vous en effet que produise une doctrine d'enthousiasme sur les hommes, dont le plus grand nombre est toujours porté à l'absurdité? et quel frein pourraient-ils connaître, si une raison plus éclairée ne rendait à la fin leur cruel fanatisme odieux et ridicule? Le fait est que cette religion [chrétienne] n'a cessé d'exciter des troubles depuis qu'elle s'est montrée parmi les hommes; et s'ils sont aujourd'hui moins dangereux, peut-on donner une autre cause de ce changement que les progrès des lettres et de la raison? Je ne sais, toutefois, comment nous osons nous vanter de mœurs plus douces et d'un siècle plus éclairé. Je doute qu'il y ait trace dans l'histoire d'une atrocité plus déplorable que celle qui vient d'arriver à Toulouse. Rousseau sait faire jusqu'à l'apologie du fanatisme; il le trouve préférable à la philosophie par plusieurs bonnes raisons qu'il indique; et moi, je trouve qu'un tel écrivain serait digne d'être l'apologiste des juges de l'infortuné Calas.[100]

Although the passage just cited is primarily concerned with heaping scorn on Rousseau's "apology" for religious fanaticism, it is evident that the issue involved is a much broader one: the opposition of enthusiasm to enlightenment. It was on this question that the *philosophes* felt compelled to take a stand after the publication of *La Nouvelle Héloïse* and *Emile*, countering Rousseau's insistence on the abuses of reason with an equal insistence on the abuses of enthusiasm. Diderot himself, of course, was an enthusiast of sorts who never tired of proclaiming the benefits of the "great passions"; but his enthusiasm must have been appreciably dampened when he saw Jean-Jacques push the paradox to its ultimate limit by his defence of fanaticism in *Emile*. He continued to wrestle with the problem, as is shown by several pages of the *Salon de 1767* (A.T., XI, 130–2) and especially by the *Paradoxe sur le comédien*; it is in *Le Neveu de Rameau*, however, that he comes to grips with his antagonist in a hand-to-hand struggle. We have seen already on several occasions that the conflict between Lui and Moi can be interpreted as a dramatic debate between enthusiasm and enlightenment; and there is every reason to think that Rousseau's invidious comparison of fanaticism and philosophy in *Emile* might have inspired Diderot in the creation of his two characters.

### The Compleat Egoist
The third passage of *Emile* that concerns us here is part of the brief sec-

99 Ibid., 633 n.                                    100 *Corr. lit.*, v, 136–7.

tion following immediately upon the *Profession de foi* in which Rousseau sets out to explain how Emile's introduction to the religious dimension of life fits into the overall scheme of the boy's formation. Having pointed out that justice is beyond the reach of those unenlightened by divine faith because without such faith men are unable to see what interest they have in being just, Rousseau elaborates on this idea with a statement which, for sheer callousness and irresponsibility, can be compared only to the closing paragraph of his *Lettre sur la musique française*:

Sortez de là [i.e. the love of God], je ne vois plus qu'injustice, hypocrisie et mensonge parmi les hommes; l'intérest particulier qui, dans la concurrence, l'emporte necessairement sur toutes choses, apprend à chacun d'eux à parer le vice du masque de la vertu. Que tous les autres hommes fassent mon bien aux dépends du leur, que tout se rapporte à moi seul, que tout le genre humain meure, s'il le faut, dans la peine et dans la misére pour m'épargner un moment de douleur ou de faim; tel est le langage intérieur de tout incrédule qui raisone. Oui, je le soutiendrai toute ma vie; quiconque a dit dans son cœur : il n'y a point de Dieu, et parle autrement, n'est qu'un menteur, ou un insensé.[101]

The impact which these words must have had on Diderot can best be appreciated if they are seen as the final blow struck in the Rousseau-Diderot quarrel. They were written, we shall recall, by the same Jean-Jacques who had himself been stung to the quick, in 1757, upon reading a similar categorical statement from the pen of his closest friend: "Il n'y a que le méchant qui soit seul."[102] The opportunity to reply in kind came with Rousseau's next published work, the *Lettre à M. d'Alembert sur les spectacles*; there, he let the world know the reason for his disenchantment with the Encyclopedist by the following remark introduced into a footnote: "Je n'entens point ... qu'on puisse être vertueux sans Religion : j'eus long-tems cette opinion trompeuse, dont je suis trop désabusé."[103] Diderot, of course, was highly incensed by the implications of this verdict; his reaction is recorded in the *Tablettes*: "Il dit qu'il a cru qu'on pouvoit avoir de la probité sans religion, mais que c'est un préjugé dont il est revenu, parce que méprisé de tous ceux qui le connoissent, et surtout de ses amis, il ne seroit pas fâché de les faire passer pour des coquins."[104] Now, four years later, comes the terrible pronouncement that we have just read where Jean-Jacques refines upon his earlier judgment by branding all unbelievers as complete and utter

101 *Emile*, Pléiade ed., IV, 636–7.
102 *Le Fils naturel*, Act IV, Sc. 3 (A.T., VII, 66). For Rousseau's reaction, see *Confessions*, Pléiade ed., I, 455.
103 Critical edition by M. Fuchs, p. 130 n.
104 In *Diderot Studies*, III (1961), 317.

egoists who hide their real sentiments behind the mask of virtue. It would be strange indeed if Diderot were not even more outraged by this than he had been by the *Lettre à d'Alembert*; and it would be stranger still if there were no connection between Rousseau's hypocritical egoist, unveiled in the summer of 1762, and the outspoken egoist painted by Diderot at about the same time in his satire, *Le Neveu de Rameau*.

The three passages from *Emile* that we have examined seem to show that Diderot might well have been prompted by Rousseau's treatise on education to draw a caricature of his former friend as an anti-intellectual, enthusiastic egoist. But, although the motivation for such a procedure undoubtedly existed, it still remains to be demonstrated that *Emile* did in fact impel the author of *Le Neveu de Rameau* to express himself satirically in this way. If a textual comparison of the two works were to bring to light an abundance of parallel passages, little doubt would remain that *Emile* provided the principal inspiration of Diderot's satire.

In seeking to bring into focus the outlines of the caricature by a study of *Emile*, we must keep in mind the fact that the artistry of our dialogue was guided by a fundamental working principle which we have encountered already on several occasions: the author chose to obviate any possible accusations of envy by employing the "confessional" form of satire. We may expect, therefore, that the portrait of Rousseau-Lui will be to some extent a self-portrait – that is to say, many of Lui's words will reproduce, either faithfully or in a distorted manner, ideas expressed by the author of *Emile*. If our hypothesis is correct, *Le Neveu de Rameau* will prove to be a kind of "*Emile* travesti."

This observation is of the utmost importance, for it is possible that we have here the key to the mystery of Diderot's satire. As we have seen, Lui is representative of the spirit of his age; and we have presumed throughout that Diderot, in a mood of sombre pessimism, painted his age in the blackest possible colours. But what if Lui represents his age, not as Diderot saw it, *but as Rousseau described it in* Emile *and elsewhere*? What more malicious irony than to create a literary character who incarnates all the vices for which Rousseau the cynic had reprimanded his contemporaries – and to endow that character with the unmistakable features of the citizen of Geneva! Surely, no satirist had ever imagined a more perfect scheme for the working out of his revenge! If this is indeed the satirical procedure employed in *Le Neveu de Rameau*, the text of the satire will bear eloquent witness to the fact.

### The "Méchant"
One of the interesting features of *Emile* – one which Diderot could not have failed to recognize – is that Rousseau's reflections on human

wickedness are full of echoes from Plato's *Republic*. The image of the tyrant appears early in the work, in the description of a wilful child: "Heureux, lui! C'est un Despote; c'est à la fois le plus vil des esclaves et la plus misérable des créatures" (Pléiade IV, 314). And the depraved life of Plato's tyrannical man is reflected in the youthful libertines, "la crapule de la jeunesse," who debauch their virtuous companions:

Vils et lâches dans leurs vices mêmes, ils n'ont que de petites ames parce que leurs corps usés ont été corrompus de bonne heure; à peine leur reste-t-il assés de vie pour se mouvoir. Leurs subtiles pensées marquent des esprits sans étoffe; ils ne savent rien sentir de grand et de noble; ils n'ont ni simplicité ni vigueur. Abjets en toutes choses et bassement méchans ils ne sont que vains, fripons, faux, ils n'ont pas même assés de courage pour être d'illustres scelerats (Pléiade IV, 665).

It is evident from this that one of Lui's essential moral traits – mediocrity – could have been derived from Plato's *Republic* through the intermediary of *Emile*.

There are many more passages in *Emile* that are borrowed from Plato, all of them expressing commonplaces related to the notion that virtue brings happiness and freedom whereas vice is the source of interior suffering. We need not dwell on these, for they are relatively unimportant in comparison with Rousseau's own remarks on the state of the wicked soul which find their place in the portrait of Lui in *Le Neveu de Rameau*. Let us take as our first example this statement found in a footnote: "Le méchant tire avantage de la probité du juste et de sa propre injustice; il est bien aise que tout le monde soit juste excepté lui" (Pléiade IV, 523 n.); Diderot's Lui says precisely the same thing when he declares that he would be happy to see egoists like himself remain few in number (Fabre, p. 9). Rousseau tells us too that, if men were naturally evil, they would feel remorse for virtuous actions rather than for vicious ones (Pléiade IV, 596); and Lui, accordingly, is made to express his horror at the thought of his being a virtuous man as follows: "Cela me feroit crever de faim, d'ennui, et de remords peut être" (Fabre, p. 46). Furthermore, when Lui excuses himself for his vices on the pretext that he is no worse than the multitude of men (Fabre, pp. 35, 39, 44, 55), he is acting out Rousseau's description of the young man exposed too soon to the ways of the world: "Il s'accoutumera ... au spectacle du vice, et à voir les méchans sans horreur comme on s'accoutume à voir les malheureux sans pitié. Bientôt la perversité générale lui servira moins de leçon que d'exemple; il se dira que si l'homme est ainsi, il ne doit pas vouloir être autrement" (Pléiade IV, 526).

One of the most impressive pantomimes in *Le Neveu de Rameau* is that in which Lui illustrates his cleverness in seducing young girls; it is introduced (Fabre, p. 22) in order to prove to Moi that his interlocutor sometimes suffers from "le mepris de soi" and it ends (p. 24) with a reaffirmation by Lui that he is well acquainted with that sentiment. This scene appears to have had its origin in these words of Rousseau, aimed at the inconsistency of vicious men:

Pourquoi cette barbare avidité de corrompre l'innocence, de se faire une victime d'un jeune objet qu'on eut dû protéger et que de ce premier pas on traîne inévitablement dans un gouffre de misères dont il ne sortira qu'à la mort? Brutalité, vanité, sotise, erreur et rien davantage. Ce plaisir même n'est pas de la nature, il est de l'opinion, et de l'opinion la plus vile, puisqu'elle tient au mépris de soi. Celui qui se sent le dernier des hommes craint la comparaison de tout autre et veut passer le prémier pour être moins odieux (Pléiade IV, 684).

Rousseau's explanation of what he means by "le mépris de soi" helps us to understand what Diderot had in mind when he translated these lines of *Emile* into action.

Another important passage of *Emile*, one which was aimed particularly at Diderot and other rational optimists, can be seen as the source of Lui's ego-centred philosophy:

La vertu, disent-ils, est l'amour de l'ordre; mais cet amour peut-il donc et doit-il l'emporter en moi sur celui de mon bien-être? Qu'ils me donnent une raison claire et suffisante pour le préférer. Dans le fond leur prétendu principe est un pur jeu de mots; car je dis aussi, moi, que le vice est l'amour de l'ordre, pris dans un sens différent. ... le méchant ordonne le tout par raport à lui (Pléiade IV, 602).

Lui, of course, is much more down to earth: "Le point important est que vous et moi nous soyons, et que nous soyons vous et moi. Que tout aille d'ailleurs comme il pourra. Le meilleur ordre des choses, a mon avis, est celui ou j'en devois etre; et foin du plus parfait des mondes, si je n'en suis pas" (Fabre, pp. 14–15). In this, as in many of Lui's observations on life, Diderot is painting the "méchant" as Rousseau described him: "Le méchant se craint et se fuit; il s'égaye en se jettant hors de lui-même; il tourne autour de lui des yeux inquiets, et cherche un objet qui l'amuse; sans la satire amère, sans la raillerie insultante il seroit toujours triste; le ris moqueur est son seul plaisir" (Pléiade IV, 597).

There is one further aspect of "méchanceté" to be considered that is most significant for our interpretation of *Le Neveu de Rameau*; it is the question of total perversity. Rousseau, as we know, had accused Diderot

– along with all other unbelievers – of being a systematic egoist who would gladly purchase his personal well-being at the expense of the whole human race. Now, that is precisely what Diderot meant by the word "méchant"; it is also what Plato meant by the word "tyrant." In 1758, Diderot had expressed his suspicions concerning Rousseau in this regard: "Si cet homme n'a pas un système de dépravation tout arrangé dans sa tête, que je le plains! Et s'il s'est fait des notions de justice et d'injustice qui le réconcilient avec la noirceur de ses procédés, que je le plains encore!"[105] With the years, however, he seems to have resolved his doubt; the *Réfutation d'Helvétius* absolves Jean-Jacques of any systematic perversity: "Rousseau ... n'est point un méchant par système, c'est un orateur éloquent, la première dupe de ses sophismes."[106]

This lenient interpretation of Rousseau's actions is not really as generous as it at first appears, for Diderot was convinced at heart that total perversity is impossible for man. So, for that matter, was Rousseau, and he makes a point of saying so in *Emile*:

Mais quel que soit le nombre des méchans sur la terre, il est peu de ces ames cadavereuses, devenues insensibles, hors leur interêt, à tout ce qui est juste et bon. ... Enfin l'on a, malgré soi, pitié des infortunés; quand on est témoin de leur mal, on en souffre. Les plus pervers ne sauroient perdre tout-à-fait ce penchant : souvent il les met en contradiction avec eux-mêmes (Pléiade IV, 596–7).

But these sentiments did not prevent Jean-Jacques, a few pages farther on (ibid., 602), from painting the atheist as one who follows a system of reasoned egoism. It is noteworthy that this passage was the object of Diderot's first specific criticism of *Emile* that has come down to us:

Je n'ai point lu le *Traité de l'Education*; mais, l'ayant trouvé l'autre jour sur une cheminée, j'en ouvris un volume au hasard, et j'y lus ces paroles : « Si la Divinité n'est pas, il n'y a que le méchant qui raisonne; le bon n'est qu'un insensé. » Je jetai le livre, et je dis : Il ne faut pas réfuter un auteur qui sent ainsi; il faut le plaindre. ... Dites à Rousseau ... qu'aussi longtemps que le méchant ne sera pas aussi franchement méchant que le bon est franchement bon, qu'aussi longtemps que le premier n'osera se perfectionner comme le second, je croirai la sanction de mes lois morales hors de toute atteinte : car aucun être ne peut sortir de sa nature, et celle de l'homme

---

105 Letter to Sophie Volland, 2 June 1759 (*Corr.*, ed. Roth, II, 145).

106 A.T., II, 412. This does nothing to invalidate the conclusion drawn by Robert Niklaus in his article entitled "Le 'Méchant' selon Diderot," *Saggi e ricerche di letteratura francese*, II (1961), 142: "dans un sens important et jusqu'à la fin de sa vie, le *Méchant* pour Diderot ne sera autre que Jean-Jacques Rousseau, le diable incarné, le seul véritable diable dans un monde sans Dieu."

veut qu'il aime la vertu et qu'il abhorre le vice; il ne dépend pas de lui d'être autrement.[107]

The idea of the perfectly evil man – full of memories from Plato's *Republic* – continued to haunt Diderot for several months thereafter; his major preoccupation, of course, is to justify a purely natural morality in opposition to Rousseau's God-centred ethic. In a letter to Sophie Volland, we read: "la nature a laissé dans l'âme des méchants une petite place qui n'est pas tout à fait pourrie, qui vit, qui est douloureuse, et où de tems en tems ils sont frappés."[108] And again, a short time later:

Il est impossible d'éteindre en soi tout sentiment de vérité, de bonté, de justice, d'honnêteté. Les méchants exigent ces qualités des autres. Les méchants les cultivent en eux en cent occasions diverses. Les méchants ne cessent pas d'être tout à fait des hommes. Quels que soient leurs succès, ils en rougissent quelquefois.[109]

These reflections of Diderot, undoubtedly inspired by his reaction to *Emile*, are translated into satire in *Le Neveu de Rameau*. Try as he may, Lui is incapable of attaining the state of complete depravity to which he aspires; Moi leaves him in no doubt on this score: "en depit du role miserable, abject, vil, abominable que vous faites, je crois qu'au fond, vous avez l'ame delicate" (Fabre, p. 56); "Je vous trouve de tems en tems vacillant dans vos principes" (p. 72). We may conclude from this that, despite the pessimism that marks Lui's attitude to life, *Le Neveu de Rameau* can justly be considered to express a position of relative optimism on the part of the author. Perhaps "optimism" is too strong a word to characterize the implied belief that man ineluctably desires self-perfection; however, we must remember that the context detracts considerably from this notion, to which Diderot was in reality sincerely attached. His main purpose here, it would seem, is less to defend human nature than to avenge himself for the insult to his moral integrity found in *Emile* – a goal which he achieves by ironically painting Rousseau not as an utter villain, but as a pitiful, would-be "méchant" who finds it beyond his power to extinguish within himself the last feeble spark of his humanity.

### Genius
Lui's hatred of genius (Fabre, p. 9) is founded, according to him, on the fact that the discoveries made by great men upset the carefree function-

107 *Corr. lit.*, v, 137 (1 August 1762).
108 *Corr.*, ed. Roth, IV, 210 (31 October 1762).
109 Ibid., 220 (to Sophie Volland, 11 November 1762).

ing of a world dedicated to folly: "Si je scavois l'histoire, je vous montrerois que le mal est toujours venu ici bas, par quelque homme de genie." This is apparently a burlesque treatment of Rousseau's words concerning the modest intellectual aspirations of his pupil Emile:

Ne courant jamais après les idées neuves il ne sauroit se piquer d'esprit. Je lui ai fait sentir que toutes les idées salutaires et vraiment utiles aux hommes ont été les prémiéres connües, qu'elles font de tous tems les seuls vrais liens de la societé, et qu'il ne reste aux esprits transcendans qu'à se distinguer par des idées pernicieuses et funestes au genre humain (Pléiade IV, 670).

The anti-intellectual implications of these lines are ironically brought out in *Le Neveu de Rameau* by Lui's further statement: "Mais je ne scais pas l'histoire, parce que je ne scais rien. Le diable m'emporte, si j'ai jamais rien appris; et si pour n'avoir rien appris, je m'en trouve plus mal" (p. 9).

### History and Truth

Immediately following upon these words of Lui comes an affirmation of the utility of lies and the harmfulness of truth (Fabre, p. 9). These are not Rousseau's sentiments, of course, any more than they are Diderot's; but Jean-Jacques had been guilty of turning the "utility of truth" argument against the *philosophes* in a scathingly sarcastic observation found in the *Profession de foi*: "Jamais, disent-ils, la vérité n'est nuisible aux hommes : je le crois comme eux, et c'est à mon avis une grande preuve que ce qu'ils enseignent n'est pas la vérité" (Pléiade IV, 632). This attack could not go unpunished; and fortunately, Rousseau had left himself open to reprisals by a footnote of *Emile* in which he condemned historical erudition as useless:

Les anciens historiens sont remplis de vües dont on pourroit faire usage quand même les faits qui les présentent seroient faux : mais nous ne savons tirer aucun vrai parti de l'histoire; la critique d'érudition absorbe tout, comme s'il importoit beaucoup qu'un fait fut vrai, pourvu qu'on en pût tirer une instruction utile. Les hommes sensés doivent regarder l'histoire comme un tissu de fables dont la morale est très appropriée au cœur humain (Pléiade IV, 415 n.).

### Education

Some of the parallels between *Le Neveu de Rameau* and *Emile* that are concerned with education have already been mentioned in Chapter 6 above (pp. 111–12). There are a number of others that deserve our attention.

First, Lui's opinion that harpsichord lessons should be commenced at the tender age of four (Fabre, p. 30) seems to reflect an observation made by Rousseau about the supposed inaptitude of young children to make progress in the playing of musical instruments. After citing several cases of child prodigies he had known – one who had mastered the harpsichord and another the violin – Jean-Jacques draws the following conclusion:

Tous ces exemples et cent-mille autres prouvent, ce me semble, que l'inaptitude qu'on suppose aux enfans pour nos exercices est imaginaire, et que si on ne les voit point reussir dans quelques uns, c'est qu'on ne les y a jamais exercés (Pléiade IV, 403).

Much more succinct is Lui's comment concerning the musical education of Moi's eight-year-old daughter: "Huit ans! il y a quatre ans que cela devroit avoir les doigts sur les touches."

Secondly, when Lui insists that a young girl should be "jolie, amusante et coquette" (Fabre, p. 30), we are reminded that Rousseau heartily approved of coquettish behaviour as natural to Sophie and the other members of her sex (Pléiade IV, 703, 735, 739). And, in the same context, Lui's expression of enthusiasm for lessons in singing and dancing in the training of female children (p. 30) is comparable to the favour with which they were regarded by Rousseau in *Emile* (Pléiade IV, 715, 717). We may be certain that this section of *Le Neveu de Rameau* was inspired by Rousseau's ideas on the "pleasing arts" in the education of girls.

Thirdly, and much more important, is Diderot's attack on "natural education." In *Emile*, Rousseau had repeated constantly his conviction that early education must be negative: "empêcher *que rien ne soit fait*" (Pléiade IV, 251); "en commençant par *ne rien faire*, vous auriez fait un prodige d'éducation" (ibid., 324); "Eh point de beaux discours! *rien du tout*, pas un seul mot. *Laissez venir* l'enfant ..." (ibid., 328). It is these principles, of course, that Diderot is satirizing when he has Lui describe the manner in which he conducts the education of his own child: "*Je n'y fais rien a present. Je le laisse venir.* Je l'examine. Il est deja gourmand, patelin, filou, paresseux, menteur. Je crains bien qu'il ne chasse de race."[110] The mockery is made more biting by the fact that Lui recognizes the importance of heredity – a matter which Rousseau had chosen to ignore: "Posons pour maxime incontestable que les premiers mouvemens de la nature sont toujours droits ..." (Pléiade IV, 322); "il est impossible qu'ils [les enfans] deviennent indociles, méchans, men-

110 Fabre, p. 90. The italics in all these quotations are mine.

teurs, avides, quand on n'aura pas semé dans leurs cœurs les vices qui les rendent tels" (ibid., 341).

## *Imitation*

Closely related to the problem of education is the theme of imitation. In accordance with his particular interpretation of Plato's *Republic* and *Laws*, Rousseau's answer to the age-old question "Can virtue be taught?" is that virtue cannot be taught by an appeal to reason but that it can be instilled by good example. Continually throughout *Emile* he stresses the futility of moral maxims and of verbal instruction[111] while extolling the efficacy of example and of object lessons: "L'exemple, l'exemple! sans cela jamais on ne reussit à rien auprès des enfans" (Pléiade IV, 722); "Les choses, les choses! Je ne répéterai jamais assés que nous donnons trop de pouvoir aux mots : avec nôtre éducation babillarde nous ne faisons que des babillards" (ibid., 447; cf. p. 347). In view of Rousseau's insistence on imitation in opposition to Diderot's intellectualist approach to education, we may consider the burlesque "leçon de choses" in *Le Neveu de Rameau* to be one of the most significant pieces of satire in the work:

De l'or, de l'or. L'or est tout; et le reste, sans or, n'est rien. Aussi au lieu de lui farcir la tete de belles maximes qu'il faudroit qu'il oubliât, sous peine de n'etre qu'un gueux; lors que je possede un louis, ce qui ne m'arrive pas souvent, je me plante devant lui. Je tire le louis de ma poche. Je le lui montre avec admiration. J'eleve les yeux au ciel. Je baise le louis devant lui. Et pour lui faire entendre mieux encore l'importance de la piece sacrée, je lui begaye de la voix; je lui designe du doigt tout ce qu'on en peut acquerir, un beau fourreau, un beau toquet, un bon biscuit. Ensuite je mets le louis dans ma poche. Je me promene avec fierté; je releve la basque de ma veste; je frappe de la main sur mon gousset; et c'est ainsi que je lui fais concevoir que c'est du louis qui est la, que nait l'assurance qu'il me voit (Fabre, p. 92).

There is, then, at least in this instance, a close relationship between the educational doctrine of imitation and the pantomimic nature of Lui. However, the education of children is only a small part of the overall picture; it is the general problem of imitation in the life of man that is treated in *Le Neveu de Rameau*, and therefore the question that must be answered is, why did Diderot choose to make Lui an accomplished mime? Some light may be thrown on this matter if we read what Rousseau has to say about imitation in *Emile*:

111 Pléiade ed., IV, 303, 316, 321, 324, 327, 346, 546, 645.

L'homme est imitateur, l'animal même l'est; le goût de l'imitation est de la nature bien ordonée, mais il dégénere en vice dans la societé. Le singe imite l'homme qu'il craint, et n'imite pas les animaux qu'il méprise; il juge bon ce que fait un être meilleur que lui. Parmi nous, au contraire, nos Arlequins de toute espéce imitent le beau pour le dégrader, pour le rendre ridicule; ils cherchent dans le sentiment de leur bassesse à s'égaler ce qui vaut mieux qu'eux, ou s'ils s'efforcent d'imiter ce qu'ils admirent on voit dans le choix des objets le faux gout des imitateurs; ils veulent bien plus en imposer aux autres ou faire applaudir leur talent que se rendre meilleurs ou plus sages (Pléiade IV, 340).

At first sight the ideas contained in this passage do not strike the reader as being of any particular significance for *Le Neveu de Rameau*; to inform us, as Rousseau does, that there are various forms of imitation – that a man can imitate what is good out of genuine emulation or in a spirit of ridicule, and that he can also imitate what is inferior out of misguided admiration – is to tell us what is common knowledge. However, the cynicism with which Rousseau clothes his observations must surely have attracted Diderot's notice; and especially worthy of remark are the two images employed by Jean-Jacques: the image of the monkey and that of Harlequin. If it is true, as we have suggested above, that Diderot created Lui according to Rousseau's jaundiced view of modern man, he must have been tempted to give a certain relief to these images, which correspond to two of the fundamental aspects of mimesis: mimicry and parody. Let us examine each of them in turn.

First, the monkey. Rousseau's cynical observation that monkeys imitate only what is superior whereas men are prone to imitate what is inferior might conceivably have guided Diderot in his depiction of Lui as an imitator of "great criminals." But this was merely a starting-point for Diderot, who went on to fill out the picture with his own moral observations about monkeys. Notice, for example, the perfect correlation between the portrait of Lui and that of the "homme singe" described in the *Eléments de physiologie*:

J'ai vu un homme singe. Il ne pensait pas plus que le singe. Il imitait comme le singe. Il était malfaisant comme le singe. Il s'agitait sans cesse comme le singe. Il était décousu dans ses idées comme le singe. Il se fâchait, il s'apaisait, il était sans pudeur comme le singe (A.T., IX, 424).

Furthermore, if we glance at Diderot's *Satire première*, another dimension is added to the portrait: "Méfiez-vous de l'homme singe. Il est sans caractère, il a toutes sortes de cris" (below, p. 229). This allusion to the moral inconsistency of the monkey-man justifies our concluding that all the essential traits with which Lui is endowed, both physical and moral, are common also to Diderot's image of the monkey – an animal which is by nature a caricature of a man. We might add, in corroboration of this, that there is a tradition going back to Pliny's *Natural History* (VII. ii.24) to the effect that satyrs are a species of monkey – a tradition to which Rousseau himself alludes in his *Discours sur l'inégalité*.[112]

This last-mentioned work, with its stress on the animality of primitive man and its lengthy tenth footnote speculating on the humanity of orang-outangs, would seem to be cause enough for Diderot to have drawn a caricature of Jean-Jacques as a monkey-man. The *philosophe* had not taken kindly to Rousseau's declaration that reason is merely a by-product of social living, a faculty that would never have developed without the historical accident that brought society into being; both he and Grimm were constant in affirming that rationality is essential to human nature.[113] The fact that Rousseau was widely reputed to have reduced man to the brute gives reason to suspect that he is responsible not only for the monkey image of our satire, but also for the animalism that is one of its most striking characteristics.[114]

In addition to this, we must take into account the great popularity enjoyed by "singeries" in the satirical art of the period. Watteau and Chardin had been the greatest French practitioners of pictorial satire involving monkies; the "Singe peintre," the "Singe sculpteur," the "Singe antiquaire" were among the outstanding works of this type.[115]

112 In note x: "Nos voyageurs font sans façon des bêtes sous les noms de *Pongos*, de *Mandrills*, d'*Orang-Outang*, de ces mêmes êtres dont sous les noms de *Satyres*, de *Faunes*, de *Silvains*, les Anciens faisoient des Divinités. Peut-être après des recherches plus exactes trouvera-t-on que ce sont des hommes" (Pléiade ed., III, 211).

113 Even before the *Discours sur l'inégalité* was published, we find Grimm answering Rousseau's attack on the utility of scientific knowledge in this vein: "la faculté de réfléchir, qui est proprement la source de tous les maux, est essentielle à l'homme; et qui dit un homme, dit un être qui réfléchit et la première réflexion a engendré toutes les autres. Il est évident que M. Rousseau a confondu l'état de l'homme et de la bête : ce dernier est constant et immuable; le premier est, par sa nature, sujet à mille changements bons ou mauvais qu'aucune philosophie n'est capable d'arrêter" (*Corr. lit.*, 15 February 1754, II, 321). And Diderot, in his article "Droit naturel," was also replying to Rousseau when he wrote: "il faut raisonner en tout, parce que l'homme n'est pas seulement un animal, mais un animal qui raisonne ..." (A.T., XIV, 298). Cf. Diderot's frequent statements to this effect in the *Réfutation d'Helvétius*, A.T., II, 303, 365, 388, 397.

114 *Le Neveu de Rameau* is a veritable bestiary, as is indicated by the following frequency list of animals named therein: animal (7), autruche, bête, butor, cerf, chat (3), chenille, cheval (3), chien (11), cochon, coq (2), doguin, grue, guenon, insecte, lion, loup (2), oie (2), oiseau, panthère, perroquet, pinson, poisson, polype, rossignol, singe (4), tigre (3), ver.

115 See André Blum, *L'Estampe satirique et la caricature en France au XVIIIe siècle* (Paris, Gazette des Beaux-Arts, 1910), 45–9. The extent of Diderot's debt to the pictorial caricature of his time, especially in *Le Neveu de Rameau*, is deserving of careful study.

If we were to place *Le Neveu de Rameau* in this tradition, we should have to inscribe beneath the portrait of Lui the title "Le Singe philosophe," an inscription which, in Diderot's eyes, would have suited perfectly a caricature of Jean-Jacques Rousseau. And indeed, Diderot would not have been alone in so thinking; it was thus that Fréron saw Jean-Jacques, as is attested by his criticism of the Preface to *La Nouvelle Héloïse*:

Ce ton dur & haut est-il donc le langage de la Philosophie? C'étoit celui de Diogène qui de son tonneau jugeoit l'univers, & se croyoit un être important pour avoir insulté *Alexandre*, qui fut assez grand pour mépriser le singe Philosophe.[116]

It is possible that this description of Diogenes the Cynic, and the comparison with Jean-Jacques, were instrumental in the creation of our caricature.

Turning now to the Harlequin image used by Rousseau in *Emile*, we find that he gives the word a pejorative meaning; his "Arlequins de toute espèce" are those who ape what is good in order to degrade it. Knowing the distaste which Jean-Jacques affected for the theatre (a few years earlier he had been known to frequent the Comédie Italienne assiduously[117]), we need not take this too seriously. What is important for our purpose is the fact that Harlequin, the best-known character of Italian comedy, was the conventional resource of dramatic parody in the eighteenth century. The name Harlequin was synonymous with pantomime, if we take that word in its literal sense; for there was no human character, no profession, no state of life that had not been parodied on the stage by casting Harlequin in the leading role. Thus he had become the symbol of changeability, an amorphous figure whose infinite adaptability was undoubtedly one of the qualities Diderot had in mind when he insisted, in his *Paradoxe sur le comédien*, that the great actor plays all roles equally well because he has no character of his own.[118] Moreover, the Harlequin costume, like the motley of the fool, had become a universal sign of the mental fragmentation and discontinuity normally associated with folly.

In *Le Neveu de Rameau*, with its mad saturnalian setting and the all-pervasive atmosphere of the "Querelle des Bouffons," there are numerous echoes of the literary and theatrical traditions of folly and buffoonery, all of them converging in the figure of Lui. The names Harlequin, Pulcinella, and Pantalone are each mentioned once (Fabre,

116 *Année littéraire*, 5 April 1761, Tome II, 313.

117 *Confessions*, Pléiade ed., I, 352.

118 A.T., VIII, 398-9. Diderot was also prone to see actors as "sans caractère" in the moral sense of that expression (ibid., 399).

pp. 98, 99, 105), and the "habit d'Arlequin" is invoked early in the
satire as the image of a disorderly world in which folly reigns supreme
(p. 9).

It seems possible, in view of what we have seen, that Rousseau's comments on the falseness of society, however commonplace they may have
been in substance, might have been the occasion of the confluence in
Diderot's mind of ideas already familiar to him which helped to guide
him in the creation of his pantomime buffoon.

## A Caricature in Mosaic

The scrupulous care with which Diderot composed the portrait of Lui
is attested by the fact that his dialogue might almost be described as a
mosaic of passages found in *Emile* – distorted, of course, for purposes
of satire, but nonetheless clearly recognizable. Let us begin with some
of the ideas expressed by Lui.

LUI

"un garçon charbonnier parlera
toujours mieux de son metier que
toute une academie, et que tous
les Duhamels du monde"
(Fabre, p. 82).

ROUSSEAU

"il n'y a point de petit paysan à
douze [ans] qui ne sache se servir
d'un levier mieux que le prémier
mécanicien de l'academie"
(Pléiade IV, 369).

LUI

"si je deviens jamais riche ... Je
ferois comme tous les gueux
revetus; je serois le plus insolent
maroufle qu'on eut encore vu.
C'est alors que je me rapellerois
tout ce qu'ils m'ont fait souffrir;
et je leur rendrois bien les avanies
qu'ils m'ont faites. J'aime a
commander, et je commanderai.
J'aime qu'on me loue et l'on me
louera. ... nous nous enyvrerons;
nous ferons des contes; nous
aurons toutes sortes de travers et
de vices. Cela sera delicieux"
(Fabre, pp. 38–9).

ROUSSEAU

"si j'etois riche, j'aurois fait tout
ce qu'il faut pour le devenir; je
serois donc insolent et bas,
sensible et délicat pour moi seul,
impitoyable et dur pour tout le
monde, spectateur dédaigneux
des miséres de la canaille; car je
ne donnerois plus d'autre nom
aux indigens, pour faire oublier
qu'autrefois je fus de leur classe.
Enfin je férois de ma fortune
l'instrument de mes plaisirs dont
je serois uniquement occupé; et
jusques là, je serois comme tous
les autres" (Pléiade IV, 678).

LUI

"Je n'entends pas grand chose a
tout ce que vous me debitez la.
C'est apparemment de la philo-

ROUSSEAU

"Mon enfant, n'attendez de moi
ni des discours savans, ni de
profonds raisonemens. Je ne suis

sophie; je vous previens que je ne
m'en mele pas" (Fabre, p. 15).

pas un grand philosophe, et je me
soucie peu de l'être"
(Pléiade IV, 565).

LUI
"et qu'est ce qu'une bonne education, sinon celle qui conduit a
toutes sortes de jouissances, sans
peril, et sans inconvenient"
(Fabre, pp. 95–6).

ROUSSEAU
"Le plus heureux est celui qui
souffre le moins de peines; le plus
misérable est celui qui sent le
moins de plaisirs. Toujours plus
de souffrances que de joüissances;
voila la différence commune à
tous" (Pléiade IV, 303).

LUI
[Speaking of the possibility that
his young son might become a
musician like his father]
"Un musicien ! un musicien !
quelquefois je le regarde, en
grinçant des dents; et je dis, si tu
devois jamais scavoir une note, je
crois que je te tordrois le col"
(Fabre, p. 91).

ROUSSEAU
"Je veux absolument qu'Emile
apprenne un métier. Un métier
honnête, au moins, direz-vous?
Que signifie ce mot? Tout métier
utile au public n'est-il pas
honnête ? ... je ne veux qu'il soit
ni musicien, ni comedien, ni
faiseur de Livres" (Pléiade IV,
473).

LUI
"Tenez, mon philosophe, j'ai dans
la tête que la physique sera toujours une pauvre science; une
goutte d'eau prise avec la pointe
d'une aiguille dans le vaste ocean;
un grain detaché de la chaine des
Alpes; et les raisons des pheno-
menes ? en verité, il vaudroit
autant ignorer que de scavoir si
peu et si mal ..." (Fabre, p. 32).

ROUSSEAU
"L'intelligence humaine a ses
bornes ... le nombre des vérités est
inépuisable comme celui des
erreurs. ... Il ne s'agit point de
savoir ce qui est, mais seulement
ce qui est utile. ... Que d'abîmes
je vois creuser par nos vaines
sciences autour de ce jeune
infortuné [Emile] ! ... Souviens-toi,
souviens-toi sans cesse que l'ignorance n'a jamais fait de mal, que
l'erreur seule est funeste ..."
(Pléiade IV, 428).

LUI
"S'il est destiné a devenir un
homme de bien, je n'y nuirai pas.
Mais si la molecule vouloit qu'il

ROUSSEAU
"Entraînés par la nature et par les
hommes dans des routes contraires,
forcés de nous partager entre ces

fut un vaurien comme son pere, les peines que j'aurois prises, pour en faire un homme honnete lui seroient tres nuisibles; l'education croisant sans cesse la pente de la molecule, il seroit tiré comme par deux forces contraires, et marcheroit tout de guingois, dans le chemin de la vie" (Fabre, p. 90).

diverses impulsions, nous en suivons une composée qui ne nous mêne ni à l'un ni à l'autre but. Ainsi combatus et flotans durant tout le cours de nôtre vie, nous la terminons sans avoir pu nous accorder avec nous, et sans avoir été bons ni pour nous ni pour les autres" (Pléiade IV, 251).

Although we have not yet exhausted the catalogue of parellel thoughts expressed by Lui and by Rousseau,[119] let us turn to three other examples of apparent influence, this time involving lines which Diderot gave to Moi or for which he himself, as the author, took responsibilty. We may begin with a passage from *Emile* that seems to have provided Diderot with the striking image employed on the opening page of his satire – that of the young libertines and their female partners strolling in the Palais Royal gardens (Fabre, p. 3). This image first appears in his works in a letter to Sophie Volland dated 2 September 1762: "Un jeune libertin se promène au Palais-Royal. Il voit là un petit nez retroussé, des lèvres riantes, un œil éveillé, une démarche délibérée ..."[120] It is possible that Diderot's train of thought was set in motion by his reading of what Rousseau, with his customary forthrightness, had to say about the fatuity of French youth:

Les promenades publiques des villes sont pernicieuses aux enfans de l'un et de l'autre sexe. C'est là qu'ils commencent à se rendre vains et à vouloir être regardés; c'est au Luxembourg, aux Tuilleries, surtout au Palais-Royal que la belle jeunesse de Paris va prendre cet air impertinent et fat qui la rend si ridicule et la fait hüer et détester dans toute l'Europe (Pléiade IV, 393 n.).

Farther on in the prologue we find Diderot commenting on "cette fastidieuse uniformité que notre education, nos conventions de société, nos bienseances d'usage ont introduite" (Fabre, p. 5). And Rousseau, in *Emile*: "Les bienséances, les modes, les usages qui dérivent du luxe et du bon air renferment le cours de la vie dans la plus maussade uniformité" (Pléiade IV, 686).

119 Diderot's Lui shares the sentiments of the author of *Emile* concerning self-seeking benefactors (Fabre, p. 68; cf. Pléiade IV, 521), and also concerning the desirability of bourgeois mediocrity (Fabre, p. 12; cf. Pléiade IV, 691). It should be noted, moreover, that Lui's son is referred to three times as "le petit sauvage" (Fabre, pp. 90, 95), and that the word "sauvage" is applied to Emile by Rousseau on several occasions (Pléiade IV, 484, 535, 551).

120 *Corr.*, ed. Roth, IV, 130–1.

Finally, Diderot's Moi appears to be indebted to Rousseau for an important series of observations assigned to him by the author – important because they are the occasion for Lui to display for the last time his mastery of pantomime. In each case there is question of the subservience of superiors to their inferiors insofar as the former have need of the latter:

MOI

"Quiconque a besoin d'un autre, est indigent et prend une position. Le roi prend une position devant sa maitresse et devant Dieu; il fait son pas de pantomime. Le ministre fait le pas de courtisan, de flatteur, de valet ou de gueux devant son roi. La foule des ambitieux dan-sent vos positions, en cent manieres plus viles les unes que les autres, devant le ministre" (Fabre, p. 105).

ROUSSEAU

[Jean-Jacques addresses an imag-inary sovereign as follows] "Tu as beau faire; jamais ton autorité réelle n'ira plus loin que tes facultés réelles. Sitôt qu'il faut voir par les yeux des autres, il faut vouloir par leurs volontés. Mes peuples sont mes sujets, dis-tu fiérement. Soit; mais toi, qu'es-tu? Le sujet de tes ministres, et tes ministres à leur tour que sont-ils? Les sujets de leurs commis, de leurs maitresses, les valets de leurs valets" (Pléiade IV, 309).

In *Le Neveu de Rameau*, the above passage leads up to the idea that only the philosopher is self-sufficient (p. 106); in *Emile*, on the other hand, Rousseau's observations are directed at affirming his ideal of total independence: "L'homme vraiment libre ne veut que ce qu'il peut et fait ce qu'il lui plait. Voila ma maxime fondamentale" (Pléiade IV, 309). However, it is not the freedom of the philosopher that Jean-Jacques craves, but the freedom of the savage; we have his own admis-sion to that effect in a later statement on human needs:

Tout nous importe depuis que nous sommes dépendans de tout, et nôtre curiosité s'étend nécessairement avec nos besoins. Voila pourquoi j'en donne une très grande au philosophe et n'en donne point au sauvage. Celui-ci n'a besoin de personne; l'autre a besoin de tout le monde, et surtout d'admira-teurs (ibid., 483).

These lines, I believe, throw light on the closing pages of *Le Neveu de Rameau*. They explain both Lui's refusal to admit that Diogenes was free (Fabre, p. 106) and the ironical appeal made by Moi to the simple nourishment enjoyed by savages (ibid.).

There is one further passage that should be taken into account, one which involves Rousseau the man rather than the author of *Emile*. In his prologue to the *Profession de foi* Jean-Jacques relates some of his adventures as a boy, beginning with his conversion to Catholicism at the hospice in Turin.[121] Speaking of himself in the third person, he outlines the reasons that led him to the hospice, where "il changea de réligion pour avoir du pain" (Pléiade IV, 559). Scandalized by what he saw and heard there, he tried to flee but was locked up and punished. His distress at this injustice knew no bounds: "Des larmes de rage couloient de ses yeux, l'indignation l'étouffoit. Il imploroit le Ciel et les hommes, il se confioit à tout le monde et n'étoit écouté de personne" (ibid.).

Now let us read what appears to be a burlesqued version of this incident, the hero of which is Diderot's Lui:

Il s'etoit introduit, je ne scais comment, dans quelques maisons honnêtes, ou il avoit son couvert, mais a la condition qu'il ne parleroit pas, sans en avoir obtenu la permission. Il se taisoit, et mangeoit de rage. Il etoit excellent a voir dans cette contrainte. S'il lui prenoit envie de manquer au traité, et qu'il ouvrit la bouche; au premier mot, tous les convives s'ecrioient, o Rameau! Alors la fureur etincelloit dans ses yeux, et il se remettoit a manger avec plus de rage (Fabre, p. 6).

It would seem from this that Lui the parasite does not owe all of his characteristics to models from ancient literature. "La voix de la conscience et de l'honneur, est bien foible, lorsque les boyaux crient," he exclaims (p. 38); and Rousseau, speaking of the pitiable state into which he himself had fallen, makes the same excuse: "Il est un dégré d'abrutissement qui ôte la vie à l'ame, et la voix intérieure ne sait point se faire entendre à celui qui ne songe qu'à se nourrir" (Pléiade IV, 562).

Our examination of *Emile* has been limited to its most striking parallels with *Le Neveu de Rameau*; much more could have been said concerning the topics that are common to the two works,[122] but this would have taken us away from our study of the character Lui. In his adaptation of the passages from *Emile* that we have examined, Diderot has shown himself a master of parody; a complete study of the matter might appreciably deepen our knowledge of his literary art.

121 The great admiration manifested by Lui for the renegade of Avignon (Fabre, p. 72) undoubtedly contains an ironical allusion to the fact that Jean-Jacques himself was a renegade Calvinist for twenty-five years of his life.

122 In addition to the broader topics – utility, necessity, virtue and happiness, appearance and reality – which recur continually in both works, more specific examples of parallelism are not uncommon: the "puer robustus" of Hobbes (Pléiade IV, 288, 314; cf. Fabre, p. 95); the "singeries" of the dancing-master Marcel, presented as typical of the extravagance of the French (Pléiade IV, 391 and note; cf. Fabre, pp. 104–6); the abuses of favouritism (Pléiade IV, 471–2; cf. Fabre, p. 97); talent and practice in the formation of an artist (Pléiade IV, 474–5; cf. Fabre, pp. 26–8); admiration for heroic actions (Pléiade IV, 596; cf. Fabre, pp. 72–6); Socratic martyrdom (Pléiade IV, 599; cf. Fabre, p. 11).

The evidence that we have seen has not only supported convincingly the hypothesis that Diderot's Lui is largely a caricature of Rousseau, but has also given us a glimpse of the manner in which the portrait must have been composed. However much our interpretation of the data needs to be refined, it appears to be fairly well established that Jean-Jacques Rousseau played an essential role in the motivation, the conception, and the execution of *Le Neveu de Rameau*. It is up to each reader to judge whether it is Jean-Jacques or Rameau's nephew whose name deserves to figure in the title of our satire.

Before making this judgment, however, we should recall that Diderot, in the first edition of his *Essai sur les règnes de Claude et de Néron* (1778), sought to discredit in advance the "calumny" of himself and his friends that he knew to be contained in the yet unpublished *Confessions* by revealing what he considered to be Rousseau's true nature. To this end, he drew for his readers the portrait of a malicious hypocrite (A.T., III, 90–1) – unnamed, but obviously intended to represent the author of the *Confessions* – who is willing to display his own turpitude before the world in order the better to blacken the reputation of others. He concludes artfully with these words: "Mais ce monstre a-t-il jamais existé? Je ne le pense pas."

Diderot was criticized severely for this attack on a man recently deceased. In the second edition of the *Essai* (1782) he made the following defence of his action:

Ce Jean-Jacques a-t-il fait un ouvrage tel que celui que je désigne ? A-t-il calomnié ses anciens amis ? A-t-il décelé l'ingratitude la plus noire envers ses bienfaiteurs ? A-t-il déposé sur sa tombe la révélation de secrets confiés ou surpris ? ... Je dirai, j'écrirai sur son monument : *Ce Jean-Jacques que vous voyez fut un pervers.* ...

Jean-Jacques n'a-t-il rien fait de pareil ? Ce n'est plus de lui que j'ai parlé.

Existe-t-il, a-t-il jamais existé un méchant assez artificieux pour donner de la consistance aux horreurs qu'il débite d'autrui par les horreurs qu'il confesse de lui-même ? J'ai protesté que je n'en croyais rien. Censeurs, à qui donc en voulez-vous ? S'il y a quelqu'un à blâmer, c'est vous; j'ai ébauché une tête hideuse, et vous avez écrit le nom du modèle au-dessous (A.T., III, 91–2).

The critic's responsibility is indeed a grave one. Mindful of this warning, one ought perhaps to conclude that the immediate model of Lui was neither Rousseau nor Rameau, but the "modèle idéal" of a parasite buffoon constructed by Diderot's fertile imagination.

# 8
# Miscellaneous reflections

THE heading of this chapter is gratefully borrowed from Shaftesbury, who gave the title "Miscellaneous Reflections" to the last of his six collected essays that make up the famous *Characteristics* of 1711. We shall be discussing Shaftesbury, and also miscellanies, in the course of these pages; but the principal reason for the borrowing is simply that no title could be more apt to describe what will follow: a series of conjectures regarding the sources, the structure, and the meaning of Diderot's multi-faced satire. Each of these conjectures will be presented as briefly and as objectively as possible in order to avoid the appearance of special pleading. It is hoped that their cumulative effect will be to corroborate our previous findings and to open up for future exploitation the hidden riches of *Le Neveu de Rameau*.

## POLARITY

It is a commonplace observation that Diderot's thought is marked by a native bi-polarity that finds expression in almost all his writings. What has not been sufficiently stressed is the fact that this propensity of his for dialogue and dialectic is essentially the development to a high degree of a tendency that is characteristic also of the ancient Greek mind: the tendency to see the world in terms of binary oppositions. We know, of course, that "thinking in opposites" is fundamental to all human reasoning;[1] but we know equally well that the ancients were especially given to antithetical thinking. It is as though Heraclitus, who conceived of all life as a harmony of warring forces – the so-called "complementarity of opposites" – had cast his imprint on subsequent ages; for the eristic spirit is as typical of the philosophy of the Greeks as the agonistic spirit is typical of their whole culture – a culture devoted to the worship of the goddess of Victory (Nike) and to its expression in athletic, rhetorical, theatrical, and musical contests (*agones*). These uni-

[1] See Paul Roubiczek, *Thinking in Opposites* (London, Routledge and Kegan Paul, 1952).

versally accepted cultural-historical generalizations, which we owe to
the insight of Jacob Burckhardt and other nineteenth-century scholars,
were undoubtedly sensed, however vaguely, by a man of Diderot's profound erudition; at least, they are implicit in his choice of the musical
*agon* between Apollo and Marsyas as the allegorical basis of *Le Neveu
de Rameau.*

We should not be surprised, therefore, to find in our satire – imbedded
in the structure or playing ironically beneath the surface – those paired
opposites (one and many, equal and unequal) without which no conversation involving Socrates would be complete.[2] But *Le Neveu de
Rameau* cannot be taken seriously as an exercise in empirical dialectic,
for the author begins with a fixed set of values in terms of what is
superior and what is inferior. "C'est un composé de hauteur et de
bassesse, de bon sens et de deraison"; thus is Lui described near the
beginning of the prologue (Fabre, p. 4), and thereafter the opposition
of "high" and "low" becomes a prominent theme.[3] The high and low
on the musical scale are the basic pattern with which Diderot is working.
To these correspond the sublime and the mediocre in art as well as the
noble and base in moral activity. Indeed, it is true to say that the opposition of "high" and "low" subsumes all the forms of "inequality" dealt
with in our dialogue: inequality of rank, of fortune, of intellect, of
temperament, of talent.[4] Where high and low are indiscriminately
mingled – as in the case of Lui – the result is inconsistency in action
and mediocrity in art.[5] And the ill-starred Lui – fragmented, direction-

2 Xenophon (*Memorabilia*, 1.i.16) stresses this aspect of Socrates' character:
"His own conversation was ever of human things. The problems he discussed were,
What is godly, what is ungodly; what is beautiful, what is ugly; what is just, what is
unjust; what is prudence, what is madness; what is courage, what is cowardice ..."
(trans. E. C. Marchant).

3 See the remarks on this subject by Michel Launay in *Entretiens sur "Le Neveu
de Rameau,"* 80 ff.

4 It was not only Rousseau's egalitarianism that Diderot found objectionable, but
also that of Helvétius. The latter's theory of man is described by Ernst Cassirer as "a
leveling process which threatens to deny the living wealth of human consciousness
and to look upon it merely as a disguise" (*The Philosophy of the Enlightenment*, 25–
6). Cassirer continues: "Analytical thinking removes this disguise from psychological
phenomena; it exposes them, and in so doing reveals their naked sameness rather
than their apparent diversity and inner differentiation. Differences in form as well
as in value vanish and prove to be delusions. As a result, there is no longer a 'top'
and 'bottom' or a 'higher' and a 'lower' in the realm of psychological phenomena.
Everything is on the same plane – equal in value and validity" (p. 26).

5 See the *Dictionnaire de l'Académie* (1762), s.v. "Haut": "On dit ... d'Un
homme d'humeur inégale, qu'*Il a du haut & du bas dans l'humeur. Il y a bien des
hauts & des bas dans son humeur.*" Cf. Rousseau, *Confessions*, Pléiade ed., I, 91:
"Dans l'ordre successif de mes gouts et de mes idées, j'avois toujours été trop haut
ou trop bas; Achille ou Thersite, tantot heros et tantôt vaurien."

less – is contrasted with three individuals who have attained to a certain unity: the genius who has sacrificed everything to a single intellectual passion; the "grand criminel" who relentlessly pursues his dominant vice; and the philosopher-sage who has achieved unity of virtue. The dialectical movement of the dialogue is not to be found in the argumentation but in the interplay of all these characters.

Other dialectical idea-patterns of *Le Neveu de Rameau* can be reconstructed around two key concepts already touched upon in Chapter 6. One of them is purely conceptual: *physis-nomos*[6] (nature-law); the other is mythical: Dionysus-Apollo (the god of nature and the god of reason). They express, in effect, a single antithesis – the antithesis that lies at the heart of the problem of man in society – that of Nature and Culture. (The words "Nature" and "Culture" must be taken here in their broadest sense: everything that is elemental, irrational, orgiastic, opposed to what is structured, reasoned, controlled.)

The Dionysian-Apollonian contrast has been a commonplace, of course, only since the time of Nietzsche.[7] But, because of the intimate relationship between this concept and the well-known *physis-nomos* antithesis, we need not fear that we are falsifying Diderot's thought in using these terms to interpret a work written a century before *The Birth of Tragedy*. Nietzsche's was the broader and deeper view, and his analysis of the tragic spirit bears mystic overtones that are the reflection of his individualistic temperament and of his particular philosophical formation. Diderot, on the other hand, was more concerned with the human comedy than with the human tragedy; nonetheless, his treatment of the question remains highly serious beneath the façade of buffoonery. His principal interests are those of a moralist and social philosopher: the conflict of the individual with society, and the relative claims of Nature and Art. Quite naturally, both of these problems are given a special bias by the fact that they are seen in the context of the Rousseau-Diderot quarrel.

The following schema can be said to represent the most important intellectual, moral, and aesthetic aspects of the Nature-Culture opposition with which we are dealing in *Le Neveu de Rameau*:

6 See Felix Heinimann, *Nomos und Physis. Herkunft und Bedeutung einer Antithese im griechischen Denken des 5. Jahrhunderts* (Basel, Friedrich Reinhardt, 1945). For the evolution of the concept of *physis*, see R. G. Collingwood, *The Idea of Nature* (Oxford, The Clarendon Press, 1945).

7 *Die Geburt der Tragödie aus dem Geiste der Musik* was first published in 1872. See also Carl Gustav Jung's well-known application of the Apollonian and Dionysian to psychology, in *Psychological Types, or the Psychology of Individuation*, trans. H. Godwin Baynes (London, Routledge and Kegan Paul, 1923), 170–83.

| PHYSIS (DIONYSIAN) | NOMOS (APOLLONIAN) |
|---|---|
| Enthusiasm | Philosophy |
| Temperament | Education |
| Individuality | Humanity |
| Chaos | Cosmos (Order) |
| Melody | Harmony |
| Nature | Art |

These paired concepts, some of which have already been touched upon, will be matter for discussion below. It should be noted here, however, that the pairing of such terms by no means implies that they are irreconcilably opposed. These and the other manifold tensions of which man is the focus make human life to be truly dialectical; it is their complementarity, not their opposition, that has the greater significance. So it was for Diderot. His classical (Apollonian) training was deeply ingrained in him; but he also had a deep awareness of the importance of enthusiastic (Dionysian) individualism – a lesson he had learned from long familiarity with the works of Shaftesbury. He was therefore particularly sensitive to the *physis-nomos* dichotomy and to the questions it raises for art and morality.

It was, of course, a personal problem for him as it is for everyone, and to that extent it is true to say that *Le Neveu de Rameau* is an attempt to paint the two faces of Denis Diderot – but only insofar as he shared the nature of "homo duplex" and saw both tendencies in himself as well as in all other men. The surest indication of the stand taken by the author in the dialogue – aside from the fact that Lui is a vicious fool and Moi a virtuous philosopher – is the notion of harmony that underlies the whole argument; and by "harmony" we must understand not only the meaning attached to that word since the Middle Ages – the simultaneous blending of dissimilar elements as in a musical chord – but also the Greek concept of harmony as a relative proportionality – the joining of several elements, or the disposition of the parts of a whole, according to a just ratio.[8] It is the contrast between Lui and Moi that bears the author's message: only when *physis* and *nomos* complement one another in their proper proportion – that is, when reason directs the primitive energies of men – will moral, social, and artistic progress become possible.

8 See R. G. Collingwood, *The Idea of Nature*, 52–3 and note. A most useful discussion of harmony in the context of literature is that of John Hollander, *The Untuning of the Sky: Ideas of Music in English Poetry, 1508–1700* (Princeton, N.J., Princeton University Press, 1961), 3–51. On this particular subject, see Hollander, pp. 26–7.

## Enthusiasm and Philosophy

The opposition between enthusiasm and philosophy is one that is never openly expressed in *Le Neveu de Rameau*, but it may nonetheless be more important than any other for our appreciation of Diderot's thought. Diderot, as we know, was prone to extol "great passions"; enthusiasm, for him, was an essential element of sublimity in moral action as well as in art.[9] However, there are few occasions when his praise of enthusiasm is not accompanied by a warning against excess.[10] And there are reasons for seeing the contrast between Lui and Moi in our dialogue as another affirmation that enthusiasm must be tempered by rational control, for this is a point on which Rousseau and Diderot seem to have been at odds.

What follows is pure speculation. In the second of the *Entretiens sur le Fils naturel*, Diderot paints the character Dorval rather sympathetically as a melancholy enthusiast (A.T., VII, 102–3). Now, although there can be no doubt that Dorval is made to express Diderot's own views throughout the work, it is fairly well established that, both in the *Entretiens* and in *Le Fils naturel*, he has been endowed with certain traits of Jean-Jacques Rousseau.[11] It would seem that Diderot is here gently mocking his friend's enthusiastic temperament. Of course, the depiction of Dorval is by no stretch of the imagination a satirical portrait; but it could easily have been taken for such by the melancholy Rousseau, especially in view of the fact that *Le Fils naturel* contained the impertinent dictum aimed at him, "Il n'y a que le méchant qui soit seul."[12]

It was some time after the appearance of *Le Fils naturel* (February 1757) that Rousseau expanded the original four parts of his novel *La Nouvelle Héloïse*, adding the religious theme and making Julie's husband, M. de Wolmar, an atheist.[13] Like Diderot's Dorval (whose name

---

9 See the first five *Pensées philosophiques* (A.T., I, 127–8). Also the article "Eclectisme" of the *Encyclopédie*: "J'observerai ici en passant qu'il est impossible en poésie, en peinture, en éloquence, en musique, de rien produire de sublime sans enthousiasme" (A.T., XIV, 322).

10 The fourth *Pensée* insists that the passions must be controlled: "Etablissez entre elles une juste harmonie, et n'en appréhendez point de désordres" (A.T., I, 128). The article "Eclectisme" is much more forceful: "il faut un très-grand sens pour balancer l'enthousiasme. L'enthousiasme n'entraîne que quand les esprits ont été préparés et soumis par la force de la raison; c'est un principe que les poëtes ne doivent jamais perdre de vue dans leurs fictions ..." (A.T., XIV, 323).

11 See Diderot, *Œuvres esthétiques*, ed. P. Vernière, 73–4; Blandine McLaughlin, "A New Look at Diderot's *Fils naturel*," *Diderot Studies*, x (1968), 109–19; Herbert Dieckmann, "Currents and Crosscurrents in *Le Fils naturel*," *Linguistic and Literary Studies in Honor of Helmut A. Hatzfeld* (Washington, The Catholic University of America Press, 1964), 107–16.

12 Act IV, Sc. 3 (A.T., VII, 66).

13 See the editor's introduction in the Pléiade edition, II, xl. Rousseau had completed his novel by September 1758 (ibid., lv).

is so similar to his own), M. de Wolmar expresses many of the author's own ideas; but, despite a certain sympathy in the portrayal of his character, he is essentially the cold, indifferent philosopher whom Rousseau had turned to ridicule on two previous occasions.[14] Neither sad nor gay, Wolmar seldom laughs; everything, even his love for Julie, seems to be regulated by reason (Pléiade II, 370). His cold rationality is constantly stressed (ibid., 370, 490, 492, 561) and is even satirized on one occasion.[15] His first meeting with Julie had inspired in him the only emotion he had ever experienced (p. 492), and her death draws from him the first tears he has ever shed (p. 721). He feels no compassion for humanity (pp. 490, 491), but enjoys playing the role of dispassionate observer (pp. 370, 491, 561). His life is one of perfect orderliness (p. 371), and his "goût naturel de l'ordre," the mainspring of all his activity, allows him to enjoy the spectacle presented by the human comedy "comme une belle simétrie dans un tableau, ou comme une piece bien conduite au théâtre" (pp. 490–1). He is "sans passion" (p. 429), "integre et severe" (p. 443), "tranquille et contemplatif" (p. 507) – in a word, his entire existence is ruled by "le sens-froid d'un philosophe" (p. 561). But, despite his many virtues, M. de Wolmar's atheism is a constant source of pain to the devout Julie; and indeed, the contrast between his upright conduct and his unbelief serves to increase her sorrow: "Cet homme si sage, si raisonnable, si loin de toute espece de vice, si peu soumis aux passions humaines, ne croit rien de ce qui donne un prix aux vertus, et, dans l'innocence d'une vie irréprochable, il porte au fond de son cœur l'affreuse paix des méchans" (p. 588).

It is quite conceivable that Rousseau's portrait of M. de Wolmar is a companion-piece to Diderot's Dorval. Wolmar's cold indifference stands in direct contrast to the pitiful emotional weakness of Dorval as he appears in Le Fils naturel, especially in the third scene of Act IV where we find not only Diderot's statement about the "méchant" but also certain allusions to Rousseau's fears concerning his children.[16] It would no doubt be an exaggeration to say that M. de Wolmar is a caricature of Diderot; but it is not unreasonable to suggest that Julie's husband, who condemns the "trompeur enthousiasme" by which Julie and her lover had been led astray (Pléiade II, 495), bears a message that

14 See Rousseau's Preface to Narcisse, Pléiade ed., II, 967, and the Discours sur l'inégalité, Pléiade ed., III, 156. When Rousseau tells us (Confessions, Pléiade ed., I, 389 n.) that this last portrait was suggested to him by Diderot, we can only conclude that Jean-Jacques failed to perceive the sarcasm that dictated Diderot's suggestion!

15 "Wolmar lui-même, le froid Wolmar se sentit ému. O sentiment, sentiment! douce vie de l'ame! quel est le cœur de fer que tu n'as jamais touché? quel est l'infortuné mortel à qui tu n'arrachas jamais de larmes?" (Pléiade II, 599).

16 A.T., VII, 66–8. See Blandine McLaughlin, "A New Look at Diderot's Fils naturel," 115–17.

was directed at Diderot, just as the enthusiastic character of Dorval was intended as a rebuke to Jean-Jacques. It seems entirely possible, therefore, that *La Nouvelle Héloïse*, which was published in France in January 1761, set Diderot to preparing a reply – the original *portrait-charge* of Rousseau that was to become, after the appearance of *Emile* in 1762, the satire known as *Le Neveu de Rameau*.

## Temperament and Education

It was suggested in Chapter 4 above that *Le Neveu de Rameau* treats of education at its most fundamental level. Is nature modifiable? Are men perfectible? Can virtue be taught? These are some of the questions posed by the interplay of character and argument; and to all of them it is Lui, not Moi, who gives a resounding negative reply. Believing that the failure he has experienced is ineluctable – whether it be explained by heredity, education, environment, lack of inspiration, or simply by fate – the musician literally makes a virtue of necessity and rejoices in the fact that his vicious life, however meagre its material rewards, is at least in conformity with the character that nature has given him (Fabre, p. 44). All of Moi's suggestions for self-improvement – hard work, courage, discipline, asceticism – are blithely dismissed as impossible or undesirable. Both for himself and for his son, Lui prefers to let nature run her course (p. 90); and this is his last word on the subject: "je ferois mal de prendre une autre allure qui me peneroit, et que je ne garderois pas" (p. 108).

Moi, on the other hand, firmly believes in the efficacy of a good education. The lessons in ethics that he prescribes for his daughter (p. 31) indicate his belief in the teachability of virtue; and it is with some reluctance that he is brought to admit, in the closing lines, that he has before him a man beyond hope of moral enlightenment. The satirical implication, of course, is that the multitude of his contemporaries whom Lui represents are equally incorrigible.

If we are to understand fully the significance of the educational theme, we must not neglect the fact that Diderot had constantly before his mind the parallel between his own age and antiquity. Socrates, in his debates with Protagoras and others concerning the teachability of virtue, defends a series of paradoxical propositions that are the basis of his so-called "intellectualism." A recent book on the subject sets them forth as follows: "These paradoxes are: no one does wrong willingly; no one wishes evil; virtue can be taught; virtue is an art like medicine or carpentry; virtue is knowledge; vice is ignorance."[17] The *Meno*, the

17 Michael J. O'Brien, *The Socratic Paradoxes and the Greek Mind* (Chapel Hill, University of North Carolina Press, 1967), 16.

*Hippias Minor,* the *Protagoras,* the *Gorgias,* are largely devoted to discussing various aspects of these statements. The *Meno* concludes that, if virtue can be taught, it must be a form of knowledge (87c), but that no one has yet proved that it can be taught successfully. The *Republic* finally answers the question affirmatively by showing *how* virtue can be taught; but such teaching is strictly limited to those who are fortunate enough to be born with a "philosophic nature."

In *Le Neveu de Rameau,* the Platonic doctrine of education and the Socratic paradoxes provide a kind of intellectual background to the satire. Diderot's dialogue is not, as many have believed, the product of a momentary lapse into immorality; much less is it the final self-revelation of a hypocritical preacher of virtue. On the contrary, it is a powerful affirmation of Socratism, of faith in virtue and happiness through reason, dramatically stated in the ironical confrontation of an ideal sage with an unhappy wretch, no less ideal, whose foolish sophistries have brought him to a state of utter abjection. Woven into the character of Lui are traits borrowed from certain opponents of the Platonic Socrates – from the "great sophist" Protagoras for whom the individual is the measure of all things; from Ion the inspired rhapsode whose imitations of Homer are mechanical and unintelligent; from Hippias who pretended to know all things and who failed signally to know himself; from the immoralists Thrasymachus and Callicles, and perhaps from many more. Like those works of Plato which are aporetic, Diderot's satire appears on the surface to end in *aporia* or uncertainty; but, when we consider the mock-heroic treatment of Lui's downfall, the interplay of character with its all-pervading irony, and especially the underlying allegory, we must come to the conclusion that the author is not posing questions but making statements. Paradoxical statements, it is true, but presented with a force that only satire can command: virtue is knowledge, especially self-knowledge; vice is ignorance of where true human happiness lies; virtue and happiness are arts, like music; virtue, like music, can be taught – but not to all.

## Individuality and Humanity

In the prologue of *Le Neveu de Rameau,* the author introduces Lui as an unusual character whose "natural individuality" has successfully resisted the levelling effects of education and social convention.[18] The unique qualities of this bizarre personage immediately attract our interest; but it is not long before it appears that we are dealing not only with

18 Fabre, p. 5. It is of interest to note that the neologism "individualité," which Littré finds first in 1760 (see Fabre, p. 272), is used by Jean-Jacques Rousseau in his first version of the *Contrat social,* written in 1755 or 1756 (Pléiade ed., III, 284).

a fascinating individual but with an individualist of the most cynical type. Despite his engaging talents, Lui is a moral solipsist whose only law is that of self-interest. He is the "puer robustus" of Hobbes; he is the "raisonneur violent" of Diderot's article "Droit naturel"; his spirit of revolt parodies the naked individualism that breathes through Rousseau's second *Discours*.

The most striking example of individualism in the dialogue (and there are many) is the theory of the "idiotismes moraux" propounded by Lui (Fabre, pp. 36–7). It is indeed ironical that this passage, frequently cited to prove Diderot's immoralism, must have been intended by the author to be a criticism of Rousseauist individualism. We know, of course, that the general tendency of Rousseau's philosophy is not individualistic; nonetheless, a recent editor of *La Nouvelle Héloïse* has pointed out that the dictum "être soi!" is "la loi fondamentale de la vie morale selon Rousseau."[19] The same impulse towards self-realization exists, to be sure, in Diderot; but Hubert Gillot, whose study of the *philosophe* includes a chapter entitled "Etre soi," comes to the conclusion that "Diderot n'a garde de sacrifier aux prétentions de l'individualisme anarchique les droits imprescriptibles de l'intérêt général."[20] Diderot, like Socrates, was violently opposed to any individualist interpretation of the "homo-mensura" principle enunciated by the great sophist Protagoras and implicit in the doctrine of Rousseau, "le grand sophiste" of the eighteenth century. For the Encyclopedist it is mankind, not the individual man, that is the measure of all things.

Two firmly held principles underlie Diderot's ethical thinking in this regard: first, that the recognition of oneself as part of a larger system (the human race) bears with it a moral imperative;[21] and second, that it is erroneous, in our reasoning concerning man, to argue from purely animal nature as Rousseau and Helvétius were prone to do.[22] Against Rousseau's individualism in the *Discours sur l'inégalité* he declared: "Je suis homme, et je n'ai d'autres *droits naturels* véritablement inaliénables

19 Pléiade ed., ii, 1534, n. 1 to p. 334.

20 Hubert Gillot, *Denis Diderot. L'homme; ses idées philosophiques, esthétiques, littéraires* (Paris, 1937), 98.

21 This notion, an intellectualized version of Shaftesburian doctrine, might be called the theme of the article "Droit naturel" (A.T., xiv, 296–301). A most illuminating discussion of the virtue of "humanité" is found in Paul Vernière, "L'Idée d'humanité au xviii^ème siècle," *Studium Generale*, xv (1962), 171–9; for the relative positions of Diderot and Rousseau on this question, see pp. 173, 176–7. See also Rousseau's first version of the *Contrat social* (Pléiade ed., iii, 281–9), written in refutation of Diderot.

22 *Réfutation d'Helvétius*, A.T., ii, 388: "l'homme n'est point une bête, il ne faut pas négliger cette différence dans le jugement que l'on porte de ses actions." Text corrected according to Roland Desné, in *Diderot Studies*, x (1968), 43.

que ceux de l'humanité";[23] and against the ingenuous mechanistic doctrine of Helvétius: "je suis homme, et il me faut des causes propres à l'homme."[24] In *Le Neveu de Rameau*, the "Je suis homme" of Diderot-Moi is opposed to the "Je suis moi" of Rousseau-Lui; the cry of humanity: "Songeons au bien de notre espece" (Fabre, p. 14) is answered by the cry of individuality: "Le point important est que vous et moi nous soions, et que nous soions vous et moi" (ibid.). We may conclude, therefore, that at this level the debate betwen Lui and Moi is a confrontation of the individual with the species, of egoism with enlightened self-interest, of savagery with civilization.[25]

## Chaos and Cosmos

In 1748, Diderot began to divest himself of the influence of Shaftesbury and sentimentalism. The first sign of this emancipation is found in one of his mathematical essays published in that year, where he propounds a theory of moral and aesthetic judgment conceived as "la perception des rapports."[26] He had still not relinquished entirely the possibility that aesthetic appreciation might be a matter of sentiment for the multitude (A.T., IX, 106); but the article "Beau" of the *Encyclopédie* dismisses completely the "sixth sense" theory (A.T., X, 20–4) and affirms that moral and aesthetic appreciation is not innate but empirical, not an act of sentiment but an act of understanding (ibid., 25–8). It is the intellect alone that can seize "rapports," a term which Diderot uses to include

23 Article "Droit naturel," A.T., XIV, 300.

24 *Réfutation d'Helvétius*, A.T., II, 300.

25 In *The Political Writings of Jean-Jacques Rousseau* (Cambridge, at the University Press, 1915, 2 vols.), C. E. Vaughan suggested that Diderot's "raisonneur violent" of the article "Droit naturel" was intended by the author to represent Jean-Jacques, and he adduced certain corroborative arguments (1, 427–8). Rousseau's refusal to accept either reasoned virtue or enlightened self-interest forced him to pose the question of justice in anti-intellectualist terms: "Il ne s'agit pas de m'apprendre ce que c'est que justice; il s'agit de me montrer quel intérest j'ai d'être juste" (*Contrat social*, first version, Pléiade ed., III, 286). In *Le Neveu de Rameau*, Lui's insistence on seeing everything from the viewpoint of self-interest (Fabre, p. 56) indicates that he belongs to the same family as Rousseau and the "raisonneur violent."

26 *Principes généraux d'acoustique*, A.T., IX, 104: "Le plaisir, en général, consiste dans la perception des rapports. Ce principe a lieu en poésie, en peinture, en architecture, en morale, dans tous les arts et dans toutes les sciences. Une belle machine, un beau tableau, un beau portique ne nous plaisent que par les rapports que nous y remarquons : ne peut-on pas même dire qu'il en est en cela d'une belle vie comme d'un beau concert? La perception des rapports est l'unique fondement de notre admiration et de nos plaisirs ..." This theory has its foundation in music; indeed, Diderot gives Pythagoras credit for its discovery: "Pythagore posa les premiers fondements de la science des sons. Il ignora comment l'oreille apprécie les rapports; il se trompa même sur leurs limites; mais il découvrit que leur perception était la source du plaisir musical" (ibid., 85).

"ordre," "arrangement," "symétrie," and so forth, "car tous ces mots ne désignent que différentes manières d'envisager les rapports mêmes" (ibid., 28).

During these same years, he took the decisive step of rejecting a universe ordered by Providence in favour of a universe in which order is the temporary equilibrium of necessary physical forces. By 1749 at the latest, the "spectacle of nature" no longer speaks to Diderot's heart of an intelligent creator any more than it speaks to the blind eyes of Saunderson.[27] How, then, do we explain the marvellous order in nature and the apparent interdependence of all things? "Ce sont des êtres métaphysiques qui n'existent que dans votre esprit," he tells Voltaire, though once again disguising himself with the mask of Saunderson.[28] And he continues, with tongue in cheek: "Je crois en Dieu, quoique je vive très bien avec les athées. Je me suis aperçu que les charmes de l'ordre les captivoient malgré qu'ils en eussent; qu'ils étoient enthousiastes du beau et du bon ..."[29]

"Les charmes de l'ordre," "l'amour de l'ordre," "le goût de l'ordre" – these are the terms by which Diderot characterizes man's ineluctable inclination towards truth, beauty, and goodness.[30] Man is an ordering animal by virtue of his intellect; although living in a universe of heterogeneous matter in continual flux, he is drawn to admire the provisional configurations of things that he sees around him and he strives to create order in his material environment, in his moral life, in society, and in his own artistic activity. The "love of order," then, is not a blind submission to Providence or to the necessity imposed by material forces; it is a natural intellectual activity, the source of virtue, of social harmony, and of art. When properly exercised, it overflows into a fervent enthusiasm for the true, the good, and the beautiful. It is neither cold rationalism nor rabid fanaticism; it is both the philosophy-*eros* described by Socrates in Plato's *Symposium* and the serene heroism of his death. It frees the individual from the chaos of "sensibilité," it frees society from the dis-

---

27 *Lettre sur les aveugles*, A.T., I, 307–11. The argument for the existence of God based on the order of the universe was the only proof that Diderot had explicitly accepted in the *Pensées philosophiques* (*Pensée* XX, A.T., I, 133–4) – and his adherence to it was already seriously undermined by his scepticism concerning the argument from motion (*Pensée* XXI).

28 Letter to Voltaire, 11 June 1749. *Corr.*, ed. Roth, I, 77.

29 Ibid., 78.

30 *Entretiens sur le Fils naturel*, A.T., VII, 127: "Je définis la vertu, le goût de l'ordre dans les choses morales. Le goût de l'ordre en général nous domine dès la plus tendre enfance; il est plus ancien dans notre âme ... qu'aucun sentiment réfléchi ... il agit en nous, sans que nous nous en apercevions; c'est le germe de l'honnêteté et du bon goût; il nous porte au bien, tant qu'il n'est point gêné par la passion ..." For a later exposition of this doctrine in a wider context, see Diderot's letter to Falconet, 4 October 1767, *Corr.*, ed. Roth, VII, 163–4.

cord of injustice, and it frees the artist from the tyranny of the "disparate."

Rousseau too was attracted to the notion of "love of order"; for him, however, it was not the source of virtue but a sentiment intimately related to his faith in Providence. When he endows M. de Wolmar with "le goût naturel de l'ordre" and "l'amour de l'ordre" (Pléiade II, 490, 492), he goes on to say that love of virtue is a passion, not a function of reason (p. 493); and Wolmar, moreover, is made to express a certain passive optimism that is really that of Jean-Jacques: "Tout concourt au bien commun dans le sistême universel. Tout homme a sa place assignée dans le meilleur ordre des choses, il s'agit de trouver cette place et de ne pas pervertir cet ordre" (ibid., 563). The editor of the Pléiade edition comments on this passage as follows: "Ce qui revient à dire que non seulement nous ne pouvons pas corriger la nature, mais que nous ne le devons pas. Ce serait offenser la volonté de son auteur" (p. 1674).

It is this doctrine that is parodied in Le Neveu de Rameau when Lui proclaims: "Le meilleur ordre des choses, a mon avis, est celui ou j'en devois etre; et foin du plus parfait des mondes, si je n'en suis pas" (Fabre, pp. 14–15). Rousseau, in Emile, had written: "j'acquiesce à l'ordre qu'il [Dieu] établit, sûr de joüir moi-même un jour de cet ordre, et d'y trouver ma félicité : car quelle félicité plus douce que de se sentir ordonné dans un sistême où tout est bien?" (Pléiade IV, 603). In view of this, we may conclude that it is not Diderot's determinism but Rousseau's fatalistic optimism that lies behind Lui's supine acceptance of the character that nature has given him (Fabre, pp. 44, 90, 108). For Diderot as for Moi, order in the soul, in society, and in art is a prize to be won by conquest, and the success of our efforts depends upon the proper marshalling of the forces of reason.

### Melody and Harmony

One of the major sources of disagreement between the Encyclopedists and Jean-Philippe Rameau was the fact that for them, as for Plato, music was an imitative art; and we must understand "imitation" in this context to mean not servile reproduction but dynamic expressionism. If music is imitative, what does it imitate? Nothing other than the interior movements of the soul. And since this is the case, it is melody, not harmony, that is the soul of music.[31] Harmony can at best imitate only

31 Paul-Marie Masson, in an article entitled "Les Idées de Rousseau sur la musique" (Revue Musicale, July–August 1912, p. 5), writes thus: "l'harmonie est dans la musique un élément secondaire et accessoire, tandis que la mélodie est l'élément primitif et essentiel. Sur ce point Rousseau s'oppose nettement à Rameau, et cette question du primat de l'harmonie ou de la mélodie forme le principal objet de leur polémique."

natural sounds, as indeed Rameau had imitated instrumentally the croaking of frogs in his *Platée*; it is melody that expresses the passionate responses of an individual or the spirit of a national group. Harmony has conventional beauties, melody is nature beautified. Harmony speaks to the ear, melody to the heart. Harmony is a science – geometry imposed on music; it is only by virtue of melody that music can be called an art. These ideas, to which Rousseau returned again and again, are found most clearly expressed in Chapters xii to xix of his *Essai sur l'origine des langues*, written in 1754.

It is easy to see how Rousseau's expressionistic doctrine fits into the overall plan of *Le Neveu de Rameau*; but what exactly is Diderot's position on the musical question? I would suggest that he was too much the scientist and philosopher to reduce harmony in music to the subordinate position given it by Rousseau. We know, of course, that he considered Rameau's exaggeration of the importance of harmony to be an aberration,[32] and we must surmise that he believed Rousseau's enthusiasm for melody to be equally extreme. As early as 1748 Diderot had given recognition to the truly scientific nature of music and had expressed his awareness of the dangers of "le scepticisme musical" attached to a purely empirical approach.[33] Although he was not inimical to the basic implications of the "cri de la passion" (Fabre, pp. 86–7), it is very doubtful that he saw eye to eye with Rousseau on the question of melody.

## Nature and Art

We have spoken above of the precarious balance between enthusiasm and rationalism in Diderot's thought. It is generally recognized that at some point between 1757 and 1770 – that is, between the publication of the *Entretiens sur le Fils naturel* and the time when the *Paradoxe sur le comédien* began to take shape in his mind – his distrust of enthusiasm became more pronounced. The article "Eclectisme" of 1755 had warned that enthusiasm is not far removed from folly (A.T., xiv, 323); the article "Théosophes," written some time after the break with Rousseau, still praises enthusiasm – but the accompanying warning shows the influence of Diderot's reflections on the "grand criminel": "L'enthousiasme est le germe de toutes les grandes choses, bonnes ou mauvaises"

32 *Encyclopédie*, Vol. vi, "Avertissement des Editeurs," p. ii. Here, as in *Le Neveu de Rameau* (Fabre, p. 6), it is a question of the "visions inintelligibles" in which Rameau tended to see harmony as the key to the universe.

33 *Principes généraux d'acoustique*, A.T., ix, 85–6. Diderot here takes a middle position between the rigid mathematization of music by the followers of Pythagoras and the empiricism espoused by Aristoxenus and his school. There can be little doubt that Diderot recognized the parallel between the Pythagorean-Aristoxenian dispute and the Rameau-Rousseau controversy, just as he saw a relationship between the "Querelle des Bouffons" and the Dorian-Phrygian quarrel.

(A.T., XVII, 245). It seems that during these years, partly because of his experience with the enthusiast Rousseau and partly owing to his studies in biology, Diderot tended to consider enthusiasm as the effect of *sensibilité*, that physical weakness by which one is impelled either to sublime action or to folly and vice. His famous definition of *sensibilité* in the *Paradoxe sur le comédien* concludes as follows: "Multipliez les âmes sensibles, et vous multiplierez en même proportion les bonnes et les mauvaises actions en tout genre ..." (A.T., VIII, 393).

The hesitation of Diderot's thought in this regard is described by Yvon Belaval in *L'Esthétique sans paradoxe de Diderot*:

rien ne saurait être plus dangereux pour l'art, la morale et l'ordre public que les prédications à la Rousseau en faveur de la sensibilité. Le plus heureux est sans doute l'homme sensible : mais ce bonheur est égotiste. Dans la société, le bonheur de chacun dépend des vertus raisonnables. La Nature devient raison progressivement découverte. La supériorité de l'ordre rationnel sur le désordre de la sensibilité s'impose tellement à Diderot qu'il ne recule plus devant les conséquences (pp. 284–5).

It is the gradual crystallization of these ideas that seems to have produced the *Paradoxe*, in which Diderot, without disturbing the traditional equilibrium between Nature and Art (natural talent and artistic rules) – both of which, for him as for Horace (*Ars poet.*, 408–11), remain equally indispensable – attempts to demythologize inspiration or enthusiasm by making rational insight the mark of the great actor as it is for the genius in every order. And this doctrine, according to M. Belaval (pp. 291–2), is quite consistent with his general philosophical orientation: "En réalité, Diderot n'a jamais dénoncé les droits de la raison : le fond constant de sa doctrine se définirait, s'il était permis de s'exprimer ainsi, comme un intellectualisme empiriste."

I would propose that the *Paradoxe sur le comédien* is the final manifestation of Diderot's intellectualism, first expressed in 1748 in his theory of aesthetic appreciation as the "perception des rapports" (A.T., IX, 104; X, 25–8). Other recognizable steps in the process are the exorcism of the demon of Socrates in *De l'interprétation de la nature* (A.T., II, 24) and in the article "Théosophes" (A.T., XVII, 242–3), the theory of the "modèle idéal" in *De la poésie dramatique* (A.T., VII, 390–4), and the whole tenor of the argument in *Le Neveu de Rameau*. In this last-named work, Diderot's admiration for the natural genius of Lui (and, we must infer, for that of Jean-Jacques Rousseau) is evident in the striking talents conferred upon the pantomime musician; but the author cannot fully endorse an artist in whom *sensibilité* is not balanced by rational control. As he tells us in the *Observations sur Garrick*, nature untempered by art and reason cannot be consistently sublime: "ce n'est pas que la pure nature n'ait ses moments sublimes; mais je conçois que si quelqu'un est sûr de leur conserver leur sublimité, c'est celui qui les aura pressentis et qui les rendra de sang-froid" (A.T., VIII, 350). We may sum up his thoughts concerning Nature and Art in terms of mimesis: man is by nature an imitative animal; but mimicry and artistic imitation are two completely different things.

GRAVE AND GAY

One of the most difficult problems posed by *Le Neveu de Rameau* is the function in the dialogue of the elements of buffoonery and farce. In his Introduction to the satire, Jean Fabre stresses the fact that farce is combined with pathos in the character Lui, whose façade of clownish gaiety is unable to conceal his utter failure to realize himself as a person: "Sa tragédie est une farce, sa farce une tragédie" (p. lxxxiii). This opinion represents a sensitive reading of the work, and its validity cannot be questioned; but the conception of the satire as "farce-tragédie" is only one aspect of the total picture. With the adjustment of perspective authorized by our previous findings, it is possible to propose a more general explanation of the buffoonery that will relate it both to the structure and to the characterization. As we have seen, *Le Neveu de Rameau* owes its principal inspiration to ancient literature; it would seem probable, in consequence, that Moi and Lui, the philosopher and the buffoon, were intended by the author to incarnate the spirit that characterizes all Greek satirical writings as well as the Socratic dialogues – that mixture of the serious and the laughable which the Greeks called *to spoudaiogeloion* and which Lucilius adopted in his creation of the Roman literary genre named *satura*.[34]

The question of the serio-comic is so closely linked to that of satire that we should be well advised to study them together in a separate section. There is, however, one aspect of the matter that can usefully be considered here. Although Diderot formed his ideas on the serio-comic by direct contact with Greek and Roman sources, his approach to it in *Le Neveu de Rameau* seems to have been influenced considerably by a commentary on ancient literature from the pen of one of his favourite modern authors. I am referring to the third of the six essays that make up Shaftesbury's *Characteristics*, entitled *Soliloquy, or Advice to an Author*.[35]

This treatise of Shaftesbury's contains a particularly interesting pas-

34 On this concept, see Mary A. Grant, *The Ancient Rhetorical Theories of the Laughable* (Madison, Wisconsin, 1924), 20, 56–9.

35 All references to the *Characteristics* are to the edition of J. M. Robertson (London, 1900), reprinted in 1963 (Gloucester, Mass., Peter Smith, 2 vols.). Cited as Robertson.

sage pertaining to our subject. The question under discussion is the influence of critics on the gradual refinement of taste and style in the ancient Greek theatre (Pt. II, Sec. 2); in this connection, he draws a parallel between the historical beginnings of the theatre and those of philosophy (Robertson, I, 163 ff.). First, the theatre. According to Aristotle, says Shaftesbury, comedy was a later invention than tragedy (which he calls "the Sublime"); and he concludes from this historical fact that the "familiar airy muse" of comedy must have been introduced to serve as a natural corrective to false sublimity, having the function of "a sort of counter-pedagogue against the pomp and formality of the more solemn writers." Then, turning to philosophy, he shows that there occurred about the same time a similar succession of styles in that discipline:

in opposition to the sublime philosopher [Socrates], and afterwards to his grave disciple and successor in the Academy [Plato], there arose a comic philosophy in the person of another master and other disciples [Diogenes and the Cynics], who personally, as well as in their writings, were set in direct opposition to the former; not as differing in opinions or maxims, but in their style and manner; in the turn of humour and method of instruction (Robertson, I, 165–6).

Enlarging upon this theme, Shaftesbury points out that in the same way as all forms of poetry – "the tragic, the comic, and every other kind" – were said to be derived from Homer, so Socrates was the source of the various styles in which philosophy found expression in antiquity:

His disciple of noble birth and lofty genius [Plato], who aspired to poetry and rhetoric, took the *Sublime* part, and shone above his other condisciples. He of mean birth and poorest circumstances [Antisthenes], whose constitution as well as condition inclined him most to the way we call satiric, took the reproving part, which in his better-humoured and more agreeable successor [Diogenes] turned into the comic kind, and went upon the model of that ancient comedy which was then prevalent (Robertson, I, 166–7).

In these passages we have, I believe, the master pattern that guided the portrayal of character in Diderot's dialogue: Moi represents the sublime and serious philosophical school of Socrates and Plato, Lui the vulgar, comic side of Cynicism. It is true that we do not ordinarily think of Lui in terms of philosophy; yet he is far more than the "pauvre diable de bouffon" he represents himself to be (Fabre, p. 12), for he pretends to direct his life according to a system, that of ruthless individualism (pp. 9, 61, 94). It is his adoption of this system that dooms him to failure as a human being; built on the shifting sands of impulse and self-gratification, it proves to be no system at all and dissolves into corrosive universal cynicism. He has, of course, none of the high ideals of the Cynics, merely their buffooning manner; his spirit is that of the decadent age described by Diderot in the article "Cyniques" of the *Encyclopédie*, when "tout ce qu'il y avait, dans les villes de la Grèce et de l'Italie, de bouffons, d'impudents, de mendiants, de parasites, de gloutons et de fainéants ... prit effrontément le nom de *cyniques*" (A.T., XIV, 255).

### SATIRE AND COMEDY

Despite the title *Satyre 2$^{de}$* which Diderot gave to his dialogue, despite its sardonic tone and the miscellaneous character of the topics discussed, *Le Neveu de Rameau* cannot be said to coincide exactly with any of the literary forms usually designated by the term "satire." This does not mean, however, that the title is an inappropriate one; on the contrary, it is no exaggeration to say that this unique piece of writing is the very quintessence of satire. From the time of Lucilius, the inventor of the genre proper, the distinguishing characteristic of satire has been the disparate or miscellaneous nature of the subject matter; Diderot, in adopting this procedure, extended it to include not only the subject matter but also the form itself of the work. *Le Neveu de Rameau* fails to match any of the traditional patterns of satire for one very excellent reason: its author, in constructing it, drew on all the satirico-comic forms known to ancient literature from its very beginnings to the end of the classical age.

"J'ai un peu étudié le système dramatique des Anciens" (A.T., VII, 124). This laconic remark of Diderot in the *Entretiens sur le Fils naturel* was no idle boast; we have only to look at his article "*Comédie (Hist. anc.)*" of the *Encyclopédie* (III, 669) to be assured that he was familiar with the standard commentaries on this subject. Let us review some of the other literary traditions that he must have gleaned from his readings: that the origins of comedy, if we are to believe Aristotle, are to be found in the pseudo-Homeric mock-epic entitled *Margites*;[36] that Plato's dialogues were traditionally considered to be literary mimes like those of Sophron;[37] that the first Latin works called "saturae" were farcical stage pieces with musical accompaniment;[38] and that Roman satire, according to Horace, had been modelled after the Old Comedy of Aristo-

---

36 *Poetics*, IV, 1448b.

37 Diogenes Laertius, III, 18. On this subject, see Hermann Reich, *Der Mimus* (Berlin, 1903, 2 vols.), I, 380–99, 405–13. More generally, William C. Greene, "The Spirit of Comedy in Plato," *Harvard Studies in Classical Philology*, XXXI (1920), 63–123.

38 Livy, VII, 2. See J. Wight Duff, *Roman Satire* (Berkeley, University of California Press, 1936), 19–20. Also G. Michaut, *Sur les tréteaux latins* (Paris, Fontemoing & C$^{ie}$, 1912), 51–87.

phanes, with its great freedom of expression (*parrhesia*) and its mixture of grave and gay.[39]

We shall touch upon all these matters as we proceed; their juxtaposition above serves merely to indicate that comedy, satire, mock-epic, Socratic dialogue, and mime are interrelated forms of expression whose confluence in the *Satyre 2^{de}* has a certain historical justification – especially when we see presiding over the work the traditional notion of satire as medley or miscellany. The concept of satirical mixture, however, is not sufficient to clarify Diderot's intention in *Le Neveu de Rameau*; if Plato's views on music and imitation have helped us to see the philosophic basis for objecting to uncontrolled multiplicity, Shaftesbury is able to throw light on the artistic aspect of the question. In the ironical first chapter of his *Miscellaneous Reflections* he observes with wry humour that regularity, order, and simplicity were once considered essential to works of art, but that now "mere wit" is in the ascendancy. Scorning the discipline and effort required by classic kinds and forms, the new school has had recourse to the miscellany as a means of expression:

A manner therefore is invented to confound this simplicity and conformity of design; patchwork is substituted; cuttings and shreds of learning, with various fragments and points of wit, are drawn together and tacked in any fantastic form. If they chance to cast a lustre and spread a sort of sprightly glare, the miscellany is approved and the complex form and texture of the work admired. The eye, which before was to be won by regularity, and had kept true to measure and strict proportion, is by this means pleasingly drawn aside to commit a kind of debauch and amuse itself in gaudy colours and disfigured shapes of things. Custom in the meanwhile has not only tolerated this licentiousness, but rendered it even commendable, and brought it into the highest repute.[40]

It is important to note that, in order to drive home the point of this satire on democratic taste and makeshift artistry, Shaftesbury himself proceeds to write a miscellany, defined as "a kind of work which, according to modern establishment, has properly neither top nor bottom, beginning nor end."[41] It is this procedure that Diderot followed in *Le Neveu de Rameau*; and it is only when we see that his miscellany too contains an implicit condemnation of popular taste in matters of art that we begin to appreciate the wedding of form and sense that makes his satire a model of literary irony.

39 Horace, *Sat.*, I.iv.1–7; I.x.1–19.
40 Robertson, II, 159.
41 Ibid., 161.

We may return to ancient satire by way of another passage from Shaftesbury. In *Soliloquy, or Advice to an Author*, his discussion of the various styles that are proper to critical writing leads him to remark that neither the sublime form (Plato) nor the methodic form (Aristotle) has any chance of touching modern hearts. There remains, he says, a single expedient:

The only manner left in which criticism can have its just force amongst us is the ancient comic; of which kind were the first Roman miscellanies or satiric pieces; a sort of original writing of their own, refined afterwards by the best genius and politest poet of that nation [Horace], who, notwithstanding, owns the manner to have been taken from the Greek comedy above mentioned. And if our home wits would refine upon this pattern, they might perhaps meet with considerable success.[42]

We must now attempt to determine to what extent Diderot followed this sage advice.

The one thing everyone knows about Diderot's dramatic theories is that he attempted to establish the poetics of a genre intermediate between tragedy and comedy.[43] His meditations on this subject brought various possibilities to his fertile mind, and the plays which he published in 1757 and 1758 were only two of them:

J'ai essayé de donner, dans *le Fils naturel*, l'idée d'un drame qui fût entre la comédie et la tragédie. *Le Père de famille*, que je promis alors, et que des distractions continuelles ont retardé, est entre le genre sérieux du *Fils naturel*, et la comédie. Et si jamais j'en ai le loisir et le courage, je ne désespère pas de composer un drame qui se place entre le genre sérieux et la tragédie (A.T., VII, 308).

He was well aware that the idea of an intermediate genre was not a new one. His own century had already seen the rise of the "comédie larmoyante" in France and of domestic tragedy in England; and even in antiquity such a theatrical form was known to exist. The ancient genre was less well known for the simple reason that only one example of it had survived the ages: the satyr-play of Euripides entitled *The Cyclops*.
    Let us first see what Diderot knew about satyr-drama from his reading of the *Discours sur le Cyclope d'Euripide et sur le spectacle satyrique* in

---

42 Ibid., I, 169.
    43 A.T., VII, 307 ff. (*De la poésie dramatique*). See Felix Vexler, *Studies in Diderot's Aesthetic Naturalism* (New York, 1922), 9–87.

Brumoy's *Théâtre des Grecs*.[44] After several pages of apology for presenting to his readers the analysis of a genre marked by "des bouffon-
neries faites pour la dernière classe d'une populace républicaine et liber-
tine" (x, 4), the Jesuit author explains that "le poëme satyrique n'est
ni tragédie, ni comédie. Mais il tient le milieu entre l'une & l'autre"
(p. 8). Satyr-plays, he says, were short after-pieces comparable to the
"petites pièces" of the French theatre but closer to tragedy than to comedy (pp. 11–12). Because of the character that tradition had given
them – "cynique, mordant, pétulant et lâche" – satyrs on the stage were
"les bouffons de la populace" (p. 17). But the atmosphere of low comedy seems to have been redeemed by the allegorical nature of these productions: "les pièces satyriques étoient des allégories qui receloient un
sens plus fin que celui qui se présentoit d'abord" (p. 19). And indeed,
Brumoy admits, if these plays had contained nothing but buffoonery,
singing, and dancing with no element of allegory or parody, they would
not have been worthy of the pen of a Euripides (p. 22).

Far more interesting for our purpose is the well-documented article
"Satyre (*Poésie*)" furnished by De Jaucourt for the fourteenth volume
of the *Encyclopédie* (pp. 697b–703a), which contains not only an excellent study of the origins and nature of satyr-drama (697b–698b) but
also a summary of the arguments advanced by Isaac Casaubon to prove
that the word "satire," despite an ancient tradition, was not derived
from the "satyric" element of Greek drama.[45] De Jaucourt stresses
the fact that the singing, dancing chorus of satyrs with their clownish
postures and audacious raillery gave to these spectacles the gaiety and
laughter by which they were marked off from tragedy, and that this element was balanced by the introduction of gods, demi-gods, and heroes
whose presence lent an air of dignity to the action and prevented it from
descending to the merely burlesque. He concludes:

En un mot, la *satyrique* ... tenoit alors le milieu entre la tragédie et l'ancienne comédie. ... Voilà presque le comique larmoyant de nos jours, dont
l'origine est toute grecque, sans que nous nous en fussions douté (698a).

44 Diderot probably owned a copy of the *Théâtre des Grecs* by Pierre Brumoy,
first published in 1730. On 30 September 1760 he calls the attention of Sophie Volland to a passage in it (*Corr.*, ed. Roth, III, 112). References are to the Paris edition
of 1787 in ten volumes, of which Vol. x contains the *Discours sur le Cyclope d'Euri-
pide* and a translation of Euripides' play by Brumoy.

45 *Encycl.*, XIV, 698b–699b. Modern scholars support Casaubon (*De satyrica
Graecorum poesi et Romanorum satira* [Paris, 1605]). The present state of the
question is summed up by C. A. Van Rooy, *Studies in Classical Satire and Related
Literary Theory* (Leiden, E. J. Brill, 1965). See especially Ch. IV, "The Satirical
Elements in Greek Literature," Ch. VI, "*Satura* and *Satyroi*: The Development of
Greek Satyr-Drama and the *Rapprochement* of Literary Terms," and Ch. VII, "Latin
Satire, Greek Satyr-Drama, and Attic Old Comedy in Literary Theory and Termi-
nology."

Diderot, we may be sure, was not startled by this revelation. But, however ancient the origins of the serio-comic theater may have been, he felt he had a certain proprietary right over the *drame* and was personally insulted when Jean-Jacques treated it with scorn: "il dit du mal du comique Larmoyant parce que c'est mon genre."[46] Reason enough, perhaps, for his employing the serio-comic in a counterattack against Rousseau.

It is not known exactly when this commentary of De Jaucourt on satire and satyr-plays passed through the hands of the editor of the *Encyclopédie*, but it was undoubtedly no later than 1762, perhaps much earlier. It therefore constitutes a possible, though by no means a necessary, source of inspiration for the procedures adopted in *Le Neveu de Rameau*. We may presume that Diderot knew the *Cyclops* of Euripides, at least in the translation that Brumoy had given; but nowhere do we find him commenting on it. It might be helpful, therefore, to glance at the section entitled "Satyre dramatique (*Art dramat.*)" appended by De Jaucourt to his article on satire (*Encycl.*, xiv, 702b–703a). He begins by stating that the *Cyclops* is the only extant satyr-drama, then goes on to describe the characters of this unique work:

Les personnages de cette pièce sont Polyphème, Ulysse, un silène & un chœur de satyres. ... Le caractère du cyclope est l'insolence, & une cruauté digne des bêtes féroces. Le silène est badin à sa maniere, mauvais plaisant, quelquefois ordurier. Ulysse est grave & serieux, de maniere cependant qu'il y a quelques endroits où il paroît se prêter un peu à l'humeur bouffonne des silènes. Le chœur des satyres a une gravité burlesque, quelquefois il devient aussi mauvais plaisant que le silène.

It would appear that *Le Neveu de Rameau*, at least insofar as its two characters are concerned, has the characteristics of the play described by De Jaucourt.

If a playwright were intending to compose a satyr-drama, there could be some embarrassment as to where exactly to begin. Not, however, if he were as familiar as Diderot with Horace's *Ars poetica*. There (vv. 220–50) we find not only certain minute directions concerning that genre but also, in the midst of these, one of the most serious challenges ever presented to a literary artist:

Not mine shall it be [Horace says] ... if writing Satyric plays, to affect only the plain nouns and verbs of established use ... My aim shall be poetry, so moulded from the familiar that anybody may hope for the same success, may sweat much and yet toil in vain when attempting the same: such is the

46 *Tablettes,* in *Diderot Studies,* iii (1961), 317.

power of order and connexion, such the beauty that may crown the commonplace.[47]

Many an author through the ages has memorized these famous verses
and striven to carry out their prescriptions; very few, I am sure, have
applied them in the medium for which they were intended – the satyr-
play.

The discussion of satyr-drama in the *Ars poetica* bears almost exclusively upon language and style, and it is here that we shall find its importance for Diderot. Horace had two recommendations to make in this
regard; first, he specifies the sort of speech that is befitting the god or
hero of the play, then that which is appropriate to satyrs. The hero or
god, says Horace, must be allowed to retain some of the dignity associated with his role in tragedy, and his speech must be neither too vulgar
nor too high-flown.[48] (It may be said, I believe, that the language of
Diderot's Moi seems to follow this pattern.) And the satyrs, "brought
from the woodland," should beware of speaking as though they were
natives of Rome and frequenters of the Forum, whether it be the senti-
mental language of young poets or the coarse and shameless talk of the
populace.[49] We cannot help being reminded of Diderot's Lui, who declares: "Si je scavois m'enoncer comme vous. Mais j'ai un diable de
ramage saugrenu, moitié des gens du monde et des Lettres, moitié de la
Halle" (Fabre, p. 94). It would be difficult to imagine a clearer indication that Diderot's artistic triumph in *Le Neveu de Rameau*, especially
his creation of Lui, is largely due to his successful implementation of

47 Non ego inornata et dominantia nomina solum
      verbaque, Pisones, Satyrorum scriptor amabo,
      nec sic enitar tragico differre colori,
   ut nihil intersit, Davusne loquatur et audax
   Pythias, emuncto lucrata Simone talentum,
   an custos famulusque dei Silenus alumni.
      ex noto fictum carmen sequar, ut sibi quivis
      speret idem, sudet multum frustraque laboret
      ausus idem : tantum series iuncturaque pollet,
      tantum de medio sumptis accedit honoris.
(*Ars poet.*, 234–43. Trans. Fairclough)
48 Verum ita risores, ita commendare dicaces
      conveniet Satyros, ita vertere seria ludo,
   ne quicumque deus, quicumque adhibebitur heros,
   regali conspectus in auro nuper et ostro,
   migret in obscuras humili sermone tabernas,
   aut, dum vitat humum, nubes et inania captet.
(*Ars poet.*, 225–30)
49 Silvis deducti caveant me iudice Fauni,
      ne velut innati triviis ac paene forenses
   aut nimium teneris iuvenentur versibus umquam,
   aut immunda crepent ignominiosaque dicta ...
(*Ars poet.*, 244–7)

Horace's prescriptions for satyr-drama. As De Jaucourt had remarked in commenting on the Horatian formula at the end of his article on satire: "il est aisé de dire quelques mots avec naïveté; mais de soutenir long-tems ce ton sans être plat, sans laisser du vuide, sans faire d'écarts, sans liaisons forcées, c'est peut-être le chef-d'œuvre du goût & du génie" (XIV, 703a).

Are we to say, then, that Le Neveu de Rameau is a satyr-play? Most of the elements would seem to be present in the work: parody of a mythical theme, a god speaking with a satyr, the blend of grave and gay – and we can even conceive of Lui's musical and pantomimic performances as representing the singing and dancing of a chorus of satyrs. But we must also recognize the fact that there are obviously other elements involved – the Socratic dialogue, the mime, the Horatian satire – that seem to have influenced the dialogue. There is reason, therefore, for believing that Diderot set out to compose a comic *satura* in the sense of a medley of different comic genres. The fact that Lui has certain traits of the mock-hero (his calamitous dismissal from Bertin's house) and that he is presented as an abject failure in life as well as in art reminds us that, according to Aristotle, one of the first examples of the comic in regular literature was the *Margites*, a mock-epic poem whose hero was a ne'er-do-well.[50] We have noted too that the stress on freedom of speech (Lui's frankness) bestows on our satire the spirit of *parrhesia* for which Aristophanic comedy was famous; and there is perhaps a further parallel in the fact that Aristophanes' play *The Clouds*, in which he pilloried Socrates, is remarkable for the comic *agon* in which Just Reason is matched against Unjust Reason.[51] When we add to these observations the fact that the mixture of genres is a procedure similar to that used by Varro in his Menippean satire, we may reasonably conclude that the format and spirit of the satyr-play were supplemented with elements of several satirico-comic forms brought together by Diderot in his *Satyre 2^{de}*.

If it can be taken as established that Le Neveu de Rameau is a miscellany of ancient comic forms, we have yet to consider the reasons why a work such as this should have been conceived and executed by an eighteenth-century Frenchman. The answer, I believe, lies in the extraordinary popularity of theatrical entertainment around 1760 and in the

50 The *Second Alcibiades*, falsely attributed to Plato, preserves a verse from the pseudo-Homeric *Margites* at 147: "Full many a thing he knew / But he knew them all badly." And Aristotle quotes a similar verse in the *Nichomachean Ethics* (VI, 1141a): "Him did the gods make neither a digger nor yet a ploughman / Nor wise in anything else." Shaftesbury describes the *Margites* as "a concealed sort of raillery intermixed with the Sublime" (Robertson, I, 130).

51 *The Clouds*, vv. 890 ff. On the qualities of this *agon*, see Francis M. Cornford, *The Origin of Attic Comedy* (Cambridge, at the University Press, 1934), 78, 114–16.

abuses that beset any process of democratization, especially in the field of artistic production. One need not be an aristocrat but merely a man of refinement to deprecate the ephemeral enthusiasms of the crowd, the vulgarity of taste, the gaudy display, especially the prevalence of parody – that refuge of mediocre minds – and of makeshift songs in which words are fitted to music instead of the reverse.[52] It was in reaction to all this that Diderot set his dialogue against a backdrop of popular theatre – in particular the new French comic opera, fruit of the "Querelle des Bouffons," for which Grimm held such high hopes and which Diderot himself did not fail to appreciate. But, as Aristotle had said, both art and virtue are concerned with what is harder; and comic opera, for all its merit as entertainment, is by classical standards an inferior form of art. Similar to other kinds of popular comedy – mime, farce, *parade* – it is frequently a haphazard mixture thrown together with one object in mind – the applause of the vulgar.[53]

Such thoughts could scarcely have been avoided by one, like Diderot, who had recently been made a subject of public amusement in a "farce,"[54] and whose own attempt at serious drama had gone unappreciated by that same public. Fitting thoughts for the year 1762, which had seen the Opéra-Comique merged with the Comédie-Italienne in February, and in August the arrival in Paris of Goldoni, that prolific writer of scenarios. In November we find Diderot magnanimously affirming that, although his own tastes incline him toward the beauties of ancient sculpture, he does not underestimate the value of entertainment of the popular sort:

Au reste il faut avoir un peu d'indulgence pour les hommes occupés d'affaires sérieuses pendant toute la journée. Il leur faut des bagatelles qui les délassent. Disserter, examiner, combiner, analyser, seroit un nouveau travail pour eux. En général ces gens, le soir, préfèrent Arlequin à Cinna; et je n'en suis pas surpris.[55]

52 Since the time of Plato it had been a commonplace that music must follow the words of the poet (*Republic*, 398d), and the flouting of this rule by writers of comic opera in France met Grimm's censure (*Corr. lit.*, 15 Feb. and 1 June 1762, v, 45, 97).

53 The *Correspondance littéraire* for 15 August 1762 devotes two pages to discussing the great difficulties involved in writing good farce (v, 141–3). An excellent study of Diderot's familiarity with and appreciation of various forms of low comedy is found in Jacques Proust, "A propos d'un plan d'opéra-comique de Diderot," *Revue d'Histoire du Théâtre*, vii (1955), 173–88. The decline in matters of popular taste was perceived by many of Diderot's contemporaries. See Oscar G. Brockett, "The Fair Theatres of Paris in the Eighteenth Century: the Undermining of the Classical Ideal," in *Classical Drama and its Influences: Essays Presented to H. D. F. Kitto*, ed. M. J. Anderson (London, Methuen, 1965), 249–70.

54 Grimm refers to Palisott's play *Les Philosophes* as a farce, *Corr. lit.*, 1 June 1760, iv, 240.

55 To Sophie Volland, 7 November 1762 (*Corr.*, ed. Roth, iv, 215).

This reference to Harlequin as the epitome of gay buffoonery in opposition to all that is serious and high-minded must not be passed over as a mere commonplace. If Arlecchino, with his patchwork costume, is the greatest of all comic creations, it is because he embodies the very essence of farce, distilled through centuries of popular theatre. The Age of Enlightenment, in its preoccupation with the origins of institutions, was not unaware of theatrical traditions. It is interesting to read De Jaucourt's remarks in this regard with reference to the satyr-drama of the Greeks:

Je crois qu'on retrouve chez nous, à peu de chose près, les *satyres dramatiques* des anciens dans certaines pieces italiennes; du-moins on retrouve dans arlequin les caracteres d'un satyre. Qu'on fasse attention à son masque, à sa ceinture, à son habit collant, qui le fait paroître presque comme s'il étoit nud, à ses genoux couverts, & qu'on peut supposer rentrans; il ne lui manque qu'un soulier fourchu. Ajoutez à cela sa façon mievre & déliée, son style, ses pointes souvent mauvaises, son ton de voix; tout cela forme assurément une maniere de satyre. Le satyre des anciens approchoit du bouc; l'arlequin d'aujourd'hui approche du chat; c'est toujours l'homme déguisé en bête. Comment les satyres jouoient-ils, selon Horace? avec un dieu, un héros qui parloit du haut ton. Arlequin de même paroît vis-à-vis Samson; il figure en grotesque vis-à-vis d'un héros; il fait le héros lui-même ...[56]

It is perhaps fanciful to trace the history of Italian comedy back to the Greek satyr-drama, although this is one theory that has been proposed.[57] A more likely explanation for this modern theatrical phenomenon, one which became current in the eighteenth century and which has been seriously challenged only in the twentieth, is that Italian popular comedy is a direct descendant of the mimes and "Atellan farces" of Roman antiquity.[58] The two theories are not unconnected, for the Atellan farce had long been considered the Roman equivalent of the Greek satyr-drama.[59] The article "Atellanes (*Littérat.*)" of the *Encyclopédie* (I, 797) repeats the opinion of Vossius that these spectacles were similar to the Greek satyr-plays because they often mixed the serious with the laughable, and that they could be called "comédies satyriques" despite

56 *Encyclopédie*, XIV, 703a.
57 See Albrecht Dieterich, *Pulcinella* (Leipzig, 1897).
58 See Allardyce Nicoll, *Masks, Mimes and Miracles. Studies in the Popular Theatre* (London, Harrap, 1931), 214–15. On the Atellana, see Margarete Bieber, *The History of the Greek and Roman Theater*, 2nd ed. (Princeton, Princeton University Press, 1961), 145–50; W. Beare, *The Roman Stage*, 3rd ed. (London, Methuen, 1964), 137–48; George E. Duckworth, *The Nature of Roman Comedy* (Princeton, Princeton University Press, 1952), 10–13; also the article "Atellana" in the *Enciclopedia dello spettacolo*, Vol. I, and G. Michaut, *Sur les tréteaux latins*, 225–79.
59 Editions of Horace's *Ars poetica*, including that of Dacier, normally repeated the observation of the scholiast Porphyrion to the effect that the passage concerning satyr-plays was intended to apply to the Atellanae.

the fact that the actors were pantomimes who did not wear the satyr's mask. Diderot, in his article "Comédie (*Hist. anc.*)," describes the Atellana as "un tissu de plaisanteries" composed of "de la musique, de la pantomime, & de la danse" (*Encycl.*, III, 669). Neither of these articles mentions the tradition – a commonplace, nonetheless, since Luigi Riccoboni's *Histoire du théâtre italien* of 1730 – to the effect that the improvised farces called Atellanae, taken over by pantomime artists, had survived the fall of Rome and the barbarian invasions to become the modern Italian popular theatre.[60] This relationship, however, did not escape the notice of that indefatigable researcher, De Jaucourt, in his article "Exode (*Littérat.*)" in the sixth volume of the *Encyclopédie* (VI, 267b–268b).

The Atellana, described by Livy (VII, 2) as an after-piece (*exodium*), is defined by De Jaucourt as follows: "Poëme plus ou moins châtié, accompagné de chants & de danses, & porté sur le théâtre de Rome pour servir de divertissement après la tragédie" (267b). He continues, paraphrasing Livy: "Les plaisanteries grossieres s'étant changées en art sur le théâtre des Romains, on joüa l'Atellane, comme on joue aujourd'hui parmi nous la piece comique à la suite de la piece sérieuse." He then goes on to describe the extreme liberty with which the Atellanae ridiculed serious matters and held up to mockery the vices and crimes of the emperors themselves (268a). Finally, he establishes the historical connection between these ancient spectacles and the Italian comedy, ending with the same severe judgment found in all the articles of the *Encyclopédie* ("Comique," "Farce," "Parade," etc.) that deal with the low comic:

Les *exodes* se joüerent à Rome plus de 550 ans, sans avoir souffert qu'une légere interruption de quelques années; & quoique sous le regne d'Auguste elles déplussent aux gens de bon goût, parce qu'elles portoient toûjours des marques de la grossiereté de leur origine, cependant elles durerent encore long-tems après le siecle de cet empereur. Enfin elles ont ressuscité à plusieurs égards parmi nous : car quel autre nom peut-on donner à cette espece de farce, que nous appellons *comédie italienne*, & dans quel genre d'esprit peut-on placer des pieces où l'on se moque de toutes les regles du théâtre? des pieces où dans le nœud & dans le dénouement, on semble vouloir éviter la vraisemblance? des pieces où l'on ne se propose d'autre but que d'exciter à rire par des traits d'une imagination bisarre? des pieces encore où l'on ose avilir, par une imitation burlesque, l'action noble & touchante d'un sujet dramatique? Qu'on ne dise point, pour la défense de cette Thalie bar-

60 Louis Riccoboni, *Histoire du théâtre italien, depuis la décadence de la comédie latine* (Paris, 1730, 2 vols.), I, 2–6, 21–6.

bouillée, qu'on l'a vû plaire au public autant que les meilleures pieces de Racine & de Moliere : je répondrois que c'est à un public mal composé, & que même dans ce public il y a quantité de personnes qui connoissent très-bien le peu de valeur de ce comique des halles ... (268b).

This article of De Jaucourt is important for the light it sheds on Diderot's intentions in *Le Neveu de Rameau*. The Atellan farce, as we have just seen, was an after-piece; so was the Greek satyr-play, presented after the tragic trilogy at the dramatic festivals; and so also was the *opera buffa* brought to Paris in 1752. The last-named genre, properly called *intermezzo* in Italian and *intermède* in French, was originally a short musical *entr'acte*; but the *intermèdes* that precipitated the "Querelle des Bouffons" were normally performed following the presentation of a longer opera,[61] and the word came to be synonymous with *opéra bouffon*.[62] The fact that Jean-Jacques Rousseau had composed one of the most popular *intermèdes* of the 1750s – *Le Devin du village* – cannot be ignored in our evaluation of Diderot's choice of literary form in his satire. There is good reason, too, why he should have seen the mimicry and improvisation that marked the history of theatrical buffoonery as a suitable context in which to castigate the folly and the artistic corruption of his age.

It is clear, I think, that *Le Neveu de Rameau* is much more than a satire in the sense given to that word today. The title must be considered as part of the mystification, for *Satyre 2^{de}* can be interpreted as meaning both satyr-play and *satura* (a dish of mixed ingredients, a medley or miscellany); these had been the two commonly-accepted origins of the Latin word "satura" ("satire") until the time of Casaubon.[63] Thus, *Le Neveu de Rameau* can properly be described as a medley of satirico-comic forms, a kind of encyclopedia of low comedy based on the historical accounts found in ancient authors. It would seem that Diderot, while retaining the structure and the language of the satyr-play, had also in mind Livy's description of the dramatic *satura* and of the Atellana (VII, 2), the literary mimes of Sophron and the Socratic dialogues, and the satires of Lucilius and Horace. Like the mimes, the dialogues and the satires, *Le Neveu de Rameau* seems to have been conceived by the author as a dramatic creation destined for reading rather than for stage

---

61 Louisette Richebourg, *Contribution à l'histoire de la "Querelle des Bouffons,"* 28 ff.

62 *Encyclopédie*, art. "Intermede (Belles-lettres & Musique)," VIII, 831a: "c'est un poëme burlesque ou comique en un ou plusieurs actes, composé par le poëte pour être mis en musique; un *intermede* en ce sens, c'est la même chose qu'un opéra bouffon."

63 See C. A. Van Rooy, *Studies in Classical Satire*, Ch. 1.

presentation. After the poor reception accorded to *Le Père de famille*, Diderot may well have preferred, like Horace, to "entrust himself to a reader rather than to bear the disdain of an insolent spectator" (*Epist.* II.i.214–15).

FLUTE AND LYRE

There remains to be examined the question of musical instrumentation. As we saw in Chapter 6, it is possible to consider our dialogue as a contest between flute and lyre; and since Diderot, like Plato, was fond of comparing the human body to a musical instrument,[64] there is every justification for applying this comparison literally to the satire. It is perhaps not too fanciful, for example, to see Lui's "inequality" as the "unequal temperament" of an instrument adjusted to an irregular scale-system and Moi's "aequabilitas" as the "equal temperament" of an instrument tuned to a system of equalized semitones.[65]

Lui, moreover, was undoubtedly meant to be identified with the flute, as is indicated by the admonition he addressed to himself as a young man: "Qu'as tu, Rameau? tu reves. Et a quoi reves tu? que tu voudrois bien avoir fait ou faire quelque chose qui excitat l'admiration de l'univers. Hé, oui; il n'y a qu'a souffler et remuer les doigts" (Fabre, p. 99). We are perhap justified, as a consequence, in interpreting the dialogue as a musical composition; it might even be said: a solo concerto, in which a flautist virtuoso is matched against the orchestra of humanity. Or conversely, the lone philosopher against the ignorant multitude ...

MYSTIFICATION

The ambivalence of Diderot's attitude towards enthusiasm is reflected in the mixed admiration and scorn with which he treats the "Théosophes" in the article devoted to them in the *Encyclopédie* (A.T., XVII, 242–68). This lengthy article has aroused a certain interest in recent years, and some attention has been accorded to Diderot's contacts with

64 See Jacques Proust, "Variations sur un thème de l'*Entretien avec d'Alembert*," *Revue des Sciences Humaines*, n. s., CXII (1963), 453–70.

65 It was in terms of "just temperament" that Diderot explained his degree of identification, as spectator, with the hero or heroine of a tragedy: "Si je m'oublie trop et trop longtemps, la terreur est trop forte ; si je ne m'oublie point du tout, si je reste toujours un, elle est trop faible : c'est ce juste tempérament qui fait verser des larmes délicieuses" (*Salon de 1767*, A.T., XI, 120). In a book review written in 1770, he gives a rather simple explanation of temperament based on Rameau's version of mean-tone temperament (A.T., IX, 449–50). For the technical background of this question, see J. Murray Barbour, *Tuning and Temperament. A Historical Survey*, 2nd ed. (East Lansing, Michigan State College Press, 1953).

esoteric thinkers.[66] There is, of course, no suspicion that he shared the views of these "philosophes par le feu"; nonetheless, his fascination with the Hermetic-Cabalist tradition can scarcely be denied.

Although there is no evidence of any early influence of this school upon Diderot, we must remember that in 1751 his *Lettre sur les sourds et muets* gave considerable place to a theory of poetry as "emblem" and "hieroglyph" that attests a certain familiarity with the lore of Egyptology.[67] Some ten years later he wrote *Le Neveu de Rameau*, in which we find not only a hidden portrait, but also the favourite themes of the occult practitioners: enthusiasm, harmony, and imitation, with an underlying allegory involving Apollo, the god of light. Should not these facts be taken into account in our appraisal of Diderot the "mystificateur"?[68]

## THE CHESS-BOARD

One might be inclined to see the motif of Harlequin's patchwork costume repeated in the squares of the chess-board which our imagination sees as forming part of the décor of the opening scene of *Le Neveu de Rameau*. There is some merit in this suggestion – but we must not allow

66 See Jean Fabre, "Diderot et les théosophes," *Cahiers de l'Association Internationale des Etudes Françaises*, XIII (1961), 203–22; and Jean Ehrard, "Matérialisme et naturalisme : Les Sources occultistes de la pensée de Diderot," ibid., 189–201.

67 See James Doolittle, "Hieroglyph and Emblem in Diderot's *Lettre sur les sourds et muets*," *Diderot Studies*, II (1952), 148–67. For hieroglyphs in general, and their relation to occultism, see Erik Iversen, *The Myth of Egypt and its Hieroglyphs in European Tradition* (Copenhagen, 1961).

68 The following pertinent observations might be made about *Le Neveu de Rameau*: (1) It is possible that Lui's physiognomy, so carefully detailed on Fabre, p. 8, reflects Diderot's view of Rousseau's character, and that each of Lui's features as he describes them will be found to be related to a corresponding inner disposition catalogued in some treatise belonging to the Hermetic tradition. (2) Lui is very conscious of the power of the stars for good or ill: "et l'astre! l'astre!" (p. 96). The idea of a malevolent influence presiding over Lui's birth is expressed in the epigraph, "Vertumnis, quotquot sunt, natus iniquis." (3) The trinity of true, good, and beautiful, invoked by Lui (p. 82), could reflect a reading of *The Divine Names* of the Pseudo-Dionysius, who was steeped in magical lore. (4) The image of the sun striking the statue of Memnon (p. 100) recalls one of the famous myths of Egyptian religion – the animating of statues by drawing spirits into them. On this question, see Frances A. Yates, *Giordano Bruno and the Hermetic Tradition* (London, Routledge and Kegan Paul, 1964), 9–10. (5) The Brière edition of *Le Neveu de Rameau* (1823), based on a manuscript obtained by Brière from Diderot's daughter, gives the reading "élève" for "neveu" and "maître" for "oncle" throughout the dialogue (see A.T., v, 389 n.). This manuscript has disappeared without trace. Did Brière make these alterations gratuitously? Perhaps; but it is possible that the readings "élève" and "maître" are true variants that reflect an earlier state of the text. The Hermetic treatises were usually in the form of a dialogue between a master and his disciple; and it may well be that Diderot's original plan was to caricature Rousseau as the enthusiastic disciple of the great Rameau, whose "visions inintelligibles" are satirized on p. 6 of the Fabre edition.

our attention to be distracted from the pieces on the board. Especially
the one called "le fou," which Diderot had described in the article "*Fou
(Jeu)" of the *Encyclopédie*. "Le *fou* qui occupe la case noire," he tells
us, "ne marche qu'obliquement, & toûjours sur les cases noires. Celui qui
est sur les blanches, y marche toûjours aussi de biais" (VII, 212). We
are immediately reminded of the mediocre "especes" who, as Lui tells
us, "[marchent] tout de guingois, dans le chemin de la vie" (Fabre, p.
90).

### CHESS-PLAYERS

"Lorsqu'un ami commun, Daniel Roguin, vaudois d'origine, les présenta
l'un à l'autre au Café de la Régence vers la fin de 1742, Rousseau et
Diderot ont trente ans ..."[69] Rousseau was skilled in chess and had decided to excel in the game as the best way of attracting attention and
beginning his rise to fortune.[70] This first meeting may well have taken
place over a chess-board, for the two friends frequently played the game
together – though Diderot was no match for Jean-Jacques.[71]

Twenty years later, Diderot sets out to draw a literary caricature of his
former friend, now his bitterest enemy. Their fifteen-year friendship
flashes before his eyes. Where to begin? ... At the beginning, of course!
Recreate the place, the atmosphere, the players ... recreate Jean-Jacques
... not as he was then, but as you know him now ...

69 Jean Fabre, "Deux Frères ennemis : Diderot et Jean-Jacques," p. 157.
70 *Confessions*, Pléiade ed., I, 220–1. Cf. ibid., 288.
71 A.T., XI, 127 (*Salon de 1767*). See I. Grünberg, "Rousseau joueur d'échecs,"
*Annales J.-J. Rousseau*, III (1907), 157–74.

# 9
# Conclusion

In the course of these eight chapters there has emerged a new vision of *Le Neveu de Rameau* that I believe to be both comprehensive and self-consistent. The word "vision" seems more suitable than "explanation," for, far from reducing Diderot's masterpiece to a tidy formula, our investigations have tended rather to extend its horizons and to show the astonishing range of the literary mind that conceived it. More significant perhaps than any of the individual discoveries that we have made is the fact that the inner unity of the dialogue has been seen to flow from the author's psychology as we know it and to reflect the historical situation in which he found himself.

Our first conclusion concerns the genesis of the satire. In 1761, perhaps in reaction to the portrait of Wolmar in *La Nouvelle Héloïse*, Diderot set about composing in dialogue form an idealized confrontation of himself with Jean-Jacques Rousseau. It is impossible to say exactly how much of the work was written at that time. The following year, with the publication of *Emile*, Diderot's inspiration received a new impulsion; the dialogue seems to have been brought to completion between mid-July 1762 (Diderot had read *Emile* by that time) and January 1763.

The feeling of suppressed excitement that runs through the letters to Sophie Volland in October and November 1762 was undoubtedly due in large part to the fever of creative activity on the part of the Encyclopedist. He remained close to home, his wife being ill and Grimm being absent from Paris; his friends, curious to know what had been occupying his attention, sent Georges Le Roy to investigate.[1] Early in October, Diderot wrote a book review for Grimm in which he speaks both of Marsyas and of the Cyclops.[2] On 21 November we find the following

---

1 To Sophie Volland, 11 November 1762 (*Corr.*, ed. Roth, IV, 220–1).
2 To Sophie Volland, 14 October 1762 (ibid., 192). Diderot's remarks, which appeared in the *Corr. lit.* in February 1763, are reproduced by Assezat: "Nous détournerions les yeux avec horreur de la page d'un auteur ou de la toile d'un peintre

cryptic statement: "Je suis au tiers de ma cinquième revision. Si je vais passer quatre jours à la Briche, comme on [Madame d'Epinay] me le propose, j'achèverai."[3] This forecast, if it refers to *Le Neveu de Rameau*, was somewhat optimistic; we can place the completion of the dialogue shortly after 11 January 1763, the date on which Dauvergne's *Polixène* was presented at the Opéra.[4]

The final form of the work – whether we consider it as a satyr-play, a mime, or a Socratic dialogue – is intimately related to the Rousseau-Diderot quarrel. The *philosophe* had more than one reason to represent Rousseau as a satyr;[5] chief among them, of course, was his tendency to interpret Jean-Jacques as an advocate of the unleashing of instinctive forces. This aspect of the dialogue, moreover, is related to the notion of moral imitation. Diderot considered Rousseau to be a hypocrite,[6] one of those who, in the words of Juvenal, simulate virtue while leading a life dedicated to Bacchanalian vice; his aim in *Le Neveu de Rameau* is that stated in his analysis of satire in the article "Encyclopédie": "d'arracher le masque à de graves personnages, *Qui Curios simulant, et Bacchanalia*

---

qui nous montrerait le sang des compagnons d'Ulysse coulant aux deux côtés de la bouche de Polyphême, ruisselant sur sa barbe et sur sa poitrine, et qui nous ferait entendre le bruit de leurs os brisés sous ses dents. Nous ne pourrions supporter la vue des veines découvertes et des artères saillantes autour du cœur de Marsyas écorché par Apollon" (A.T., XIII, 38–9).

3 To Sophie Volland, *Corr.*, ed. Roth, IV, 227.

4 This is not the first time it has been suggested that the *Polixène* of Antoine Dauvergne is the opera referred to on the last page of *Le Neveu de Rameau* as being performed the very day on which the interview with Lui takes place. Some critics have used this ambiguous reference to date a supposed conversation between Diderot and Jean-François Rameau that might have inspired the composition of our satire. Such a conversation – or rather, many such conversations – did undoubtedly occur, but their importance for the dialogue has been greatly exaggerated. *Le Neveu de Rameau* is the fruit of fifteen years spent with Jean-Jacques and not of an afternoon spent in the company of Jean-François Rameau.

5 Lubricity and drunkenness are two well-known characteristics of satyrs. The first may pass without comment except to say that Rousseau's sylvan trysts with Saint-Lambert's mistress, Madame d'Houdetot, in 1756–7 could well have caused the *philosophe* to think of Jean-Jacques not only as a satyr but also as Polyphemus, the cruel, ugly Cyclops who lived alone, a law unto himself ("Il n'y a que le méchant qui soit seul"), and who fell ridiculously in love with Galatea (Ovid, *Metam.*, XIII, 744 ff.). As for drunkenness, we must admit that the Citizen of Geneva scarcely qualifies to wear the satyr's mask. Diderot himself brings Rousseau's sobriety to our attention in *Jacques le fataliste*: "Platon et Jean-Jacques Rousseau, qui prônèrent le bon vin sans en boire, sont ... de faux frères de la gourde" (A.T., VI, 224). This is perhaps why Lui of our dialogue quenches his thirst with beer (Fabre, p. 88).

6 The nameless portrait of Rousseau in the *Essai sur les règnes de Claude et de Néron* (A.T., III, 91) suggests that he had led "une vie cachée pendant plus de cinquante ans sous le masque le plus épais de l'hypocrisie." Cf. Diderot's definition of satire in the *Paradoxe sur le comédien* (A.T., VIII, 389): "La satire est d'un tartuffe, et la comédie est du Tartuffe. La satire poursuit un vicieux, la comédie poursuit un vice."

*vivunt.*"[7] And finally, as a Socratic dialogue, *Le Neveu de Rameau* is a debate between Diderot-Socrates and the "sophist" Rousseau, with "Platon Diderot" (as Voltaire was wont to call the Encyclopedist) manipulating the strings of his marionettes. Lui, like the sophists, is a master of mere appearances; the *Logos* is far beyond his ken. Among his failures he can count that of failing to be improved by a conversation with Socrates: "Adieu, Mr le philosophe. N'est-il pas vrai que je suis toujours le meme?" Because of similar mutual incomprehension, Diderot and Rousseau had parted ways in 1758.

Since the satyr-play is considered to belong to the tragic rather than to the comic genre, we are justified in seeing *Le Neveu de Rameau* as the theatrical piece that Diderot had proposed in 1758 in the *Discours sur la poésie dramatique* when he wrote: "si jamais j'en ai le loisir et le courage, je ne désespère pas de composer un drame qui se place entre le genre sérieux et la tragédie" (A.T., VII, 308). It is much more than this, however, for it was to become his answer – hermetically sealed and left for posterity – to the eventual publication of Rousseau's *Confessions*. The threat of Jean-Jacques' revelations hung over the head of the *philosophe* for more than twenty years – the same years during which he returned again and again to his dialogue to perfect it as the instrument of his vengeance. Rousseau intended to speak from the tomb shortly after his death; Diderot planned to do the same, but much later. It was with terrible irony that he put these closing words on the lips of Rousseau-Lui: "Rira bien qui rira le dernier"!

Whatever we may think of satire as a genre, it must be granted that *Le Neveu de Rameau* stands in a class by itself and that it cannot be judged by ordinary standards. This unique work has always been appreciated as a brilliant piece of writing; in the light of what we have seen, one might, at the risk of exaggerating, make the following claims: that Diderot is a conscious literary artist truly deserving of the name "poet" in the broadest sense of the word; that his satire is unsurpassed for depth of thought and mastery of execution by anything contemporary with it in French literature; and finally, that the one-dimensional "esprit" of other eighteenth-century authors pales in comparison with the scintillating qualities of this imaginative satire, which is perhaps the most perfect illustration, in England or in France, of what the term "wit" signified for Shaftesbury and for Pope.

7 A.T., XIV, 465. The quotation is from Juvenal, *Sat.*II.3. The application is made to Rousseau in the *Tablettes*; Diderot cites Juvenal's words inaccurately, but their meaning cannot be mistaken: "Il faisoit passer la vie la plus malheureuse à la mère, et à la fille [Thérèse], il étoit bien alors de ceux *qui curios simulant et vivant[sic]*" (*Diderot Studies*, III [1961], 318).

One of the most striking aspects of our satire – and one of the surest proofs of the author's genius – is the manner in which form and sense correspond at every level. It is especially worthy of note that this mimetic procedure extends even to the creative act itself. *Le Neveu de Rameau*, as it has already been suggested, implies on every page that Diderot believed his age to be a period of moral and cultural decline.[8] He shared this sentiment with Longinus, who long ago had devoted the last chapter of his *De sublimitate* to analysing the reasons for the "world shortage" of men who might produce sublime works of literature. Longinus leaves us with no solution to the problem; but it seems to be implied in his whole treatise that the practice of mimesis – imitating the sublime authors of antiquity and being "lifted up" to their level – is the surest way of achieving sublimity in any age, however corrupt.[9] And this, in fact, is what Diderot succeeded in doing. In the very act of writing about the bankruptcy of his age, he so perfectly "imitated" the writings of the ancients – especially the *Republic* of Plato and the *Ars poetica* of Horace – that he was able to create a work which, for sheer artistry and originality, stands second to none in the literature of his country.

8 Diderot's views on this matter are summed up by Henry Vyverberg, *Historical Pessimism in the French Enlightenment* (Cambridge, Mass., Harvard University Press, 1958), 189–200.

9 For an interesting discussion of this question, see Charles P. Segal, " ΥΨΟΣ and the Problem of Cultural Decline in the *De sublimitate*," *Harvard Studies in Classical Philology*, LXIV (1959), 121–46.

# EPILOGUE
# Midas judgment

AMONG the many questions concerning *Le Neveu de Rameau* which this inquiry has made no attempt to answer, there is one of more than passing interest to those who are fascinated by the functionings of a creative mind: to what extent did Diderot deliberately set out to mystify his readers? Certainly he tried to obscure the fact that Plato was his starting-point by placing at the head of his dialogue the motto from Horace. He also took pains to conceal Rousseau's involvement in the satire and the underlying allegory – and succeeded in this perhaps better than he might have wished. Thus far, we may call *Le Neveu de Rameau* a mystification. But is it possible that the author foresaw all the difficulties his work would present to critics? Could he have imagined that some day there would be schools of thought concerning his meaning in this dialogue?

There would seem to be solid reasons for thinking otherwise. Did he not, after all, call one of his characters "Moi," whereas he could have given him any other name? And did he not make it evident that the adversary Lui is a vicious fool? Such procedures are scarcely those of one who wishes to mask his hand. It is true, of course, that he saw fit to lend to Lui certain ideas which he himself had expressed frequently as his own, and this fact has done more perhaps than anything else to raise doubts as to where the author stood in the debate between his two characters. But, if we look on the matter from Diderot's point of view, this was clearly unavoidable under the circumstances. Did not literary tradition oblige him to give to his fool a few flashes of wisdom? And what does consider wise except one's own intimate convictions? These observations make it appear likely that the opposition between Moi and Lui was intended to speak for itself and that much of the confusion on this score has been of our own making. The contrary opinion – that Diderot realized he had left his satire open to various interpretations – remains nonetheless a distinct possibility.

Our judgment in this matter is not without consequence, for upon it depends the attitude we must take to another delicate question, one which involves the Marsyas-Apollo myth. Among the several versions of this myth which have come down to us, perhaps that found in Ovid (*Metam.*, xi, 146 ff.) is the most widely known. According to Ovid's latinized account of the story, the two participants in the musical contest are Phoebus and Pan. At the conclusion of the trials, Phoebus is proclaimed the winner; but one lone voice rises in dissent from this verdict. It is that of foolish King Midas, who prefers the music of Pan. As punishment for his stupidity, Midas' ears are transformed into the ears of an ass.

We are obliged, in the light of this, to accuse Diderot of having bequeathed his satire to posterity with playfully malicious intent. The question is: how malicious? If we agree that he spared no effort (apart from the allegory) to make his meaning in the dialogue stand clear, the Midas story must have appeared to him as simply an amusing rhetorical device; if, however, we hold that he deliberately created certain obscurities in *Le Neveu de Rameau*, we must give to that work the distinction of being a literary trap which is absolutely unique. It would seem to be impossible to escape one of these two conclusions. If there are some who prefer to believe that Diderot had no such mischief in mind, they would do well to turn to his *Salon de 1767*. There, he reviews a painting by a certain Bounieu who had presented to the Academy as his *tableau de réception* a canvas entitled "Le Jugement de Midas." His opening remarks are most revealing:

Voilà un sujet plaisamment choisi pour une réception, pour une composition qu'on présente à des juges. C'est presque leur dire : « Messieurs, prenez-y garde; si je vous déplais, c'est vous que j'aurai peints : portez les mains sur vos oreilles, et voyez si elles ne s'allongent pas » (A.T., xi, 336–7).

# Appendices

# Appendix 1

*Satire première*: A CRITICAL EDITION

The *Satire première* was distributed in manuscript form to the subscribers of Grimm's *Correspondance littéraire* in October 1778. It appeared in print for the first time in 1798, in the ninth volume of the works of Diderot published by Jacques-André Naigeon.[1] This edition is designated as N. All subsequent editions have been based on N, either directly or indirectly.[2] The printed tradition, therefore, poses no difficulty for the establishing of the text.

No autograph manuscript of the *Satire première* is known to exist. There are six manuscript copies:

L: Leningrad State Public Library, Diderot Collection, Tome XVIII, 225–38. Consulted on microfilm at the Bibliothèque Nationale. The contents of Vol. XVIII are described by Maurice Tourneux, *Les Manuscrits de Diderot conservés en Russie* (Paris, 1885), 21. The copyist, Roland Girbal, has been identified by Paul Vernière, *Diderot, ses manuscrits et ses copistes* (Paris, Klincksieck, 1967), 27 n.

VI: Bibliothèque Nationale, Nouv. acq. fr. 13760, ff. 3–17. Described by Herbert Dieckmann, *Inventaire du fonds Vandeul*, 71–2. See also Paul Vernière, *Diderot, ses manuscrits et ses copistes*, 36.

1 *Œuvres de Denis Diderot*, publiées sur les manuscrits de l'auteur, par Jacques-André Naigeon (Paris, Desray et Déterville, an VI-1798), 15 vols., IX, 492–514.
2 The principal editions are: *Œuvres de Denis Diderot* (Paris, A. Belin, 1818–19), 8 vols., I, 577–86; *Œuvres de Denis Diderot* (Paris, J.-L.-J. Brière, 1821–3), 21 vols., III, 170–89; *Œuvres complètes de Diderot*, ed. J. Assézat and M. Tourneux (Paris, Garnier Frères, 1875–7), 20 vols., VI, 303–16; Diderot, *Œuvres*, ed. André Billy (Paris, Gallimard, 1951), 1217–29; Diderot, *Chefs-d'œuvre* (London, Dent & Sons; Paris, Gillequin, 1911), 2 vols., II, 191–203; Denis Diderot, *Satires*, ed. Roland Desné (Paris, Club des Amis du Livre Progressiste, 1963), 153–84.
Belin based his edition on a faulty reimpression of Naigeon's text published in 1800; Brière collated Naigeon and Belin; Assézat used Brière; the Dent edition and the Pléiade edition adopted Assézat's text. R. Desné was the first to go back to Naigeon.

v2: Bibliothèque Nationale, Nouv. acq. fr. 13765, ff. 57–65. Described by H. Dieckmann, *Inventaire*, 85. See also the article by the same author, "Observations sur les manuscrits de Diderot conservés en Russie," *Diderot Studies*, IV (1963), 65.

v3: Bibliothèque Nationale, Nouv. acq. fr. 13782, ff. 115–24. Described by H. Dieckmann, *Inventaire*, 111. See also Paul Vernière, *Diderot, ses manuscrits et ses copistes*, 29.

H: October 1778 issue of the *Correspondance littéraire*, Royal Library, The Hague, 128 F 14, Vol. VII, item 2, paginated 1–19. Described by Jean de Booy, "Inventaire provisoire des contributions de Diderot à la *Correspondance littéraire*," *Dix-huitième Siècle*, No. 1 (1969), 387–8. Consulted on microfilm.

G: October 1778 issue of the *Correspondance littéraire* preserved at the Forschungsbibliothek, Gotha, East Germany. Described by Jean de Booy, loc. cit. Thus far unobtainable; not used for this edition.

The order in which the manuscripts have been presented above indicates their relative value. The least complete is H, for it lacks the lengthy postscript; one or two of their variant readings seem to reflect an earlier state of the text. We may disregard v3, which is patently copied from v2 with the exception of the title.[3] The other three manuscripts are remarkably similar, and the few common faults which link them are so minute that we are scarcely justified in drawing conclusions as to their filiation. If we suppose the existence of a common model, L was copied first and most accurately; then VI, after a series of corrections to the model; finally v2, after the suppression of certain proper names in the model. Unquestionably the best manuscript that we possess is L.

There is reason to believe, as it was shown above (p. 8, n. 15), that Naigeon was at one time in possession of the original of the *Satire première* or at least of a direct copy. To what degree, in his capacity as editor, did he allow himself to alter the author's text? His edition shows very few divergencies from the manuscript tradition, none of them of any great consequence. It was probably Naigeon who supplied the subtitle (see above, p. 4) as well as some of the proper names that appear as *** in all the manuscripts. We may be certain that in two instances he intervened to

3 Instead of "Satire première" we find "Satyre a Mʳ Naigeon." This title is repeated in the "Table des matières" of the volume (f. 1 verso). Such a bold departure is surprising in a manuscript that slavishly copies all the errors of v2, but any significance that it may have is not apparent.

correct the form of quoted matter in Diderot's text;[4] all the other variations could be due to scribal error or to stylistic changes introduced by Diderot's son-in-law Vandeul. One thing is certain: Naigeon has given us a text that is more complete and more accurate than that contained in the manuscripts.

Although Naigeon undoubtedly took certain liberties with the text of the *Satire première*, it must be said that, in adding a subtitle to the work for the sake of clarity and in correcting what he considered to be faulty quotations, he did not far overstep the bounds of his duties as editor. We are obliged to adopt his edition as giving the best available text. Naigeon's spelling and punctuation have been preserved save for the correction of one or two obvious errors.[5] No subsequent edition has been taken into account. As for the manuscripts, only those readings have been retained which can be considered true variants.

4 See below, p. 228, n. 16 and p. 230, n. 25.

5 Naigeon's use of the *tiret* to mark off dialogue has been supplemented by quotation marks for the sake of clarity. It was found useful, in the dialogued interchange of the author with Naigeon (below, p. 237 ff.) to begin each *réplique* on a new line while retaining the original disposition of the paragraphs. In Naigeon's edition, a horizontal rule separates the title and subtitle from the dedication "A Mon Ami M. Naigeon." This line has been removed, and the dedicatory formula set in smaller type in order to give the title its due importance.

# SATIRE PREMIERE,[a]

sur les caractères et les mots de caractère, de profession, &c.[b]

> – Quot capitum vivunt, totidem studiorum
> Millia.
>
> Horat. Sat. lib. ii.[1c]

### A MON AMI M. NAIGEON,[2]
sur un passage de la première satire du second livre d'Horace :
> Sunt, quibus in satyrâ videar nimis acer, et ultra
> Legem tendere opus.[3]

N'avez-vous pas remarqué, mon ami, que telle est la variété de cette prérogative qui nous est propre, et qu'on appelle raison, qu'elle correspond seule à toute la diversité de l'instinct des animaux ? De-là vient que, sous la forme bipède de l'homme, il n'y a aucune bête innocente ou malfaisante, dans l'air, au fond des forêts, dans les eaux, que vous ne puissiez reconnoître. Il y a l'homme loup, l'homme tigre, l'homme renard, l'homme taupe, l'homme pourceau, l'homme mouton, et celui-ci est le plus commun. Il y a l'homme anguille ; serrez-le tant qu'il vous plaira, il vous échappera. L'homme brochet, qui dévore tout. L'homme serpent, qui se replie en cent façons diverses. L'homme ours, qui ne me déplaît pas. L'homme aigle, qui plane au haut des cieux. L'homme corbeau, l'homme épervier, l'homme et l'oiseau de proie. Rien de plus rare qu'un homme qui soit homme de toute pièce ; aucun de nous qui ne tienne un peu de son analogue animal.

Aussi, autant d'hommes, autant de cris divers.[4]

Il y a le cri de la nature, et je l'entends lorsque Sara dit du sacrifice de son fils : *Dieu ne l'eût jamais demandé à sa mère.*[5] Lorsque Fontenelle, témoin des progrès de l'incrédulité, dit : *Je voudrois bien y être dans soixante ans, pour voir[d] ce que cela deviendra* ; il ne vouloit qu'y être. On ne veut pas mourir, et l'on finit toujours un jour trop tôt.[6] Un jour de plus,

a Satire Par M. Diderot H / b *Le sous-titre manque dans les mss.* / c *L'épigraphe manque dans* H / d savoir LVI – scavoir V2

1 *Sat.*, ii, i, 27–8 : « Autant de têtes de vivants, autant de goûts par milliers » (Villeneuve). La pensée est proverbiale : « Quot homines, tot sententiae ; suus cuique mos » (Térence, *Phorm.*, 454).

2 Jacques-André Naigeon (1738–1810), ami et disciple de Diderot.

3 *Sat.*, ii, i, 1–2 : « Aux yeux de certains, j'ai trop d'âpreté dans la satire, et je force le genre au-delà de ses lois » (Villeneuve).

4 Cf. l'épigraphe, « Quot capitum vivunt, totidem studiorum millia ».

5 Manlio D. Busnelli (*Diderot et l'Italie*, Paris, Champion, 1925, p. 170 n.) n'a pu retrouver ces mots dans l'œuvre de Métastase, bien que Diderot les lui attribue dans une lettre à Sophie Volland du 8 août 1762 (*Corr.*, éd. Roth, t. iv, pp. 94–5).

6 Lieu commun qui se trouve chez Lucrèce (*De rerum natura*, iii, 951–2) comme chez Horace (*Sat.*, i, i, 117–19). Diderot affectionne cette idée, qu'il exprime également dans l'article « Homme » de l'*Encyclopédie* (A.T., t. xv, p. 138) et dans un fragment de lettre sans date (*Lettres à Sophie Volland*, éd. André Babelon, Paris, Gallimard, 1938, 2 vol., t. ii, pp. 277–8).

et l'on eût découvert la quadrature du cercle.[7]

Comment se fait-il que dans les arts d'imitation, ce cri de nature, qui nous est propre, soit si difficile à trouver ? Comment se fait-il que le poète qui l'a saisi, nous étonne et nous transporte ? Seroit-ce qu'alors il nous révèle le secret de notre cœur ?

Il y a le cri de la passion, et je l'entends encore dans le poète, lorsqu'Hermione dit à Oreste : *Qui te l'a dit ?*[8] lorsqu'à, *ils ne se verront plus,* Phèdre répond : *Ils s'aimeront toujours ;*[9] à côté de moi, lorsqu'au sortir d'un sermon éloquent sur l'aumône, l'avare dit : *Cela donneroit envie de demander* ; lorsqu'une maîtresse surprise en flagrant délit, dit à son amant : *Ah! vous ne m'aimez plus, puisque vous en croyez plutôt ce que vous avez vu que ce que je vous dis ;*[10] lorsque l'usurier agonisant dit au prêtre qui l'exhorte : *Ce crucifix, en conscience, je ne saurois prêter là-dessus plus de cent écus, encore faut-il m'en passer un billet de vente.*[11]

Il y eut un temps où j'aimois le spectacle et sur-tout l'opéra.[12] J'étois un jour à l'opéra entre l'abbé de Cannaye[13] que vous connoissez, et un certain Montbron,[14] auteur de quelques brochures où l'on trouve beaucoup de fiel et peu, très-peu de talent. Je venois d'entendre un morceau pathétique, dont

7 Selon Pierre Hermand (*Les idées morales de Diderot*, p. 242 n.), Diderot relisait pendant son séjour en Hollande l'*Eloge de Bernouilli* de Fontenelle. Dans la *Réfutation* on peut lire : « Lisez Bernouilli, et il vous dira que l'art des probabilités présente des questions qui ne sont ni plus ni moins difficiles que la quadrature du cercle » (A.T., t. II, p. 352). Cf. Fontenelle : « Cependant M. Bernouilli, qui possédoit fort cette matière, assuroit que ce problême étoit beaucoup plus difficile que celui de la Quadrature du Cercle, et certainement il seroit sans comparaison plus utile » (*Œuvres de Monsieur de Fontenelle*, Paris, 1766, t. v, p. 110).

8 Racine, *Andromaque*, v, 3.

9 Racine, *Phèdre*, iv, 6.

10 Souvent cité au xviiie siècle, ce mot est donné en exemple par Helvétius, *De l'esprit*, Disc. I, Ch.II, « Des erreurs occasionnées par nos passions ».

11 Cette anecdote se trouve dans le *Dictionnaire d'anecdotes* de Jacques Lacombe (Paris, 1766), p. 677. Selon Jean Pommier, Balzac se serait inspiré de ce passage de la *Satire première* en décrivant la mort de l'avare Grandet (« Comment Balzac relaie Diderot », *Revue des Sciences Humaines*, avril–sept., 1951, p. 163). Il est vraisemblable que Balzac ne fait que relayer Lacombe, dont le recueil fut maintes fois réédité au cours du xviiie siècle.

12 « Lorsque ces acteurs [Dufresne et Montménil] étaient au théâtre, il était assidu au spectacle ; mais depuis environ vingt ans, il n'y a été qu'en passant, pour voir de temps en temps quelque nouvelle pièce, par courtoisie pour l'auteur » (note de Grimm datant de 1770, A.T., t. VIII, p. 354).

13 L'abbé Etienne de Canaye (1694–1782), membre de l'Académie des Inscriptions et Belles-Lettres, dont le grand enthousiasme pour l'opéra était connu des Parisiens de l'époque. Cf. le *Neveu de Rameau*, éd. Jean Fabre, pp. 109, 242.

14 Louis-Charles Fougeret de Monbron (1706–60), auteur cynique du *Cosmopolite* et de *Margot la ravaudeuse*. La publication de ce dernier roman a entraîné l'exil de Monbron en novembre 1748. Voir Franco Venturi, *Jeunesse de Diderot*, pp. 36–40; et J. H. Broome, « "L'homme au cœur velu" : the Turbulent Career of Fougeret de Monbron », *Studies on Voltaire and the Eighteenth Century*, t. xxiii (1963), pp. 179–213.

les paroles et la musique m'avoient transporté. Alors, nous ne connoissions
pas Pergolèse,[15] et Lulli étoit un homme sublime pour nous. Dans le trans-
port de mon ivresse je saisis mon voisin Montbron par le bras, et lui dis :
« Convenez, monsieur, que cela est beau. » L'homme au teint jaune, aux
sourcils noirs et touffus, à l'œil féroce et couvert, me répond : « Je ne sens
pas cela. – Vous ne sentez pas cela ? – Non ; j'ai le cœur velu... » Je fris-
sonne, je m'éloigne du tigre à deux pieds ; je m'approche de l'abbé de
Cannaye, et lui adressant la parole : « Monsieur l'abbé, ce morceau qu'on
vient de chanter comment vous a-t-il paru ? » L'abbé me répond froidement et avec dédain : « Mais assez bien, pas mal. – Et vous connoissez
quelque chose de mieux ? – D'infiniment mieux. – Qu'est-ce donc ? – Certains vers qu'on a faits[a] sur ce pauvre abbé Pellegrin :

> Sa culotte attachée avec une ficelle,
> Laisse[b] voir par cent trous un cul plus noir qu'icelle.[16]

C'est-là ce qui est beau ![17] »

Combien de ramages divers, combien de cris discordans dans la seule forêt
qu'on appelle société ! « Allons ! prenez cette eau de riz. – Combien a-t-elle
coûté ? – Peu de chose. – Mais encore, combien ? – Cinq ou six sous peut-
être. – Et qu'importe que je périsse de mon mal ou par le vol[c] et les
rapines ?[18] » – « Vous, qui aimez tant à parler, comment écoutez-vous cet
homme si longtemps ? – J'attends ; s'il tousse ou s'il crache, il est perdu. » –
« Quel est cet homme assis à votre droite ? – C'est un homme d'un grand
mérite, et qui écoute comme personne. » Celui-ci dit au prêtre qui lui an-

---

a ʟᴠɪᴠ2 *omettent* qu'on a faits / b Laissait ʟᴠɪ – Laissoit ᴠ2ʜ / c les vol ʟᴠɪ –
les vols ᴠ2

15 Gian Battista Pergolesi (1710–36). *La Serva padrona* de Pergolèse, dont la
représentation par la Comédie Italienne avait passé presque inaperçue en 1746, fut
le premier d'une série d'opéras bouffes représentés sur la scène de l'Opéra à partir
de 1752. C'est donc de 1752 que date la grande renommée de Pergolèse parmi les
encyclopédistes, laquelle tempéra du même coup l'enthousiasme qu'ils éprouvaient
pour la musique de Jean-Baptiste Lulli (1632–87).

16 L'abbé Simon-Joseph Pellegrin (1662–1745). « L'abbé Pellegrin, écrit Fréron,
étoit né malheureusement sans fortune ; ce qui le mit dans la nécessité de multiplier
ses veilles et les fruits de son travail. ... Une chose encore qui a pû contribuer au
décri où il étoit tombé, fut sa négligence sur son extérieur » (*Lettres de Madame la
Comtesse de \*\*\* sur quelques écrits modernes*, Genève, 1746, p. 85). D'après une
lettre de Diderot à Sophie Volland du 9 novembre 1760, le sujet de ce couplet peu
laudatif serait l'abbé de la Marre (*Corr.*, éd. Roth, t. ɪɪɪ, p. 246). Comme les manuscrits de la *Satire première*, cette lettre porte la leçon « laissoit », que Naigeon se
serait donc permis de remplacer par « laisse ».

17 Dans la *Réfutation*, Diderot évoque cette expérience, preuve directe du fait
que la sensibilité du diaphragme est plus forte chez un homme que chez un autre :
« C'est grâce à sa diversité qu'au moment où je suis transporté d'admiration et de
joie, où mes larmes coulent, l'un me dit « Je ne sens pas cela, j'ai le cœur velu ... » ;
l'autre me fait une plaisanterie très-burlesque » (ᴀ.ᴛ., t. ɪɪ, pp. 337–8).

18 Ce petit dialogue est tiré textuellement d'Horace, *Sat.*, ɪɪ, iii, 155–7. La leçon
« les vols » correspond au texte d'Horace, qui comporte un pluriel (*furtis*).

nonçoit la visite de son Dieu : *Je le reconnois à sa monture : c'est ainsi qu'il entra dans Jérusalem...* [19] Celui-là, moins caustique, s'épargne dans ses derniers momens l'ennui de l'exhortation du vicaire qui l'avoit administré, en lui disant : *Monsieur, ne vous serois-je plus bon à rien ?...* Et voilà le cri de caractère.

Méfiez-vous de l'homme singe. Il est sans caractère, il a toutes sortes de cris.

« Cette démarche ne vous perdra pas, vous, mais elle perdra votre ami. – *Eh ! que m'importe, pourvu qu'elle me sauve ?* – Mais votre ami ? – *Mon ami, tant qu'il vous plaira ; moi d'abord.*[20] » – « Croyez-vous, monsieur l'abbé, que madame Geoffrin vous reçoive chez elle avec grand plaisir ? – *Qu'est-ce que cela me fait, pourvu que je m'y trouve bien ?*[21] » Regardez cet homme-ci lorsqu'il entre quelque part ; il a la tête penchée sur sa poitrine, il s'embrasse, il se serre étroitement pour être plus près de lui-même.[22] Vous avez vu le maintien et vous avez entendu le cri de l'homme personnel,[23] cri qui retentit de tout côté. C'est un des cris de la nature.

« *J'ai contracté ce pacte avec vous, il est vrai ; mais je vous annonce que je ne le tiendrai pas.* – Monsieur le comte, vous ne le tiendrez pas ! et pourquoi cela, s'il vous plaît ? – *Parce que je suis le plus fort...* » Le cri de la force est encore un des cris de la nature...[24] « *Vous penserez que je suis un infâme, je m'en moque...* » Voilà le cri de l'impudence.

« *Mais ce sont, je crois, des foies d'oie de Toulouse ?* – Excellens ! délicieux ! – *Eh ! que n'ai-je la maladie dont ce seroit là le remède !...* » Et c'est l'exclamation d'un gourmand qui souffroit de l'estomac.

---

19 Mot souvent attribué à Rabelais.

20 C'est ce caractère égoïste que Diderot prête au Commandeur dans son *Père de famille* : « c'est ton ami, ce n'est pas toi. Germeuil, soi, soi d'abord, et les autres après si l'on peut » (A.T., t. VII, p. 359).

21 C'est l'abbé Morellet que vise Diderot dans ce portrait. Une différence fondamentale de tempérament explique sans doute, en partie, l'antipathie de Diderot pour Morellet. Ni l'un ni l'autre n'étaient bienvenus chez Madame Geoffrin ; Diderot n'insista pas, tandis que Morellet s'imposa à la bonne dame. « Je dois même dire, écrit celui-ci, ce qu'elle me disoit elle-même, qu'*elle avoit pour moi quelqu'éloignement.* ... Je lui disois quelquefois qu'elle m'aimeroit un jour, et que je la priois seulement de me supporter jusqu'à ce que ce jour fût venu. Il vint. Depuis ce moment elle n'a cessé de me combler de bontés et de marques d'intérêt » (*Portrait de Madame Geoffrin*, in *Eloges de Madame Geoffrin* par MM. Morellet, Thomas et d'Alembert, Paris, 1812, p. 32). Marie-Thérèse Geoffrin (1699–1777).

22 « L'abbé, dont notre bonne baronne a dit qu'il allait toujours les épaules serrées en devant pour être plus près de lui-même ... » (A.T., t. VI, p. 393). Il s'agit de Morellet.

23 L'adjectif « personnel », dans le sens de « qui est égoïste, qui n'est occupé que de soi », était fort à la mode après 1760. Il ne figure pas dans le *Dictionnaire de l'Académie* avant 1798. L'« abbé Personnel » dont Diderot parle dans une lettre à Sophie Volland est certainement Morellet (28 août 1768, *Corr.*, éd. Roth, t. VIII, p. 102).

24 Diderot revient à plusieurs reprises sur la « loi du plus fort » dans la *Réfutation* (A.T., t. II, pp. 397, 446).

– Vous leur fîtes, seigneur,
En les croquant,[a] beaucoup d'honneur...[25]

Et voilà le cri de la flatterie, de la bassesse et des cours. Mais ce n'est pas tout.
Le cri de l'homme prend encore une infinité de formes diverses de la
profession qu'il exerce. Souvent elles déguisent l'accent du caractère.

Lorsque Ferrein[26] dit : *Mon ami tomba malade, je le traitai, il mourut,
je le disséquai* ; Ferrein fut-il un homme dur ? Je l'ignore.

« Docteur, vous arrivez bien tard. – *Il est vrai. Cette pauvre mademoiselle
du Thé*[27][b] *n'est plus.* – Elle est morte ! – *Oui. Il a fallu assister à l'ouverture
de son corps ; je*[c] *n'ai jamais eu un plus grand plaisir de ma vie...* » Lorsque
le docteur parloit ainsi, étoit-il un homme dur ?[d] Je l'ignore. L'enthousiasme
de métier, vous savez ce que c'est, mon ami.[28] La satisfaction d'avoir deviné
la cause secrète de la mort de mademoiselle du Thé,[e] fit oublier au docteur
qu'il parloit de son amie. Le moment de l'enthousiasme passé, le docteur
pleura-t-il son amie ? Si vous me le demandez, je vous avouerai que je n'en
crois rien.[29]

*Tirez, tirez ; il n'est pas ensemble.* Celui qui tient ce propos d'un mauvais
Christ qu'on approche de sa bouche, n'est point un impie. Son mot est de
son métier, c'est celui d'un sculpteur agonisant.[30]

Ce plaisant abbé de Cannaye, dont je vous ai parlé, fit une petite satire
bien amère et bien gaie des petits dialogues de son ami Rémond de Saint-
Mard.[31] Celui-ci qui ignoroit que l'abbé fût l'auteur de la satire, se plaignoit
un jour de cette malice à une de leurs communes amies.[32] Tandis que
Saint-Mard, qui avoit la peau tendre, se lamentoit outre mesure d'une

a En les croquant, Seigneur, vous leur fîtes *les mss.* / b de Thé LVIH – de T***
v2 / c et je LV2 / d bien dur H / e de Thé LVIH – de T*** v2
25 La Fontaine, *Fables*, VII, i, 37–8. Helvétius avait cité ces vers dans son livre
*De l'homme*, Sec. II, Ch. XVIII, n. 24. La version inexacte que portent les manuscrits
de la *Satire première* (« En les croquant, Seigneur, vous leur fîtes beaucoup d'honneur ») a été corrigée sans doute par Naigeon. Dans la *Réfutation*, Diderot ne manque pas d'estropier à nouveau ces mêmes vers : « Seigneur, en les dévorant vous
leur faites beaucoup d'honneur » (A.T., t. II, p. 447).
26 Antoine Ferrein (1693–1769), anatomiste célèbre.
27 « Quelle est cette demoiselle du Thé ? Ce n'est à coup sûr pas la fameuse cour-
tisane qui ne mourut qu'en 1820 » (note d'Assézat). Le mystère n'a toujours pas été
pénétré.
28 « il y a deux sortes d'enthousiasme : l'enthousiasme d'âme et celui du métier.
Sans l'un, le concept est froid ; sans l'autre, l'exécution est faible ; c'est leur union
qui rend l'ouvrage sublime » (*Pensées détachées sur la peinture*, A.T., t. XII, p. 88).
29 Dans la *Réfutation*, l'exemple du chirurgien, que la pratique de son art a
rendu dur et cruel paraît plusieurs fois (A.T., t. II, pp. 379, 413).
30 Ce mot figure également dans une lettre à Sophie Volland du 27 janvier 1766
(*Corr.*, éd. Roth, t. VI, p. 34).
31 Toussaint Rémond de Saint-Mard (1682–1757), auteur des *Nouveaux Dialogues des dieux, ou Réflexions sur les passions* (1711).
32 « Madame Geoffrin » (note de Naigeon).

piqûre d'épingle, l'abbé, placé derrière lui et en face de la dame, s'avouoit auteur de la satire, et se moquoit de son ami en tirant la langue. Les uns disoient que le procédé de l'abbé étoit malhonnête, d'autres n'y voyoient qu'une espièglerie.[33] Cette question de morale fut portée au tribunal de l'érudit abbé Fenel,[34] dont on ne put[a] jamais obtenir d'autre décision, sinon, que *c'étoit un usage chez les anciens Gaulois de tirer la langue*... Que conclurez-vous de-là ? Que l'abbé de Cannaye étoit un méchant ? Je le crois. Que l'autre abbé étoit un sot ? Je le nie. C'étoit un homme qui avoit consumé ses yeux et sa vie à des recherches d'érudition, et qui ne voyoit rien dans ce monde de quelqu'importance en comparaison de la restitution d'un passage ou de la découverte d'un ancien usage. C'est le pendant du géomètre, qui, fatigué des éloges dont la capitale retentissoit lorsque Racine donna son *Iphigénie*, voulut lire cette *Iphigénie* si vantée. Il prend la pièce ; il se retire dans un coin ; il lit une scène, deux scènes, à la troisième il jette le livre en disant : *Qu'est-ce que cela prouve ?*...[35] C'est le jugement et le mot d'un homme accoutumé dès ses jeunes ans à écrire à chaque bout de page : *Ce qu'il falloit démontrer*.

On se rend ridicule, mais on n'est ni ignorant, ni sot, moins encore méchant, pour ne voir jamais que la pointe de son clocher.

Me voilà tourmenté d'un vomissement périodique, je verse des flots d'une eau caustique et limpide. Je m'effraie, j'appelle Thierry.[36b] Le docteur regarde en souriant le fluide que j'avois rendu par la bouche, et qui remplissoit toute une cuvette. « Eh bien ! docteur, qu'est-ce qu'il y a ? – Vous êtes trop heureux : vous nous avez restitué la *pituite vitrée* des anciens que nous avions perdue...[37] » Je souris à mon tour, et n'en estimai ni plus ni moins le docteur Thierry.

Il y a tant et tant de mots de métier, que je fatiguerois à périr un homme

---

a peut v1v2 / b le médecin Thierry н

33 «Quelquefois malin, jamais caustique ni méchant, il se bornoit à employer cette plaisanterie douce, aimable, qui avertit les autres de se tenir sur leurs gardes, les atteint sans les blesser ... » (Joseph Dacier, « Eloge de l'abbé de Canaye », in *Mémoires de l'Académie des Inscriptions et Belles-Lettres*, t. xlv, 1783, pp. 183–4).

34 Jean-Basile-Pascal Fénel (1695–1753) fut l'auteur d'un « Plan systématique de la religion et des dogmes des anciens Gaulois », publié dans les *Mémoires de l'Académie des Inscriptions et Belles-Lettres*, t. xxiv, 1753, pp. 345–88.

35 Ce mot de Gilles Personne, Sieur de Roberval, professeur de mathématiques au Collège Royal et ennemi acharné de Descartes, fut maintes fois cité au xviiie siècle pour mettre en lumière l'abîme profond qui sépare la raison scientifique de la sensibilité artistique. Diderot rappelle ce mot dans une lettre à Sophie Volland, où il est question des *Réflexions sur la poésie* de d'Alembert (31 août 1760, *Corr.*, éd. Roth, t. iii, p. 46).

36 François Thierry, docteur-régent de la Faculté de Paris, médecin-consultant de Louis xv et de Louis xvi.

37 Voir la lettre à Sophie Volland du 31 octobre 1762 (*Corr.*, éd. Roth, t. iv, p. 211), et la note de G. Roth, t. iv, pp. 235–6. L'ancienne médecine divisait la pituite en *vitrée, salée, douce* et *acide*.

plus patient que vous, si je voulois vous raconter ceux qui se présentent à ma mémoire en vous écrivant. Lorsqu'un monarque, qui commande lui-même ses armées, dit à des officiers qui avoient abandonné une attaque où ils auroient tous perdu la vie sans aucun avantage : *Est-ce que vous êtes faits pour autre chose que pour mourir ?*... il dit un mot de métier.

Lorsque des grenadiers sollicitent auprès de leur général la grace d'un de leurs braves camarades surpris en maraude, et lui disent : *Notre général, remettez-le entre nos mains. Vous le voulez faire mourir ; nous savons punir plus sévèrement un grenadier : il n'assistera point*[a] *à la première bataille que vous gagnerez...* ils ont l'éloquence de leur métier. Eloquence sublime ! Malheur à l'homme de bronze qu'elle ne fléchit pas ! Dites-moi, mon ami, eussiez-vous fait pendre ce soldat si bien défendu par ses camarades ? Non. Ni moi non plus.

« Sire, et la bombe ! – *Qu'a de commun la bombe avec ce que je vous dicte ?*...[38] » – « *Le boulet a emporté la timbale ; mais le riz n'y étoit pas...* » C'est un roi qui a dit le premier de ces mots ; c'est un soldat qui a dit le second, mais ils sont l'un et l'autre d'une ame ferme ;[b] ils n'appartiennent point à l'état.

Y étiez-vous lorsque le castrat Cafarielli[39] nous jetoit dans un ravissement que ni ta véhémence, Démosthène ! ni ton harmonie, Cicéron ! ni l'élévation de ton génie, ô Corneille ! ni ta douceur, Racine ! ne nous firent jamais éprouver ? Non, mon ami, vous n'y étiez pas.[40] Combien de temps et de plaisir nous avons perdu sans nous connoître !... Cafarielli a chanté ; nous restons stupéfaits d'admiration. Je m'adresse au célèbre naturaliste Daubenton,[41] avec lequel je partageois un sofa. « Eh bien ! docteur, qu'en dites-vous ? – Il a les jambes grêles, les genoux ronds, les cuisses grosses, les hanches larges, c'est qu'un être privé des organes qui caractérisent son sexe, affecte la conformation du sexe opposé... – Mais cette musique angélique !... – Pas un poil de barbe au menton... – Ce goût exquis, ce sublime pathétique, cette voix ! – C'est une voix de femme. – C'est la voix la plus belle, la plus égale, la plus flexible, la plus juste, la plus touchante !... » Tandis que le virtuose nous faisoit fondre en larmes, Daubenton l'examinoit en naturaliste.

L'homme qui est tout entier à son métier, s'il a du génie, devient un

a pas v2H / b forte H
38 Anecdote tirée du huitième livre de l'*Histoire de Charles XII* de Voltaire (éd. Moland, t. XVI, p. 332).
39 Caffarelli (né Gaetano Maiorano, 1710–83), dont la superbe voix enchanta les amateurs parisiens en 1753.
40 Naigeon exagère sans doute en affirmant qu'il avait « passé avec ce philosophe les vingt-huit dernières années de sa vie » (*Mémoires historiques et philosophiques sur la vie et les ouvrages de Diderot*, Paris, Brière, 1823, p. 386), ce qui ferait remonter leurs relations à 1757.
41 Louis-Jean-Marie Daubenton (1716–99).

prodige ; s'il n'en a point, une application opiniâtre l'élève au-dessus de la médiocrité. Heureuse la société où chacun seroit à sa chose, et ne seroit qu'à sa chose ! Celui qui disperse ses regards sur tout, ne voit rien ou voit mal ; il interrompt souvent, et contredit celui qui parle et qui a bien vu.

Je vous entends d'ici, et vous vous dites : Dieu soit loué ! J'en avois assez de ces cris de nature, de passion, de caractère, de profession, et m'en voilà quitte... Vous vous trompez, mon ami. Après tant de mots malhonnêtes ou ridicules, je vous demanderai[a] grace pour un ou deux qui ne le soient pas.

« *Chevalier, quel âge avez-vous ? –* Trente ans. *– Moi j'en ai vingt-cinq ; eh bien ! vous m'aimeriez une soixantaine d'années, ce n'est pas la peine de commencer pour si peu...*[42] » – C'est le mot d'une bégueule. – Le vôtre est d'un homme sans mœurs. C'est le mot de la gaieté, de l'esprit et de la vertu. Chaque sexe a son ramage ; celui de l'homme n'a ni la légéreté, ni la délicatesse, ni la sensibilité de celui de la femme. L'un semble toujours commander et brusquer ; l'autre se plaindre et supplier... Et puis celui du célèbre Muret, et je passe à d'autres choses.

Muret[43] tombe malade en voyage ; il se fait porter à l'hôpital. On le place dans un lit voisin du grabat d'un malheureux attaqué d'une de ces infirmités qui rendent l'art perplexe. Les médecins et les chirurgiens délibèrent sur son état. Un des consultans propose une opération qui pouvoit également être salutaire ou fatale. Les avis se partagent. On inclinoit à livrer le malade à la décision de la nature, lorsqu'un plus intrépide dit : *Faciamus experimentum in animâ vili.* Voilà le cri de la bête féroce. Mais d'entre les rideaux qui entouroient Muret, s'élève le cri de l'homme, du philosophe, du chrétien : *Tanquam foret anima vilis, illa pro qua Christus non dedignatus est mori !* Ce mot empêcha l'opération, et le malade guérit.[44]

A cette variété du cri de la nature, de la passion, du caractère, de la profession, joignez le diapason des mœurs nationales, et vous entendrez le vieil

a demande H
42 « Il m'en faut tout au moins un siècle bien compté / Car trente ans, ce n'est pas la peine ». C'est ainsi que La Fontaine sollicite les faveurs de la Volupté dans le deuxième livre de son roman *Psyché* (*Œuvres*, Paris, Hachette, 1883–93, t. VIII, p. 233). L'on retrouve la même anecdote dans le fragment non daté d'une lettre, vraisemblablement adressée à Madame de Maux (*Lettres à Sophie Volland*, éd. cit., t. II, p. 281).
43 Marc-Antoine Muret (1526–85), humaniste célèbre, professeur de Montaigne au Collège de Guyenne.
44 Tous les biographes de Muret affirment que c'est lui, et non un autre, comme le prétend Diderot, qui faillit servir de cobaye aux médecins. Le philosophe revient sur cette anecdote dans son *Essai sur les règnes de Claude et de Néron* (A.T., t. III, p. 362), traduisant cette fois les phrases latines : « Faisons essai sur une âme vile » ; « Comme si elle était vile, cette âme pour laquelle le Christ n'a pas dédaigné de mourir ! »

Horace dire de son fils, *qu'il mourût* ;[45] et les Spartiates dire d'Alexandre :
*Puisque Alexandre veut être Dieu, qu'il soit Dieu.*[46] Ces mots ne désignent
pas le caractère d'un homme, ils marquent l'esprit général d'un peuple.

Je ne vous dirai rien de l'esprit et du ton des corps. Le clergé, la noblesse,
la magistrature ont chacun leur manière de commander, de supplier et de
se plaindre. Cette manière est traditionnelle. Les membres deviennent vils
et rampans, le corps garde sa dignité. Les remontrances de nos parlemens
n'ont pas toujours été des chefs-d'œuvre ;[47a] cependant Thomas, l'homme
de lettres le plus éloquent, l'ame la plus fière et la plus digne, ne les auroit
pas faites ; il ne seroit pas demeuré en deçà, mais il seroit allé au-delà de
la mesure.[48]

Et voilà pourquoi, mon ami, je ne me presserai jamais de demander quel
est l'homme qui entre dans un cercle. Souvent cette question est impolie,
presque toujours elle est inutile. Avec un peu de patience et d'attention on
n'importune ni le maître ni la maîtresse de la maison, et l'on se ménage le
plaisir de deviner.

Ces préceptes ne sont pas de moi ; ils m'ont été dictés par un homme très-
fin,[49] et il en fit en ma présence l'application chez mademoiselle Dornais,[50b]
la veille de mon départ pour le grand voyage,[51] que j'ai entrepris en dépit
de vous. Il survint sur le soir un personnage qu'il ne connoissoit pas ; mais
ce personnage ne parloit pas haut, il avoit de l'aisance dans le maintien, de
la pureté dans l'expression et une politesse froide dans les manières. « C'est,
me dit-il à l'oreille, un homme qui tient à la cour. » Ensuite il remarqua
qu'il avoit presque toujours la main droite sur sa poitrine, les doigts fermés

a chef-d'œuvres NH / b D*** *les mss*

45 Corneille, *Horace*, II, 6. Diderot partageait avec tout son siècle une admiration
profonde pour ce vers sublime. Cf. A.T., t. II, p. 332 ; t. x, p. 30 ; t. xv, p. 36.

46 Diderot a pu trouver cet exemple du caractère laconique des Lacédémoniens
dans les *Histoires diverses d'Elien, traduites du grec avec des remarques,* par J.-B.
Dacier, Paris, 1772, p. 66. « Cette courte réponse, dit Elien, conforme à leur génie,
étoit un trait sanglant contre l'extravagance d'Alexandre ».

47 Durant les quinze années qui précédèrent la réforme du Parlement en 1770, les
remontrances des cours souveraines avaient été faites sur un ton de plus en plus hardi.
D'après Madame de Vandeul, Diderot aurait plus d'une fois prêté sa plume aux
magistrats (*Mémoires sur Diderot,* A.T., t. I, p. li).

48 Antoine-Léonard Thomas (1732–85), académicien connu par son grand talent
dans le genre de l' « éloge », associé intime et apprécié des philosophes. Thomas
tombait souvent dans l'emphase et l'exagération, à tel point que Diderot pouvait
traiter son *Eloge du Dauphin* d'« un amas d'hyperboles » (*Corr. lit.,* 1 avril 1766, t.
VII, p. 17).

49 « Rulhières » (note de Naigeon). Claude-Carloman de Rulhière (1735–91),
poète et historien.

50 Mademoiselle Dornet, maîtresse du prince Galitzine, joue un rôle important
dans la *Mystification, ou Histoire des portraits* de Diderot. Voir *Quatre contes,* éd. J.
Proust, Genève, Droz, 1964, pp. 1–39, 135–40.

51 « Celui de Hollande et de Russie » (note de Naigeon). Diderot quitta Paris
dans les premiers jours de juin, 1773.

et les ongles en dehors. « Ah ! ah ! ajouta-t-il, c'est un exempt des gardes du corps, et il ne lui manque que sa baguette. » Peu de temps après, cet homme conte une petite histoire. « Nous étions quatre, dit-il, madame et monsieur tels, madame de \*\*\*, et moi... » Sur cela mon instituteur continua : « Me voilà entièrement au fait. Mon homme est marié, la femme qu'il a placée la troisième est sûrement la sienne, et il m'a appris son nom en la nommant. »

Nous sortîmes ensemble de chez mademoiselle Dornais.[a] L'heure de la promenade n'étoit pas encore passée ; il me propose un tour aux Tuileries ; j'accepte. Chemin faisant, il me dit beaucoup de choses déliées et conçues dans des termes fort déliés ; mais comme je suis un bon homme, bien uni, bien rond,[52] et que la subtilité de ses observations m'en déroboit la vérité, je le priai de les éclaircir par quelques exemples. Les esprits bornés ont besoin d'exemples. Il eut cette complaisance, et me dit :

« Je dînois un jour chez l'archevêque de Paris.[53] Je ne connois guère le monde qui va là ; je m'embarrasse même peu de le connoître ; mais son voisin, celui à côté duquel on est assis, c'est autre chose. Il faut savoir avec qui l'on cause, et, pour y réussir, il n'y a qu'à laisser parler et réunir les circonstances. J'en avois un à déchiffrer à ma droite. D'abord l'archevêque, lui parlant peu et assez sèchement, ou il n'est pas dévot, me dis-je, ou il est janséniste. Un petit mot sur les jésuites m'apprend que c'est le dernier. On faisoit un emprunt pour le clergé ;[54b] j'en prends occasion d'interroger mon homme sur les ressources de ce corps. Il me les développe très-bien, se plaint de ce qu'ils sont surchargés, fait une sortie contre le ministre de la finance,[55] ajoute qu'il s'en est expliqué nettement en 1750 avec le contrôleur général.[56] Je vois donc qu'il a été agent du clergé.[57] Dans le courant de la conversation, il me fait entendre qu'il n'a tenu qu'à lui d'être évêque. Je le

a D\*\*\* *les mss* / b sur le clergé LV1V2

52 Naigeon aurait savouré la finesse de cette allusion au sage des stoïciens, « teres atque rotundus » (Horace, *Sat.*, ii, vii, 86).

53 Christophe de Beaumont (1703–81), archevêque de Paris depuis 1746 jusqu'à sa mort, s'évertua sans relâche pour extirper le jansénisme de son diocèse.

54 La leçon donnée par Naigeon (« pour le clergé ») s'impose. Il s'agit du « don gratuit » que le clergé français offrait au roi à l'occasion de son Assemblée Générale. Le roi autorisait l'emprunt des fonds nécessaires. De tels emprunts se firent en 1755, 1758, 1760, 1762, 1765, 1770 et 1772. Voir Gabriel Lepointe, *L'Organisation et la politique financières du clergé de France sous le règne de Louis XV*, Paris, 1923, pp. 278–307.

55 On donnait au ministre des finances le titre de « contrôleur général ».

56 Jean-Baptiste de Machault d'Arnouville (1701–94), contrôleur général en 1750, commença en cette même année sa fameuse lutte, vouée à l'échec, contre le clergé français. Voir Marcel Marion, *Machault d'Arnouville*, Paris, 1891, pp. 239–329.

57 Toutes les affaires financières du clergé français étaient remises entre les mains de deux agents généraux, nommés pour une période de cinq ans par l'Assemblée Générale. En 1750, les deux anciens agents, l'abbé de Nicolaï et l'abbé de

crois homme de qualité ; mais comme il se vante plusieurs fois d'un vieil oncle lieutenant-général, et qu'il ne dit pas un mot de son père, je suis sûr que c'est un homme de fortune qui a dit une sottise. Comme il me conte les anecdotes scandaleuses de huit ou dix évêques, je ne doute pas qu'il ne soit méchant. Enfin il a obtenu, malgré bien des concurrens, l'intendance de *** pour son frère. Vous conviendrez que si l'on m'eût dit, en me mettant à table, c'est un janséniste sans naissance, insolent, intrigant, qui déteste ses confrères, qui en est détesté, enfin c'est l'abbé de ***,[58] on ne m'auroit rien appris de plus que ce que j'en ai su, et qu'on m'auroit privé du plaisir de la découverte. »

La foule commençoit à s'éclaircir dans la grande allée. Mon homme tire sa montre et me dit : « Il est tard, il faut que je vous quitte, à moins que vous ne veniez souper avec moi. – Où ? – Ici près, chez Arnoud.[59] – Je ne la connois pas. – Est-ce qu'il faut connoître une fille pour aller souper chez elle ? Du reste, c'est une créature charmante, qui a le ton de son état et celui du grand monde. Venez, vous vous amuserez. – Non, je vous suis obligé ; mais comme je vais de ce côté, je vous accompagnerai jusqu'au cul-de-sac Dauphin...[60] » Nous allons, et en allant il m'apprend quelques plaisanteries

Breteuil, ayant présenté à l'Assemblée le bilan de leur charge, furent remplacés par l'abbé Coriolis d'Epinouse et l'abbé de la Croix de Castries de Meyrargues. Selon la coutume, le roi fut prié de récompenser les services des anciens agents en les élevant à l'épiscopat. Voir *Collection des procès-verbaux des assemblées générales du Clergé de France*, éd. Antoine Duranthon, Paris, 1767–78, Tome VIII, première partie, p. 246.

58 L'abbé dont parle ici Diderot doit être l'un des quatre mentionnés dans la note précédente. Chacun des anciens agents avaient eu une altercation avec Machault en 1750. « L'abbé de Breteuil, agent du clergé, a encore eu une violente dispute avec lui [Machault] », rapporte le Marquis d'Argenson, « on dit que cela a été fort loin » (*Journal et mémoires*, Paris, 1859–68, 9 vol., t. VI, p. 16). E.-J.-F. Barbier nous informe que « M. l'abbé de Nicolaï ... a parlé un peu trop haut sur ces affaires-ci à M. le contrôleur général ; il n'en faut pas davantage pour l'empêcher d'être jamais évêque » (*Journal historique*, Paris, 1847–56, 4 vol., t. III, p. 174). L'abbé de Nicolaï, cependant, fut nommé évêque de Verdun en 1754, et il s'y signala bientôt par ses mesures rigoureuses contre les jansénistes (*Nouvelles ecclésiastiques*, 1766, p. 80). L'abbé de notre anecdote ne peut donc être qu'Elisabeth-Théodose Le Tonnelier, abbé de Breteuil (1710–81), frère de la « divine Emilie », marquise du Châtelet. Il est permis de douter de l'exactitude des faits rapportés par Diderot. Le « vieil oncle lieutenant général » est vraisemblablement le mari d'Emilie, le marquis Florent-Claude du Châtelet-Lomont (1695–1766), nommé lieutenant général en 1744. L'abbé de Breteuil n'avait pas à l'époque de frère pour qui il pût obtenir un poste d'intendant; mais il avait, en effet, en tant que chancelier du duc d'Orléans, obtenu le poste d'ambassadeur en Russie pour son neveu, Louis-Auguste Le Tonnelier, Baron de Breteuil. Il est à noter que Rulhière avait accompagné le baron de Breteuil en Russie en 1760, en qualité de secrétaire d'ambassade.

59 Sophie Arnould (1740–1802) « fille d'Opéra » connue tant par ses talents extraordinaires que par ses nombreuses affaires de cœur. Rulhière figurait régulièrement parmi les hôtes à ses soupers. Voir E. et J. de Goncourt, *Sophie Arnould*, édition définitive, Paris, 1884, p. 56 n.

60 La rue du Dauphin, aujourd'hui partie de la rue Saint-Roch, s'appelait familièrement « cul-de-sac Dauphin » à cause de la barrière qui en fermait l'extrémité

cyniques d'Arnoud et quelques-uns de ses mots ingénus et délicats.[61] Il me parle de tous ceux qui fréquentent là, et chacun d'eux eut son mot... Appliquant à cet homme même les principes que j'en avois reçus, moi, je vois qu'il fréquente dans de la bonne et de la mauvaise compagnie...

– Ne fait-il pas des vers, me demandez-vous ?[62]

– Très-bien.

– N'a-t-il pas été lié avec le maréchal de Richelieu ?[63a]

– Intimement.

– Ne fait-il pas sa cour à la comtesse de Grammont ?[64b]

– Assiduement.

– N'y a-t-il pas sur son compte ?...

– Oui, une certaine histoire de Bordeaux, mais je n'y crois pas. On est si méchant dans ce pays-ci, on y fait tant de contes, il y a tant de coquins intéressés à multiplier le nombre de leurs semblables !

– Vous a-t-il lu sa *Révolution* de Russie ?[65c]

– Oui.

a maréchal de *** LVIV2 / b Comtesse de *** LVIV2 – comtesse d'Egmont H / c Révolution de *** LVIV2

sud. Sophie Arnould et Rulhière habitait chacun un appartement dans la même maison, rue du Dauphin. En 1771 Sophie emménagea rue Neuve-des-Petits-Champs. C'est donc avant cette date que la conversation entre Rulhière et Diderot dut avoir lieu.

61 « On pourrait faire un petit recueil des bons mots de Sophie, qui ont tous le ton de fille, mais d'une fille de beaucoup d'esprit » (*Corr. lit.*, 1 février 1770, t. VIII, pp. 453–4). Cf. Albéric Deville, *Arnoldiana*, Paris, 1815, et E. et J. de Goncourt, *Sophie Arnould*, pp. 56–60.

62 Le *Discours en vers sur les disputes* de Rulhière était connu à l'époque, ayant paru dans l'article « Dispute » du *Dictionnaire philosophique* (Voltaire, *Œuvres*, éd. Moland, t. XVIII, pp. 397–402). Diderot fait l'éloge de ce poème dans une lettre à Sophie Volland du 10 septembre 1768 (*Corr.*, éd. Roth, t. VIII, p. 152).

63 Louis-François-Armand Duplessis de Richelieu, Maréchal de France (1696–1788). Rulhière avait servi d'aide de camp à Richelieu en 1758–9, quand celui-ci était gouverneur de la Guyenne. Il fut le protégé de la fille de Richelieu, la comtesse d'Egmont, jusqu'à la mort de celle-ci en 1773.

64 Antoine-Adrien-Charles, comte de Gramont (1726–62), gouverneur du Béarn à partir de 1756, commandait toutes les troupes françaises du secteur de la Guyenne qui était dans la Généralité d'Auch. C'est en Guyenne, sans doute, que sa femme, née Marie-Louise-Sophie de Faoucq, avait connu Rulhière. Après son veuvage en 1762, elle resta à Paris jusqu'à la Révolution. Elle émigra alors à Brunswick, où elle mourut en 1798. Voir Comte Agénor A. A. de Gramont, *Histoire & Généalogie de la Maison de Gramont*, Paris, 1874, pp. 296–7.

65 « Il a écrit l'histoire de la dernière révolution de Russie avec une témérité incroyable. Ce qui l'est peut-être encore davantage, c'est l'étourderie avec laquelle il lit ce morceau, depuis plusieurs années, de cercle en cercle » (*Corr. lit.*, 1 avril 1770, t. VIII, p. 493). Grimm, Diderot et Madame Geoffrin firent l'impossible pour faire supprimer cet ouvrage dans l'intérêt de Catherine II. Rulhière promit de ne pas publier son livre, terminé en 1768, avant la mort de Catherine. Bien que Diderot doutât de sa bonne foi (lettre à Falconet, mai 1768, *Corr.*, éd. Roth, t. VIII, p. 33), Rulhière tint parole. Son *Histoire ou Anecdotes sur la révolution de Russie en 1762* ne parut qu'en 1797.

– Qu'en pensez-vous ?

– Que c'est un roman historique assez bien écrit et très-intéressant, un tissu de mensonges et de vérités que nos neveux compareront à un chapitre de Tacite.[66]

Et voilà, me dites-vous, qu'au lieu de vous avoir éclairci un passage d'Horace, je vous ai presque fait une satire à la manière de Perse.[67]

– Il est vrai.

– Et que vous croyez que je vous en tiens quitte ?

– Non.

Vous connoissez Burigny ?[68]

– Qui ne connoît pas l'ancien, l'honnête, le savant et fidèle serviteur de madame Geoffrin ?[a]

– C'est un très-bon et très-savant homme.[b]

– Un peu curieux.

– D'accord.

– Fort gauche.

– Il en est d'autant meilleur. Il faut toujours avoir un petit ridicule qui amuse nos amis.

– Eh bien ! Burigny ?

Je causois avec lui, je ne sais plus de quoi. Le hasard voulut qu'en causant, je touchai sa corde favorite, l'érudition ; et voilà mon érudit qui m'interrompt, et se jette dans une digression qui ne finissoit pas.

– Cela lui arrive tous les jours, et jamais sans qu'on n'en soit plus instruit.

– Et qu'un endroit d'Horace qui m'avoit paru maussade, devient pour moi d'un naturel charmant, et d'une finesse exquise.

– Et cet endroit ?

– C'est celui où le poète prétend qu'on ne lui refusera pas une indulgence qu'on a bien accordée à Lucilius, son compatriote. Soit que Lucilius fût Appulien ou Lucanien, dit Horace, je marcherai sur ses traces.[69]

– Je vous entends, et c'est dans la bouche de Trébatius, dont Horace a

---

a Madame de *** LVIV2 / b *L'absence du tiret dans* NH *rattache à tort cette réplique à la précédente*

66 « Sur ce que j'ai pu lui dire de réminiscence de la relation de Rulhières, il m'a semblé que ce n'était qu'un tissu romanesque, sans connaissance réelle des faits et des personnes, et qui aura pourtant avant deux siècles toute l'autorité de l'histoire » (*Sur la Princesse Dashkoff*, A.T., t. XVII, p. 492). Passage signalé par Naigeon.

67 Peu de temps auparavant, Diderot avait annoté les *Satires* de Perse pour son ami l'abbé Guillaume-Antoine Lemonnier, qui préparait une seconde édition de la traduction qu'il avait faite de cette œuvre. Voir G. Charlier et L. Hermann, « Diderot, annotateur de Perse », *Revue d'Histoire Littéraire de la France*, t. XXXV, 1928, pp. 39–63.

68 Jean-Lévesque de Burigny (1692–1785), savant membre de l'Académie des Inscriptions et Belles-Lettres. Il avait publié de nombreuses dissertations dans les *Mémoires* de cette société, ainsi que des livres biographiques et historiques.

69 Il s'agit de la première satire du deuxième livre, où Horace « prend une consultation juridique au sage et vieux Trébatius sur la violence ou la faiblesse de

touché le texte favori, que vous mettez cette longue discussion sur l'histoire ancienne des deux contrées.[70] Cela est bien et finement vu.

– Quelle vraisemblance, à votre avis, que le poète sût ces choses ! Et quand il les auroit sues, qu'il eût assez peu de goût pour quitter son sujet, et se jeter dans un fastidieux détail d'antiquités !

– Je pense comme vous.

– Horace dit : *Sequor hunc, Lucanus, an Appulus.*[a] L'érudit Trébatius prend la parole à *Anceps*,[71] et dit à Horace : « Ne brouillons rien.[b] Vous n'êtes ni de la Pouille, ni de la Lucanie ; vous êtes de Venouse, qui laboure sur l'un et l'autre finage. Vous avez pris la place des Sabelliens après leur expulsion. Vos ancêtres furent placés là comme une barrière qui arrêtât les incursions des Lucaniens et des Appuliens. Ils remplirent cet espace vacant, et firent la sécurité de notre territoire contre deux violens ennemis. C'est du moins une tradition très-vieille ».[72]

– L'érudit Trébatius, toujours érudit, instruit Horace sur les chroniques surannées de son pays.

– Et l'érudit Burigny, toujours érudit, m'explique un endroit difficile d'Horace, en m'interrompant précisément comme le poète l'avoit été par Trébatius.

– Et vous partez de là, vous, pour me faire un long narré des mots de nature et des propos de passion, de caractère et de profession ?

– Il est vrai. Le tic d'Horace est de faire des vers, le tic de Trébatius et de Burigny, de parler antiquités,[c] le mien de moraliser, et le vôtre...[73]

– Je vous dispense de me le dire : je le sais.

a Horace dit : Soit qu'il fût Lucanien ou Appulien H / b L'érudit Trebatius l'interrompt là et dit : Ne brouillons rien H – LV1 V2 *omettent* Ne brouillons rien / c antiquité H

ses satires » (Lejay). Trébatius lui conseille de s'abstenir, mais Horace répond qu'il ne saurait renoncer à sa marotte, qui est de composer des satires à la mode de Lucilius (vv. 1–33). Horace poursuit : « Sequor hunc, Lucanus an Apulus, anceps » (v. 34). La traduction de ce vers que donne ici Diderot pèche par plus d'un endroit. C'est à tort, surtout, qu'il fait de Lucilius, né en Campanie, le compatriote d'Horace. On s'accorde pour traduire : « Je suis son exemple, moi, Lucanien ou Apulien, je ne sais trop ... » (Villeneuve).

70 Il est question ici des vv. 35–9, que Diderot traduit plus loin. Tous les commentateurs modernes les attribuent à Horace. Trébatius ne reprend la parole qu'au v. 60.

71 « Je ne sais trop ». Diderot a fait un contresens en rattachant le mot « anceps » au vers suivant.

72 Nam Venusinus arat finem sub utrumque colonus,
   Missus ad hoc, pulsis, vetus est ut fama, Sabellis,
   Quo ne per vacuum Romano incurreret hostis,
   Sive quod Apula gens seu quod Lucania bellum
   Incuteret violenta.

(*Sat.*, II, i, 35–9)

73 « Ce passage ne peut avoir aucun sens pour le public ; mais il étoit très-clair pour Diderot et pour moi : et cela suffisoit dans une lettre qui pouvoit être interceptée et compromettre celui à qui elle étoit écrite. Comme il n'y a plus aujourd'hui

– Je me tais donc. Je vous salue ; je salue tous nos amis de la rue Royale[74] et de la cour de Marsan,[75] et me recommande à votre souvenir qui m'est cher.

P.S.[a] Je lirois volontiers le commentaire de l'abbé Galiani sur Horace, si vous l'aviez.[76] A quelques-unes de vos heures perdues, je voudrois que vous lussiez l'ode troisième du troisième livre, *justum et tenacem propositi virum*,[77] et que vous me découvrissiez ailleurs la place de la strophe : *Aurum irrepertum, et sic melius situm*,[78] qui ne tient à rien de ce qui précède, à rien de ce qui suit, et qui gâte tout.

Quant aux deux vers de l'épître dixième du premier livre,

Imperat aut servit collecta pecunia cuique,

Tortum digna sequi potiùs, quàm ducere funem,[79]

voici comme je les entends.

Les confins des villes sont fréquentés par les poètes qui y cherchent la solitude, et par les cordiers qui y trouvent un long espace pour filer leur

---

a *Le post-scriptum manque dans* H

aucun danger à donner le mot de cette énigme, qui peut d'ailleurs exciter la curiosité de quelques lecteurs, je dirai donc que Diderot, souvent témoin de la colère et de l'indignation avec lesquelles je parlois des maux sans nombre que les prêtres, les religions et les dieux de toutes les nations avoient faits à l'espèce humaine, et des crimes de toute espèce dont ils avoient été le prétexte et la cause, disoit des vœux ardens que je formois, *pectore ab imo* [Lucrèce, *De rer. nat.*, III, 57], pour l'entière destruction des idées religieuses, quel qu'en fût l'objet, que *c'étoit mon tic*, comme celui de Voltaire étoit *d'écraser l'infâme*. Il savoit de plus que j'étois alors occupé d'un dialogue entre un déiste, un sceptique et un athée ; et c'est à ce travail dont mes principes philosophiques lui faisoient pressentir le résultat, qu'il fait ici allusion ; mais en termes si obscurs et si généraux, qu'un autre que moi n'y pouvoit rien comprendre : et c'est précisément ce qu'il vouloit » (note de Naigeon – qui n'a guère besoin de commentaire !)

74 Résidence du baron d'Holbach.

75 Résidence de Madame de Maux, amie intime du philosophe.

76 Il s'agit d'un manuscrit de cet ouvrage, dont Suard et Arnaud avaient publié une partie, bien que l'auteur s'y opposât, dans la *Gazette littéraire de l'Europe* de 1765. Voir Fausto Nicolini, *Gli studi sopra Orazio dell'abate F. Galiani*, Naples, 1910, p. vii.

77 Horace, *Od.*, III, iii, 1. Diderot cite ce premier vers afin de localiser la strophe dont il veut parler. L'ode débute par un éloge de « l'homme juste et ferme dans ses desseins ».

78 Horace, *Od.*, III, iii, 49–52. Diderot ne cite ici que le premier vers de cette strophe, dont Villeneuve donne la traduction suivante : « [Rome] mettant son courage à dédaigner l'or et à le laisser enfoui et caché sous la terre, sa meilleure place, plutôt qu'à l'amasser d'une main prompte à ravir pour l'usage de l'homme toute chose sacrée ». On trouve dans ces vers, ainsi que dans ceux de l'épître, qui vont suivre, deux idées chères à Diderot : le mépris de l'or et l'usage bien entendu des richesses. Diderot ne se trompe pas dans sa critique d'Horace : « Parmi les éditeurs, les uns rattachent cette strophe à la précédente, les autres à la suivante ... » (Plessis).

79 Horace, *Ep.*, I, x, 47–8 : « L'argent amassé est notre tyran ou notre esclave, mais ce qui lui revient, c'est de suivre la corde de chanvre tordu, non de la tirer » (Villeneuve).

corde. *Collecta pecunia,* c'est la filasse entassée dans leur tablier. Alternativement, elle obéit au cordier, et commande au chariot. Elle obéit, quand on la file; elle commande, quand on la tord. Pour la seconde manœuvre, la corde filée est accrochée d'un bout à l'émérillon du rouet, et de l'autre à l'émérillon du chariot, instrument assez semblable à un petit traîneau.[80] Ce traîneau est chargé d'un gros poids qui en ralentit la marche, qui est en sens contraire[a] de celle du cordier. Le cordier qui file s'éloigne à reculons du rouet, le chariot qui tord s'en approche. A mesure que la corde filée se tord par le mouvement du rouet, elle se raccourcit, et en se raccourcissant, tire le chariot vers le rouet. Horace nous fait donc entendre que l'argent, ainsi que la filasse, doit faire la fonction du chariot, et non celle du cordier, suivre la corde torse, et non la filer, rendre notre vie plus ferme, plus vigoureuse, mais non la diriger. Le choix et l'ordre des mots employés par le poète indiquent l'emprunt métaphorique d'une manœuvre que le poète avoit[b] sous les yeux, et dont son goût exquis a sauvé la bassesse.[81]

a marche en sens contraire v1 v2 / b qu'il avait lv1 – qu'il avoit v2

80 « On peut se représenter, au lieu d'une laisse, une corde de halage, le câble d'une machine, etc. » (Villeneuve).

81 « On presseroit jusqu'à la dernière goutte tous les commentaires et les commentateurs passés et présens, qu'on n'en tireroit pas de quoi composer, sur quelque passage que ce soit, une explication aussi naturelle, aussi ingénieuse, aussi vraie, et d'un goût aussi délicat, aussi exquis. Ces deux vers m'avoient toujours arrêté ; et le sens que j'y trouvois ne me satifaisoit nullement. Les interprêtes et les traducteurs d'Horace n'ont pas même soupçonné la difficulté de ce passage : et leurs notes le prouvent assez. Il falloit, pour l'entendre, avoir la sagacité de Diderot, et sur-tout connoître comme lui la manœuvre des différens arts mécaniques, particulièrement de celui auquel le poète fait ici allusion : et j'avoue, à ma honte, que la plupart de ces arts dont je sens d'ailleurs toute l'importance et toute l'utilité, n'ont jamais été l'objet de mes études. Je suis bien ignorant sur ce point ; mais il n'est plus temps aujourd'hui de réparer à cet égard le vice de mon éducation, et, je crois aussi, celui de beaucoup d'autres. Ces différentes connoissances dont on a si souvent occasion de faire usage dans le cours de sa vie, ne sont pas du genre de celles qu'on peut acquérir par la méditation, par des études faites à l'ombre et dans le silence du cabinet. Ici il faut agir, se déplacer ; il faut visiter toutes les sortes d'ateliers, faire, comme Diderot, travailler devant soi les artistes, travailler soi-même sous leurs yeux, les interroger, et, ce qui est encore plus difficile, savoir entendre leurs réponses souvent obscures, parce qu'ils ne veulent pas se rendre plus clairs ; et quelquefois aussi parce qu'ils n'en ont pas le talent » (note de Naigeon).

# Appendix 2

*Lui et Moi*: TEXT AND NOTES

*Lui et Moi* appeared for the first time among the "Œuvres diverses" brought together in the seventeenth volume of the Assézat-Tourneux edition of Diderot's works (pp. 481–5). In a prefatory note to the "Œuvres diverses" (p. 474), Maurice Tourneux states that he has based his edition of *Lui et Moi* on a manuscript lent to him by the well-known bibliophile E.-J.-B. Rathery shortly before the latter's death. The catalogue of Rathery's collection, sold at auction in April 1876, describes the work thus (p. 56): "Diderot. *Lui et Moi*, pièce autographe, 3 p. in -4. Dialogue entre le philosophe et un écrivailleur qu'il a obligé et qui a publié une satire contre lui. Pièce fort curieuse" (Bibl. Nat., Δ 34759). The successors of Etienne Charavay, the expert who handled the sale, are unable to supply information as to the purchaser. Since there is no copy of *Lui et Moi* either in the Fonds Vandeul or in the Leningrad Collection, we are obliged to follow the text of the A.T. edition.

## Lui et Moi

Personne n'a jamais su comme lui combien j'étais bête ; il doit, il m'emprunte de l'argent pour payer ses dettes et s'en sert pour faire imprimer une satire contre moi. Avant que de faire imprimer sa satire, il me la lit. Je lui montre qu'elle est mauvaise et il se sert de mes conseils pour la rendre meilleure. Quand il croit avoir tiré de moi tout le parti qu'un coquin peut tirer d'un sot, il vient me voir, il me dit qu'il est un coquin, me laisse clairement entendre que je suis un sot, me tire sa révérence et s'en va.[1]

1 « Vous qui savez tout, savez-vous de l'histoire naturelle ? – Tout le monde en sait. – Vous avez entendu parler du formicaleo ? – Oui. – C'est un petit animal fort adroit. Il établit sa demeure au fond d'un sable fin. Là il se fait une niche en entonnoir renversé. Il couvre la surface de cet entonnoir d'une surface de sable très-légère et très-mobile. Si un autre insecte inconsidéré vient se promener sur cette surface, il s'enfonce et tombe au fond du trou où le formicaleo s'en saisit, le dévore et lui dit : « Monsieur, je suis bien votre serviteur » (note de Diderot). Le philosophe connaissait déjà les caractéristiques de cet insecte, décrits par Daubenton dans l'article « Fourmi-lion » de l'*Encyclopédie* (t. VII, pp. 231–2).

Au bout de cinq à six mois, je le retrouve au coin de la rue Mâcon.[2] Il rasait le mur, il n'avait pas pour vingt sous de hardes sur tout son corps. Il était maigre, sale et hâve. Il paraissait accablé de misère et de vilaines maladies. Il m'arrête et nous causons.

MOI.

Comme vous voilà !

LUI.

Il est vrai que je suis fort mal.

MOI.

Pardieu, je m'en réjouis.

LUI.

Comment ! Vous vous en réjouissez.

MOI.

Assurément. Vous avez le sort que vous méritez et je vois qu'il faut tôt ou tard que justice se fasse.

LUI.

Toujours de la gaieté et de l'imagination. Sans plaisanter, vous m'avez dit il y a quelque temps que s'il ne me manquait qu'une centaine de francs par an pour me soutenir et m'aider à reprendre la robe de palais,[3] vous me les donneriez volontiers.

MOI.

Je m'en souviens, mais j'ai changé d'avis.

LUI.

Et pourquoi cela ?

MOI.

C'est que vous êtes un brigand et qu'il y a dans la société vingt mille honnêtes gens qui souffrent.

LUI.

Vous avez bien mauvaise opinion de moi.

MOI.

Très-mauvaise. Mais qu'est-ce que cela vous fait ?

LUI.

Peu de chose.

2 A.T. : « rue Maçon ». Selon Jacques Hillairet (*Dictionnaire historique des rues de Paris*, Paris, Editions de Minuit, 1963, 2 vol.), la rue Mâcon « reliait les rues de la Harpe et Saint-André-des-Arts » (t. II, p. 472).

3 « Ceux qui, après avoir quitté la profession d'Avocat, veulent la reprendre, n'ont rang sur le Tableau que du jour qu'ils ont repris l'exercice de la profession » (Boucher d'Argis, *Histoire abrégée de l'Ordre des Avocats*, p. 112). On n'admettait au Tableau que ceux qui avaient « un domicile certain et connu » ainsi que « des meubles, une bibliothèque, et surtout des in-folios de droit » (Francis Delbeke, *L'Action politique et sociale des avocats au XVIIIe siècle*, Bruxelles et Paris, 1927, pp. 72, 113).

MOI.

Oh ! je sais que la seule chose que vous regrettiez, c'est l'argent que vous ne m'attraperez plus.

LUI.

Vous ne savez pas combien vous êtes bon.

MOI.

Mais, en revanche, je sais combien vous l'êtes peu. A quel propos aussi me faire cet impertinent apologue de la fourmi et du fourmilion ?

LUI.

Vous pensez encore à cela ?

MOI.

Si j'y pense ! cet apologue pouvait me coûter fort cher : il ne fallait que le différer jusqu'aujourd'hui, par exemple.

LUI.

Le conseil est bon et j'en userai. Imaginerez-vous que dans l'état déplorable où vous me voyez j'ai fait un livre ?

MOI.

Une satire contre un bienfaiteur ?

LUI.

Ah ! l'horreur !

MOI.

C'est donc une apologie des persécuteurs ou des sangsues de la nation ?

LUI.

Ah ! ah !

MOI.

Mais n'est-ce pas au moment où je vous empêchais de mourir de faim au coin d'une borne, ou sur la paille dans une prison, que vous avez fait imprimer *les Zélindiens* ?[4]

LUI.

Qu'est-ce que cela ?

MOI.

Une satire contre mes amis et moi.

LUI.

Et de qui cette satire ?

MOI.

De vous.

LUI.

Cela n'est pas possible.

---

4 « *Les Zélindiens*, par Mlle F***, sont un petit conte insipide que personne n'a regardé » (Grimm, *Corr. lit.*, 1 juin 1762, t. v, p. 90).

MOI.

Vous êtes un impudent. Songez donc que vous me l'aviez lue manuscrite ! Allons donc, à votre rôle ! Il ne faut pas me dire : « Je ne sais pas ce que c'est que *les Zélindiens* », mais : « Il est vrai que j'ai fait cette satire. Que voulez-vous ? Je n'avais pas le sol, et ce coquin d'Hérissant,[5] qui court après tout ce qu'on écrit contre les encyclopédistes, m'en offrait quatre louis ». Je suis homme à me payer de ces raisons. Si je fais la sottise de réchauffer un serpent, je ne serai pas surpris qu'il me pique.[6]

LUI.

Il fait un froid de diable. Si nous entrions au café ?

MOI.

Serviteur.

LUI.

Ma foi ! vous êtes un rare corps. Entrons un moment. J'ai un plaisir infini à causer avec vous.

MOI.

Moi, je ne saurais souffrir les gens sans caractère. Quand on a le vice, encore faut-il savoir en tirer parti.

LUI.

Entrons un moment et vous m'apprendrez tout cela.

MOI.

Serviteur.

LUI.

Quoi que vous pensiez de mon caractère, je ne néglige pourtant rien pour m'en donner un bon.

MOI.

Temps perdu. Peut-être qu'avec plus d'intrépidité...

LUI.

Eh bien ! Que ferais-je ?

MOI.

Mais si vous aviez un père âgé qui vécût trop longtemps...

5 Claude-Jean-Baptiste Hérissant, imprimeur-libraire, avait publié les multiples volumes de la *Religion vengée, ou Réfutation des auteurs impies,* par Soret et Hayer (1757–63), et les *Préjugés légitimes contre l'Encyclopédie* de Chaumeix (1758–9). « Les six presses de Hérissant gémissent à la fois », dit l'abbé Morellet, en faisant allusion à la publication de cette dernière œuvre (*Mémoire pour Abraham Chaumeix contre les prétendus Philosophes, Diderot et d'Alembert,* Amsterdam, 1759, p. 32).

6 Dans le *Neveu de Rameau,* Lui exprime la même idée sous forme de confession dans laquelle il avoue la nature instinctive de sa méchanceté : « Il y a un pacte tacite qu'on nous fera du bien, et que tôt ou tard nous rendrons le mal pour le bien qu'on nous aura fait. Ce pacte ne subsiste-t-il pas entre l'homme et son singe ou son perroquet ? » (éd. Jean Fabre, p. 68).

LUI.

Je n'ai point de père.

A ce mot, l'horreur me saisit. Je m'enfuis, lui me criant : « Philosophe, écoutez donc, écoutez donc. Vous prenez les choses au tragique ». Mais j'allais toujours et j'étais bien loin de cet homme que je m'en croyais encore trop près. M. Le Roy[7] m'a dit qu'il avait beaucoup de pareils. Ma foi, je ne saurais le croire.

7 Charles-Georges Le Roy (1723–89), ami de Diderot.

# Appendix 3

1 Extract from Madame de Vandeul's *Mémoires sur Diderot* as found in
A.T., I, xlviii–l:

Il avait ramassé, je ne sais où, un M. Rivière, beau, jeune, éloquent, ayant
le masque de la sensibilité, le don des larmes, pauvre, malheureux : le quart
de tout cela aurait suffi pour intéresser mon père ; il l'aida dans quelques
ouvrages, et plusieurs fois lui donna quelques louis. Le désir de rendre son
sort plus doux l'engage à faire à cet homme plusieurs questions sur sa famille
et le parti qu'il pourrait en tirer. « J'ai un frère ecclésiastique et fort riche,
il pourrait me secourir, mais il me hait ; dans ma jeunesse je lui ai fait
quelques espiègleries, et dans l'âge mûr je l'ai empêché d'être évêque. –
Mais comment diable empêche-t-on un homme d'être évêque ? – Rien n'est
plus simple ; il prêcha un carême devant le roi ; ses sermons étaient élo-
quents et hardis, la cour en fut satisfaite, on devait le nommer au premier
évêché vacant ; je fis cent plaisanteries sur ses talents, et dis à tout venant
que les sermons étaient de moi. – Mais cette conduite est fort ridicule ;
malgré cela votre frère peut être un homme de bien. Je veux essayer de vous
raccomoder ; je le verrai demain ; et si vous ne gâtez pas ma besogne avec
de nouvelles frasques, nous en obtiendrons peut-être quelque chose... »
Mon père s'habille, va chez l'abbé, se fait annoncer ; on le reçoit avec
politesse. A peine a-t-il prononcé les premiers mots du sujet qui l'amène,
que l'abbé s'agite, ses yeux s'allument. « Monsieur, dit-il à mon père, un
homme sage ne sollicite jamais qu'il ne connaisse le sujet qu'il recommande.
Connaissez-vous mon frère ? – Je le crois, et il ne m'a célé aucun des motifs
qu'il vous a donnés de vous plaindre de lui. – Il est impossible, monsieur,
qu'il ait osé vous dire ce que je vais vous raconter... » Alors il enfile un tissu
de bassesses, de noirceurs, de scélératesses plus fortes les unes que les autres.
Pendant son récit, mon père, étourdi de ce torrent d'horreurs et d'infamies,
regardait du coin de l'œil l'endroit où il avait déposé sa canne et son
chapeau, et méditait une prompte retraite. Heureusement l'abbé parla trop
longtemps, mon père reprit sa tranquillité, et attendit avec patience la fin

d'une narration aussi violente que longue. Enfin, l'abbé s'arrêta. « Je savais tout cela, monsieur, et vous ne m'avez pas encore tout dit. – Juste ciel ! monsieur, et que pouvez-vous savoir de plus ? – Vous ne m'avez pas dit qu'un soir, lorsque vous reveniez de matines, vous l'aviez trouvé à votre porte ; qu'il avait tiré un poignard qu'il tenait sous son manteau, et qu'il avait voulu vous l'enfoncer dans la poitrine. – Si je ne vous ai pas dit cela, monsieur, c'est que cela n'est pas vrai... » Alors mon père se lève, s'approche de l'abbé, lui prend le bras et lui dit : « Eh bien, quand cette action serait vraie, il faudrait encore donner du pain à votre frère. » Il ne faut qu'un mot pour ébranler l'âme la plus ferme, le premier mouvement donné rend tout le reste facile. Cet homme un peu étonné finit par être persuadé, et promit à mon père de donner six cents livres de rentes à son frère.

Celui-ci revient savoir le succès de la négociation. « Monsieur, lui dit mon père, vous m'avez trompé, vous n'êtes pas un homme vrai ; vous avez fait cent actions abominables, mais je n'en ai pas moins réussi ; votre frère vous donnera de quoi vivre. Renoncez, s'il est possible, à un caractère aussi odieux, qui ferait le malheur de votre vie, le tourment de votre famille et la honte de vos amis. » Rivière, fort content, remercie mon père et de ses services et de ses conseils, cause encore un quart d'heure et prend congé de lui ; mon père le reconduit. Quand ils sont sur l'escalier, Rivière s'arrête, et dit à mon père : « Monsieur Diderot, savez-vous l'histoire naturelle ? – Mais un peu ; je distingue un aloès d'une laitue, et un pigeon d'un colibri. – Savez-vous l'histoire du *Formica-leo* ? – Non. – C'est un petit insecte très-industrieux ; il creuse dans la terre un trou en forme d'entonnoir, il le couvre à la surface avec un sable fin et léger, il y attire les insectes étourdis, il les prend, il les suce, puis il leur dit : « Monsieur Diderot, j'ai l'honneur « de vous souhaiter le bonjour. » Mon père rit comme un fou de cette aventure. Quelque temps après il sort ; un orage l'oblige d'entrer dans un café, il y trouve Rivière; cet homme s'approche et lui demande comment il se porte. « Eloignez-vous, lui dit mon père ; vous êtes un homme si méchant et si corrompu, que, si vous aviez un père riche, je ne le croirais pas en sûreté dans la même chambre avec vous. – Hélas ! malheureusement, je n'ai point de père riche. – Vous êtes un abominable homme. – Allons donc, philosophe, vous prenez tout au tragique. »

2 Passage from Diderot's *Paradoxe sur le comédien*, A.T., VIII, 384–5, corrected according to the text given by Paul Vernière (*Œuvres esthétiques de Diderot*, 332–3) :

Un littérateur, dont je tairai le nom, était tombé dans l'extrême indigence. Il avait un frère, théologal et riche. Je demandai à l'indigent pourquoi son frère ne le secourait pas. C'est, me répondit-il, que j'ai de grands torts avec

lui. J'obtins de celui-ci la permission d'aller voir M. le théologal. J'y vais.
On m'annonce ; j'entre. Je dis au théologal que je vais lui parler de son
frère. Il me prend brusquement par la main, me fait asseoir et m'observe
qu'il est d'un homme sensé de connaître celui dont il se charge de plaider
la cause; puis, m'apostrophant avec force : « Connaissez-vous mon frère ?
– Je le crois. – Etes-vous instruit de ses procédés à mon égard ? – Je le crois.
– Vous le croyez ? Vous savez donc ?... » Et voilà mon théologal qui me
débite, avec une rapidité et une véhémence surprenante, une suite d'actions
plus atroces, plus révoltantes les unes que les autres. Ma tête s'embarrasse,
je me sens accablé ; je perds le courage de défendre un aussi abominable
monstre que celui qu'on me dépeignait. Heureusement mon théologal, un
peu prolixe dans sa philippique, me laissa le temps de me remettre; peu à
peu l'homme sensible se retira et fit place à l'homme éloquent, car j'oserai
dire que je le fus dans cette occasion. « Monsieur, dis-je froidement au théologal, votre frère a fait pis, et je vous loue de me céler le plus criant de ses
forfaits. – Je ne cèle rien. – Vous auriez pu ajouter à tout ce que vous m'avez
dit, qu'une nuit, comme vous sortiez de chez vous pour aller à matines, il
vous avait saisi à la gorge, et que tirant un couteau qu'il tenait caché sous
son habit, il avait été sur le point de vous l'enfoncer dans le sein. – Il en est
bien capable ; mais si je ne l'en ai pas accusé, c'est que cela n'est pas vrai... »
Et moi, me levant subitement, et attachant sur mon théologal un regard
ferme et sévère, je m'écriai d'une voix tonnante, avec toute la véhémence et
l'emphase de l'indignation : « Et quand cela serait vrai, est-ce qu'il ne
faudrait pas encore donner du pain à votre frère ? » Le théologal, écrasé,
terrassé, confondu, reste muet, se promène, revient à moi et m'accorde une
pension annuelle pour son frère.

3 From the fragment entitled *S'il est plus aisé de faire une belle action
qu'une belle page,* first published in A.T., III, 539. Reprinted with punctuation modernized by Georges Roth, *Correspondance,* X, 180:

Il m'en coûte beaucoup pour être éloquent ; il ne m'en coûte presque rien
pour être bon. Je suis bon quand on veut et tant qu'on veut. Pour éloquent,
c'est autre chose. Je n'ai mémoire de l'avoir été qu'une fois ; mais dans ce
moment, je n'aurois pas été fâché d'être entendu de Démosthène ou de
Cicéron. Ce fut le jour que je visitai le théologal de Notre-Dame ; je fis
alors une belle page comme tous les hommes peuvent faire une belle action.

4 Excerpt from Madame de Vandeul's *Mémoires sur Diderot* as given in
A.T., I, xlvii–xlviii:

Un matin arrive un jeune homme avec un manuscrit ; il prie mon père de vouloir bien le lire et de mettre ses observations en marge ; c'était une satire amère de sa personne et de ses ouvrages. Le jeune homme revient. « Monsieur, lui dit mon père, je ne vous connais point, je n'ai jamais pu vous désobliger ; pourriez-vous m'apprendre le motif qui vous a déterminé à me faire lire une satire pour la première fois de ma vie ? Je jette ordinairement ces espèces d'ouvrages dans mon seau. – Je n'ai pas de pain ; j'ai espéré que vous me donneriez quelques écus pour ne pas l'imprimer. – Vous ne seriez pas le premier auteur dont on payerait volontiers le silence ; mais vous pouvez tirer un meilleur parti de cette rapsodie. Le frère de M. le duc d'Orléans est retiré à Sainte-Geneviève ; il est dévot ; il me hait ; dédiez-lui votre satire, faites-la relier avec ses armes ; portez-lui cet ouvrage un matin, et vous en obtiendrez quelques secours. – Mais je ne connais point ce prince, et l'épître dédicatoire m'embarrasse. – Asseyez-vous là, et je vais vous la faire. » Mon père écrit l'épître ; l'auteur l'emporte, va chez le prince, en reçoit vingt-cinq louis, et revient quelques jours après remercier mon père, qui lui conseilla doucement de prendre un genre de travail moins avilissant.

5  Passage from Diderot's letter to Falconet of 6 September 1768, *Corr.*, ed. Roth, VIII, 109–10:

J'avois retiré de la misère un jeune littérateur qui n'étoit pas sans talent. Je l'avois nourri, logé, chaussé, vêtu pendant plusieurs années. Le premier essai de ce talent que j'avois cultivé, ce fut une satyre contre les miens et moi. Le libraire que je ne connoissois pas, plus honnête que l'auteur, m'envoya les épreuves et me proposa de supprimer l'ouvrage. Je n'eus garde d'accepter cette offre. La satyre parut ; l'auteur eut l'impudence de m'en apporter lui même le premier exemplaire. Je me contentai de lui dire : « Vous êtes un ingrat. Un autre que moi vous feroit jeter par les fenêtres. Mais je vous sçais gré de m'avoir bien connu. Reprenez votre ouvrage, et portez le à mes ennemis ; à ce vieux duc d'Orléans qui demeure de l'autre côté de ma rue. » J'habitois alors l'Estrapade. La fin de ceci, c'est que je lui dressai moi même, contre moi, un placet au duc d'Orléans ; que le vieux fanatique lui donna cinquante louis ; que la chose se sçut ; et que le protecteur resta bien ridicule et le protégé bien vil.

6  Melchior Grimm's review of *Les Zélindiens*, 1 June 1762, in *Corr. lit.*, ed. M. Tourneux, V, 90:

*Les Zélindiens*, par Mlle F\*\*\*, sont un petit conte insipide que personne n'a regardé. Vous jugez bien que les Zélindiens sont les Parisiens ; qu'on parle beaucoup des Zélindiennes, et que tout cela fait un recueil de petites peintures, de mesquineries, de platitudes, qui vous affadissent l'esprit et le cœur, deux substances que les écrivains de cette espèce aiment à accoupler ensemble, comme les théologiens le corps et l'âme. Mon esprit et mon cœur ne se sentent pas propres à être échauffés par l'esprit et le cœur de Mlle F***.

7 Footnote appended to the above passage by the editor, Maurice Tourneux:

*Les Zélindiens* sont-ils bien de Mlle Fauque, que Grimm désigne ici et à qui Mme Briquet et l'abbé de La Porte les attribuent aussi, ce dernier en ajoutant qu'il n'en dira rien « parce qu'ils ne sont pas assez intéressants » ? Nous avons exposé nos doutes sur l'exactitude de cette attribution, tome xvii, page 477 des *Œuvres* de Diderot, et depuis lors ils ne se sont pas dissipés, car cette brochure ne nous est point encore passée sous les yeux.

# Select Bibliography

MANUSCRIPTS

Paris Archives of the Archevêché
    Card catalogue assembled by Abbé Paul Pisani
Paris Archives Nationales
    x$^{1a}$ 9327 (Parlement Register of Lawyers, 1706–51)
    Family papers of Abbé Jean-François Rivière:
    T202-1 (2 June and 22 June 1753)
    T202-12 (10 September 1713)
Paris Bibliothèque Nationale
    MSS *Nouvelles acquisitions françaises*:
    13760 ff. 3–17 (Diderot *Satire première*)
    13765 ff. 57–65 (Diderot *Satire première*)
    13782 ff. 115–24 (Diderot *Satire première*)
Leningrad State Public Library
    Diderot Collection
    Vol. XVIII ff. 225–38 (*Satire première*)
The Hague Royal Library
    *Correspondance littéraire* October 1778
    128 F 14 Vol. VII Item 2 (*Satire par M. Diderot*)

WORKS BY DIDEROT

*Chefs-d'œuvre* 2 vols. London, Dent & Sons; Paris, Gillequin 1911
*Correspondance* ed. Georges Roth. Paris, Editions de Minuit 1955 ff.
    14 vols. to date
(Ed.) *Encyclopédie, ou Dictionnaire raisonné des sciences, des arts et des*
    *métiers, par une société de gens de lettres* 17 vols. Paris 1751–65
*Le Neveu de Rameau* Edition critique par Jean Fabre. Geneva, Droz 1950
*Lettre sur les sourds et muets* Edition commentée et présentée par
    Paul Hugo Meyer. Geneva, Droz 1965 (*Diderot Studies* VII)

*Lettres à Sophie Volland* ed. André Babelon 2d ed. 2 vols. Paris,
   Gallimard 1938
*Œuvres* ed. André Billy. Paris, Gallimard 1951 (Bibliothèque
   de la Pléiade)
*Œuvres* ed. Jacques-André Naigeon 15 vols. Paris, Desray-Déterville
   an VI-1798
*Œuvres complètes* ed. Jean Assézat and Maurice Tourneux 20 vols.
   Paris, Garnier 1875–7
*Œuvres* 8 vols. Paris, A. Belin 1818–19
*Œuvres* 21 vols. Paris, J.-L.-J. Brière 1821–3
*Œuvres esthétiques* ed. Paul Vernière. Paris, Garnier 1959
*Quatre Contes* Edition critique avec notes et lexique par Jacques Proust.
   Geneva, Droz 1964
*Salons* ed. Jean Seznec and Jean Adhémar 4 vols. Oxford, Clarendon
   Press 1957–67
*Satires* ed. Roland Desné. Paris, Club des Amis du Livre Progressiste 1963
*Tablettes* see Pappas, John


OTHER SOURCES

Alembert, Jean le Rond d' *Mélanges de littérature, d'histoire, et de
   philosophie* Nouv. éd. 5 vols. Amsterdam, Châtelain 1773
Anderson, Warren D. *Ethos and Education in Greek Music* Cambridge,
   Mass., Harvard University Press 1966
Arnold, E. Vernon *Roman Stoicism* Cambridge, Cambridge University
   Press 1911
Attinger, Gustave *L'Esprit de la commedia dell'arte dans le théâtre
   français* Paris, Librairie Théâtrale 1950
Bar, Francis *Le Genre burlesque en France au XVII° siècle. Etude de
   style* Paris, D'Artrey 1960
Barricelli, Jean-Pierre "Music and the Structure of Diderot's *Le Neveu
   de Rameau*" *Criticism* V (1963) 95–111
Belaval, Yvon *L'Esthétique sans paradoxe de Diderot* Paris,
   Gallimard 1950
— "Note sur Diderot et Leibniz" *Revue des Sciences Humaines*
   n.s. CXII (1963) 435–51
Blum, André *L'Estampe satirique et la caricature en France au XVIII°
   siècle* Paris, Gazette des Beaux-Arts 1910
Boyd, John D. *The Function of Mimesis and its Decline* Cambridge,
   Mass., Harvard University Press 1968

Brun, A. "Aux origines de la prose dramatique : le style haletant" in
  *Mélanges de linguistique offerts à M. Charles Bruneau* Geneva,
  Droz 1954, 41–7

Busnelli, Manlio D. *Diderot et l'Italie* Paris, Champion 1925

Cassirer, Ernst *The Philosophy of the Enlightenment* trans. Fritz Koelln
  and James P. Pettigrove. Boston, Beacon Press 1955

Charlier, G. and Hermann, L. "Diderot, annotateur de Perse" *Revue
  d'Histoire Littéraire de la France* xxxv (1928) 39–63

Chouillet, Jacques "Le Mythe d'Ariste, ou Diderot en face de lui-même"
  *Revue d'Histoire Littéraire de la France* LXIV (1964) 565–88

Cicero, Marcus Tullius *De officiis* trans. Walter Miller. London,
  Heinemann 1913 (Loeb Classical Library)

— *Tusculan Disputations* trans. J. E. King. London, Heinemann 1927
  (Loeb Classical Library)

Condillac, Etienne Bonnot de. *Œuvres philosophiques* ed. Georges Le Roy
  3 vols. Paris, Presses Universitaires de France 1947–51

Crocker, Lester G. *Rousseau's Social Contract: an Interpretive Essay*
  Cleveland, Case Western Reserve University Press 1968

— "*Le Neveu de Rameau*, une expérience morale" *Cahiers de
  l'Association Internationale des Etudes Françaises* XIII (1961) 133–55

— "The Priority of Justice or Law" *Yale French Studies* No. 28
  (1961–2) 34–42

Curtius, Ernst Robert *European Literature and the Latin Middle Ages*
  trans. Willard R. Trask. New York, Pantheon Books 1953

Derathé, Robert *Le Rationalisme de J.-J. Rousseau* Paris, Presses
  Universitaires de France 1948

Desné, Roland *Diderot et Le Neveu de Rameau. Essai d'explication*
  Paris, Centre d'Etudes et de Recherches Marxistes, n.d.

— "*Le Neveu de Rameau* dans l'ombre et la lumière du xviiiᵉ siècle"
  *Studies on Voltaire and the Eighteenth Century* xxv (1963) 493–507

— "Monsieur le Philosophe et le Fieffé Truand" *Europe* Nos. 405–6
  January–February 1963, 182–98

Desnoiresterres, Gustave *La Comédie satirique au XVIIIᵉ siècle* Paris,
  Perrin 1885

Dieckmann, Herbert *Inventaire du fonds Vandeul et inédits de Diderot*
  Geneva, Droz 1951

— "Currents and Crosscurrents in *Le Fils naturel*" in *Linguistics and
  Literary Studies in Honor of Helmut A. Hatzfeld* ed. Alessandro S.
  Crisafulli. Washington, The Catholic University of America Press
  1964, 107–16

— "Observations sur les manuscrits de Diderot conservés en Russie"
  *Diderot Studies* IV (1963) 53–71

— "The Relationship Between Diderot's *Satire I* and *Satire II*"
  *Romanic Review* XLIII (1952) 12–26

Doolittle, James *Rameau's Nephew. A Study of Diderot's "Second
  Satire"* Geneva, Droz 1960

— "Hieroglyph and Emblem in Diderot's *Lettre sur les sourds et muets*"
  *Diderot Studies* II (1952) 148–67

Duchet, Michèle and Michel Launay (eds.) *Entretiens sur "Le Neveu
  de Rameau"* Paris, Nizet 1967

Ehrard, Jean "Matérialisme et naturalisme : les Sources occultistes de la
  pensée de Diderot" *Cahiers de l'Association Internationale des
  Etudes Françaises* XIII (1961) 189–201

Epinay, Louise Florence Pétronille de La Live, madame d' *Histoire de
  Madame de Montbrillant* ed. Georges Roth 3 vols. Paris, Gallimard
  1951

Fabre, Jean "Deux Frères ennemis : Diderot et Jean-Jacques"
  *Diderot Studies* III (1961) 155–213

— "Diderot et les théosophes" *Cahiers de l'Association Internationale
  des Etudes Françaises* XIII (1961) 203–22

Fellows, Otis "Metaphysics and the *Bijoux indiscrets*: Diderot's Debt to
  Prior" *Studies on Voltaire and the Eighteenth Century*
  LVI (1967) 509–40

— "The Theme of Genius in Diderot's *Neveu de Rameau*"
  *Diderot Studies* II (1952) 168–99

Feugère, Anatole "Pourquoi Rousseau a remanié la Préface de la *Lettre
  à d'Alembert*" *Annales J.-J. Rousseau* XX (1931) 127–62

Folkierski, Wladyslaw *Entre le Classicisme et le Romantisme. Etude sur
  l'esthétique et les esthéticiens du XVIIIᵉ siècle* Paris, Champion 1925

François, Alexis *Histoire de la langue française cultivée des origines à nos
  jours* 2 vols. Geneva, Jullien 1959

— "Précurseurs français de la grammaire 'affective' " in *Mélanges de
  linguistique offerts à Charles Bally* Geneva, Georg 1939, 369–77

Freer, A. J. "L'Exemplaire du *Devin du village* offert par Rousseau à
  Diderot" *Revue d'Histoire Littéraire de la France* July-September
  1966, 401–8

Freud, Hilde H. *Palissot and "Les Philosophes"* Geneva, Droz 1967
  (*Diderot Studies* IX)

Gillot, Hubert *Denis Diderot. L'homme; ses idées philosophiques,
  esthétiques, littéraires* Paris, Courville 1937

Grannis, Valleria Belt *Dramatic Parody in Eighteenth-Century France*
  New York, Institute of French Studies 1931

Grant, Mary A. *The Ancient Rhetorical Theories of the Laughable*
  Madison, University of Wisconsin Press 1924 (University of

Wisconsin Studies in Language and Literature No. 21)

Greene, William Chase "The Spirit of Comedy in Plato" *Harvard Studies in Classical Philology* xxxi (1920) 63–123

Grimm, Friedrich Melchior, Diderot, Raynal, Meister, et al. *Correspondance littéraire, philosophique et critique* ed. Maurice Tourneux 16 vols. Paris, Garnier 1877–82

Grout, Donald S. "Opéra bouffe et Opéra-comique" in *Histoire de la musique* Paris, Gallimard 1960–3, 2 vols. ii 5–25 (Encyclopédie de la Pléiade)

Guillemin, Henri "Les Affaires de l'Ermitage (1756–57). Examen critique des documents" *Annales J.-J. Rousseau* xxix (1941–2) 59–258

Havelock, Eric A. *Preface to Plato* Cambridge, Mass., Harvard University Press 1963

Havens, George R. "Diderot, Rousseau, and the *Discours sur l'inégalité*" *Diderot Studies* iii (1961) 219–62

Helvétius, Claude-Adrien *De l'esprit* Paris, Durand 1758

Hendel, Charles W. *Jean-Jacques Rousseau, Moralist* 2 vols. London, Oxford University Press 1934

Hermand, Pierre *Les Idées morales de Diderot* Paris, Presses Universitaires de France 1923

Hirzel, Rudolf *Der Dialog: Ein literarhistorischer Versuch* 2 vols. Leipzig, S. Hirzel 1895

Horatius Flaccus, Quintus *Epîtres* Texte établi et traduit par François Villeneuve 3rd ed. Paris "Les Belles Lettres" 1955

— *Odes, Epodes et Chant Séculaire* Publiés par Frédéric Plessis. Paris, Hachette 1924

— *Odes et Epodes* Texte établi et traduit par François Villeneuve 6th ed. Paris "Les Belles Lettres" 1959

— *Satires* Texte établi et traduit par François Villeneuve 5th ed. Paris "Les Belles Lettres" 1958

— *Satires* Publiées par Paul Lejay. Paris, Hachette 1911

— *Satires and Ars poetica* trans. H. Rushton Fairclough. London Heinemann 1947 (Loeb Classical Library)

Hyppolite, Jean *Genèse et structure de la "Phénoménologie de l'esprit" de Hegel* Paris, Aubier 1946

Jaeger, Werner *Paideia: The Ideals of Greek Culture* trans. Gilbert Highet 3 vols. New York, Oxford University Press 1943

Jimack, Peter D. *La Genèse et la rédaction de l'Emile de J.-J. Rousseau* Geneva, Institut et Musée Voltaire 1960 (*Studies on Voltaire and the Eighteenth Century* xiii)

Josephs, Herbert *Diderot's Dialogue of Gesture and Language: Le Neveu de Rameau* Columbus, Ohio State University Press 1969

Knight, Isabel F. *The Geometric Spirit: The Abbé de Condillac and the French Enlightenment* New Haven, Yale University Press 1968

Koller, H. *Die Mimesis in der Antike: Nachahmung, Darstellung, Ausdruck* Berne, A. Francke 1954

Lakoff, Sanford A. *Equality in Political Philosophy* Cambridge, Mass., Harvard University Press 1964

Laufer, Roger "Structure et signification du *Neveu de Rameau* de Diderot" *Revue des Sciences Humaines* n. s. c (1960) 399–413

Launay, Michel "Etude du *Neveu de Rameau*, hypothèses pour une recherche collective" *La Pensée* No. 118 (December 1964) 85–92

Lioublinski, V. S. "Sur la trace des livres lus par Diderot" *Europe* January–February 1963, 274–90

Lippman, Edward A. *Musical Thought in Ancient Greece* New York, Columbia University Press 1964

Lloyd, G. E. R. *Polarity and Analogy: Two Types of Argumentation in Early Greek Thought* Cambridge, Cambridge University Press 1966

Manuel, Frank E. "From Equality to Organicism" *Journal of the History of Ideas* XVII (1956) 54–69

Marrou, Henri-Irénée *A History of Education in Antiquity* trans. George Lamb. London, Sheed and Ward 1956

Maurer, Karl "Die Satire in der Weise des Horaz als Kunstform von Diderots *Neveu de Rameau*" *Romanische Forschungen* LXIV (1952) 365–404

Mauzi, Robert *L'Idée du bonheur dans la littérature et la pensée française au XVIII' siècle* 3rd ed. Paris, A. Colin 1967

May, Georges *Quatre Visages de Denis Diderot* Paris, Boivin 1951

—— "L'Angoisse de l'échec et la genèse du *Neveu de Rameau*" *Diderot Studies* III (1961) 285–307

Mayer, Jean *Diderot, homme de science* Rennes, Imprimerie Bretonne 1959

McLaughlin, Blandine "A New Look at Diderot's *Fils naturel*" *Diderot Studies* X (1968) 109–19

Mesnard, Pierre *Le Cas Diderot. Etude de caractérologie littéraire* Paris, Presses Universitaires de France 1952

Michaut, G. *Sur les tréteaux latins* Paris, Fontemoing & C$^{te}$ 1912

Moore, Alexander Parke *The Genre Poissard and the French Stage of the Eighteenth Century* New York, The Institute of French Studies 1935

Morize, André *L'Apologie du luxe au dix-huitième siècle et le Mondain de Voltaire* Paris, Didier 1909

Mornet, Daniel "La Véritable Signification du *Neveu de Rameau*" *Revue des Deux Mondes* 7th per. XL (August 1927) 881–908

Mortier, Roland *Diderot en Allemagne* Paris, Presses Universitaires de France 1954

— "Diderot et la notion de 'peuple' " *Europe* No. 405–6 (January–February 1963) 78–88

— "The 'Philosophes' and Public Education" *Yale French Studies* No. 40 (1968) 62–76

Moutsopoulos, Evanghélos *La Musique dans l'œuvre de Platon* Paris, Presses Universitaires de France 1959

Nettleship, R. L. *The Theory of Education in Plato's Republic* London, Oxford University Press 1935 (reprint of 1880 edition in *Hellenica*)

— *Lectures on the Republic of Plato* London, Macmillan 1937 (reprint of 1897 edition)

Nicoll, Allardyce *The World of Harlequin: a Critical Study of the Commedia dell'Arte* Cambridge, Cambridge University Press 1963

Niklaus, Robert "Le 'Méchant' selon Diderot" *Saggi e ricerche di letteratura francese* II (1961) 139–50

North, Helen *Sophrosyne: Self-knowledge and Self-restraint in Greek Literature* Ithaca, Cornell University Press 1966

O'Brien, Michael J. *The Socratic Paradoxes and the Greek Mind* Chapel Hill, University of North Carolina Press 1967

Oliver, Alfred R. *The Encyclopedists as Critics of Music* New York, Columbia University Press 1947

Palissot, Charles *Œuvres complètes* 7 vols. Liège, Bastien 1778

Pappas, John and Roth, Georges "Les 'Tablettes' de Diderot" *Diderot Studies* III (1961) 309–20

Plato *The Republic* trans. Paul Shorey 2 vols. London, Heinemann 1930–5 (Loeb Classical Library)

— *Lysis, Symposium, Gorgias* trans. W. R. M. Lamb London, Heinemann 1925 (Loeb Classical Library)

Pommier, Jean "Comment Balzac relaie Diderot" *Revue des Sciences Humaines* n. s. (April–September 1951) 161–6

Pouilloux, Jean-Yves "L'Esthétique dans le *Neveu de Rameau*" *La Pensée* No. 129 (October 1966) 73–90

Proust, Jacques *Diderot et l'Encyclopédie* 2nd ed. Paris, A. Colin 1967

— "A propos d'un plan d'opéra-comique de Diderot" *Revue d'Histoire du Théâtre* VII (1955) 173–88

— "Variations sur un thème de l'*Entretien avec d'Alembert*" *Revue des Sciences Humaines* n. s. CXII (1963) 453–70

Raymond, Marcel "J.-J. Rousseau. Deux Aspects de sa vie intérieur (intermittences et permanence du 'Moi')" *Annales J.-J. Rousseau* XXIX (1941–2) 5–57

Richebourg, Louisette *Contribution à l'histoire de la "Querelle des*

*Bouffons*" Paris, Nizet et Bastard 1937

Robinson, T. M. *Plato's Psychology* Toronto, University of Toronto Press 1970

Rousseau, Jean-Jacques *Correspondance complète* ed. R. A. Leigh. Geneva, Institut et Musée Voltaire 1965 ff. 10 vols. to date

— *Lettre à Mr. D'Alembert sur les spectacles* Edition critique par M. Fuchs. Geneva, Droz 1948

— *Œuvres complètes* ed. Bernard Gagnebin and Marcel Raymond. Paris, Gallimard 1959 ff. 4 vols. to date (Bibliothèque de la Pléiade)

— *Œuvres complètes* 13 vols. Paris, Hachette 1909

Rudd, Niall *The Satires of Horace* Cambridge, Cambridge University Press 1966

Sachs, Curt *The Rise of Music in the Ancient World, East and West* New York, W. W. Norton 1943

Schlesinger, Kathleen *The Greek Aulos* London, Methuen 1939

Schlösser, Rudolf *Rameaus Neffe. Studien und Untersuchungen zur Einführung in Goethes Üebersetzung des Diderotschen Dialogs* Berlin, Duncker 1900 (*Forschungen zur neuren Litteraturgeschichte* xv)

Schwartz, Jerome *Diderot and Montaigne: the* Essais *and the Shaping of Diderot's Humanism* Geneva, Droz 1966

Seiden, Milton F. "Jean-François Rameau and Diderot's Neveu" *Diderot Studies* I (1949) 143–91

Seznec, Jean *Essais sur Diderot et l'Antiquité* Oxford, Clarendon Press 1957

Shaftesbury, Anthony Third Earl of. *Characteristics of Men, Manners, Opinions, Times, etc.* ed. John M. Robertson 2 vols. Gloucester, Mass., Peter Smith 1963 (reprint of 1900 edition)

Smith, D. W. *Helvétius: a Study in Persecution* Oxford, Clarendon Press 1965

— "The Publication of Helvétius's *De l'esprit*, 1758–9" *French Studies* xviii (1964) 332–44

Spitzer, Leo *Classical and Christian Ideas of World Harmony* Baltimore, The Johns Hopkins Press 1963

Taylor, Samuel S. B. "Rousseau's Contemporary Reputation in France" *Studies on Voltaire and the Eighteenth Century* xxvii (1963) 1545–74.

Thomas, Jean *L'Humanisme de Diderot* 2nd ed. Paris "Les Belles Lettres" 1938

Topazio, Virgil "Diderot's Supposed Contributions to Helvétius' Works" *Philological Quarterly* xxxiii (1954) 313–29

Tourneux, Maurice *Les Manuscrits de Diderot conservés en Russie* Paris, Imprimerie Nationale 1885

Trahard, Pierre *Les Maîtres de la sensibilité française au XVIII* siécle*
    *(1715-1789)* 4 vols. Paris, Boivin 1931-3
Trousson, Raymond *Socrate devant Voltaire, Diderot et Rousseau : la*
    *Conscience en face du mythe* Paris, Minard 1967
Van Rooy, C. A. *Studies in Classical Satire and Related Literary Theory*
    Leiden, E. J. Brill 1965
Venturi, Franco *Jeunesse de Diderot (1713-1753)* traduit de l'italien
    par Juliette Bertrand, Paris [Skira] 1939
Verdenius, W. J. *Mimesis. Plato's Doctrine of Artistic Imitation and its*
    *Meaning to Us* Leiden, E. J. Brill 1949
Vernière, Paul *Diderot, ses manuscrits et ses copistes* Paris, Klincksieck
    1967
—    "Histoire littéraire et papyrologie : à propos des autographes de
    Diderot" *Revue d'Histoire Littéraire de la France* July-September
    1966, 409-18
—    'L'Idée d'humanité au XVIII* siècle" *Studium Generale* xv
    (1962) 171-9
Vexler, Felix *Studies in Diderot's Aesthetic Naturalism* New York,
    Columbia University Press 1922
Vicaire, Paul *Platon, critique littéraire* Paris, Klincksieck 1960
Voltaire, François Marie Arouet de. *Correspondence* ed. Theodore
    Besterman 107 vols. Geneva, Institut et Musée Voltaire 1953-65
—    *Œuvres complètes* ed. Louis Moland 52 vols. Paris, Garnier 1877-85
Vyveberg, Henry *Historical Pessimism in the French Enlightenment*
    Cambridge, Mass., Harvard University Press 1958
Waites, M. C. "Some Features of the Allegorical Debate in Greek
    Literature" *Harvard Studies in Classical Philology* XXIII (1912) 1-46
Wartofsky, Marx W. "Diderot and the Development of Materialist
    Monism" *Diderot Studies* II (1952) 279-329
Wild, John *Plato's Theory of Man: an Introduction to the Realistic*
    *Philosophy of Culture* Cambridge, Mass., Harvard University Press
    1946
Wilson, Arthur M. *Diderot: The Testing Years, 1713-1759* New York
    Oxford University Press 1957
Yates, Frances A. *Giordano Bruno and the Hermetic Tradition* London,
    Routledge and Kegan Paul 1964
Xenophon *Memorabilia and Oeconomicus* trans. E. C. Marchant
    London, Heinemann 1923 (Loeb Classical Library)

# Index

# UNIVERSITY OF TORONTO ROMANCE SERIES

This book
was designed by
ELLEN HUTCHISON
under the direction of
ALLAN FLEMING
University of
Toronto
Press